THE BEST
of *British*
MEN

Printed and bound by Bath Press, England
Typeset by Mainline Typesetters Ltd, St. Leonards-on-Sea
B/W origination by GH Graphics, St Leonards-on-Sea

Front cover illustrations:
Clockwise from top left: Nigel Kennedy, Terry Waite MBE, Lennox Lewis, Sir Anthony Hopkins, Antony Worrall-Thompson, Eric Clapton

Rear cover illustrations:
Left to right: Peter Kertesz, Kenneth Branagh, Lord Montagu of Beaulieu

Spine illustration:
Lord David Sutch

ISBN 0 951863 11 8

First published in Great Britain in 1993 by Best of British Publications, Eldon Lodge, 52 Victoria Road, London W8 5RQ. Tel 071-937 4276. Fax 071-937 1137

THE
BEST
of British
MEN

CONTENTS

ACKNOW

THE TEAM

In addition to the people whose contributions are acknowledged on this page, I would particularly like to give credit for the skill and dedication of the following members of the BEST OF BRITISH team, without whose efforts the books would not have been produced at all:

THE RESEARCHERS

The job of gathering and collating formation on the number of people featured in the BEST OF BRITISH is one requiring a great deal of patience, perseverance and, not least, charm. The reward has been the opportunity of speaking to and getting to know the most extraordinary and successful members of our society in every walk of life. The research team burned the midnight oil for many months, chivvying and cajoling for information, photographs ad biographies and I would particularly like to mention Angela Breheny, Jenny Tobin, Donna Allen-Eggison, Lloyd Stanton, Patrick Fuller, Sandi Mollod, Kim Bolton, Debbie Collinson and Jonny Ffinch.

THE WRITERS

The principal writers, Richard Bundy, Amelia Maiden and Richard Dawes, who summarised, expanded and edited the information provided until man and machine became one.

THE ART DEPARTMENT

Art director John Clement, ably assisted by Tasha Miller, who made the pictures fit the text and the text fit the pages.

Accountancy Age Newspaper; Acorn Entertainments; Dr Helen Agnew, Institute of Physics; Linda Agran, Paravision; The Airds Hotel; Amanda, Laister Dickson Ltd; Carol Ames, Eagle Star Investment Managers Ltd; Anderson O'Day Gallery; Stuart Anderson; Annely Juda Fine Art; Dr Barbara Ansell; Eve Arnold; Arts Review Magazine; Dr Margaret Ashwell, British Nutrition Foundation; Association of British Introduction Agencies; Aurelia PR; Austin-Desmond Gallery; Kit Bailey, Adastra; Martin Bailey; Roy Bailey; Lorraine Baldry; Dennis Ball, The Foundry; Nick Ballantine; Prof John Barrow, Univ of Sussex; Guy Batham, National Federation of Spiritual Teachers; BBC News Publicity; BBC Picture Publicity; BBC Publicity Office; The Beeson Gallery; Sasha Behrendt, Storm; Jean Bennett; Hazel Bently, International Journal of Alternative & Complementary Medicine; Beverley Cable PR; Lt David Bird; Dr Carol Black; Tim Bourne, Amalgam Gallery; William Boustead, The Toffee Shop, Penrith; Wendy Bridgman; British Film Institute; British Institute of Management; The British Tourist Board; Nikki Brokenshire, Mail on Sunday; Twink Burton, Alison Price Catering; Ann Bush, Alan Mann Helicopters; Elizabeth Butler-Sloss, Royal Courts of Justice; Liz Calder, Bloomsbury; Campaign Magazine; Eileen Campbell, Thorson Publications; Dee Carpenter; Axel Chaldecott, Howell Henry Chaldecott Lury; Julie Ivelaw Chapman, Chester Music; Stephanie Churchill; Nick Clarke, English National Ballet;

Classical Music Magazine; Tony Cobb, Royal College of Art; David Cole, British Microlight Commission; Helen Constantindes, PBJ Management; The Cooling Gallery; Graham Coombs, British Rail; Jackie Cooper; Paul Cordy, Dail Mail; Sue Cottam, Design Council; Anne Cox, Thorson Publications; The Crafts Council; Ilse Crawford, Elle Deco; Creative Review Magazine; Alan Cristea, Waddington Gallery; Paul Crocetta; Alan Crompton-Batt; Dianne Crowder, Shell UK; Jane Curtis; Andy Cutting; Marcelle D'Argy-Smith, Cosmopolitan; Beverly D'Silva, Cosmopolitan; Jackie Daya, Reed Regional Newspapers; Sally Dellow, Prime Performers; Clarissa Dickson-Wright, Books for Cooks; Mike Dinsdale, English Karate Commission; Steve Dixon, Caterer's Magazine; Michael Donovan, Alison Hargreaves; Sarah Doukas, Storm; April Ducksbury, Models One; Richard Dudley, The Custome Studio; Mairi Eastwood, Eastwood Consulting; Janet Eiger, London Contemporary Dance School; Andrew Eliel, Egon Ronay Guides; Elle Magazine; Dr Brent Elliott; Peter Ellwood, TSB; John Emmett; John and William Emmett; Michael Endicott, Institute of Complementary Medicine; Yvonne Eskenzi, London Enterprise Agency; Mary Evans, British Council on Ballroom Dancing; Baroness Ewart-Biggs; Steven Farish; E Fellows; Andrew Ferguson; Scott Findlay; Folk Roots; Jose Fonseca, Models One; John Fordham, Evening Standard; Annie Forster-Firth; William Fotheringham, Cycling Weekly; Erika Frei;

LEDGEMENTS

Gabbitas Truman & Thring; Gerry Gajadharsingh; Rosie Gerrard-Wright; Robin Gibson, National Portrait Gallery; Peggy Gibson; Rod Gilchrist, The Mail on Sunday; Martin Glanville, CBD Research Ltd; Johnny Gold, Tramp Nightclub; Joy Goodman; Goring PR; Paul Green, London Regional Transport; Henrietta Green; John Grig, British Dietetic Association; Isaac Guillory; Philip Gunn; Tim Haigh, Psychic News; Hairdressers Journal; Theresa Hale, Hale Clinic; Robin Hall, CINVen; Rev Douglas Hamilton-Ashby; Harold Holt Ltd; Paul Harris; Harrison Parrott Ltd; Anne Harvey; Richard Havers, Rushman-Lloyd Communications; Carol Hayes; Clare Henry; Peter Heppel, The Stage; Simon Higman, BBC; Hilary Shaw Management; Mark Hindle, The Mousetrap Cheese Shop; Mark Hindle; Lt Peter Hingley, Royal Astronomical Society; Chris Hodgekins, Jazz Services; Jane Holden, West Riding Milk Testing Service; John Home; Horrowitz Music Management Ltd; Barry Hugman, British Boxing Association; Ian Hutchinson; IMG Artists; Independent Television News Press Office; Hugh Inge-Innes-Lillingston; Brian Ingles; Ingpen & Williams; J Gurnett Personal Management Ltd; JRA Management; Jeremy James, Helicopter Club of Great Britain; Helen Jameson, Lilliput Ltd; Pervella Jeffries, Spotlight Casting; John Roseman Associates; John Kenny; Elizabeth Kershaw, Harpers & Queen; Leslie Knevitt, Prince of Wales Innovation Awards; Nicolas Lander, Financial Times; Jean Lee,

Corporate Hospitality & Event Association; Tac Lee, Harrods; Dr Robert Lefever; Suzanne Lewis; Lies Askonas Ltd; Hugh Lillingston; Jo Lloyd, Automobile Association; Ashley Lloyd-Jennings; Joanne Logan, Predictions Magazine; London Weekend Television Press Office; John Lowe; Edward Lucie-Smith; Anthony Lyman-Dixon, Arne Herbs; Mainline Typesetters Ltd; Arthur Map, British Ju Jitsu Association; Marlborough Fine Art; Jack Masserik, The Guardian; Martin Matthews; Anne Mayer, Royal Court Theatre; Leslie Mayer, London Fire Brigade; Sam McCarthy, British Marble Board of Controls; Helen McKay, Associated Newspapers; Rod McNeil, Theunissen; Greig McPherson, P Wigham-Richardson Ltd; Deidre McQuillen, Food Journalist; Jane McWhirter, All Hallow's Clinic; Anna Mei, Chadwick Gallery; Peter Miall, National Trust; Maureen Michaelson; Mike Henton Photography; John Miles; Bobbie Mitchell, BBC Photo Library; Edward Mitchell, NEVS; Modern Painters Magazine; Jonathon Monckton, Research Council for Complementary Medicine; Kate Moon, Speakeasy; Debbie Moore, Pineapple Studios; Becky Morris, Smallworld Music; Robert Morris, Koestler Chair of Parapsychology; Stephen Morris; Jonathan Morrish, Sony Music; Martin Mortimer, Tomorrow's World, BBC; National Pawbrokers Association; James Nicoll; Richard O'Donoghue, The Society of Designer-Craftsmen; Terry O'Neil; Dr Paul Oldershaw; Tony Ortzen, Psychic News; The Oxford

Gallery; PR Unlimited; Sue Parker, Blank Space Studios; Brad Parsons, Elite Premier; Brian Pearse, Midland Bank; The Photographers Gallery; Pomeroy Purdy Gallery; Margarita Porter; Stephen Pottle, Designer Sale Studio; PR Consultants Association; Kim Prior, You & Your Wedding; E Pugh, The Society of West End Theatres; Peter Pugson, Pugson's Food & Wine; Dr Richard Ralph, London Contemporary Dance School; Christopher Ramus; John Renbourn; Mark Rhodes, Angels & Bermons; Jo Richardson, MP; Gloria Ricks, National Magazine; William Robson; Roger Forrester Management; Barry Rolfe, Royal Aero Club of the UK; Gwen Rolfe, Martial Arts Commission; Michael Roosen; Derek Ross, British Airways; Prof rchie Roy, Univ of Glasgow; The Royal Geographical Society; Nicky and Nigel Rushman, Rushman-Lloyd Communications; Annette Russell, Tuff; Debbie Saldana, Prime Performers; Katrina Scetter, Larraine Ashton; Amber Webster, John Swannell Studios; Bert Weedon; The Welsh Tourist Board; Charles Westhead; Barbara Westmore, Harper Collins; Carol White, Elite Premier; Dr Roger Whitehead, Dunn Nutrition Centre; Andrew Wickham; Beverley Wickham; John Williams, British Bridge Union; Stan Willis, Society of Golden Keys; Shane Wilson, Expedition Advisory Centre; Women in Film & TV; Women's Journal; Celia Wood, Jazz Services; Chris Wood; Alex Woodcock-Clarke.

A MAJOR DECISION

At the time of going to press, we learned that John Major is proposing to adopt the Best of British method of nomination for the sadly anachronistic honours system. This is enormously pleasing to us, because the whole ethos of the Best of British is to acknowledge excellence in every field regardless of political favour. The honours system has long been a mystery to the man in the street; some jobs, particularly in the Civil Service, seem to carry such honours as CMG (call me God), KCMG (kindly call me God) and GCMG (God calls me God) as part of the promotional package. The range of honours available has also been remarkably confusing, for instance, in the 1992 New Year's list two television personalities were honoured, one with the CBE and one with the MBE, a nice but baffling distinction. When honours were first bestowed on members of Parliament they were a form of recompense for those who sacrificed their time performing a service to the community. Nowadays, being an MP is an extremely well-paid job when jobs are not easy to come by and to present a knighthood to someone who has done little or nothing except vote in the right direction, sit on the back benches and keep his nose clean seems a long way from slaying dragons or searching for the Holy Grail. In a rapidly changing society in which the Queen pays tax, her children make telephone calls like ordinary mortals and the Courts occassionally admit their fallibility. THE BEST OF BRITISH would like to welcome Mr Major's decision which, like this book, is intended to recognise people for what they do and not for what they are.

Martin was born in Worthing in 1946 and educated at the local secondary modern school. He became a freelance photographer and local radio journalist on leaving school, before co-founding Lyle Publications, in 1968. He has a rare talent for restoring period buildings – the larger the better – and left his mark in the South of England for the five years after leaving Lyle, until, in 1979, he started Miller's Antiques Guide, now the biggest selling antiques yearbook in the world. Martin's obsession with property has stayed with him and he is a director and co-founder of the highly successful Kent-based company, Milroy Developments. In 1984, he bought Chilston Park, at the time an uninhabitable virtual ruin, which he opened in 1985 as a country house hotel. The success of Chilston has been a tribute to Martin's vision and it now boasts 40 bedrooms, all individually furnished with antiques, and two stars in the restaurant guide for its food. Martin lives in Eldon Lodge, in Kensington, a Victorian mansion which, again, he restored from the uninhabitable. Aside from the Best of British books, Martin's recent publishing successes have included The Miller's Christmas Book, various books on period styles and details and the Essential Address Books. His latest venture is The Martin Miller Design Partnership, through which he combines his knowledge of antiques and buildings with his flair for decoration and restoration for the benefit of selected clients.

INTRODUCTION

When Martin Miller first conceived the idea of THE BEST OF BRITISH yearbooks, he did so with more knowledge than most people would have had of the scale of the undertaking. He had, after all, been publishing books since he co-founded Lyle Publications in 1968 and could boast amongst his publishing achievements MILLER'S ANTIQUES PRICE GUIDE, the biggest selling yearbook in the world. The first edition of THE BEST OF BRITISH MEN and its companion volume, THE BEST OF BRITISH WOMEN, have taken four years from conception to production.

The first problem was to decide on the categories, over 135 of them in each volume, and, realising that it was impossible to include every possible field of endeavour in a single volume, it was reasoned that, as a yearbook, we could concentrate on certain areas for 1993 which we may leave out in 1994. For instance, 1992 being an Olympic year, we have emphasised the achievements of our Olympians and, particularly, Paralympians at the expense of our association footballers, cricketers and boxers, who will get their turn in 1994.

The next major consideration involved establishing the criteria for 'the best'. Obviously, there are any number of areas in which this is a very subjective judgement – for instance, the best pub is often the pub where you are best known and the best smoked salmon to some may be thoroughly offensive to others. It was reasoned that there were two reliable ways to judge standards of excellence and the first of these – and the easiest – was by taking the results of current awards. The second method was by recommendations. Thus, ten names were extracted from one leading exponent in a given field and then ten from each of them and so on until a broad consensus was reached. In this way it became possible to say that, whilst people appearing in the book are not indisputably 'the best', there are very few better. To ascertain this information, a team of expert and experienced researchers was assembled, each with a specialised knowledge of a particular field. With 12 researchers working full time, the information started to flood in and the book began to take shape.

It was our intention to include under the various categories only those people who are currently active at the top of their chosen fields of endeavour and who have made a particular impact in the past year. This has left room for a separate section entitled HALL OF FAME, dedicated to those people who may not have made a particular contribution in 1992, but whose impact on British life over the years is impossible to ignore. Thus, Ian Botham may no longer be amongst the top five cricketers in the country, but as a fund-raiser, TV performer and personality, he certainly deserves a place among THE BEST OF BRITISH. The HALL OF FAME also contains people whom media exposure has brought to prominence, sometimes through no achievement of their own. Finally, there are some, although very few, people who requested that they should be left out of the book – there is, for instance, a well-known omission in the Horse Racing section – and their wishes have been respected.

Should the reader find what he considers to be a glaring omission – or an unfair inclusion – he is welcome to contact us with nominations for the 1993 BEST OF BRITISH.

HOW TO NOMINATE

If you wish to nominate anyone for inclusion in the 1994 BEST OF BRITISH book, in an existing category or one which you may feel we have overlooked, then fill in the form at the back of the book and send it to us. To avoid defacing your book you may reproduce the form as often as you wish.

ELDON LODGE · 52 VICTORIA ROAD · KENSINGTON · LONDON · W8 5RQ

071-937 4276

NICK SMALLWOOD AND SIMON SLATER

Nick Smallwood and Simon Slater won the 1992 CATEY Award for Restaurateur of the Year, for their two Kensington restaurants, Launceston Place and Kensington Place. Simon built up an extensive knowledge of wines and hotel and restaurant management after leaving school, and enhanced this through extensive travel in Europe, Southern Africa and the USA. On his return, he was appointed manager of Zanzibar, and left there in 1984 to become general manager of 192 Kensington Park Road. Nicholas Smallwood attended Westminster Hotel School, and continued his training at Claridges, leaving there to run a Scottish shooting lodge, a small Chelsea restaurant and subsequently to become general manager of the Hard Rock Cafe. He spent a year travelling, and returned to open Morton's in Berkeley Square with Peter Morton. In 1976, he opened Zanzibar with four partners who went on to found the Groucho Club, and Nick went on to be general manager at l'Escargot for four years.

In 1986, Nick and Simon got together to open their own restaurant, Launceston Place, and two years later opened Kensington Place. Due to their popularity, both places have considerably increased in size since their opening, and they have distinctly different characters whilst providing excellent quality. Launceston is discreet and fairly plush, Kensington noisy, full and the most fashionable watering-hole in London.

CHRISTOPHER CORBIN AND JEREMY KING

Chris Corbin left school in Bournemouth at 16 to become an apprentice aircraft fitter. In 1973, he changed direction and became a waiter, firstly in Bournemouth, and subsequently at the Rib Room in Burlington Street, London. He took an OND in Hotel & Catering Management, and in 1977, after a variety of kitchen and restaurant jobs, joined Langan's as a station waiter, progressing through the ranks to become restaurant manager by 1981.

Jeremy King started his working life at a merchant bank, and moved into the restaurant business in 1974, first at Searcy's and later becoming manager of Charco's in the King's Road. In 1976 he became a director of La Grenouille, a Battersea French restaurant and wine importing company, and in 1979 moved to become Maitre d'Hotel of Joe Allen, until 1981.

In 1981, Chris and Jeremy opened Le Caprice, and by 1983 had become independent of their financial backers. Le Caprice is probably the best loved restaurant in London, great food, lovely decor and service which is unfailing and indiscriminate. In 1990 they opened the Ivy, in West Street, WC2, and the same proprietorial insistence on quality persists.
Photograph by John Swannell

PAUL HEATHCOTE

Paul Heathcote's eponymous Lancashire restaurant was the winner of the 1992 CATEY Award for "Newcomer of the Year". Born in Bolton in 1960, Paul started his culinary career cooking packet soups in a Scottish hotel, but set his sights on more exotic things. His ambition took him to the Sharrow Bay Hotel, the Connaught, le Manoir aux Quatre Saisons and his first head position at Broughton Park Hotel, Preston. This period as executive chef added financial management to his portfolio of catering expertise, and in July 1990 the doors opened on his own establishment. Apart from the CATEY, representing the accolade of his peers, Paul has also quickly collected his first Michelin and Egon Ronay stars.

JOHN TOVEY

John Tovey was born in Lancashire in 1933. At the age of 16, he emigrated to Rhodesia, and worked in Central and West Africa for nine years. On returning to England, he first became involved with a repertory company in Barrow-in-Furness, and then was appointed private secretary/assistant manager at a well established lakeland hotel. John had obviously found his métier, and rose to be general manager of three hotels before he saw, bought and opened Miller Howe in 1971. John Tovey is the "arch-exponent" of good regional British cooking, and although he has now stood down as chef to concentrate on his writing (including an annual cookery book) and broadcasting, the tradition which he started in this lovely Edwardian house overlooking Lake Windermere is as strong as ever and has carried over into his other outlets.

Photograph by Graham Edwards

RICHARD SHEPHERD

Richard Shepherd was born in Weston-super-Mare, and spent most of his school holidays working in hotels and restaurants. In 1960, he became apprenticed at the Mount Pleasant Hotel in Worcestershire, moving to the Savoy as commis chef in 1963. In 1964 he went to France to be chef de partie at La Reserve in Beaulieu, where he met his wife, Christine. Returning to England in 1969, he worked at the Dorchester until 1971, when he went to the Capital as chef de cuisine, and where, in 1974, he became the first Englishman in London to receive the distinction of a Michelin star. In 1977 he joined Langan's Brasserie as chef de cuisine, in partnership with Peter Langan and Michael Caine and the rest, as they say, is history. Langan's has been the restaurant phenomenon of the 1970s, 80s and it seems, the 90s. Still THE place in London to see and be seen, and to eat simple or complex food at less than exhorbitant prices.

DAVID WILSON

David Wilson was born near Glasgow, and started his career in sales and marketing. His marketing career took him to England, but his love of food, and the encouragement of his wife, led him to resign his position to learn to cook, firstly at the Pheasant Inn, Keyston, and then at other places until he bought the Peat Inn in 1972. After humble beginnings, the Inn is now established as one of Britain's most respected "Restaurants with Rooms".

David Wilson was the first Scottish chef to earn a Michelin star in Scotland, and he was the recipient of the CATEY Award for Best Restaurateur 1989. David was elected a fellow of the RSA in 1992, and has featured in many books and on television. The Peat Inn is in Cupar, Fife.

CHRISTOPHER GILMOUR

Son of former Cabinet Minister Lord Gilmour, Christopher developed a taste for simple unpretentious American food during his 11 years in the USA as a commodities trader. He returned to England in 1989 determined to open a restaurant in the style of the classic American lobster and steak houses, and in December 1991 the doors opened on "Christopher's – The American Grill" in Covent Garden.

RICK STEIN

Rick Stein, 45, is the chef and owner of the Seafood Restaurant in Padstow, Cornwall. With wife Jill, he opened the restaurant in an old granary on the quay 18 years ago, and it has become internationally famous, drawing customers from Japan, Hong Kong, Australia and the USA. Rick is also the author of English Seafood Cookery (Penguin), which won the Glenfiddich Food Book Award in 1989, and he is currently working on another book of fish recipes discovered during his travels in the closed season.

Photograph by Janet Young

SIMON HOPKINSON ▲

Simon Hopkinson is chef/partner at Bibendum, housed in the old Michelin building in the Fulham Road. He was born in Lancashire, and started cooking as an apprentice chef at the Normandie Hotel, near Manchester. From there he moved to the Hat and Feather in Knutsford, and thence to St. Non's Hotel in Dyfed. He followed this with a year as chef/proprietor at the Shed restaurant in Fishguard. For the next two years, he was an inspector for Egon Ronay and then a private chef before moving to head Hilaire, where he stayed until 1987, and won his Egon Ronay star. His happy association with Sir Terence Conran and Paul Hamlyn at Bibendum goes from strength to strength. Simon's menu is extensive and wide ranging, and if it is not the cheapest place in London, it is extraordinarily good.
Photograph by Martin Brigsdale

◄ PAUL GAYLER

Paul Gayler, the chef at the Lanesborough Hotel, was first employed at the Royal Garden Hotel, between 1975 and 1980, where he rose to become the direct understudy of the executive chef, with a total brigade of 88 chefs. He went on to the Dorchester where he was employed as sous chef to Anton Mosimann for two years before moving to the late and lamented Inigo Jones, as head chef for seven years with responsibilities for costings and menus as well as day to day running. Paul then spent two years in contributing to the design and organisation of the back of the house of the Halkin Hotel, which opened in 1992, by which time he had taken up his present appointment.

ALASTAIR LITTLE →

Alastair Little is the only top British chef to have an MA in archaeology. He was born in 1950 in Colne in Lancashire, where his mother was a very adequate cook, but it was on exchange visits to France that food became a passion with him. Although Alastair has had no formal training as a chef, he has learned through experience in a number of establishments, including Parsons in the Fulham Road, where he was a waiter, the Old Compton Wine Bar, Le Routier in Suffolk where he was chef/partner, Simpson's in Putney, l'Escargot, and 192, where he met his Danish wife and partner, Kirsten Pederson. His eponymous restaurant in Frith Street has been a cult ever since it opened, and Alastair's idea of simple food has become everyone's idea of gourmet eating. He has become much more interested in lecturing these days, and teaches in Italy every year. The talent and dedication of his co-chef Juliet Peston allows him more time these days to indulge these pursuits and others such as studying dinosaur bones and The Times crossword.
Photograph by Anthony Blake

DAVID CHAMBERS →

David Chambers career is remarkable in that he started at the Piccadilly Hotel as a 16-year-old apprentice, and returned as executive chef 15 years later in 1985. In 1986, when the hotel became Le Meridien, David continued in his key role, and has earned for the Oak Room, the hotel's gourmet showcase, a Michelin star. As executive chef, David Chambers' career is with the consultant chef, Michel Lorain, and it is a tribute to both their culinary expertise and, indeed, their patience, that they communicate without a common language.

GARY RHODES ↑

Gary Rhodes joined the Greenhouse in November 1990, and the restaurant was voted Times Restaurant of the Year in 1991. Born in 1960, Gary trained at Thanet Technical College, before becoming commis chef rising to chef saucier at the Amsterdam Hilton. He has since worked at the Reform Club, The Capital, the Whitehall Restaurant in Essex and the Castle Hotel in Taunton, where he was chef for four years, and during which time he cooked at the Singapore Hilton for a three week Castle promotion in 1989. Gary is married with two sons, whom he is training as sous chefs.

CHEFS

BRIAN TURNER ▶

Brian Turner, "Purveyor of Yorkshire Puds to the Discriminating", is the chef/patron of the award winning Turner's restaurant in Walton Street, London. He has trained at some of the most prestigious hotels and restaurants, starting with Simpson's in the Strand and the Savoy Grill, with Richard Shepherd and under Louis Virot. After honing his skill in classical cuisine at the Beau Rivage Palace, in Lausanne, Brian returned to Claridge's, and then became Chef de Cuisine at the Michelin starred Capital Hotel. He opened Turner's in 1986.

SHAUN HILL ▶

Shaun Hill is the chef and director of the lovely Gidleigh Park, in Devon, and the Egon Ronay Guide Chef of the Year 1993. Born in 1947 of London Irish parentage, Shaun's career has taken him from Carrier's Restaurant (1967-71), to the Gay Hussar (1972-74), The Intercontinental (1975/76), The Capital (1976/77), Blake's (1978-80), The Lygon Arms (1981/82), Hills Restaurant (1983-85), and Gidleigh Park thereafter, Shaun is a senior member of the Académie Culinaire de France, and a Master Chef. Shaun is book reviewer for the Caterer Magazine, and lists his pastimes as drinking and spending more than he earns.

DAVID CAVALIER ▶

David Cavalier joined the Bell Inn at Aston Clinton as head chef in March 1992. Born in 1962, David was educated at Aylesbury and Ealing, where he received credits and distinctions in all his City and Guilds catering subjects. Between 1980 and 1984 he travelled variously at the Royal Garden, the Grosvenor House and the Dorchester hotels and, in 1984, moved to the Berkeley Hotel as senior sous chef. In 1985 David bought Pebbles Restaurant, Aylesbury, and in 1987 opened his eponymous restaurant in Battersea, where he won his Michelin and Egon Ronay stars, and was awarded Nigel Dempster's

Restaurant of the Year 1989. David has been consultant chef to National Leisure Catering for the past year.

ANTONY WORRALL-THOMPSON ←

Antony Worral-Thompson is the great innovator of the London restaurant scene, the man who always seems to leave all his competitors two steps behind in the race to be fashionable. He keeps such a high profile, and is so exposed by the media, that it is easy to overlook the fact that he is a very good chef indeed. Leaving Westminster College in 1971, with an HND in Hotel & Catering Management, Antony worked in several provincial establishments before taking over as head chef at Brinkley's Restaurant in the Fulham Road in 1978. A six month educational sabbatical in various three star establishments in France changed Brinkley's menus substantially and, when he took over as head chef of Dan's Restaurant in 1980, Antony propelled it from café to haute cuisine. The opening of Mènage a Trois in 1981 signalled the real start of the Worral-Thompson revolution – the place that served only starters and main courses. Mènage was followed by Mis-en-Place Limited, a factory kitchen to supply his outside catering business, and then the opening of One Ninety Queen's Gate, a unique club designed exclusively for the restaurant industry, and Bistrot 190, the noisy, stylish and highly affordable restaurant next door. Antony's most recent ventures are dell'Ugo, the three tiered giant in Frith Street, and the Fish Bistro at 190, both of which are well-judged for these recessionary times, and are packing them in. The winner of many awards and accolades, Antony Worral-Thompson is Meilleur Ouvrier de Grande Bretagne.

Photograph by Martin Brigdale

JOHN BURTON-RACE ▼

John Burton-Race is the owner and chef at L'Ortolan in Shinfield, Berkshire, where he has firmly established himself as one of Britain's best chefs. Born in Hampshire, his first catering appointment was as an apprentice at the Wessex Hotel in Winchester. He progresssed through various positions to sous chef at the Manoir aux Quat' Saisons, then head chef and manager of Le Petit Blanc, Oxford, 1984-86, before opening l'Ortolan in 1986. His list of honours and distinctions is extraordinary, but includes three stars in Egon Ronay (Restaurant of the Year 1991), a Two Star Michelin 1991-92, Personalité de l'Année Chef Laureat (Paris) 1991, four stars AA, 5/5 in the Good Food Guide, Relais Gourmand 1990 and Mumm Prizewinner 1987. He is a member of the Académie Culinaire Filiale Grande Bretagne, and the Chambre Syndicale de Haute Cuisine Française – and a truly terrific cook.

Photograph by Martin Brigdale

THE McCOY BROTHERS ▼

Although Tom McCoy is the chef at McCoy's in North Yorkshire, it is impossible to write about him without mentioning his brothers, Eugene and Peter, since they have been in business together since they opened a coffee bar called the Purple Onion in 1968. McCoy's is an old Coaching Inn, and a lighthearted way with the menu does not disguise the fact that Tom's cooking, self-taught, is seriously good. He enjoys giving people food that they wouldn't cook for themselves – he sees no point in doing what you could do at home for less!

MICHAEL WILSON ▼

Michael Wilson is head concierge at the Savoy Hotel. His father was head concierge at the Westbury and a founder member of the Society of Golden Keys. Michael began his career in 1966 at the age of 18, as a messenger boy at the Carlton Tower, joining the Society his father founded six years later and in 1981 he moved to the Shangri-La Hotel in Hong Kong. In 1986 he was made head concierge at the Connaught. He moved to the Savoy in 1992 where he heads a team of 24 people dedicated to providing a traditional service of the highest standard.

◄ THOM BROADBENT

Current president of the Society of Golden Keys Great Britain, Thom Broadbent is head concierge at Duke's Hotel, London. Born in Edinburgh in 1936, Thom spent his early adult life in the army, travelling extensively and gaining the rank of sergeant. His activities during this time included teaching Chinese students to play basketball and winning the inaugural race around Hong Kong island. Civilian life saw Thom as technical advisor for Shell, project manager for the Scottish Coal Board and a writer for direct sales companies, before joining Duke's in 1974. A concierge of distinction, Thom lists some of the required qualities as patience, enthusiasm, integrity and an undying sense of humour.

PETER LINNINGTON ▶

Head hall porter at Chewton Glen Hotel, Health and Country Club, Peter Linnington started his career at Cunard before moving to Zambia where he worked on the construction of the Kariba Dam. In 1972, at the age of 21, he joined Chewton Glen where he met his wife, Jane, who was assistant housekeeper.

PATRICK McGOVERN ▲

Patrick McGovern began working as a coal miner at the age of 15, a job he continued for ten years before an accident persuaded him to leave. After a spell in the construction industry, Patrick joined the Hilton, Livingston, where he has been night porter for the last three years.

EDDIE MATTINGLY ▲

Starting as page boy at the Grosvenor Hotel when he was just 14 years old, Eddie Mattingly's next post, as hall porter at Browns Hotel was interrupted by national service. He went on to the Piccadilly Hotel before accepting the position of enquiry clerk hall porter at the opening of the Hilton Hotel, Park Lane. From here Eddie moved to the Dorchester where he spent ten years as enquiry clerk. In 1972 he moved to the Royal Bath Hotel, a five star hotel in Bournemouth, as head hall porter.

KEN FRANKLYN, BEM ▶

Ken Franklyn was awarded the British Empire Medal in 1992 in recognition of 36 years service to the hotel industry at the Marine Highland Hotel in Troon, Scotland, where he is head hall porter. Guests such as Open golf champions Arnold Palmer, Mark Calcavecchia and Tom Weiskopf call him by his first name but this hasn't helped his 16 hole handicap! A member of the Society of Golden Keys, no unusual demand is a problem for Ken; a banana sundae at midnight or a replacement dress shirt in five minutes are provided without fuss.

RON SMITH ▲

Ron Smith retired from the army in the rank of Lieutenant Colonel after 33 years of service. His military experience ensures that his responsibilities as guest services manager at Gleneagles Hotel are discharged with courtesy and efficiency, whether it be obtaining a favourite golf caddy for a guest or supplying a preferred brand of whiskey.

VICTOR RADOJEVIC

Disenchanted with the political situation in Yugoslavia, Victor Radojevic moved to London in 1975 at the age of 22. Shortly after his arrival he found a job as a kitchen porter in a London hospital. He changed paths becoming night porter at the Berkeley Hotel and most recently, doorman at the Ritz.

SHAUN GLADSTONE-HOLBROOK ▼

Head concierge at the five star Swallow Hotel in Birmingham, 32-year-old Shaun Gladstone-Holbrook will arrange tickets to shows, taxis, air travel or just showing a guest to their room, Shaun is immediately helpful. In his lapel he wears the symbol of the Clef d'Ors, the Society of Golden Keys.

PUBLICANS/B&Bs

ROBERT SPENCER ▶

Grandson of the sixth Earl Spencer, Robert Spencer was born in 1932, near the family home of Althorp in Leicestershire, and educated at Eton. He joined the XIth Hussars and saw service in Germany before going into the wine and spirit business, in which he worked in the UK and abroad until 1969. He then helped his uncle with the running of Althorp, until the latter's death in 1975. For ten years, he opened his home at Langton Hall, near Market Harborough, to visitors, after which he moved to Lord Kinnaird's home, Rossie Priory, where he now lives. Here he welcomes guests into the charming classic Gothic structure, with its glorious views over the River Tay to Fife. Aside from the delights of the sumptuous accommodation, the gardens are particularly beautiful in the spring and the beautiful Perthshire countryside invites visitors to walk, play tennis and golf and view the other historic houses round about.

◀ JAMES CLIFTON

James Clifton returned to his native Devon nine years ago, at the age of 39, after a varied career as an actor and in the fashion world in London and abroad. He spent two years renovating his 16th century Devon Longhouse, Silkhouse, and then opened it to those members of the public requiring "the complete retreat" for dinner, bed and breakfast or a full holiday. A keen conservationist and gardener, James loves cooking and entertaining. In his eight acres of grounds, he breeds rare poultry and pygmy goats, keeps six dogs and two horses and plays tennis on his all-weather court. He is a member of Wolsey Lodge, the exclusive private accommodation agency, and of the Devon Wildlife Trust, the Rare Breeds Society and Taste of the West.

STEWART BASSETT

Formally trained in hotel school and in hotels in London and Switzerland during the 1960s. He rejected formal catering when he opened his own first restaurant, Bassett's of Halesworth, where he created a totally informal atmosphere. The root of this rejection of formality he puts down to his happy and relaxed upbringing in East Anglia, where he was born in 1939. In 1983 Stewart bought the Old Rectory at Campsea Ashe, near Woodbridge, and opened it as a small hotel. Stewart's approach is splendidly autocratic, following no national trends in food, where there is no choice, or decor. However, a loyal band of interesting people enjoys his style and returns time and again.

RAYMOND PAINE ▼

Raymond Paine was born in Hornchurch in Essex, where he served his apprenticeship in electrical engineering. He entered the retail trade shortly before marrying in 1966, and attained the position of branch manager with a large national retail group. In 1980, he decided to go it alone, and bought a small news business. A lover of the English canals, when the Canal Centre, at Sandbach in Cheshire came on the market in 1987, he and Susan seized the opportunity. The business now incorporates a four bedroomed guest house, a licensed restaurant, tea rooms, a post office and general store and a small marina and boatyard. In whatever spare time Raymond has left to him, he is a keen pilot of gliders and two and four engined powered aircraft and he enjoys playing the organ.

RONNIE RUSACK ▲

The famous Rusack's Hotel in St Andrew's was built by Ronnie Rusack's great grandfather and his links with the industry have always been strong. His career began at the Great Western Hotel in Oban, where he stayed until becoming manager at Edinburgh's Doric Tavern. In 1971 he arrived at the near derelict Bridge Inn at Ratho, alongisde the disused Union Canal, and he immediately made it his mission to turn the Inn and the Canal into viable businesses. By 1974, the first Canalboat Restaurant was launched. Nowadays, dinner dances, weddings and Santa Cruises are a fact of life. In the early 1980s, Ronnie was awarded the Order of St John, by HM The Queen, in recognition of his work for the disabled and the decade culminated in his receiving Lothian's first Children's License. The pub has been the recipient of many awards, notably: The Booker Pirze for Excellence – Best Pub in Britain; British Family Pub of the Year; Children's Caterer of the Year; Pub Promotion of the Year and a Business Innovation Award for Santa Cruises.

◀ BRUCE TAYLOR

The winner of the Evening Standard London Pub of the Year Award, 1992, is The Star in Belgrave Mews West. Landlord Burce Taylor has been running the pub with his wife, Kathy, for nine years. Bruce and Kathy were both born in Hoxton and met at the local secondary modern school in 1958, when he was 16 and she 13 years old. He decided that this was the girl he would marry and announced the fact to his unimpressed family. They were married in 1963 and, for ten years, ran The Greyhound in Islington. Finding that increasing racial tension and football hooliganism were making The Greyhound uncomfortable, they moved to Heneckey's, in the Strand, which became the Lyceum Tavern. The Star was the pub that they had been looking for all their lives and, in their nine years, they have created a friendly, efficient pub, with real fires, real food – cooked by Bruce in the evenings and Kathy's brother-in-law at lunchtimes – no music and no artificial aids.

KEVIN MORAN ▲

Born into a mining community in County Durham, Kevin Moran followed tradition and went down the mines. He left mining to join the Brigade of Guards and, being London based, started to get involved in Theatreland. He swapped his military ID for an Equity Card and began to tread the boards. He soon found that stunt work was more lucrative, and he worked in the studio instead. His first pub was The Man in the Moon, in Chelsea, in the 1970s and there he set up a fringe theatre club which is still running today. After several years of running pubs for breweries, he decided that he wanted more say in how a pub was run and how it should look. He acquired the tenancy of The Nag's Head in Kinnerton Street some years ago and, more recently, the freehold. As a publican, Kevin is very involved in the local community. He believes that a good pub is created by real ale, real people and real atmosphere and The Nag's Head, the village pub in Belgravia, is now a Free House in the real sense.

SIMON McINTYRE ▼

Born in Australia in 1969, Simon McIntyre is British with a capital B and has spent almost all his life in Norfolk and Scotland. The essential barman, he took over the running of The Sporting Page, in Chelsea, in the summer of 1992, and enjoys serving a wide cross-section of customers, offering them a quiet early evening drink, or a "blast" until closing time. Simon spends his spare time drawing, painting and designing or thinking up marketing ideas for making The Sporting Page the best pub in London, not only for the evening pint of Boddingtons, but also for the essential Bloody Mary in the morning. He spends weekends off at home in Scotland, contemplating life as the youngest manager of a pub in Chelsea.

DAVID MIZEL ▼

A former London cabbie with family connections with the licensed trade, David Mizel entered the profession some 20 years ago and has been behind bars ever since. He started in the West End, at the famous Sherlock Holmes and then spent a number of years in and around Soho and its theatre pubs, learning his craft. Five years ago, he moved from Lewes to the village of Burwash in East Sussex, famous as the home of Rudyard

Kipling, where he can be found behind the bar of The Bell. The Bell was the winner of the Evening Argus Sussex Country Pub of the Year Award 1991. David runs the bar and collects agricultural ephemera and clocks and barometers with which he festoons the walls and ceilings, and his wife, Annick, manages the kitchen to great effect. Now aged 56, David's hobbies are golf, arranging quiz nights and drinking as much Guinness as he can get hold of.

MICHAEL JAMIESON ▲

The Chequers in Lymington is a mecca for the sailing community of the Solent – and from all over the world. Michael Jamieson took over as landlord in the mid-1980s, and believes that he and his wife, Maggie, have weathered the recession by concentrating on value for money and looking after their customers. Mike was involved in the licensed trade in the early 1970s in various bars, restaurants and clubs in New York City. He returned to the UK in the late 1970s and, for 18 months, worked for Egon Ronay as an inspector. The early 1980s were taken up with positions in marketing and export management in the marine trade, followed by a spell of yacht management and messing about in racing yachts, including Barracuda of Tarrant in the filming of the first two series of television's Howard's Way. After meeting and marrying his wife, a qualified chef, they looked around for a pub for a year before finally buying their local, The Chequers.

JONATHAN MEADES

Jonathan Meades started writing in 1971, and for the past seven years has been the restaurant critic for the Times. He has worked for numerous papers and magazines, and has made about 30 TV films including the series The Victorian House and Abroad in Britain and is presently filming a new series Further Abroad which is a combination of architecture and anthropology. He is also a screenplay and fiction writer, his latest book being entitled Filthy English.

Photograph by Nigel Parry

MICHAEL BROADBENT ▼

Michael Broadbent is a director of Christie's London, and head of Christie's wine department. His numerous books are translated and sold worldwide, and include The Great Vintage Wine Book II, a unique wine record dating back to the vintage of 1650, and The Pocket Guide to Wine Vintages and Wine Tasting, now in its 11th edition. Michael Broadbent is one of only four Britons in the wine field to have received l'Ordre National du Merite, one of the French Government's highest honours, and he is the only British writer to have been awarded the Grand Prix of l'Academie Internationale du Vin. In 1989 he received the rarely bestowed Gold Medal of the City of Paris.

EGON RONAY ▼

Egon Ronay was born in Hungary, and acquired a law degree from the University of Budapest. He served a three year apprenticeship at one of his family's five restaurants and obtained the Diploma of the Guild of Hoteliers and Restaurateurs, finishing his training at the Dorchester. He emigrated to England in 1946 and opened his own restaurant, the Marquee, in 1952. He founded the Egon Ronay Guides in 1957 and has contributed regular columns to the press since 1954. He was the first non-French member of l'Academie des Gastronomes. In 1983 he was awarded the Médaille de la Ville de Paris by Jacques Chirac and was made a Chevalier de l'Ordre du Mérite Agricole in 1987. He founded the British Academy of Gatronomes in 1983 and has been its president ever since. He co-founded and is the vice-president of the International Academy of Gastronomy. He lives with his wife, Barbara, in Berkshire and London.

MATTHEW FORT ▼

Born in 1947 and educated at Eton, Roedean and the Universities of Lancaster and Pennsylvania, he worked for various advertising agencies until 1988 when he became food and drink editor of the Guardian. He has been writing a food column in the Illustrated London News and articles in Business on food related matters since 1986. He currently also writes for Esquire on cookery and on out of town restaurants for Country Homes and Interiors. Matthew Fort was Glenfiddich Food Writer of the Year and Restaurateurs' Food Writer of the Year in 1991, and Glenfiddich Restaurant Writer of the Year in 1992. He also edited the Guardian Sausage Directory in 1992.

DEREK COOPER ▶

In 1967 Derek Cooper wrote The Bad Food Guide, an examination of the British attitude to eating. Since then he has continued his investigations into every aspect of food and drink in various newspapers and magazines including the Guardian, the Observer Magazine, the Listener, the Sunday Standard and currently in Scotland on Sunday and also on radio and television. He presents the award-winning Radio 4 Food Programme for the BBC and Scotland's Larder for Grampian TV. He was the first chairman of the Guild of Food Writers and is currently its president.

OZ CLARKE ▼

A multi-talented and multi-faceted man, Oz Clarke's wine career began with captaining the wine-tasting team at Oxford. In 1973 he was the youngest ever Wine Taster and ten years later was named Wine Writer of the Year. During this time he was a leading West End actor, but turned to writing professionally in 1984. He is now wine correspondent for the Daily Telegraph and his wine guide is in its eighth edition. Oz Clarke's New Classic Wine, published in 1991, recently won the Glenfiddich, the Andre Simon and the Wine Guild awards. He is a presenter of BBC TV's Food and Drink programme and is a regular panellist on Radio 4's A Question of Taste. He lives in London.

STEVEN SPURRIER ▲

In 1971 Steven Spurrier purchased the Caves de la Madeleine in Paris which rapidly developed an international reputation and, in 1972-73, he opened l'Academie du Vin, Paris's first wine tasting school. Between 1975-79 he started, with partners, several wine based establishments and between 1981-87 opened Academies in New York, Zurich, Montreal, Tokyo and Toronto. He was chairman of the Circle of Wine Writers (UK) from 1987-90 and was re-elected chairman in 1991. He is now a full time wine consultant.

HUGH JOHNSON ▲

Hugh Johnson, born in London in 1939, made his name with his unstuffy, hard-to-put-down Wine in 1966, and his fame with The World Atlas of Wine in 1971. Over 20 years this has become one of the world's biggest-selling reference books, with over 2½ million copies sold in 13 languages. His other books include his annual (since 1977) Pocket Wine Book, The Story of Wine and its accompanying 13 part TV series, and books and many articles on gardening and trees. He lives in Essex and central France and sells beautiful wine glasses from his St. James's Street shop.
Photograph by Eduard Rieben

TOM DAY ▲

Tom Day became a wine producer, by chance, in 1974. He had been a fruit grower for some 12 years in Kent, Sussex and Hertfordshire when he took on the management of the 200 acre Fairfield Fruit Farm (now Three Choirs Vineyards) in Gloucestershire. He was presented with 2,500 vines, which he planted with a degree of scepticism. However, scepticism turned to deep interest when he was rewarded with a 17,500 bottle crop in 1976. He intensified his efforts and, after 18 years of steady progress, he now has 65 acres of vines, and has invested £1m in a new winery and restaurant. Tom says that he is still learning and improving, and sees a bright future ahead for Three Choirs Wines.

ADRIAN WHITE ➤

In November 1984 Adrian White, a Dorking-based businessman and engineer, purchased the Denbies estate in Dorking, and set about major refurbishment of both the house and the land. There is a history of viticulture on the estate's south facing slopes dating back to Roman times, and chronicled by Daniel Defoe in the late 17th century, and the soil and climate are remarkably similar to those of Champagne. Adrian White was determined to plant vines in some of his poorer grazing land. A total of 250 acres has been turned over to the production of vines, more than three times the size of any other UK producer, with 275,000 vines and 20 grape varieties, and Denbies produces some of Britain's best sparkling and table wines.

IAN BERWICK ▼

Ian Berwick was born in Malaya in 1938 and educated in England. After agricultural college he spent 16 years in tropical agriculture in West Malaysia. He married Eleanor in 1964 and they have two sons. They set up their vineyard in Suffolk during the course of many visits home, so that when they returned to England permanently in 1975, it was established. Bruisyard Wines have won many awards and Ian's commitment to quality has put them at the forefront of English winegrowers. They have also established a comprehensive herb centre, and tourism is a major part of the business. Ian was a founder member of the East Anglian Wine Growers Association and is currently its chairman. He is also the present chairman of the English Vineyards Association, and serves on its technical committee. He is a member of the Ministry of Agriculture's Vine Variety Classification and Quality Wine Committees and serves on the liaison committee between the industry and the Ministry.

DAVID CARR TAYLOR ▼

David Carr Taylor was born in Huddersfield in 1939, and was taken to live in India, where his father was an engineer on a tea plantation. He left India at the age of seven, and at 17 entered his father's engineering company as an apprentice, eventually becoming managing director. He married Linda in 1966, and in 1971/72 he planted his vineyard near Hastings. David passed his Diploma in Oenology in 1976 and, in 1981, he left the engineering business to develop the vineyard and to install his winery. David now makes wines for 18 vineyards, covering 200 acres. In 1992 he produced 500,000 bottles of wine. In 1985 David produced the first commercial sparkling wine in Britain and, with this and many of his still wines, he has won numerous awards both in Britain and France.

JONATHAN (JON) ▼ LEIGHTON

Jon Leighton was born in 1934, and for 30 years his life was dominated by motor sport. He finished fourth in an Australian Grand Prix and was a team member of Renault, Ford, BMC, Honda and Nissan in long distance touring car events, scoring many wins and competed in many of Australia's Championship rallies. He also established Melbourne's Sandown International racing circuit and two successful businesses. In 1978 Jon attended the English Wine Festival in Sussex and, by the spring of 1979, had planted his first vines at Stanlake Park, Berkshire. Typically, these were new varieties to England, and his hallmark has been in experimentation in variety and method ever since. In 1988 Jon was joined by the talented Australian winemaker John Warantschak and, under their labels Valley Vineyards and The Clocktower Selection, they have produced most of the front-running wines in tastings and competitions, and have won every national trophy.

WILLIAM GRANT & SONS

The Best of Scottish Spirit

Glenfiddich is the world's favourite malt whisky – the best selling brand which has revived the fortunes of malt after a century of playing second fiddle to blended whisky.

The story of Glenfiddich is the story of one family's dedication to the craft of whisky making. The Grant family have been distilling Glenfiddich in the Highlands of Scotland for over one hundred years, since the company's founder, William Grant, built the Glenfiddich Distillery in 1887.

Today, William Grant & Sons is still owned and managed by the direct descendants of William Grant. The current Chairman, Sandy Grant Gordon, is his great grandson (see page 32). Under his guidance, the family goal of distilling the best dram in the Highlands for the enjoyment of whisky drinkers everywhere is carried on.

William Grant began his apprenticeship in the Scotch whisky industry in 1866 as book-keeper at the Mortlach Distillery near his native Dufftown. Rising swiftly to the position of manager, he soon decided to build his own distillery and the rest of his family dedicated themselves to his goal.

After 20 years of careful saving, William Grant was able to buy equipment from the Cardow Distillery for £120. He had already located

the perfect spot for his Distillery, his choice determined by the proximity of a source of pure spring water known as the Robbie Dubh, on the slopes of the Conval Hills.

As any whisky distiller will tell you, water plays a vital role in the whisky making process, from mashing the malted barley to bottling the mature spirit, when the whisky is reduced to bottling strength with the addition of water.

Unlike other malts which are transported to the central belt of Scotland where they are reduced to bottling strength using a local source of water, Glenfiddich is bottled on the premises, using the same spring water from the Robbie Dubh with which the whole process began.

The Grant family have cannily preserved this precious water supply for their exclusive use by buying over 1,000 acres of land surrounding its source.

William Grant and his seven sons built their Distillery with their own hands in a valley which gave its name to the whisky that flowed from the

stills on Christmas Day in 1887 – Glenfiddich, which in Gaelic means the 'Valley of the Deer'.

William Grant and his family then set about the task of convincing buyers to try their whisky at a time when many distilleries were finding it hard to sell their malt because of the demand for blended whisky.

The Grant family's opportunity came when an unfortunate fire at a neighbouring distillery allowed them to take over its contract for the sale of malt whisky to a large wholesalers in Aberdeen.

The pioneering spirit displayed by William Grant has always distinguished William Grant & Sons as a company, which is one of the few privately owned independent Scotch whisky distillers remaining in the industry today.

In the 1960s, William Grant & Sons laid the foundations of the modern malt whisky market when they began to export Glenfiddich south of the Scottish border. This was the first time that malt whisky had been marketed in the UK, and it was considered a risky move by many in the industry.

The twentieth century has been the century of blended whisky and it is only in recent years, with the exporting of Glenfiddich, that the idea of drinking malt whisky has caught on outside Scotland.

Since then Glenfiddich has attracted a loyal following among connoisseurs of premium spirits, making it the best selling brand of malt whisky both in Great Britain and throughout the world.

Appropriately for the leading brand of malt whisky, Glenfiddich also pioneered the educational aspect of malt whisky appreciation, becoming in 1969 the first distillery to open its doors to the public.

Almost two million people have visited the Distillery since then. Glenfiddich provides a unique insight into the making of malt whisky, as it is the only Highland Distillery where the visitor can see the whole process of whisky making, from barley to bottle, at first hand.

Little has changed at the Glenfiddich Distillery since the days of William Grant himself. The Grant family has retained the traditional wooden washbacks (where fermentation takes place), rather than replacing them with easier-to-clean stainless steel.

Glenfiddich is also rare among distilleries today in keeping its own team of coppersmiths to tend the stills and maintaining a working cooperage where the casks in which the whisky matures are repaired.

The stills at Glenfiddich are the same size and shape as those installed by William Grant, despite the fact that increasing the still size would be a logical way to increase production. The Grant family believe that to alter the still size, or indeed any other aspect of their whisky making process, would be to risk altering the distinctive taste of Glenfiddich.

In the words of Sandy Grant Gordon, Chairman of William Grant & Sons and great grandson of the founder, "Because our family name goes onto every single bottle, we take a special pride in the quality of our whisky, and we will ensure that Glenfiddich always remains the best of Scottish spirit."

William Grant, the Company founder

Workers at the Glenfiddich Distillery in 1887

The family Bible

ALEXANDER GRANT GORDON

Alexander Grant Gordon was educated at Rugby and Cambridge, where he graduated in mathematics and law. Following National Service in the Royal Artillery, he joined William Grant & Sons Ltd, the Scotch whisky distillers, in 1954. In 1956 he became a director with responsibility initially for the African market and, subsequently, for Europe. He became joint managing director in 1963 and sole managing director in 1968. On the retirement of Eric Lloyd Roberts in 1976 he became chairman while retaining the position of managing director. In September 1992 he handed over the managing directorship to his nephew, but retained the chairmanship. Alexander Grant Gordon is a member of the council of the Scotch Whisky Association. In 1988 he was made vice-chairman and appointed CBE, and in July 1989 an honorary doctorate of law was conferred on him by St Andrews University.

JAMES BRUXNER

James Bruxner was educated at Eton and Oxford and commissioned in the Greenjackets. After experience on the London Stock Exchange and ten years in advertising agencies, he spent three years as marketing manager for Guinness in the UK. In January 1970 he joined IDV as export director of Gilbeys Ltd and became managing director in 1971. In September 1973 he became managing director of export at Justerini & Brooks and retained this post until 1984, when he became chairman and managing director. He holds a number of important positions within the Scotch Whisky industry. He is currently chairman of the Public Affairs Committee of the Scotch Whisky Association and chairman of the Keepers of the Quaich. The Keepers of the Quaich is an organisation which was founded to promote Scotch Whisky around the world. The membership of the society is continually growing as people prominent in the industry are nominated by existing members. Members come from 39 countries.

KEN DON ↟

Scotsman Ken Don was born in Alloa in 1945 and joined the Ind Coope Alloa brewery in 1963 as a pupil brewer. During the next four years, he attended Heriot Watt University, graduating with a BSc in brewing and went on to work for Allied Breweries at Watford, Warrington and Burton-on-Trent. He joined Young's Brewery in Wandsworth as Head Brewer in 1980 and has overseen a complete redevelopment of both the brewhouse and the packaging lines, resulting in a brewery capable of producing a wide range of cask and bottled ales as well as keg lagers. Ken has won many awards from both the brewing industry and the Campaign for Real Ale during his career at Young's, but his proudest moment came when he was awarded the Championship Trophy for the best real ale in Britain in the 1992 Brewing Industry International Awards, the industry's most prestigious accolade.

DAVID POLDEN ▷

Born in Hertfordshire in 1949, David Polden qualified as an engineer and a brewer, and joined Morrells Brewery Limited, the oldest surviving family run business in Oxford, as Second Brewer in 1975. He became Head Brewer in 1989. In 1990 Morrells-brewed Harp Extra was the championship runner-up in the brewing industry International Awards Draught Lager competition, out of 76 British and foreign brews. In the 1992 competition, Morrells Dark Mild was judged to be the Champion Draught Mild Ale, winning the gold medal in its class.

David is in the forefront of those striving to keep the best of British traditional brewing alive and thriving.

GRAHAM SIMPSON ↟

Following a three year BSc in biochemistry at York University, Graham Simpson joined Allied Breweries as a production management trainee in 1980. During his 12 years at Allied, he gained experience as a shift brewer and a member of the packaging development team. He has held the position of Head Brewer at Tetley Walker since 1990. When Tetley Walker began to brew and supply Greenall Whitley's ale brands in August 1990, he was given the task of ensuring the consistency of taste and texture of the brand which was already an established product in the region. He was heavily involved in the Greenall product development as well as giving care and attention to all the other beers which Tetley holds in its portfolio, with the conspicuous success that won the brewery the 1992 Championship Trophy for Brewery Conditioned Ales for Greenall's Bitter.

PETER HERBERT ➤

Peter Herbert is the founder and proprietor of Gravetye Manor, probably the best known of English country house hotels. He started his catering career at the Gore Hotel Restaurant and Elizabethan Rooms, where he was managing director from 1950-67. He launched London's first floating post-war restaurant and night club with the Yardarm Club in 1954. Peter acquired Gravetye Manor in 1958, an exquisite Elizabethan Manor. Set in William Robinson's famous natural English gardens, Gravetye was Egon Ronay's Hotel of the Year 1978, and is the joint fourth longest running entry in the Good Food Guide. Peter Herbert is a past chairman of the British Branch of Chateaux & Relais, and a Fellow of the Hotel & Catering Institute & Management Association.

MARTIN SKAN ▼

Equipped with experience as an officer in the Dorset Regiment, followed by ten years in advertising and management, in 1966 Martin Skan bought Chewton Glen with his brother, who later withdrew from the partnership. At that time small country house hotels like Chewton Glen were fast becoming fashionable. Martin has long been at the forefront of this trend, with Chewton Glen winning, among other honours, the Egon Ronay Hotel of the Year Award in 1976, a Michelin Star in 1981 and the title of American Express Country Hotel of the Year in 1991 and 1992. Martin, who works closely with his Swiss-born wife and partner Brigitte, was voted Personality of the Year in 1990, Master Innholder in 1991 and Hotelier of the Year in 1991. Today Chewton Glen, attractively situated in the New Forest, offers 56 rooms, a large pool and tennis courts – both indoors, and a health club.

RONALD JONES ▲

Ronald (Ron) Jones, OBE, began his career at the Adelphi Hotel and at the age of 29, after service in the Royal Navy, became general manager of British Transport Hotels. He held a succession of important positions in the industry, including management of Scotland's Turnberry Hotel and of the Athenaeum, then Rank Hotels' flagship, for 11 years until, in 1984, he was appointed director and general manager of Claridge's. Since then Ron has seen the top-flight London hotel voted Britain's best by both American Express and Courvoisier in 1991 and 1992. Other honours received by the hotel under his management include, in 1987, its recognition by the USA's Travel and Leisure magazine as one of the "Ten Best Hotels in the World in the Grand Tradition" and, in 1990, Five Red Stars from the Automobile Association and the National Clean Kitchen Award. In 1989 Ron received the OBE for his services to the hotel industry.

JONATHAN WIX ▲

Jonathan Wix, managing director of A Way of Life plc, began buying and selling houses while he was a student in the early 1970s. Having developed properties ranging from London flats to grand country houses, in 1989 he bought four old grain warehouses in Leeds, turning them into an acclaimed 39-bedroomed luxury hotel. Opened in 1991, 42 The Calls won the Leeds Architecture Award ("altered buildings" category) the following year.

FRANCIS COULSON AND BRIAN SACK ▲

In 1948 Francis Coulson bought a "family mansion" on the edge of Ullswater. By 1949 he had created a five bedroomed hotel, the beginnings of the first country house hotel in the world. In 1952 Brian Sack joined Francis, and the Sharrow Bay Hotel was really born. Since those early days, Sharrow Bay has expanded to 28 bedrooms, but the atmosphere of an oasis where people are really made to feel that they are being cared for in every way, with no pressure from the outside world, remains. Francis and Brian have always had a great love of people, and this feeling has not diminished over the years.

CHRISTOPHER ROUSE ▼

The continuing success of Ayrshire's Turnberry Hotel, with its spa and two world-famous golf courses, reflects the outstanding abilities of its general manager since 1987, Christopher Rouse. Honours received in recent years by the Turnberry include the RAC's Five Star Hotel of the Year Award in 1989 and Five Stars from the AA in 1990. Two years later its Ailsa Course was voted the UK's number three by Golf World.

DAVID LEVIN ▼

Now aged 55, Glasgow-born David Levin has been in the restaurant and hotel business for nearly 40 years. He left school at the age of 16, and his career began with British Transport Hotels, as a trainee manager. By the age of 25 he had become a manager at Lochalsh Hotel, overlooking the Isle of Skye. At this point in his career he decided to go it alone, and bought The Royal Oak at Yattenden, which he and his wife,

Margaret, decided to turn into a pub serving top quality food. They baked their own bread, cooked duck for the sandwiches and made their own pâtés. He even imported his own sherry, and very soon was in the Good Food Guide, confirming his belief that, if you are good enough, people will find you. In 1971 David opened the 48 bedroomed Capital Hotel, in a "back street" in Knightsbridge, built to his own design. The Capital is today one of only two London members of Chateaux & Relais. In 1991 he won the Catey Award for Restaurateur of the Year, and has produced three Michelin starred chefs, Richard Shepherd, Brian Turner and now Philip Britten. David Levin now owns The Greenhouse (run by son Joseph), Le Metro and L'Hotel; his newest venture is shipping wine from his Loire vineyard. He is the chairman of the British Hospitality Association.
Photograph by Sarah Ainslie

GEORGE GORING ▲

Trained in the hotel business in Switzerland, Germany and England, George Goring became managing director of the Goring Hotel, London, SW1, and the Spa Hotel, Tunbridge Wells, in 1970, both owned and run by the Goring family. The former, opened in 1910 by George's grandfather, was the first hotel in the world to have a private bathroom and central heating to every room. George, who was Hotelier of the Year in 1990 and the following year received the OBE for services to hotelkeeping, has served for over 30 years on numerous committees concerned with training, tourism and all aspects of the hotel industry.

DAVID NAYLOR-LEYLAND ▼

Born in 1955, and educated at Eton and Sandhurst, David Naylor-Leyland started his career with four years in the Life Guards. For the next ten years he was involved in property development, in all its manifestations, initially with high quality residential developments, but progressing to include commercial and industrial. In 1988 he purchased the properties in Egerton Terrace and Gardens which were to become the Egerton House and Franklin Hotels, and involved himself in every stage of their development.

HARVEY GOLDSMITH ▲

Over two decades Harvey Goldsmith has built a reputation as Britain's leading entrepreneur in the concert business. As chief executive officer and joint managing director of the Allied Entertainments Group, formed in 1986, he is involved not only in concert promotion, but also TV and film production and video distribution. In addition to his staging of events by international artists from the Rolling Stones to Pavarotti, the Prince's Trust concerts – each raising more than £1.5 million for charity – are a continuing success. He masterminded the Live Aid concert which raised over £100 million for famine relief. In 1990 Harvey was executive producer of The Wall in Berlin, and in 1992 he organised the Tribute to Freddie Mercury concert at Wembley and was producer of the Tribute to Bob Dylan, held at New York's Madison Square Garden.

EDWARD HOARE ▶

Educated at Winchester and Oxford, Edward Hoare pursued management and accountancy training with separate employers before becoming managing director of the Warwickshire-based corporate hospitality company Elegant Days. Since 1989 he has concurrently been Treasurer of the industry's trade organisation, the Corporate Hospitality Association.

JIM BIGNAL ▲

Jim Bignal worked for Wilkinson Sword, RHM, Buitoni and the British Printing Corporation, mainly in sales and marketing, before settting up his own business in 1981. The Ealing-based Cavendish Consultancy, of which he is managing director, offers hospitality packages at a wide range of sporting, cultural and showbusiness events. Jim is also a founder member and current chairman of the hospitality industry's trade organisation, the Corporate Hospitality and Event Association (CHA).

◀ KIT PETERS

It was Kit Peters who brought paintball games to Britain in 1984. After a varied career including naval service, working as a shipping manager and selling fax and telecommunications equipment, he set up Skirmish Corporate Services in 1985 and within two years had 32 franchised paintball sites across Britain and Europe. In 1988 Kit Peters Extraordinary Events was formed, specialising in unique forms of participative corporate events. The following year Kit gave up his directorship of the Skirmish franchise operation to concentrate on his own paintball site and to develop the Surrey-based corporate entertainment business. With the help of five full-time staff and over 100 regular contractors, Kit has organised over 400 events for British, European and American companies.

PATRICK GRIFFIN

Patrick Griffin, director of Trak 1 Racing, was quick to realise the potential appeal to the corporate hospitality industry and the public alike of indoor go-karting. In 1988, with his business partner Ricky Ferdinando, he opened an impressive circuit in an Uxbridge warehouse, which since that time has played host to over 100,000 competitors. On offer are race events catering for participants ranging from novices to world-class Grand Prix champions, with 40-50 drivers usually competing. A display-and-promotional area is available for corporate use during events. Trak 1's success led to its opening a Honda Pilot dune-buggy circuit near Reading in 1990 and a twin-engine Honda Pro-kart circuit in 1992.

MIKE BEST ▼

After an army career from which he retired lieutenant-colonel in 1982, Mike Best founded and became managing director of the Westerly Sea School. His military roles, including that of chief instructor for the Joint Services Adventurous Training Centre in the UK, equipped him to set new standards of instruction in sailing and to develop a series of programmes of sailing-based corporate hospitality. In 1990 Mike joined Sunsail, an international yacht charter company based at Port Solent, where he set up and developed a corporate hospitality division. Under Mike's guidance the fleet is in constant demand for inter-company race events, leadership training and one-day fun events. He was awarded the MBE in 1980.

Photograph by Pat Collinge

NICHOLAS PRICE ▲

During his 25 years of running the family-owned Western Manor Hotel near Oxford, Nicholas Price acquired first-hand knowledge of the good food and fine wines that are so much a part of the service he now provides to corporate clients. Formed in 1986, Nick and his partner Richard Stephenson's company A Day in the Country offers a day's clay shooting, fly fishing for trout and other country sports with international experts. But, however good the sport, it is the food that rounds off the day to perfection. Simple but based on the best British ingredients, the menu includes finest Scotch salmon, best prime fillet of beef and a choice of seven or eight puddings and ice creams.

DUNCAN REVIE ▼

Cambridge-educated Duncan Revie, son of the late Don Revie who managed Leeds United and England, qualified with a City law firm before leaving in 1978 to pursue a career in sports hospitality. One of the pioneers of the industry, he set up his own company Total Sport in 1984. Since then the company has expanded to embrace sports management and event promotion in both sports and music, alongside the core business of providing stylish hospitality at events all over the world.

VICTOR CESERANI ⬆

A true veteran of the culinary world, Victor started his distinguished career in 1934 when, at the age of 15, he became apprentice chef at the Ritz. The war was spent in the Royal Fusiliers and Catering Corps and in 1942 he married his wife Letty. From 1946 to 1950 Victor continued to develop his skills at the Borders club. A year at teacher training college followed, prior to a 13-year stint as a lecturer in professional cookery. In 1964 Victor was appointed head of Ealing Catering School, a position he was to occupy for 16 years apart from a year spent as a visiting professor at Michigan State University, where he received an MBA. The author of several books on catering and cooking, including the very popular Practical Cooking and Theory of Catering, Victor has also written an autobiography, the aptly titled Catering for Life. He has been chief examiner and advisor for the City & Guilds, served on the council and educational committee for the Hotel and Catering Institute and been a judge for numerous cookery competitions. He is an honorary member of the Association of Culinaire Français, the Academie Culinaire de France, Chefs and Cookes Civile and a Fellow of Ealing College. He has received the Grand Cordon Culinaire, the Chevalier des Palmes Academiques and a Lifetime Achievement award. In 1975 he received an MBE for services to catering education.

PAUL DYSON ▼

Paul Dyson's gift for eye-catching promotion first received widespread recognition during his tenure as display and visual merchandising coordinator for Harvey Nichols from 1980-88. His work at the company embraced all aspects of visual design from house graphic styles to outside social functions and won him three Evening Standard Best Window awards. Similar success attended his move to Harrods where his Month in the Country promotion doubled store turnover for six weeks. In 1989 Paul became managing director of his own company, Paul Dyson and Associates, providing a range of services from press launches to lectures on visual merchandising. Among the notable projects undertaken by the company are the front-of-house decorations for the Royal Opera House during a state gala, the design and realisation of major parts of the Sovereign exhibition for the V&A, and the party decor for Jewels of Fantasy, also for the V&A.

ALLEN JONES ▼

Born in 1936, Allen Jones spent the first ten years after secondary school in the Merchant Navy and it was there that his catering career began – with a sharp knife and 2cwt of potatoes to be peeled by hand! From galley boy to baker, from assistant to chief cook, his life revolved around pots and pans. Back on dry land, industrial catering seemed a natural choice for Allen, leading to employment in the motorway service area, an industry then in its infancy with only a few miles of the M1 and M6 in existence. He worked as general manager of Little Chef for a number of years before starting up his own company, Welcome Break, in 1973. A merger with Happy Eater followed and Allen spent 13 successful years as managing director of the company before the vagaries of finance persuaded him to branch out on his own again with A.J.'s Family Restaurants. With over 20 restaurants bearing his name, Allen Jones' love for the catering business shows no signs of waning. He is married with two children.

◄ WILLIAM WEBER

The current manager of John (Personal Services), a catering company established in 1952 in preparation for the Coronation, William Weber continues to maintain the high standards set by its founder, John Cawston. A trained chef, William's expertise in catering stretches beyond cooking to embrace all aspects of party planning from security personnel to disco lighting, from the small function to the full-scale bash. For a company with a reputation for excellent waiting staff, traditional courtesy and classic cuisine, they have a rather frivolous motto borrowed from Miss Piggy: "Never eat more than you can lift."

TONY PAGE ▲

Tony Page, 44, has loved catering ever since his boy scout days and, on leaving Westminster School, trained at the Plaza Athenee in Paris for 18 months. After a spell at Grosvenor House, he became assistant manager at the first Moat House when it opened in Brentwood, Essex. Following this, Tony spent the next two years at Holiday Inns at Plymouth and London before joining the King David Suite where he transformed the small kosher catering company into an organisation serving almost every five-star hotel in London. In December 1991, Tony started his own company, Tony Page Ltd, where, from their state-of-the-art kitchen/warehouse in North London, Tony and his staff mastermind some of the most successful parties in the capital.

JOHN ROXBURGH ▼

Founder, along with Rolline Frewen, of the Admirable Crichton, a party design and catering company named after J. M. Barrie's punctilious butler, John Robertson Roxburgh has built a reputation by presenting stylish and imaginative food combined with an inspired flair for party design. By offering service and creativity, John has ensured that the Admirable Crichton occupies a unique position in the party catering market. Sensitive to changing times, the 12-year-old company adapted its approach during the Nineties to reflect the less ostentatious atmosphere now fashionable.

RICHARD TEAR ▲

Richard Tear's expertise is the result of a lifetime in the field. Born in Hampshire in 1945, his first catering experience was gained in the family business – a hotel between Romsey and Winchester. After studying in Bournemouth and working in several local restaurants, he began a long association with J. Lyons Catering, starting as a trainee manager before becoming one of the youngest hotel managers of the Robley Inn Group. Two years later he returned to the restaurant group, managing several establishments before being promoted to area manager. His time at J. Lyons Catering head office was spent in the leisure and concessions division until 1979 brought further success with Richard being appointed general manager of Town-and-Country Catering. Richard has fond memories of this, a varied and demanding role in which he was responsible for a substantial number of contracts and events including Wimbledon tennis championships. In 1991 Richard was invited by the Goodhew family to join the long-established firm of Searcys, where his position as chief executive ensures that his considerable talents are in constant demand.

◄ CHARLES BOYD

For the past ten years Charles Boyd and his company, Chester Boyd, have been synonymous with the City of London, providing the one-of-a-kind catering demanded by its corporate institutions. With a splendid choice of 11 livery halls for a venue or the option of an on-location service, the carefully planned catering of the company has sweetened many a Eurobond deal or multinational merger. Describing himself as almost a fashion victim of food and wine, Charles' personality is integral to the style of the company and his reputation for providing creative, top-class service with a minimum of fuss has earned him the loyalty of many in what must be London's most competitive square mile.

IAN REES ▼

Ian Rees gained much of his experience of the service industry in the Sixties while working as purser/hotel officer with the Cunard Line. In 1972, after travelling extensively throughout the world and serving aboard liners such as the Queen Mary, the QEII and the Sylvana, Ian left the world of ocean liners to found Cadogan Caterers with partner John Bateson. In the 20 years since then, Ian and John have developed their services including the production of high quality confectionery. Apart from operating catering facilities at sites such as the Royal Horticultural Society's Wisley Garden in Surrey, Windsor Great Park and the Royal Botanic Gardens at Wakehurst Place, Cadogan Caterers operates an outside division which personally tailors to corporate events, royal functions or private parties.

RICHARD BEGGS ▲

Richard Beggs is managing director of highly successful caterers, The Moving Venue, a company he started in 1984. Born in 1957 Richard's first taste of the industry came at the age of 18 when he joined the Savoy Hotel's Food & Beverage Management Training Programme, which saw him training in the kitchens of Claridges, the Berkeley and Simpsons in the Strand. Work at major London hotels followed, with Richard honing his skills in hotel management and earning a name for himself in the business. After taking time out to complete his HCIMA at Oxford Polytechnic, Richard joined the Dover Street Restaurant and Wine Bar as the overall manager of Food and Beverage. It was during this period that Richard conceived the idea that was to become The Moving Venue, an idea that is now very much reality with over 20 full-time staff serving corporate and private clients all over London.

JEREMY PAXMAN

A graduate in English from Cambridge University, Jeremy Paxman was also the editor of the University newspaper. In 1977, after working in local radio, he moved to Northern Ireland as the first full-time television reporter specialising in investigative work. In 1977 he moved to London, where he worked as a reporter on Tonight, and the documentary series The Bear Next Door. In 1979 he became a reporter for Panorama, and for six years reported from around the world. During this time he wrote (with Robert Harris) A Higher Form of Killing, a history of chemical and biological warfare and his book on Central America, Through the Volancoes. His investigation into the death of Roberto Calvi, Called to Account, won the RTS Award for international current affairs. In 1985 he returned to England to present The Six O'Clock News, and then London Plus. He moved to present Breakfast News in 1986. Since 1989, Jeremy Paxman has been presenting Newsnight for BBC 2, and is also the host of the critical programme Did You See?

PETER SISSONS ▼

Peter Sissons is the presenter of BBC's Question Time and the main presenter of the Six O'Clock News. Born in Liverpool, he read Philosophy, Politics and Economics at University College, Oxford, before joining ITN as a writer. He became a reporter in 1967. In 1968 he was wounded by gunfire whilst covering the Biafran War. He became ITN's News Editor in 1969, Industrial Correspondent in 1970 and Industrial Editor in 1972. In 1978 he became the presenter of ITN's News at One and, in 1982, he presented the newly created Channel 4 News. Peter Sissons was awarded the Royal Television Society's Judges Award in 1988.

◄¬ JOHN SIMPSON

A BBC journalist since leaving Cambridge in 1966, John Simpson was first a sub-editor then reporter and then foreign correspondent for radio news. He joined TV news in 1978 as Diplomatic Correspondent. John covered the revolution in Iran from its inception and accompanied the Ayatollah Khomeini on his flight to Tehran. From 1980 to 1988 he was the BBC's Political Editor and presenter of The Nine O'Clock News. In 1988 he was appointed Foreign Affairs Editor. He reported on the Russian withdrawal from Afghanistan, the breaching of the Berlin Wall, the peaceful revolution in Prague and the fall of Ceaucescu in Romania. He reported from Baghdad before, during and immediately after the 1990/91 Gulf War, for which he was appointed CBE. He joined the Spectator as contributing editor in 1990. John Simpson won the James Cameron Award in 1990, was RTS Journalist of the Year in 1991 and won the Richard Dimbleby Award in 1992. He is the author of two novels and books on Argentina, Iran, the fall of communism, the Gulf War and Peru.

DAVID DIMBLEBY ▲

David Dimbleby is a major presenter of current affairs programmes and documentaries for BBC Television. He learnt French in Paris and Italian in Perugia and studied politics, philosophy and economics at Christ Church, Oxford. He joined the BBC as a news reporter in Bristol, and appeared in Network programmes from 1962. During his BBC career, he has presented Panorama, 24 Hours, Nationwide and People and Power and chaired The Dimbleby Talk-In. Well known as the presenter of This Week Next Week, he also wrote and presented the award-winning series The White Tribe of Africa. David Dimbleby has been commentator for a wide range of special outside broadcast events for BBC Television and has taken part in Budget Specials and a number of Election programmes. He was anchor man for the 1983, 1987 and 1992 General Elections, and for the US Presidential programmes of 1984, 1988 and 1992, when he handled the Washington coverage.

◄¬ TREVOR McDONALD

Trevor McDonald began his career in television in his native Trinidad, where he read the nightly news and was an interviewer on local current affairs programmes. He joined ITN from the BBC World Service in 1973 as a reporter and, in 1978, became Sports Correspondent, covering the soccer World Cup in Argentina and the cricket World Series in Australia. His next job was as Diplomatic Correspondent and, in 1987, he became Diplomatic Editor of Channel 4 News. In 1990, Trevor achieved two great interviewing coups, gaining the first British television interview with the newly released Nelson Mandela, and becoming still the only Briton to be granted a televised audience with Sadam Hussein. Trevor McDonald is now the main presenter of ITN's News at Ten. He was awarded the OBE in 1992.

MARTYN LEWIS ▼

Martyn Lewis, currently a main presenter of BBC's Nine O'Clock News, has been a television journalist for 25 years, since graduating from Trinity College, Dublin. He worked for BBC Belfast, then HTV, before joining ITN in 1970. He set up and ran ITN's Northern Bureau, became a foreign correspondent, newscaster and documentary producer before returning to the BBC in 1986. Amongst his numerous documentaries are Battle for the Falklands, The Secret Hunters, Fight Cancer and Health UK. He is the author of three light-hearted books, And Finally (1983), Cats in the News (1991) and Dogs in the News (1992) and two charity books, Tears and Smiles – The Hospice Handbook (1989) and Go For It – The Essential Guide to Opportunities for Young People (1993). His extensive charity books work is focused on the Hospice Movement and disadvantaged young people. He is Chairman of Drive for Youth, a Freeman of the City of London, a Fellow of the Royal Society of Arts and a Director of the Institute for Citizenship Studies.

MARTIN BELL ▼

Martin Bell joined the BBC in 1962, after acquiring a first class degree in English from Cambridge University. He has been a BBC TV news reporter since 1965, became Diplomatic Correspondent in 1977 and Washington Correspondent in 1978. He has reported from over 50 countries and has covered two Middle East Wars, in 1967 and 1973, the Nigerian Civil War and the Vietnam War. He has also reported extensively from Northern Ireland. His US experience includes coverage of the Democratic Convention in Chicago in 1968, the 1968 race riots, the Nixon Brezhnev Summit in 1973 and President Nixon's resignation in 1974. He was appointed Berlin correspondent in 1989. During the Gulf War in 1991, Martin was attached to the Media Response Team with the 7th Armoured Brigade. In August 1992, he was hit by shrapnel in the abdomen whilst filming shelling in Sarajevo, and was operated on in a UN field hospital. Martin Bell was named RTS Reporter of the Year in 1977 and, in 1992, received the OBE for services to television news.

Photograph by BBC TV News

JOHN SUCHET ▶

John Suchet graduated MA(Hons) in Political Science and Philosophy and joined BBC TV News as sub-editor in 1971. He moved to ITN in 1972 and became a reporter in 1976. By 1979 he was newscasting as well as reporting and, in 1981, became ITN's Washington Correspondent for two years. John has reported major events all over the world; he accompanied the Ayatollah Khomeini on his return from exile and filmed behind the Mujaheddin lines following the Russian invasion of Afghanistan. In 1986 he was named Journalist of the Year by the Royal Television Society for his coverage of the Philippine elections. John Suchet is currently the presenter of ITN's early evening news.

IAN McCASKILL ▼

Ian McCaskill learned his meteorology during National Service with the RAF in Cyprus, after studying science at Glasgow University. For the next 30 years he worked at 16 meteorological offices from Wick to Malta. He started television work in 1978, and has become a very familiar figure on the screen. Recently widowed, Ian lives in Buckinghamshire with his two daughters.

MICHAEL BUERK ▼

Michael Buerk is main presenter of BBC Television's The Nine O'Clock News. He also presents and reports for BBC TV's Nature and is chairman of BBC Radio's The Moral Maze. In addition to these regular commitments, he chairs, presents, reports for and contributes to a number of other television and radio programmes. He also lectures on international issues and environmental matters and chairs conferences on current affairs and political and industrial questions. Before joining the BBC in 1973, Michael gained his journalistic experience on newspapers, completing the Thomson Organisation's graduate training scheme on the Western Mail and subsequently working on the Daily Mail. He has probably won more international awards than any other British journalist, notably for his coverage of the Ethiopian Famine in 1984/85, which was shown worldwide to an audience of billions and led to a massive international relief effort. He was named Television Journalist of the Year by the RTS in 1984 and in 1988 won the James Cameron Award for his coverage of the township uprising in South Africa. Apart from his many television and journalism awards, he has also received awards from the United Nations and the Roman Catholic Church.

MICHAEL BOGDANOV ▲

Co-founder and joint artistic director of the English Shakespeare Company, Michael Bogdanov was educated at Trinity College, Dublin, in Munich and at the Sorbonne. After leaving university he directed, produced and wrote for television in England and Ireland, before moving into the theatre. After directing for the Oxford Playhouse and the Royal Court, he joined the RSC as an assistant director. In 1971 he became an associate director of the Tyneside Theatre Company and, in 1973, became associate director of the Leicester Theatre Trust and artistic director of the Phoenix Theatre, Leicester, from where his production of The Magic Drum toured the UK, culminating in a season at the National Theatre. He became artistic director of the Young Vic from 1978 to 1980. In 1979 he received the Director of the Year award for his Taming of the Shrew for the RSC. In 1986, with Michael Pennington, Michael founded the English Shakespeare Company and his seven play history cycle, The Wars of the Roses, won him the Laurence Olivier Award for Best Director 1990. Michael was the first non-German to hold the post of intendant (artistic director) of the Deutsches Schauspielhaus in Hamburg, Germany's leading National Theatre (1989-91).

TREVOR NUNN ▼

Trevor Nunn was educated at Downing College, Cambridge. He joined the Royal Shakespeare Company in 1964 and became artistic director in 1968, running the company until his retirement from the post in 1986. He has directed over 30 productions for the RSC, including Macbeth, The Comedy of Errors, All's Well That Ends Well, Once in a Lifetime, Three Sisters, Juno and the Paycock, The Fair Maid of the West, Othello and Measure for Measure. He co-directed Nicholas Nickleby, which won five Tony awards, Peter Pan and Les Miserables, which won eight Tony awards and has become the most performed musical in the world. Productions outside the RSC include the Tony award winning Cats, Starlight Express, Aspects of Love, Chess, Timon of Athens and Heartbreak House. His work at Glyndebourne includes Idomeneo, Porgy and Bess, Cosi Fan Tutte and Peter Grimes. Among the accolades which Trevor Nunn has received for his television work are a BAFTA award for Antony and Cleopatra and an Emmy for Nicholas Nickleby. He has directed two films. He was appointed CBE in 1978.

STEVEN BERKOFF ▲

Steven Berkoff was born in Stepney and studied drama and mime in London and Paris. He worked with a number of repertory companies and, in 1968, formed the London Theatre Group. His first original stage play, East, was presented by the London Theatre Group at the Edinburgh Festival in 1975. Since 1975, among the many adaptations which he has created, directed and toured are: The Trial, Metamorphosis, Agamemnon and The Fall Of The House Of Usher. He has directed and toured Hamlet and Macbeth and directed Coriolanus and Salome. Among Berkoff's original works are Decadence, Greek, Harry's Christmas Lunch, West, Acapulco, Kvetch, Sink The Belgrano and Massage. He has published a collection of poetry and prose, America, a film journal, A Prisoner Of Rio, and a production diary, I Am Hamlet. The Theatre Of Steven Berkoff, a photographic history of his productions over the last two decades, is also available. Many of Steven's creations have been televised and filmed. Among the films in which he has appeared are: A Clockwork Orange, McVicar, Absolute Beginners, Octopussy, Rambo, Winds Of Change and The Krays. His TV acting credits include Beloved Family, Knife Edge, War And Rembrance and Michelangelo – Season Of Giants.

SIR ANDREW LLOYD WEBBER, FRCM

The prolific composer Andrew Lloyd Webber was born in 1948 into a musical family. His first musical, Joseph and the Amazing Technicolour Dreamcoat, was produced in 1968 and, since then, his stage hits have followed in rapid succession: Jesus Christ Superstar (1971), Evita (1976), Variations (1978), and Tell Me On A Sunday (1979), which he combined as Song and Dance (1982), Cats (1981), Starlight Express (1984), The Phantom of the Opera (1986) and Aspects of Love (1989). His other work includes film scores for Gumshoe (1971) and The Odessa File (1983) and his setting for the Latin Requiem mass, Requiem (1985). He composed the music for the opening and closing ceremonies of the 1992 Barcelona Olympic Games. He is the only person ever to have had three musicals running simultaneously in London and New York, a feat which he has achieved twice, and the only person ever to have six shows playing simultaneously in the West End.

MAX STAFFORD-CLARK ▼

The artistic director of the Royal Court Theatre in London, Max Stafford-Clark, was educated at Trinity College, Dublin, and started his theatrical career at the Traverse Theatre in Edinburgh. He founded the Joint Stock Theatre Company with William Gaskill in 1974 and took up his current position in 1979. Among the productions he directed for Joint Stock were The Speakers by Heathcote Williams (1974), Fanshen by David Hare (1975) and Cloud Nine by Caryl Churchill (1979). Under his direction the Royal Court has retained the revolutionary, high risk principles on which it was founded, with artistic and commercial successes too numerous to mention – and, of course, a few failures. Among the former, Caryl Churchill's Serious Money (1987) transferred to enormous acclaim to the West End and Broadway and Our Country's Good by Timberlake Wertenbaker (1988/89) transferred to the West End and successfully toured Australia and Canada.

CAMERON MACKINTOSH ▼

Cameron Mackintosh produced his first West End musical, Anything Goes, in 1969, when he was 23 years old. It was a financial disaster, but he survived to produce a number of new musicals in the 1970s, including Trelawny and The Card, as well as hit revivals of such shows as Godspell, Oklahoma! and My Fair Lady. He had great success with two musical revues, Side by Side by Sondheim and Tomfoolery, celebrating the work of Tom Lehrer. In 1981 came his first collaboration with Andrew Lloyd Webber on the musical Cats – now the longest running musical in the West End and on Broadway. Subsequently, he has co-produced Lloyd Webber's Song & Dance and the phenomenally successful Phantom Of The Opera. In 1985 he produced Boublil and Schonberg's Les Miserables, which has since become the most performed musical in the world and, in 1989, he first presented Miss Saigon, by the same authors. More recently, he has produced Five Guys Named Moe in the West End and on Broadway, and Moby Dick in the West End. His latest New York production, Putting It Together, a Sondheim revue, sees the return to the stage of Julie Andrews, after a 30-year absence. In 1992 he received the Richard Rodgers Award for Excellence in Musical Theatre, awarded previously to only three people among them, appropriately, Julie Andrews.

ACTORS

NICHOLAS LYNDHURST ▼

Nick Lyndhurst started to act professionally in 1971 and has since acquired many credits to his name. His television appearances include: Davy in Anne of Avonlea; Peter in Heidi; Canty and Prince Edward in The Prince and the Pauper; Tootles in Peter Pan; Raymond in Going Straight; Adam in Butterflies; Philip in Father's Day and Dobson in the BBC serial To Serve Them All My Days. He has also appeared as a guest on a number of shows. He is probably best known for his six series and five Christmas specials as Rodney in Only Fools and Horses. He also starred in three series of The Two of Us and three series of the Piglet Files. His films include Endless Nights; Bequest to the nation; Bullshot and Gunbus. Nick's theatre work includes: Harding's Luck, at the Greenwich Theatre and Trial Run, at the Oxford Playhouse. He toured in the Peter Shaffer double bill, Black Comedy and The Private Ear. He made his West End debut in The Foreigner, at The Albery and most recently starred in Straight And Narrow at the Aldwych Theatre.

JOHN THAW ▲

One of Britain's most popular and respected actors, John Thaw was born in 1942 and educated at RADA, where he won the Vanburgh and Liverpool Playhouse Awards. He made his stage debut in 1960 in A Shred of Evidence at the Liverpool Playhouse. Best known to the public as a television star, for many years he played the lead in The Sweeney, collecting several awards. He starred in two spin-off films of The Sweeney, for which he won The Evening Standard Best Film Actor of the Year Award in 1977. He made two series of the situation comedy, Home to Roost, for which he won the Pye Award for Best Comedy Performance and he has been the celebrated Inspector Morse since 1986. Inspector Morse won him the BAFTA for Best Actor of 1989 and, in 1990, the Variety Actor of the Year Award. John has continued to work on the stage and, amongst his credits are: Sergeant Musgrave in Sergeant Musgrave's Dance (National Theatre, 1982); Wolsey in Henry VIII and Sir Toby Belch in Twelfth Night (Stratford, 1983/4); Doolittle in Pygmalion (Shaftesbury Theatre, 1984) and, to great acclaim, he took the lead in All My Sons at the Royal Exchange, Manchester in 1988. Amongst his many film appearances, John Thaw may currently be seen as Fred Karno in Richard Attenborough's Chaplin.

SIMON CALLOW ▼

Born in 1949 and educated at the London Oratory School and Queen's University, Belfast, Simon Callow speaks fluent French and German. As an actor, his London produtions include: Schippel (1975); A Mad World My Masters (1977); Arturo Ui, Mary Barnes (1978); As You Like It, Amadeus (1979); The Beastly Beatitudes of Balthazar B, Total Eclipse, Restoratio (1981); The Relapse (1983) On The Spot (1984); Kiss of the Spiderwoman (1985); Faust I and II and Single Spies (1988). He has directed theatre and opera in the UK, Europe and the USA, most recently Carmen Jones, at the Old Vic, for which he won the 1992 Laurence Olivier Award for Best Director of a Musical, and Ballad of the Sad Cafe, in 1991. His television credits include Instant Enlightenment Inc. VAT; Wings of Song; Man of Destiny, as Napoleon; Juvenalia; La Ronde, as the poet; All The World's A Stage; Chance in a Million, the series; Handel, in the title role; David Copperfield, as Mr Micawber; Trials of Oz; Bye Bye Columbus and, most recently, he appeared as the vicar in Femmes Fatales for the BBC. His publications incude Being an Actor; A Difficult Actor; Charles Laughton and various translations.

SIR IAN McKELLEN ▲

Ian McKellen was born in the North of England in 1939. He won a scholarship to Cambridge where he graduated in English Literature and joined the Belgrade Theatre Company in Coventry in 1961. His London debut in A Scent of Flowers (1964) won him the Clarence Derwent Award and a season with the National Theatre Company at the Old Vic. Rapidly establishing himself as "the leading classical actor of his generation" (Sunday Times), Sir Ian resisted the temptation of the movies and concentrated on the stage, finally coming to the notice of a wider public as David Copperfield on BBC television in 1968. In 1971, he played Hamlet on tour in Britain and Europe, in London and on television. He was a founder member of the Actors' Company in 1972 and, from 1974 until 1978 was leading man for the Royal Shakespeare Company. He returned to the commercial West End in 1979, in Martin Sherman's Bent, and won his third successive award as Actor of the Year (1977, 78, 79). He was appointed CBE in 1979. Sir Ian won the 1981 Tony Award for his Salieri in Amadeus on Broadway. During his year on Broadway, he televised his one man show, Ian McKellen Acting Shakespeare, which is used throughout the US in schools and colleges and which he continues to tour worldwide. In 1984, Peter Hall invited Sir Ian to act at the National Theatre and to advise him on artistic planning. He won Actor of the Year Awards in 1984 and 1985 and, with Edward Petheridge, managed a group of 17 actors within the NT which proved the hit of the London season. In 1991, Ian McKellen was knighted for his services to the stage, and won the Olivier Award as Actor of the Year for his Richard III.

NIGEL HAWTHORNE ▲

Best known to the British public as Sir Humphrey Appleby in Yes Minister and Yes Prime Minister, Nigel Hawthorne was born in Coventry in 1929 and brought up in South Africa. In a distinguished career on the stage, he has won the SWET and Clarence Derwent Awards as Best Supporting Actor, 1978, for Privates on Parade, the 1991 Tony Award for Best Actor for his portrayal of C S Lewis in Shadowlands, on Broadway and, in 1992, the Olivier and Evening Standard Awards for Best Actor for his performance in the title role of Alan Bennett's The Madness Of George III at the Royal National Theatre. For his performances in Yes Minister and Yes Prime Minister, he won the BAFTA Award for Best Actor in Light Entertainment in 1982/83, 1986/87 and 1987-88. Nigel Hawthorne was appointed CBE in 1987 and has an Hon MA from Sheffield University.

TIMOTHY DALTON ▼

Timothy Dalton was trained at RADA and became a leading member of Britain's National Youth Theatre. Although he has worked with distinction in the theatre, including as a guest artist with the RSC, he is best known for his roles in feature films, notably as James Bond in The Living Daylights and Licence to Kill. His latest film is Naked In New York, in which he stars opposite Kathleen Turner.

ACTORS

JOHN GIELGUD ▼

Born in London in 1904 John Gielgud started his acting career at the Old Vic in 1921 as a scholarship student from RADA. Among his many achievements as an actor and director are Hamlet in 1934 and Romeo and Juliet in 1935. Three decades later he directed Richard Burton's Hamlet, and was the offstage recorded voice of the Ghost. During the 1970s he starred in productions such as Alan Bennett's 40 Years On, Shaffer's The Battle Of Shrivings and Pinter's No Man's Land. It was the popular success in Arthur, as Hobson, Dudley Moore's acerbic manservant, which won him an Oscar for Best Supporting Actor. Since then he has appeared in many films. His performances in The Shooting Party and Plenty won him Best Supporting Actor (Los Angeles Film Critics). Other memorable film roles include Richard III, Chimes Of Midnight and Murder On The Orient Express. His television credits include Brideshead Revisited, Wagner, Inside The Third Reich, War And Remembrance, and the title role in Oscar Wilde's The Canterville Ghost. He was knighted in 1963.

BOB HOSKINS ▲

Bob Hoskins got into acting 'completely by chance'. He had gone along to the Unity Theatre with a friend who was auditioning for a part. Left in the bar downstairs he was given a script by the director who assumed he wanted to audition. Bob followed him upstairs, read his part, and was given the leading role. He toured in Ken Campbell's Road Show, in venues ranging from tents to pubs, and then worked at the Hull Arts Centre in Yorkshire and the Royal Court, where he scored a big success as a raucous Cockney electrician in The Veterans with John Mills and John Gielgud. His first major West End performance was as Alfred Doolittle in Pygmalion at the Albery with Diana Rigg as Eliza where it ran for a six month sold out season. His performance on TV as the salesman in Dennis Potter's Pennies From Heaven made him a household name in the UK. Early films include The Long Good Friday, Coppola's The Cotton Club and Mona Lisa which confirmed his status as an international star. These were followed by A Prayer For The Dying, Who Framed Roger Rabbit?, The Lonely Passion Of Judith Hearne and The Raggedy Rawney, which he also wrote and directed. Most recently he acted in Mermaids with Cher and Winona Ryder, and played the amateur detective with a pet shop in Shattered, and Smee in Steven Spielberg's Hook.
Photograph by Terry O'Neill

ALAN RICKMAN ▼

After graduating from RADA Alan Rickman spent several seasons in regional theatre before working in London's experimental theatre. He has strong connections with the Royal Court where he has appeared in The Seagull, Snoo Wilson's Grass Widow and Aphra Behn's The Lucky Chance. He has appeared three times at the Edinburgh Festival, most recently in Tango At The End Of Winter by Kunio Shimizu, directed by Yukio Ninagawa, which transferred to the West End in 1991. He has spent two seasons with the RSC, in 1985-87 as Jacques in As You Like It, Achilles in Troilus and Cressida, Hendrik Hofgen in Mephisto and Valmont in Les Liaisons Dangereuses, a role he has played in the West End and on Broadway and for which he received a Tony nomination. In 1992 he appeared as Hamlet, directed by Robert Sturua at the Riverside Studios. His work for TV includes Benefactors by Michael Frayn and a 25 minute solo as Jacques Roux in Peter Barnes' Revolutionary Witness. His film career began with Die Hard, and has continued with The January Man; Quigley Down Under; Truly, Madly, Deeply; Closetland; Robin Hood, Prince of Thieves; Close My Eyes and Bob Roberts.
Photograph courtesy of BBC Photo Library

JEREMY IRONS ⬆

Jeremy Irons trained at the Bristol Old Vic Theatre School. His first London appearance was in Godspell with David Essex. His second film, The French Lieutenant's Woman, won him the Variety Club Award for Best Actor and a British Academy Award nomination. The title role in Swann In Love in 1983 was followed by the Broadway run of Stoppard's The Real Thing, for which he won both the Drama League Award and Tony Award for Best Actor. His films include The Mission; Dead Ringers, which won him a Best Actor Award from the Film Critics' Circle in New York and a Canadian Geney; Michael Winner's adaptation of A Chorus of Disapproval; Danny, The Champion Of The World, in which he appeared with his son; Reversal Of Fortune with Glenn Close, for which he won an Academy Award in 1991; Waterland; and, most recently, Louis Malle's Damage.

SIR ANTHONY HOPKINS ⬆

Anthony Hopkins made his London debut as Metellus Cimber in Julius Caesar at the Royal Court in 1964. He won a BAFTA for Best TV Actor in 1972 for War And Peace, an Emmy for Best Actor for The Lindbergh Kidnapping Case in 1976 and another for The Bunker (1981). He won the Variety Club Film Actor Award in 1984 for The Bounty and for Pravda in 1985 he received Laurence Olivier Awards, the Variety Club Stage Actor Award, the British Theatre Association Best Actor Award and the Observer Award For Outstanding Achievement. 84 Charing Cross Road won him Best Actor at the Moscow Film Festival. Other films for which he has been acclaimed include The Elephant Man. A Bridge Too Far, Silence Of The Lambs (for which he won an Oscar), Howards End, and, most recently Coppola's Dracula. He was presented with the CBE in 1987 and was knighted in the 1993 New Years Honours List.

SIR ALEC GUINNESS ➡

Alec Guinness was appointed CBE in 1955 and was knighted in 1959. His most memorable films include Kind Hearts And Coronets, in which he demonstrated incredible versatility and comic talent, playing a range of male and female parts, Lavender Hill Mob, Bridge On The River Kwai (for which he won the Oscar for Best Actor Of The Year), Lawrence Of Arabia and Dr Zhivago. The television productions of Tinker, Tailor, Soldier, Spy and Smiley's People both won him BAFTAs and the trio of Star Wars films brought him acclaim in the late 1970s. He won a Special Oscar for Contribution To Film in 1987, an Olivier Award for Services to the Theatre in 1989, and was made a fellow of BAFTA in 1989. He holds an Hon D Litt from Oxford.

Photograph courtesy of David Hart Photography

DANCE

PETER WRIGHT ▶

Director of the Birmingham Royal Ballet, Peter Wright's distinguished career began at Ballets Jooss in 1945. Having trained with Kurt Jooss and Vera Volkova he worked at several companies before becoming ballet master of Sadler's Wells Opera Ballet in 1956. He became fascinated with television at its inception and in the early 1960s he trained with the BBC as a director. Several of his own dance television films were screened during this time. In 1961 he joined John Cranko in Stuttgart as ballet master and here he first staged Giselle in 1966, a highly acclaimed version which he has since staged for ballet companies worldwide. Wright has been much praised over the years for his ability to give a valid new look to the traditional full length ballets. Some of the many awards he has received for his work are: the CBE for services to ballet (1985) Evening Standard Award for the Most Outstanding Achievement in Ballet in 1981, Honorary Doctorate of Music at London University (1990), and the 1991 Digital Premier Award of £30,000 which he is using for the encouragement of new choreographers.
Photograph by Anthony Crickmay

DONNIE BURNS ▲

Donnie grew up in Hamilton, Scotland. He began dancing when he was seven. The hobby soon became a passion and although he got into Glasgow University to study law, Donnie decided one and a half years into the course to leave university in order to become a professional dancer. To date he holds, with his partner of 16 years, Gaynor Fairweather, nine world professional championship titles, eight of them World Latin and one a World Segue. Now 30, he and Gaynor received MBEs in 1992 for services to ballroom dancing.

KEVIN RICHMOND ▲

Kevin Richmond is one of Britain's best known dancers, acclaimed for his character roles in full length ballets for English National Ballet. He joined the company in 1977 after an acting and dance career which took off after he left the Nottingham Academy of Speech and Drama. He has the distinction of having been chosen by Christopher Bruce to perform in all his productions for English National Ballet and was one of the original cast of Swansong, nominated for a SWET Award and later produced for television. He has appeared in several televised ballets including the film Nijinsky and has created numerous roles for the English National; most recent parts include Fate in Robert North's A Stranger I Came and The Young Man in Kim Brandstrup's White Nights.
Photograph by Bill Cooper

RICHARD ALSTON ▼

Artistic director of Rambert Dance Company, Richard Alston is a formidable talent in the world of contemporary dance. Now 44 he began his dancing career at the London School of Contemporary Dance, when this was in its infancy. He concentrated on choreography, founding Strider, his own dance company, in 1972. Richard Alston and Dancers was set up in 1978, after two years spent in America studying under Merce Cunningham. In 1980 Alston was appointed resident choreographer of Ballet Rambert and five years later he became the company's artistic director. His influence on contemporary dance in Britain has been enormous. He was instrumental in introducing the British to the Cunningham technique, and to a choreographic style that was formalist rather than expressionist. His work concerns itself with movement for its own sake, rather than as a vehicle for narrative or allusion, and his works are about making a "place" with its own language and logic. To this end he has collaborated with fine artists such as Howard Hodgkin and John Hoyland and worked closely with composers, particularly Nigel Osborne.
Photograph by Catherine Ashmore

◀ MARCUS HILTON

Born and brought up in Rochdale Marcus worked as a chauffeur, a sales rep and in a dance school, before turning professional with his partner of 15 years, and wife for six, Karen. As amateurs the pair were World Latin Champions and World Ten Dance Champions. Since then they have held every major international profesional title including the World, British Open, USBC Open, International, UK Open, World Trophy and on 10 October 1992 retained their world title at the 1992 World Standard Ballroom Championship held in Kolding, Denmark.

KENNETH THARP ▼

Kenneth Tharp had "never imagined there was an alternative to classical ballet, something just as sophisticated and refined but different", until he saw his first modern dance piece when he was 16. Up until then he had trained in Glasgow and then Cambridge under a Russian ballet teacher. Apart from his obvious dancing talent he was also a proficient sportsman and musician (cello and piano). He joined LCDS when he was 18 and worked with Janet Smith and Dancers before joining LCDT in 1982. Here he was soon picked for roles that put his dramatic talent and considerable energies to good use. He now teaches both within and outside the company and as a musician accompanies dance classes and plays with the South Bank New Music Gamelan Group.

MICHAEL CLARK ▲

As the enfant terrible of dance Michael Clark changed the face of choreography in the 1980s. The 1990s are likely to prove just as successful if the acclaim given to his latest work, Modern Masterpiece (spring 1992) is anything to go by. Clark trained at the Royal Ballet School and then for two years at the Ballet Rambert. He began his career as an independent choreographer/dancer in 1981, aged 19. With the launch of his own company in 1984 he came to the notice of the general public; some were shocked but others saw a series of very polished works with, from Michael, a remarkable sense of discipline and ability to test his own limits. Since those days Michael's company has toured worldwide and he has created many outstanding works for leading European companies. He has made several films and videos of his work, performed in numerous TV pieces and appeared in the films Comrades and Prospero's Books. Today Michael finds it hard to recruit dancers who are physically capable of performing his work – he says he will soon have to train dancers himself.

DARSHAN SINGH BHULLER ▲

One of our leading young choreographers Darshan Singh Bhuller joined LCDT as a dancer in 1980 and has choreographed within and outside the company since 1981. In 1991 he took leave of absence from the company to dance with the Siobhan Davies Company, returning last year to become assistant rehearsal director. At LCDT he collaborated with the artist Graham Dean and assisted Robert Cohan on a collaboration with the London Sinfonietta. He has also choreographed and directed several films, three of which have been televised. He choreographed and directed The Fall in 1991 for BBC 2, which got a special mention at the Paris Film Festival and was nominated for a BFI Award for Innovation.
Photograph Anthony Crickmay

The best of British writing every Sunday

Sue Arnold

Michael Coveney

Simon Hoggart

Michael Ignatieff

Richard Ingrams

William Keegan

Andrew Motion

John Naughton

Andrew Porter

Alan Watkins

Katharine Whitehorn

only in

1791

THE OBSERVER

BRITAIN'S *original* SUNDAY NEWSPAPER

TO BE THE BEST IN BRITISH CINEMA, YOU HAVE TO START AT THE BOTTOM.

That's why all our cinemas have special, ergonomically designed seats.

They're wider, more comfortable and they even have a holder for popcorn and drinks built into the arm.

They're better than the average cinema seat because we believe in giving our audiences more of an experience.

That's why we have extra-bright, full-size screens, Dolby Stereo Surround Sound and a choice of the latest movies showing on up to 12 screens.

It's also the reason we attract over 18 million customers every year.

And why we are Britain's fastest-growing multiplex chain.

We now have 212 screens established across mainland Britain and are planning further expansion all the time. Which proves that despite our success, we're not sitting still.

MORE OF AN EXPERIENCE

UCI
A Paramount/UNIVERSAL COMPANY

PARKSIDE HOUSE, 51-53 BRICK ST, LONDON W1Y 7DU. TELEPHONE 071-409 1346

FILM

STEPHEN FREARS

Stephen Frears got involved in student theatre while at Cambridge, working with, among others, David Frost and John Cleese. After graduating with a law degree Stephen was hired as an assistant to Karel Reisz. He went on to assist Lindsay Anderson and Albert Finney before directing his first feature films Gumshoe, Bloody Kids and The Hit and making films for TV with writers Alan Bennett, Tom Stoppart and Neville Smith. Stephen's first collaboration with Hanif Kureishi produced the box-office hit My Beautiful Laundrette. He then took a break from socially concerned films to work on Dangerous Liaisons. In 1989 he made The Grifters for Martin Scorsese, another American movie which won him praise from every quarter. He recently completed Hero for Columbia and is currently shooting a Roddy Doyle (writer of The Commitments) story entitled The Snapper.

MICHAEL CATON JONES

While still a student at the National Film School Michael Caton Jones won the Channel 4 European Film School competition for his film Liebe Mutter. That was in 1985. After graduating a year later he went on to direct Brond for Channel 4 and Lucky Sunil for the BBC. His first taste of international fame came with Scandal, written by Michael Thomas and produced by Steve Woolley. His latest film, This Boy's Life, stars Robert De Niro and Ellen Barkin.

BILL FORSYTH

Born and brought up in Glasgow, Bill Forsyth studied at the National Film School before working with performers at the Glasgow Youth Theatre. In 1980 he directed his own screenplay, Gregory's Girl, using members of the Youth Theatre which won instant acclaim. His next film, Local Hero, produced by David Puttnam and starring Burt Lancaster, established Forsyth as one of our most talented writers and directors.

SIR RICHARD ATTENBOROUGH ▲

The grand old man of the British film industry since the death of Sir David Lean, Sir Richard Attenborough has directed, produced and starred in hundreds of films. He became an independent producer in 1959, resulting in the innovative Whistle Down The Wind and The L-Shaped Room. He is best known for directing A Bridge Too Far, Gandhi and Cry Freedom. His most recent film is the £40 million Charlie Chaplin biopic, Chaplin. In 1992 he retired as chairman of Channel 4, Capital Radio and the British Film Institute in order to spend more time film making. He remains vice-president of BAFTA, pro-chancellor of Sussex University and chairman of both the British Screen Advisory Council and the European Script Fund.

◄ MIKE LEIGH

Mike Leigh trained at RADA, Camberwell and Central Art Schools and the London Film School. His first original play evolved from improvisation at Birmingham in 1965, and since then he has written and directed hundreds of plays, using improvisation to achieve a gritty verisimilitude. His best known works are Nuts In May, Abigail's Party, for which Alison Steadman won an Evening Standard Award and Plays and Players Best Actress of 1977 Award, High Hopes (1988), and Life Is Sweet (1990). His latest play, Too Much Of A Good Thing, was transmitted on Radio 3 in 1992.

DAVID PUTTNAM ⬆

One of our most highly regarded film-makers David Puttnam's first work as a producer was on Melody, That'll Be The Day and Mahler. He soon built a reputation as a champion of new and exciting directorial talent by backing the first pictures of Michael Apted (Stardust); Alan Parker (Bugsy Malone); Ridley Scott (The Duellists); and Adrian Lyne (Foxes). In 1977 he co-produced Midnight Express which won two Oscars. Chariots of Fire won four Oscars and three British Academy Awards, including Best Picture while The Killing Fields won Oscars for Cinematography, Supporting Actor and Editor. The same year he produced CAL for which Helen Mirren won the Best Actress Prize at Cannes. In 1985 The Mission won the Palme d'Or at Cannes, was nominated for seven Academy Awards and won cameraman Chris Menges his second Oscar. In 1986 he became chairman of Columbia Pictures. Sixteen months later he returned to Britain to produce Memphis Belle and then Meeting Venus for Warner Bros. David is currently chairman of the National Film and Television School, is on the Board of the Sundance Institute, is a trustee of the Tate Gallery, the National Aids Trust and the National Energy Foundation. In 1982 he won the Michael Balcon Award and was made a CBE.

PETER GREENAWAY ▼

Peter Greenaway trained as a painter and began working as a film editor for the Central Office of Information in 1965, a job he held for 11 years. In 1966 he started making his own films and since then he has also been producing paintings, novels and illustrated books. The Draughtsman's Contract was the first of his films to receive international critical acclaim. It was followed by A Zed And Two Noughts (1986); The Belly Of An Architect (1987); Drowning By Numbers (1988); which won Best Artistic Contribution at Cannes; and The Cook, The Thief, His Wife and Her Lover (1989). In 1991 Peter directed Prospero's Books starring John Gielgud from his own screenplay adaptation of The Tempest. His latest film, The Baby of Macon, is due for release in August.

◀ STEWART TILL

The Sky Movies supremo who spent hundreds of millions of dollars in 300 separate deals with Hollywood studios and independents, Stewart Till now occupies one of the most power movie seats in Europe as international head honcho at PolyGram. He took a degree in Business Studies and an MA in American Politics before embarking on a career in advertising at Leo Burnett and Saatchi & Saatchi. In 1983, after four years as TV project manager and marketing manager for WEA Records he joined CBS/Fox Video as sales and marketing director and was promoted to managing director of the UK company and then vice-president for North Europe. From 1986-88 he was also chairman of British Videogram Association. In November 1988 he joined Sky TV as deputy managing director, where he was responsible for the management and programme acquisition for the two film channels, Sky Movies Plus and The Movie Channel, as well as the entertainment and comedy channels. In January last year he joined PolyGram as president of International, in charge of all international film distribution, non-English language film production and worldwide video acquisition and distribution.

CHRIS MENGES ▲

One of the most prominent figures in the British film industry, Chris Menges' first job was in an estate agent's office next door to the studios of American film maker Alan Forbes. Forbes took him on as an apprentice which led to his first job as a camera assistant. He then worked for Granada Television's World In Action team, where one of his first assignments was as camera-operator on a documentary about apartheid. During the 1960s and 1970s he filmed countless documentaries all over the world, including the multi-award winning documentary The Tribe That Hides From Man, and produced and directed several programmes for TV. He returned to feature films in the 1980s with projects as diverse as The Empire Strikes Back and Neil Jordan's Angel. In 1983 he won the Evening Standard Award for best Technical Achievement for his work on Local Hero and Angel, and he won Oscars in 1985 and 1987 for Best Cinematography on The Killing Fields and The Mission. He also received BAFTA awards for The Last Summer and The Killing Fields. In 1987-88 he directed his first feature film, the critically acclaimed A World Apart, which was awarded the Cannes Grand Jury Prize, The New York Film Critics Award for Best Director and Best Actress Awards for each of its three leading actresses at Cannes. In 1990 he directed the feature Crisscross for Pathe Entertainment.

DANIEL BATTSEK →

Daniel Battsek studied PPE at Oxford Polytechnic before spending four years working and travelling in Australia. He returned to England in 1982 and joined the newly formed Palace Video Ltd. Two years later he was appointed to run the new Palace Pictures Film Distribution Company. Over the next seven years this became the leading independent film production and distribution company in the UK. In March last year he became vice-president, managing director of Buena Vista International Ltd, Disney's UK operation. Here he is responsible for distributing between ten and 20 films a year and acquiring British and European made films. The company's first film went into distribution last November.

IAN RICHES ▼

Bristol-born Ian Riches has been in building and operating traditional and multiplex cinemas for some 30 years. He became director of property for US multiplex chain, American Multi-Cinemas, in 1986. Here he was responsible for choosing and developing many of the company's prime sites during the crucial early years of the UK multiplex boom. When AMC joined ranks with chief rivals CIC to form UCI, Ian, with his unique insights on cinema going habits in the UK, was the inevitable choice for managing director, overseeing an operation which now comprises 206 screens in 22 multiplex sites.

BEN GIBSON ▲

Ben gibson studied English and Theatre at the University of Warwick and Film Studies at East Anglia. He has worked as a theatre director, a writer on cinema and co-editor of Framework Film magazine, co-founder of the London International Festival of Theatre, a repertory cinema programmer and a film studies teacher. At The Other Cinema (now Metro Pictures) he worked on acquisitions, promotion, programming and the opening of the Metro Cinema in 1986. He joined the BFI in 1987 and was responsible for setting up and producing the New Directors short film scheme from 1988, now in its sixth year. He has executive produced 12 short films for the BFI and features including Young Soul Rebels (1991), The Long Day Closes (1992) and Psychotherapy (1993).

FILM

JEREMY THOMAS ▼

Son of director Ralph Thomas and nephew of director Gerald Thomas, Jeremy has worked in most areas of film production. He produced his first film, Philippe Mora's Mad Dog Morgan in 1974, moving on to a string of highly visible features – The Great Rock 'n' Roll Swindle, The Killing Fields and Merry Christmas Mr Lawrence. In 1986 he produced Bertolucci's The Last Emperor which won nine Oscars. Since then he has completed Reisz's Everybody Wins, Bertolucci's The Sheltering Sky and David Cronenberg's film of William Burroughs' novel Naked Lunch. He is currently producing Bertolucci's Little Buddha with locations in Bhutan, Nepal and the US. In 1991 he won a BAFTA Michael Balcom Award for Outstanding Contribution to the British Film Industry. Last January he became chairman of the British Film Institute.

SIMON RELPH ▼

Simon Relph graduated from Cambridge in 1961 with a degree in Mechanical Sciences. He joined the film industry as an assistant director, working on films such as Roman Polanksi's Macbeth and John Schlesinger's Sunday Bloody Sunday. In 1974 he was employed as production administrator under Peter Hall at the National Theatre. He returned to film four years later as production supervisor on Schlesinger's Yanks and assistant director on Warren Beatty's Reds.

He began his career in independent production in1982 as co-producer of Alan Bridges' The Return of the Soldier and producer of Michael Blakemore's Privates on Parade. Other credits include co-producer of Richard Eyre's The Ploughman's Lunch and producer of Bill Douglas' Comrades. In 1985 Simon was appointed the first chief executive of British Screen, set up to support British films. He returned to independent production in 1991 as executive producer on Mike Newell's Enchanted April. He co-produced Louis Malle's Damage in 1992 and is currently producing David Hare's The Secret Rapture.

NIK POWELL ▲

Nik Powell's first success was setting up Virgin with Richard Branson in the early 1970s. When he opted out, 40 per cent of his settlement provided the financial base for Video Palace, which was soon established as Britain's leading video store. He formed Palace Video with Stephen Woolley in 1982. With releases such as Fitzcarraldo, Diva, Angel and The Evil Dead, the duo became a dominant force in the video industry. Among Palace's achievements are Mona Lisa (co-prouded by Nik) which won Best Actor at Cannes. Next came Palace's first US proudction, Shag, followed by Neil Jordan's High Spirits. Nik also executive produced Scandal, A Rage In Harlem, Waterland and The Crying Game. He will executive produce on all Scala's projects including James M. Cain's Hungry Heart, the comedy/thriller History Is Made At Night, Backbeat, the story of the Beatles' early days, the Woolley-produced Jonathan Wild and George Sluizer's Dark Blood.

STEPHEN WOOLLEY ▼

Stephen Woolley established Palace Pictures and Palace Video in partnership with Nik Powell in 1982. His first production was Neil Jordan's award-winning film The Company of Wolves, which became one of the biggest British films of the past two decades. He followed this with Absolute Beginners and Mona Lisa, directed by Neil Jordan. After High Spirits, another Neil Jordan film, came Shag and Scandal, both of which achieved high box-office ratings here and in America. More recent productions include A Rage in Harlem, The Pope Must Die, and last year Waterland and The Crying Game. In January 1992 Stephen formed a new production company, Scala Productions. Stephen and Neil Jordan have joined forces again this year on Jonathon Wild, an action adventure thriller set in 18th century London.

SIMON PERRY ▲

Simon Perry worked in theatre and television production before becoming an independent film maker in 1974. Over the next eight years he was also a trade journalist for Variety and head of the National Film Development Fund. In 1982 he set up his own production company, Umbrella Films, which has produced such films as Another Time, Another Place, Loose Connections, Nineteen Eighty-Four, Nanou, Hotel Du Paradis, White Mischief and The Playboys. In January 1991 he was appointed chief executive of British Screen Finance, the state-funded investor in UK feature film development and production, and the only remaining mechanism of British government intervention in the commercial film making sector.

SCOTT MEEK ➡

Scott Meek became deputy manager of the National Film Theatre in 1972 and spent the next five years working here while script reading for various companies and writing for Time Out and Sight and Sound. In the early 1980s he worked as feature film officer at the National Film Archive, wrote for many magazines and newspapers and co-authored Electric Shadows: A History of Chinese Cinema. He also organised the first international retrospective of Chinese Cinema. He joined Zenith Productions at its inception in 1984 and quickly rose through the ranks as Head of Development and Head of Creative Affairs to his present role as Director of Production. The company, 51 per cent owned by Carlton Communications and 49 per cent by Paramount Pictures, has a current slate of five scripts and what have been described as "very healthy six-figure sums of development money".

SIR GEORG SOLTI

Born in Budapest in 1912, Sir Georg's glittering musical career as a director began in 1946 when he was appointed music director of the Bayerischer Staatsoper. Six years later he became director of the Frankfurter Opera, and then of the Royal Opera House, Covent Garden. In the ten years that followed he appeared as a guest conductor with all the great European and American orchestras and in virtually all the leading opera houses of the world. During his subsequent 20-odd years with the Chicago Symphony Orchestra he led a number of highly successful tours around the world and at the end of their centenary season in April 1991 became

◄ ROGER VIGNOLES

Internationally acclaimed as one of the leading piano accompanists of today, Roger Vignoles regularly partners the world's finest singers and instrumentalists the world over. In the last 12 months alone his appearances have included London recitals with Brigitte Fassbaender, Dame Kiri Te Kanawa (whom he partners regularly), Joan Rodgers and Sylvia McNair, with further recitals and concerts in most of the other musical capitals of the world. One of the highlights of the year was his role as artistic director of a series of recitals at the Queen Elizabeth Hall, entitled The Young Brahms. In addition to this, the summer of 1992 saw Vignoles' debut as a conductor when he directed, from the harpsichord, in performances of Handel's Agrippina at the Buxton Festival. Currently consultant professor at the Royal Academy of Music in London, he also regularly gives classes for accompaniment and chamber music all over the world. His recordings are wide ranging, one of the most recent being the complete Canticles by Benjamin Britten.

MARK ELDER ►

Mark Elder's office as musical director of English National Opera – held since 1979 – comes to an end at the end of the 1992/93 season when he will become Principal Guest Conductor of the City of Birmingham's Symphony Orchestra. Born in 1947, Elder first gained experience as a conductor at Cambridge University and then went on to work at Glyndebourne and the Royal Opera House, Covent Garden, before spending a two-year period in Australia. Since being under his direction the English National has achieved a high reputation and notched up many new productions, including an adventurous programme of largely 20th century operas, presented in 1990/91, which contributed to Elder winning a Laurence Olivier award. His symphonic career has followed a similarly successful path; as well as conducting annually at the Proms, he has worked with all the London orchestras and the major symphony orchestras throughout the country, and has had several North American engagements. His many recordings cover a wide repertoire ranging from Verdi, Strauss and Wagner to contemporary music.

their music director Laureate. Meanwhile, in 1979, Sir Georg became principal director and artistic director of the London Philharmonic Orchestra, and later their conductor emeritus. His recent productions have included Elektra and Simon Boccanegra at Covent Garden, Ballo in Maschera at the Salzburg Festival, Zauberflote and, in 1992, Die Frau Ohne Schatten. As a recording artist he has achieved equal notoriety, claiming the highest number (30) of Grammy awards of all time and 15 Grand Prix du Disque. In recognition of his great contribution to classical music, Sir Georg has received many accolades and was made a Knight Commander of the British Empire in 1972.

JOHN TAVENER ▶

The considerable musical talents of London-born John Tavener were evident by the time he reached secondary school and from there he went on to the Royal Academy of Music, where he won several major prizes for composition: in 1965 his dramatic cantata, The Whale, took its audience by storm. Always of a reflective nature, Tavener joined the Russian Orthodox Church in 1977 and since then his spiritual commitment has become evident in all his work. Important recent examples of this include the Akathist of Thanksgiving, The Protecting Veil for solo cello and strings and two large-scale choral and orchestral works, Resurrection and We Shall See Him As He Is (the latter recorded by Chandos at its 1992 Prom performance). Tavener divides his time between his home in the Sussex countryside and visits to Greece – a country which provides him with great inspiration for his music.

Photograph by Clive Barda

GRAHAM VICK ▼

Established as one of Britain's leading opera producers, Graham Vick is currently artistic director of the City of Birmingham Touring Opera. Having previously been associated with exciting productions for English National Opera, Scottish Opera, Opera North, Glyndebourne and English Music Theatre, he made a triumphant debut at the Royal Opera House, Covent Garden, with a new production of Berio's Un Re In Ascolto conducted by the composer. This was repeated in 1991 at the Bastille in Paris, along with Otello in Berlin and War and Peace in Leningrad during the same year. One of his most recent and highly acclaimed engagements included Queen of Spades for the Glyndebourne Festival.

STEVEN ISSERLIS ▶

Internationally recognised as one of the leading musicians of his generation, 35-year-old cellist Steven Isserlis regularly performs with many of the world's leading orchestras and conductors. In recital, and as a chamber musician, he is invited to play in leading centres such as London, Paris, Amsterdam, Berlin and Washington and, in 1992, was Artist-in-Residence to the Adelaide Festival in Australia. Highlights of the 1991/92 season included his New York debut with the Orchestra of St Luke and Roger Narrington, and a major tour of South America with the Halle Orchestra and Stanislaw Skrowaczewski. Steven has been the subject of a number of international television programmes and will be a featured soloist in the forthcoming Channel 4 series, Concerto. Recordings to his credit are substantial, with his extraordinarily successful interpretation of John Tavener's The Protecting Veil becoming the only classical recording to be nominated for the 1992 Mercury Music Prize.

CLASSICAL MUSIC

◀ SIMON RATTLE

Liverpool-born Simon Rattle was just 19 years old when he won the John Player Conductors' Award and, 13 years later received a CBE for his services to music. Beginning his spectacular career as Assistant Conductor of both the Bournemouth Symphony and Sinfonietta, he subsequently held titles with the Royal Liverpool Philharmonic, BBC Scottish Symphony and the Rotterdam Philharmonic. In 1980 he took up the post of principal conductor and artistic director of the Birmingham Symphony Orchestra, and became its music director in 1991. The partnership has proved highly successful, with Rattle leading the CBSO on many European and Scandinavian tours, and their first tours to the Far East and North America. Of his many notable productions, of particular importance have been The Cunning Little Vixen, with which he made his Glyndebourne debut in 1977 and his Royal Opera House debut in 1990, Porgy and Bess (recorded by EMI in 1988), and The Marriage of Figaro and Cosi Fan Tutte with the Orchestra of the Age of Enlightenment of which he became principal guest conductor in 1992. Many international recording awards have also come his way, including France's most prestigious award, the Grand Prix in Honorem de l'Academie Charles Cros, in 1990 for his recordings of Porgy and Bess, and discs of Schoenberg, Weber, Berg and Debussy.

◀ JAMES GALWAY

One of that rare breed of artists that can transcend musical boundaries, James Galway is a classical flautist known to millions. Born in Belfast, where as a boy he played the penny whistle, James began his career at the Sadlers Wells Opera and the Royal Opera Covent Garden. Following several years with the London Symphony Orchestra, the Royal Philharmonic and the Berlin Philharmonic, he launched himself as a soloist in 1975. Since then he has travelled extensively, performed in a wide spectrum of musical events featuring both classical and contemporary programmes, including new works that have been specially written for him, and made frequent international television appearances. Recently he has toured the States with the USA's major orchestras and performed in Germany with the WKO. He has over 50 best-selling albums to his name and among his latest releases is a recording of chamber works for flute by Beethoven, Mozart Flute Concerti, 4 Concerti by Quantz and the Bach B Minor Suite.

SIR HARRISON BIRTWHISTLE

Born in 1934, Harrison Birtwhistle began to compose in his early teens but it was not until after he had studied the clarinet at the Royal Manchester College of Music and the Royal Academy of Music that composition came to the fore. He first gained widespread acclaim with his Tragoedia for ten instruments in 1965 and after studying at Princeton University on a scholarship formed the Pierrot Players, which became one of the most renowned new music groups in the late 1950s. Various commissions followed, including the Mask of Orpheus while he was teaching in America. This was left unfinished, but during his eight years as music director at the National Theatre, during which time he wrote incidental music, culminating in a score for Peter Hall's production of Aeschylus's The Oresteia, the opera was completed and had its première in 1986. Sir Harrison was awarded the Grwemeyer Prize by the University of Louisville for this work, and was knighted a year later. His recent works include

JOHN HARLE

Recently awarded a Fellowship at the Guildhall School of Music and Drama where he was appointed Professor of Saxophone in 1988, John Harle conducts, composes and performs in the fields of classical, jazz and rock music. As a saxophonist he has made various concert appearances in Europe, America and the Far East, as well as being featured on the soundtrack of many major films including Passage to India and Tender is the Night. He was also the subject of a BBC television special One Man and His Sax. During 1991/92 John performed with the English Chamber, the Scottish National, the London Festival and the BBC Concert orchestras, world premièreing Richard Rodney Bennett's Concerto for Stan Getz. He has an equally high reputation as a recording artist and one of his most recent recordings has been The Shadow of the Duke, an album of the arrangements of Duke Ellington, which the John Harle Band performed on tour in the UK in 1992.

Photograph by Simon Fowler

JULIAN BREAM

A recent milestone during the career of world-renowned guitarist and lutenist Julian Bream was his 40th anniversary concert at the Wigmore Hall in March 1991, a year in which he also appeared in the Japan Festival in London, played the Malcolm Arnold concerto in a televised BBC Prom and toured Poland and Austria. Julian has performed all over the world – often appearing with colleagues and friends, including the late Sir Peter Pears, Dame Peggy Ashcroft and John Williams – and made regular television appearances which have made him known to a very wide public. At home, he has done much to widen the guitar repertoire, making transcriptions of Romantic and Baroque works, commissioning new works from contemporary composers, as well as giving practical support to instrument makers. After numerous recordings with RCA, he signed an exclusive contract with EMI classics in 1990. In March 1993 he was due to give a performance at the Wigmore Hall for his 60th birthday.

Ritual Fragment, Gawain, Four Poems by Jaan Kaplinski, Five Distances for Five Instruments and Three Settings of Celan, plus a piano concerto commissioned by the Royal Philharmonic.

GEORGE MELLY ▼

The multi-talented George Melly is one of jazz's best known personalities. He sang for many years with the Mick Mulligan Magnolia jazz band and then with John Chilton's Feetwarmers, for the last 19. In addition to his musical successes George has had 13 books published, including several on art – he is an authority on modern art – and three much acclaimed volumes of autobiography. He has been featured on countless TV shows, both as a guest and as a host. He also completed four series as presenter on Channel Four's popular Gallery series. He is a regular contributor to the national papers, wrote the Flook cartoon in the Daily Mail with Wally Fawkes and was voted Critic of the Year while at The Observer in the 1970s.

JOHN DANKWORTH ▲

It is unlikely that there is a British musician better known for a wider range of musical activities than John Dankworth. A Fellow of the Royal Academy of Music, he was awarded a Doctor of Music degree by Berklee College of Music in 1982, received a CBE, was named Variety Club's Show Business Personality of the Year (jointly with his wife Cleo Laine), and was presented with a special award for his contribution to British jazz in 1990 at the British Jazz Awards. Born in London in 1927 John was accepted for the Royal Academy of Music when he was 17. As a young professional he was named Musician of the Year by Melody Maker every year from 1949 to 1955 – the only jazz artist ever to receive such recognition. He has written several musicals and composed many film scores including Saturday Night, Sunday Morning and Return from the Ashes, for which he was nominated for an Academy Award. He founded the London Symphony Orchestra's Pops programme and has served as musical director of the orchestra since 1985. As a conductor he has directed Pops programmes for major orchestras worldwide. He has always worked to eradicate what he calls "snobbism" in music. His Wavenden Allmusic Plan – a seminal series devoted to the teaching of "all music" was set up in 1969. British Telecom are now its sponsors. He tours worldwide with Cleo Laine, this year began with a hectic six-week tour of the States.
Photograph by David Redfern

IAN CARR ▼

Trumpeter, composer, author, educator and broadcaster, Ian Carr is a major force in jazz in Britain and Europe. In 1969 he formed Nucleus, one of the earliest pioneers of electronic jazz-rock fusion. It had a seminal influence in Europe, winning first prize at the 1970 Montreux International Jazz Festival, and continuing to play a prominent part in the jazz scene for 20 years (1969-89). Since 1975 Ian has been with the highly successful The United Jazz Rock Ensemble. In 1987 Wire Magazine presented him with their special award for services to jazz. Ian is an associate Professor at the Guildhall School of Music and Drama, where he lectures on jazz history. He has also written several highly acclaimed books on his subject; the latest, an authorised biography of Keith Jarrett, was published by Paladin in 1992. Ian's most recent album Old Heartland (EMI) received praise from all quarters.

DIGBY FAIRWEATHER ↑

Jazz cornettist Digby Fairweather has worked with almost everyone in British jazz. In 1979 he won BBC Jazz Society's Musician of the Year Award and was placed in Jazz Journal's International polls in 1980. In 1987 he played a founding role in establishing the Association of British Jazz Musicans and the National Jazz Foundation Archive for jazz books and memorabilia at Loughton Central Library in Essex. He contributes to numerous publications including Grove's Dictionary of Jazz and has written several books on jazz. Since 1979 he has taught at Southport Arts Centre (he was artist in residence here with Stan Barker from 1979-86). He has worked on many radio programmes; most recently with a regular Radio 2 spot as presenter of Jazz Parade. In 1992 Digby won the Birmingham Jazz Award as first trumpeter and Freedom of the City of London for services to jazz.

COURTNEY PINE ▼

A passionate and technically superb saxophonist and bass clarinettist Courtney was the first British-born black musician to set his mark on the UK jazz scene. He played in reggae bands before, as he describes it, "falling under the spell" of American giants Sonny Rollins and John Coltrane. In the early 1980s he took part in John Stevens' workshops and by the mid-1980s was running his own. He was a founder member of the Jazz Warriors, an all-black big band which fused elements from jazz with calypso, reggae and ska. His first jazz album Journey to the Urge Within notched up sales to qualify for a silver disc while the second cracked the American jazz charts, establishing Courtney's international reputation. Courtney has played with, among others, George Russell and Art Blakey.

JOHN TAYLOR ↑

John first came to the attention of jazz enthusiasts when he partnered saxophonists Alan Skidmore and John Surman in 1969. The early 1970s saw him accompanying Cleo Laine, composing for his own sextet, and becoming a member of Ronnie Scott's quintet. In 1977 he formed Azimuth, a group described by Richard Williams as "one of the most imaginatively conceived and delicately balanced contemporary chamber-jazz groups". Azimuth has toured Europe and the US and made many recordings for ECM Records. In 1992 he was made a Professor of Jazz Piano at Cologne School of Music. He also made a solo piano recording and an album of his own music with John Surman.

◄ HUMPHREY LYTTELTON

Humphrey Lyttelton formed his first highly successful band in 1948. High spots of that early time include accompanying the great Sidney Bechet and travelling to the first international jazz festival, in Nice, where Louis Armstrong was heard to say of him: "The boy is coming on". In the late 1950s Humphrey enlarged his band and repertoire. Today it is one of the most versatile in the world. They tour regularly – to Bahrain one minute, Berlin the next. Every Monday for the last 20 years Humphrey has presented Radio 2's The Best of Jazz, and chaired the quiz show I'm Sorry I Haven't A Clue. His articles have appeared in many magazines, he has written seven books and over 120 original compositions for his band. He holds honorary degrees in letters from Warwick and Loughborough Universities, in music from Durham and Keele.

RONNIE SCOTT AND PETE KING ▼

It was Ronnie Scott's first visit to the jazz clubs of New York when he was 20 which inspired him to start up a similar venue in London. In 1959 he opened the first Ronnie Scott's in Soho's Gerrard Street with fellow sax performer Pete King (left in picture). The duo were instrumental in easing Musicians' Union restrictions in this country so that British musicians and enthusiasts could hear the great American jazz performers in person. The club was soon billing Britain's top modern jazz musicians. Ronnie Scott provided the laconic introduction to each act – Spike Milligan described him as having the vitriolic drive of a W. C. Fields or a Groucho Marx – and Stan Tracey was the club's resident pianist. Since those early days most of the world's top performers have played at Ronnie Scott's and the club still attracts the biggest names while encouraging new talent from Britain and as far afield as Cuba.

◄ JOHN SURMAN

Composer and multi-instrumentalist John Surman is one of the key figures in a generation of European musicians who expanded the horizons of jazz in the 1970s and 1980s. From the baritone saxophone to the soprano and the bass clarinet he moved on to electronics and synthesisers at a time when deviation from acoustic purity was viewed with deep suspicion by the jazz fraternity. But John is someone who has never been frightened to try out new things. He is equally affected, he says, by the melodic qualities of choral music and English folk music as by jazz. Over the years he has played with the likes of Jack De Johnette, toured with Gil Evans and collaborated as a composer with choreographer/dancer Carolyn Carlson (he was based at the Paris Opera with her company for some time). He was composer in residence at the Glasgow Jazz Festival in 1989; and his Road to St Ives (ECM label) was voted Best Album of the Year for 1990 by Jazz FM listeners.

KENNY WHEELER ▼

Kenny Wheeler studied trumpet and harmony at the Toronto Conservatory of Music before moving to England in 1952. Here he was soon much in demand, playing for big bands led by Vic Lewis and Johnny Dankworth and by the mid-1960s with Ronnie Scott, Tubby Hayes and the Clarke-Boland Orchestra. It was during these years that he began working with bands that were involved in free (abstract) improvisation such as the Tony Oxley Sextet. In the 1970s he joined John Taylor and Norma Winstone in forming the much acclaimed chamber-jazz group Azimuth. For five years he was a member of the Dave Holland quintet and for the last three years he has been touring Europe and the US with his own quintet featuring, among others, Peter Erskine and John Taylor. His latest album Kayak came out last year. *Photograph by A. Botticelli*

JULIAN JOSEPH ▲

Twenty-five year old Julian Joseph is one of Jazz's leading young talents. He was classically trained from an early age and in 1986 won a scholarship to study at Berklee College of Music in Boston where he was a finalist in the prestigious Thelonious Monk Piano Competition. On his return to London in 1989 he formed his own quartet, performing, almost exclusively, his own compositions. Securing a contract with Warner's East West label he brought out his much acclaimed debut album The Language of Truth in 1991. He also signed for Warner Classics as a classical composer and pianist and subsequently became a Steinway piano artist. In 1992 he finished writing and recording the score for a new film A Tale of Vampire, starring Julian Sands. Future plans include the premier performance of his own orchestral piece with the London Symphony Orchestra.

STAN TRACEY ▲

Stan Tracey is generally regarded as our greatest living jazz musician. A self-taught professional by the age of 16 he first came to public notice in the 1950s working as pianist, vibraphonist and arranger with the now legendary Ted Heath Orchestra. In 1960 he began a seven year stint as a resident pianist at Ronnie Scott's, playing with the likes of Sonny Rollins and Stan Getz. During this time he formed his quartet and orchestra and in 1965 produced the immortal Under Milk Wood suite, lyrical settings to Dylan Thomas's play, which brought him widespread acclaim. Official recognition has come in the form of the BASCA Award (for services to the British Music Industry), honorary membership of the Royal Academy of Music and the OBE in 1986. In 1985 he was voted International Jazz Musician of the Year and won the Wire Award for Best Composer of the Year and in 1989 received the Album of the Year Award (Jazz Journal International) and the Guardian/Wire Award for Best Composer. In 1992 Tracey won the pianist section at the British Jazz Awards. He was recently signed by Blue Note; his octet album, Portraits Plus, was released in December.
Photograph by Des Miller

ANDY SHEPPARD ▶

After first picking up the saxophone at the age of 19 Andy spent many years single-mindedly developing his talent the hard way – on the bandstand, playing for a period with Laurant Cugny's Lumière Big Band and Urban Sax in Paris and in the UK with his own group Sphere. He released his debut album with Antilles in 1987, receiving great critical acclaim and the first of many awards – Best Newcomer of the Year in the British Jazz Awards, followed by Best Instrumentalist (1988) plus Best Instrumentalist and Best Album (1989) for Introductions in

DJANGO BATES ▼

Django Bates was founder member, leading composer and inspirational keyboard and peck horn player with the famous UK big band Loose Tubes in the late 1980s. He now leads an 18-piece orchestra and has a smaller group, with fellow musicians Courtney Pine, Mike Mondesir, Steve Buckley and Martin France which toured South America in 1992. A writer and performer with Yes drummer Bill Bruford's band Earthworks and Norwegian singer Sidsel Edresen's group, Django has worked with bandleaders as varied as George Russell, George Grunz and Dudu Pukwana. He was voted Best UK Jazz Composer in 1987 and 1990 and his most recent album, Music for the Third Policeman, was voted one of the albums of the year in the UK by the Guardian and Q magazine.

the Dark, and the Big Band Award for 1991 for "Soft On the Inside". 1992 saw another direction with his electric band, In Co-Motion, and a new album. One of the most sought-after musician/composers of his generation he has worked with bandleaders like George Russell, Gil Evans, Carla Bley and collaborated with Nana Vasconcelos, Keith Tippett and Mike Mantler.

JOHN McLAUGHLIN ▼

Composer and multi-instrumentalist John McLaughlin started playing the guitar at the age of 11, having taught himself the piano. He moved to London from Yorkshire in the early 1960s where he played in R&B groups and became interested in Eastern philosophy and music and, after hearing Ravi Shankar, Indian music. His first album as leader, Extrapolation, was one of the classic albums of the decade. It anticipated the jazz-rock movements of the 1970s and showed John to be an extraordinarily fine composer and guitarist. He started his own group in1971, the Mahavishnu Orchestra, probably the greatest jazz-rock band of all time. After it disbanded John concentrated on Indian music, playing acoustic guitar with the group Shakti. From the 1970s onwards he has been making solo guitar records. One of the most complete, gifted and influential guitarists in jazz, John is as at home playing blues, bebop, free jazz, fusion, Indian music or classical. Among his feats is a densely composed and complex guitar concerto featuring himself with the Los Angeles Philharmonic, orchestrated by Mike Gibbs in 1985.

RICHARD THOMPSON ▲

The son of a policeman, Richard Thompson grew up in London in the 1950s and 1960s. By the time he reached his teens he was earning an informal reputation as a dab hand at the guitar, playing American rock 'n' roll. But, unlike most other guitar heroes of his generation, he built his epic solos not from the customary Blues but from the modes of Olde England, mixed with other, often surprising, sources and scales. These days he regularly works with fiddler Aly Bian, accordion/concertinist John Kirkpatrick on squeezy things and medieval hornman Phillip Pickett on early things. He has worked with Mitchell Froom on 1986's Daring Adventures and 1988's Amnesia and most recently on Rumour and Sigh, described by Q as "one of the most original collections of the year".

JOHN KIRKPATRICK ▲

Acknowledged as one of the best exponents of all free reed instruments and a distinguished songwriter and singer, John Kirkpatrick is one of the great names in folk music. He plays squeezeboxes of all shapes and sizes, from the accordion to the melodeon and concertina. John was involved in the creation of some of the most influential folk rock albums of the 1970s, notably Morris On and The Compleat Dancing Master. These days he tours with political singer Roy Bailey and has recently teamed up with Roy, Martin Carthy, Dave Swarbrick and Steafan Hannigan in the most exciting band of the 1990s, Band Of Hope. He also tours with two of Euroep's other leading melodeon players, Riccardo Tes from Italy and Kepa Junkera from the Basque country. He works a good deal in the theatre, was in the National Theatre production Lark Rise at Candleford and since 1980 has been contributing music, songs and choreography to several theatres around the country. He has made many appearances on radio and TV, and in 1991 presented a six-part series for Radio 2 called Squeezing Around the World, which featured some of the world's leading squeezebox players.

MARTIN CARTHY ▲

One of the giants of post-war British music, Martin Carthy performed with the Thameside Four and Three City Four in the early 1960s before establishing the solo career which brought him recognition as one of the finest interpreters of traditional music in Britain, as well as one of the most innovative. In the mid-1960s he established a partnership with Dave Swarbrick (triumphantly revived 25 years later and still active), which set the benchmark for all duos that followed. In the 1970s he made vital contributions to some classic folk line-ups with Steeleye Span and The Albion Country Band and, with John Kirkpatrick, broadened and enriched our preconceptions of what could be achieved in a folk band with the much missed Brass Monkey. He recently became involved with Band of Hope, a group comprising the finest folk musicians in the country – Martin, Roy Bailey, Steafan Hannigan, John Kirkpatrick and Dave Swarbrick.

DICK GAUGHAN ▼

One of the most experienced performers in any discipline, Dick's 23 years as a professional singer and guitarist have taken him on countless tours to most European countries and the US. He is one of the few artists to have performed extensively in the Socialist world, where he has appeared frequently on television and radio and is as highly regarded as he is in the West. Dick is involved in a wide range of fund-raising events for the Labour Party and trades union organisations.

◄ DAVE SWARBRICK

Dave took up the fiddle at an early age, but abandoned it in favour of the bass guitar, with which he led a fairly unsuccessful dance band: they once tried, and succeeded, in doing a whole evening of dance with a repertoire of one tune – Cross Over the Bridge. When the band broke up, Dave took up the fiddle again. For many years he was with the Ian Campbell group, joining up with Martin Carthy in 1966 – a duo that played an important part in the tremendous shake-up given to British folk music in the mid to late 1960s. When they parted he joined Fairport Convention and then formed Whippersnappers in 1984. Five years later he left and began working with Martin again. Since then they have performed together all over the world. In 1990 they released their critically acclaimed live album Life and Limb; their new album, Skin and Bone, was released last September.

ALY BAIN ▼

Shetland-born Aly Bain began learning the fiddle at the age of 11 under the wing of the great guru of Shetland fiddle music, the late Tom Anderson. In 1965 he got his first big break, when he was featured in a BBC radio series. He teamed up with guitarist Mike Whellans and began a busy touring schedule, performing from a mixed repertoire of Blues and traditional music. Aly and Mike then teamed up with the now internationally acclaimed Boys Of The Lough, the first band playing traditional music to turn professional. Aly has continued to pursue his solo career as a fiddler.

VIN GARBUTT ▲

Vin was born in Middlesbrough to a mother of Irish descent and an English father. He discovered folk music at the Rifle Club in Middlesbrough in 1963 when he was 15 years old and then set off hitch-hiking around Ireland in search of his musical roots. On leaving school he was steered into the safety of an apprenticeship at the ICI Wilton Chemical Plant but broke free in 1969 to become a professional musician. A summer spent busking in Spain and Morocco gave him the impetus to start writing songs and in 1972 he recorded his first album, The Valley of Tees, which established him as a songwriter of fine socially conscious and environmentally aware songs.

RORY MCLEOD ▼

In his time Rory has travelled, busked and worked his way around the world. Among his exploits are working in Mexico as a fire-eater and as a clown with a travelling circus and winning the 1980 Great Texas Harmonica Blowoff competition. As an internationalist he has played harmonica with Mali guitarist Ali Farka toured and hosted a reed workshop in North America along with Egyptian musicians from the Nile, Scottish piper Hamish Moore and Kathryn Tickell. In 1984 he won the busking championship at the Edinburgh Festival.

MICK JAGGER ▲

ERIC CLAPTON ▼

Mick Jagger's progression from rebel, through man of fashion, to establishment figure, over 30 years, is a 20th century odyssey. First discovered by Alexis Korner, he was performing with the Rolling Stones in Richmond, in 1963, when the band was spotted and signed up by Eric Easton and Andrew Loog Oldham. Their first television appearance was on Thank Your Lucky Stars on June 7th 1963, their first American tour a year later and their first No 1, It's All Over Now, in July 1964. Jagger came from a conventional, middle class family in South London and was a student at LSE when he took off as a Rock icon. He invented the strutting, androgynously sexy stage presence which has been copied by singers ever since, replacing the formation movement of those who had hitherto been the musical heroes of the young – who quickly became the young and disaffected. Drug busts and court appearances involving the Rolling Stones became daily reading to an enthusiastic youth and their increasingly bewildered parents. Brian Jones dies and the Stones gave the first free concert – in Hyde Park – with Jagger sporting a white mini-dress. World tours; the Altemont festival; the emigration to France and the marriages are all folklore, but the music goes on.

Widely acknowledged as the greatest rock guitarist in the world, Eric Clapton was born in Ripley, Surrey, in 1945 and, in spite of 25 years of non-stop globetrotting, still seems most at home in the area. He started his musical career playing in clubs along the Thames and then joined the blues-inspired group, the Yardbirds. Considering that commercial interest had prejudiced the group's musical integrity, he quit in 1965 to join the guru of British blues, John Mayall and the Bluesbreakers. With Jack Bruce and Ginger Baker, Clapton formed Cream, which in its, in retrospect, astonishingly short life, became probably the biggest influence on

popular music over the last twenty years. After a brief spell with Steve Winwood, as Blind Faith, Clapton released his eponymous solo album in 1970 before creating Derek and the Dominos in an attempt to travel with anonymity. In his 1985 album, Behind The Sun, he added his voice to his musical armoury. One of the most enthusiastic and industrious of performers, Clapton has performed on many landmark albums by other artists. With his economic stage performance and apparent shyness, combined with the traumas of his life and his massive talent, he is one of the few artists who can fill auditoria wherever, and as often as, he chooses to appear.

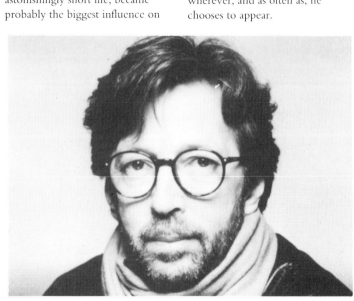

CLIFF RICHARD

Harry Rodger Webb became Cliff Richard early in 1958 and there is no truth in the rumour that a portrait in his attic has aged horribly while his appearance has remained the same. His first single, Move It, reached No. 2 in the charts and there has seldom been a time in the ensuing 35 years when he has not had a current best selling record. He famously espoused Christianity in 1966 and has preached and performed the Gospel ever since, without in any way prejudicing his success as a popular entertainer. He has not always been uncontroversial, his 1971 single, Sing A Song Of Freedom was banned in South Africa and he was refused entrance into Singapore in 1972 – but only because of the length of this hair.

PETE TOWNSHEND ▼

Born in London in 1945, the son of two musicians, Pete Townshend attended Ealing College of Art and began to write songs to be performed by himself, Roger Daltry and John Entwhistle. The Who was completed in 1964, when Keith Moon joined, and became the musical missionaries of the mod sub-culture. Their first big hit was Townshend's I Can't Explain, in 1965. Townshend was the driving force behind the group from the ground-breaking conceptual works (Tommy; Quadrophenia) to the stream of individual anthems (My Generation; Can See For Miles; Won't Get Fooled Again; Who Are You). During the 1970s, Townshend gradually broke away from the group and, in 1980, released his first full-scale solo effort, Empty Glass, and musical creations of various sorts have followed, culminating in The Iron Man – The Musical.

PAUL McCARTNEY ▶

In 1962, the Beatle's first record on the Parlophone label reached No. 17 in the charts. In 1966, they made their last public appearance, in San Francisco and, by 1970, Paul McCartney's haunting Let it Be became the group's epitaph. It had been seven years in which four working class Liverpudlians had changed the world. Since the dissolution of the Beatles, McCartney's success as a songwriter and performer has continued at a more considered pace, and his performances, solo, with his band, Wings, and with other artists such as Michael Jackson and Stevie Wonder have continued to top charts and fill auditoria wherever he has appeared. In 1977, Mull of Kintyre became the UK's best ever selling single and, in 1979, he was honoured by the Guiness Book of Records with a Triple Superlative Award for sales of over 100 million albums and 100 million singles which made him the most successful composer of popular music in history. Famously married to photographer Linda Eastman, McCartney's profile is now usually at its highest when he is championing causes, whether worldwide in conservation issues or for the retention of local hospitals.

ELTON JOHN ▼

The wearing of outrageous clothes and flamboyant glasses, the much publicised attempts to avert baldness and the generally extravagant behaviour have done nothing to diminish the quality of Elton John, the artist. In the 24 years since the release of Empty Sky, Elton has produced over 30 albums, all of great musical integrity and usually complemented by the lyrics of Bernie Taupin. Having conquered the world of music, in 1975, Elton vowed to give it all up, and spent a year concentrating on Watford Football Club, of which he is life president. However, he couldn't stay away and returned in 1978 with A Single Man and a comeback tour. In 1991, Elton won the Brits Award for Best British Male Artist and he started a world tour in 1992. All proceeds from his singles go to an AIDS charity and he is establishing the Elton John Aids Foundation.

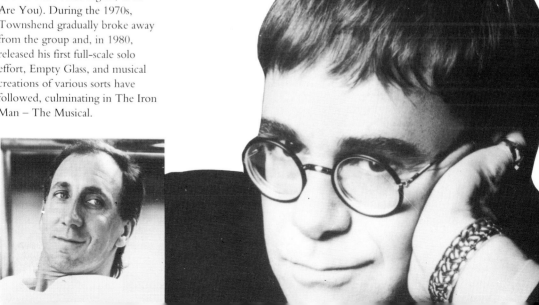

◀ BRIAN MAY

World-renowned guitarist Brian May had intended to make a career as an astronomer. To that end, he graduated BSc (Hons) from Imperial College, London, in physics and mathematics, planning to embark on a doctorate on movement of dust in the solar system. However, playing the guitar had become more and more a dominant part of May's life and, with colleague Roger Taylor, he was shortly to be joined by Freddie Mercury and John Deacon, Queen would be formed and the thesis never completed. The band rehearsed for two years, playing only the occasional college gig, before signing a deal with EMI in 1973. May's contribution to the group was as guitarist and vocalist and he played a major role in writing and production. He experimented with the multi-tracked guitar harmonies which have become his trademark. Brian May contributed three prominent tracks to the 1975 A Night At The Opera album, from which the pivotal Bohemian Rhapsody was taken. The success of Queen worldwide, culminating in the sellout trubute to Freddie Mercury at Wembley in 1990 is now the stuff of legend. Brian May's solo career – and his influence on a generation of guitarists – goes on.

PHIL COLLINS ▶

Born in London in 1951 and educated at drama school, Phil Collins first trod the boards as the Artful Dodger in Oliver. He owned his first drum kit by the time he was 12 and, after a spell with a band called Flaming Youth, he joined Genesis in 1970. He took over as vocalist in 1975, at the departure of Peter Gabriel, when the band enjoyed its first big hit, Follow You Follow Me. In 1981, Collins turned his attention to solo performing and the international success of In The Air Tonight established him as a solo performer almost overnight. He has continued to tour and record both with his own band and with Genesis and, in 1988, established himself as a film star with his performance in Buster, which won the Best Film on Video Award, while Collins himself won a Golden Glove and Best Male Singer Award.

GEORGE MICHAEL

Born Georgios Kyriacos Panayiotou in London in 1963, George Michael met his Wham! partner, Andrew Ridgeley at school. In 1981, they formed their first band, The Executives, which became Wham! very shortly afterwards. Their first hit was with their second release, Young Guns (Go For It), which reached No 3 in the UK charts. Worldwide success followed, and 72,000 people attended the Wham! farewell concert at Wembley Stadium in 1986. George's solo career was launched with the release of Careless Whisper and A Different Corner. In 1987, he released his debut solo album, Faith, from which six singles were taken. Faith reached the No. 1 spot in the UK and USA and has sold 14 million copies worldwide. He toured the world from February to October 1988. His second album, Listen Without Prejudice, was released in 1990, going straight to No 1 in the UK.

MARK KNOPFLER ▶

A journalist on the Yorkshire Evening Post and a college lecturer, in previous incarnations, Mark Knopfler founded Dire Straits in 1977. The Dire Straits hit albums, including the best ever selling UK album, Brothers In Arms (1985), have been coming ever since. Although his commercial success as a solo performer has been rather overshadowed by the phenomenon of the band, Knopfler has worked with Bob Dylan, Van Morrison, Joan Armatrading, Randy Newman and Chet Atkins, amongst others, and has won Ivor Novello, BRIT, MTV and Grammy awards. Now 43, Knopfler's latest album with Dire Straits, On Every Street, topped the UK charts in 1991.

STING ▼

Milkman's son Gordon Sumner, 41, became Sting in the early 70s and, with Police, created a new pop phenomenon. He was the sexy thinking man of rock music, appealing to everyone with any pretension to intellect. He quit Police in 1983 and, in 1985, released his first, stunningly successful solo offering, The Dream of the Blue Turtles, written at a time when he was undergoing Jungian therapy. Employing some of the most talented jazz players in America, Dream showed a more experimental and introspective approach, underlined by Nothing Like The Sun, in 1987. In recent years, Sting has been most prominent in the pursuit of causes, notably that of the salvation of the Brazilian rain forest. Still wildly successful in the USA, his fame has waned a little in this country, where we prefer our heroes to appear a little less sure of the rectitude of their views. His new album, Ten Summoner's Tales, a play on his surname, looks set to put him back to where, lyrically and musically, he belongs.

PAUL WELLER ▲

Born and bred in Woking, Weller formed his first group, The Jam, when he was 14. The band spent the next four years playing local pubs and club gigs until 1976 when Weller heard The Who's My Generation album and found the musical direction and style he was looking for. Sporting black mohair suits the band combined punk's energy and attitude with a sure grasp of melody. Three of The Jam's singles (Going Underground, Town called Malice and Beat Surrender) entered the charts at number one. Despite their great success Weller dissolved The Jam to start up The Style Council in 1982, convinced he had taken the group as far as he could. Touches of jazz, r & b, funk and soul, plus Weller's own distinctive singing talent brought the new band instant acclaim. Last year Weller signed to Go!Discs, with a debut solo album released last September.

MICK HUCKNALL ▲

Born in Manchester in 1960 Mick Hucknall took a degree in fine art before founding Simply Red. Their debut cover of the Valentine Brothers Money's Too Tight To Mention and Holding Back The Years became one of 1985's most memorable American No 1 singles. It was followed by The Right Thing, the album A New Flame, which topped the UK album chart on three separate occasions, and the number one single If You Don't Know Me By Now. After the 1989/90 world tour Mick started recording Rodger's and Hart's You Are Too Beautiful for the sax veteran Andy Hamilton's debut album. Stars was his next project, his first album without covers and consisting wholly of Hucknall originals. It has spawned five hit singles: Something Got Me Started, Thrill Me, Your Mirror, For Your Babies and Stars. Simply Red spent 1992 touring Europe, Canada, the US, Australia and the Far East.

◄ MAXI PRIEST

Regarded by many as the first artist successfully to fuse reggae, pop and r & b styles Maxi Priest joined one of the many sound systems that was part of the British reggae scene around 1978 and worked with names such as Smiley Culture and Tippa Trie before releasing his single Mi God Me King in 1980. It topped the charts in Jamaica, 'a big deal for us because this time we were exporting it (reggae) back to Jamaica'. With 1988's Wide World, a top 10 pop hit, Maxi achieved widespread recognition in America and the same year he recorded the Maxi album with Sly Dunbar, Robbie Shakespeare and Willie Lindo. In 1990 he released his album Bonafide, toured with the Reggae Sunsplash Tour and saw his song Close To You become the first reggae record to top the US pop charts and become a top r & b hit. Maxi recently made his acting debut in the film Scam with Christopher Walken and Lorraine Bracco.

SEAL ▼

Born Sealhenry Samuel in Kilburn the teenage Seal started off in a local band with whom he toured in Japan in 1989. He left them to travel around Asia for six months before returning to England, where he met up with Adamski and worked with him on Killer – a single which stayed at number one for four weeks and sold over half a million copies. Seal's next break was being signed by Trevor Horn for ZTT, with whom he brought out his first solo single, Crazy, in 1990. Crazy made number one in three countries and the top 10 in a further nine. Seal's eponymous debut album went straight to number one in the UK and sold over 500,000 copies. He is currently recording his second album in Los Angeles, due for release in 1993.

JAZZIE B ▶

Jazzie B, aka Beresford Romeo co-founded the Soul II Soul sound system in 1982 with a school friend, Philip 'Daddae' Harvey. Although he has worked as a sound engineer, Jazzie's work as a DJ, on pirate stations and in London clubs provided the training needed to create the Soul II Soul hits. Over the past three years the band has produced global hit records and videos, designed high fashion clothing and sold it through their own shops, staged a world tour and been the subject of a major documentary film. They have received numerous awards: two Grammys, three American Soul Train Awards and four British DMC awards – including World's Best Group. They have also had the fastest selling album in Virgin Record's history. Jazzie B holds an NAACP Image Award, as the first Black Briton to become 'an

outstanding role model in America'. Soul II Soul's latest album Just Right was released last year and went gold in the UK after the first week of release.

RICHARD FAIRBRASS ▶

Richard Fairbrass worked as a barman, model and bouncer before signing a deal with Capitol Records in 1987. Success came in 1991, a year after Fairbrass teamed up with his brother Fred and Rob Manzoli under the name of Right Said Fred. The band went on to secure hits with singles such as I'm Too Sexy (which sold more than 3 million copies worldwide, and earnt them an Ivor Novello Award for Most Performed Work), Don't Talk Just Kiss, which reached number three and Deeply Dippy, their first number one hit (in the position for three weeks). Their debut album, Up, went double platinum in the UK.

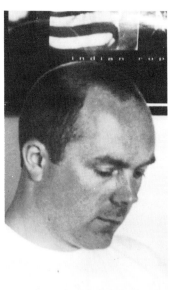

EDWIN SHIRLEY ▲

Few people know that the stage, setting and extraordinary technical display of such enormous events as Live Aid at Wembley are likely to have been built, rehearsed, transported and reconstructed from a company in West Ham. Now a world leader in his field Edwin Shirley set up Edwin Shirley Trucking in the East End in the early 1970s. He started moving tours for the Rolling Stones and Frank Sinatra before transporting productions around Europe for the RSC, London Festival ballet and what became the royal National theatre. He went on to work on the Live Aid Stage at Wembley, the 1976 Save Venice Concert in St Mark's Square for Paul McCartney and Wings, and to complete projects for the King George V Trust, the Quen's Silver Jubilee Trust and the Princes' Trust. More recently he has worked on Stones, Madonnna and Michael Jackson concerts. He received the 1992 Association of Business Sponsorship of the Arts Award for his company's sponsorship of 120 Days Of Sodom by the Marquis de Sade at Battersea Arts Centre.

PAUL RUSSELL ▼

The current chairman of Sony Music Entertainment (UK) Ltd and senior vice-president of Sony Music International, Paul Russell was appointed a solicitor in 1969 and, having acted as a lawyer for, among others, Led Zeppelin and the Moody Blues, joined CBS UK in 1973 as director of Business Affairs. Three years later he went to New York to take the post of vice-president of administration CBS Records International. Since 1982 the company has created such international stars as George Michael, Sade, Paul Young, Alison Moyet, Terence Trent D'Arby, Basia, Eighth Wonder and Beverley Craven. Paul is chairman of the BRIT Awards.

STEVE HARRISON ▲

The principal and managing director of Dead Dead Good Records, based in the South Manchester suburb of Northwich, Steve Harrison developed the label out of a record store which in turn evolved from the Northern Soul specialist mail order service he started in 1982. DDG's first release was Indian Rope by The Charlatans, which was funded by a £40,000 overdraft secured against Harrison's record stores in February 1990. The single shot to No 1 in the indie chart and achieved a top 75 national chart position. It has sold in excess of 70,000 copies and at one stage commanded rarity values of some £75 for original pressings – all this for a band other companies saw as going nowhere fast. DDG's second domestic release was I'm Alright by Katherine E, which turned out to be the biggest UK club record of 1991, with ten weeks at the top of the club charts. In August 1991 the label released what was to become the biggest selling independent single of the year, Insanity, by Oceanic. Ignored by every other record company it went on to spend 34 weeks in the indie chart and peaked at No 3 in the national top 40. 1992 saw That Uncertain Feeling rise to fame with a debut top ten indie release. Steve's latest signing, Kerosene, has already been received with an avalanche of favourable publicity from the indie

BARRIE MARSHALL ▲

Barrie Marshall started his working life a civil engineer but fate steered him in the direction of the music business, firstly as an agent, working with Arthur Howes, who was responsible for presenting all the Beatles concerts, as well as most of the artistes touring in the 1960s. In the early years Barrie represented artistes such as the Kinks and Status Quo and in the late 1960s was responsible for touring the Stax Volt Revue, featuring the likes of Otis Redding and Arthur Conley. In the late 1970s he formed Marshall Arts Ltd, and began to concentrate on promoting and coordinating tours, mostly by American performers, beginning with Smokey Robinson, The Supremes and Stevie Wonder. Since then he has worked with major talents such as Tina Turner, Lionel Ritchie, Al Jarreau, George Michael, Rod Stewart, Sting, Bryan Adams, Whitney Houston and Joe Cocker. He organised the Paul McCartney World tour in 1989-90.

CHRIS BLACKWELL ▶

Born into a wealthy Jamaican family the multi-millionaire founder of Island Records, Chris Blackwell left Harrow at the age of 16, having taken three goes to get five O levels. A short spell in accountancy was followed by a couple of years as a professional gambler, before he moved on to sell real estate and teach water-skiing. In 1962 he found his real vocation, producing and selling records in London with a captive market of Jamaican immigrants eager to buy the latest ska import. Island had its first major success in this country with Millie Small's My Boy Lollipop, the first reggae tune to make it into the pop charts. Chris went on to sign The Spencer Davis Group, who had number ones in 1965 and 1966, and Bob

TREVOR HORN ▶

Three times winner of BPI Producer of the Year Trevor has also been nominated for the title six times. He has worked with groups ranging from The Buggles, Malcolm McLaren, Yes, Frankie Goes To Hollywood, Pet Shop Boys, Seal, Grace Jones and Simple Minds to Rod Stewart, Paul McCartney and Mike Oldfield. Among his numerous awards and accolades are the Ivor Novello Award for Best Recorded Record and the BMI Award for Owner Of A Lonely Heart (Yes), Best Contemporary Song for Relax, Most Performed Work for Two Tribes (1984) (Frankie Goes To Hollywood), and Best Contemporary Song and International Hit Of The Year for Crazy (Seal, 1991). He also received a Grammy Award Best Instrumental for 90125 (Yes, 1984). He won Q Magazine and Music Week's Award for Best Proucer in 1991. Trevor was also the force behind the original 12" mix of Band Aid's Do They Know It's Christmas?

Marley in 1972 (at a time when every other company scoffed at the idea of selling reggae to a wide audience). Names Island has helped on their way to stardom include Steve Winwood, Cat Stevens, Roxy Music, Robert Palmer, Grace Jones, saxophonist Courtney Pine and U2. Island expanded into film production and distribution in the 1970s with Jamaican reggae films such as The Harder They Come and Countryman and moved on in the 1980s to American mainstream films such as Kiss Of The Spider woman and She's Gotta Have It.

PATRICK WOODROFFE ▼

Lighting designer Patrick Woodruffe's first big break came in 1977 when he was offered the job of lighting designer for Rod Stewart. In 1980 he moved to Los Angeles, where he lived for the next four eyars securing contracts with, among others, Donna Summer, Cher and Raquel Welch. He formed Woodroffe Barnett Associates in England with Jimmy Barnett in 1981 and worked with Earth Wind And Fire, The Rolling Stones and Roxy Music. In 1984 Woodroffe's work was featured at the Musee Modern in Paris in an exhibition entitled Le Jardin Musicale. For his work on the Stones tours of America and Europe in 1989 and 1990 Patrick won the Performance Magazine Lighting Designer and Lighting Director of the Year Awards. In recent years he has lit productions for Tina Turner (at the Maracana in Rio in 1988, which attracted the largest ever audience for a single performer), AC/DC, The Bee Gees, Simply Red and Seal. His TV credits include The Freddie Mercury Tribute, The Montreux Jazz Festival (one of the first shows to be shot in high definition television) and the Rock in Rio and Hollywood Rock festivals in Brazil. In 1991 he lit his first West End show, the hit musical A Tribute To The Blues Brothers.

ART

EDWARD LUCIE-SMITH ▼

Born in Kingston, Jamaica, in 1933, Edward Lucie-Smith settled in Britain in 1946. He was educated at King's School, Canterbury, and Merton College, Oxford, where he gained a degree in Modern History. After military service in the RAF, he spent ten years as an advertising copywriter before becoming a freelance author, journalist and broadcaster in 1966. He began his literary career as a poet and has published four collections of poetry with the Oxford University Press. His numerous books on art and related subjects include: Movements in Art Since 1945 (1969); A Concise History of French Painting (1971); Eroticism in Western Art (1972) [revised as Sexuality in Western Art (1991)]; Fantin-Latour (1977); Art Today (1977); A Concise History of Furniture (1979); A Cultural Calendar of the 20th Century (1979); Art in the 1970s (1980); The Story of Craft (1981); A History of Industrial Design (1983); Art of the 1930s (1985); American Art Now (1985); Lives of the Great Twentieth Century Artists (1985); Sculpture Since 1945 (1987); Art of the 1980s (1990); Art Deco Painting (1990); Fletcher Benton (1990); Jean Rustin (1990); and Harry Holland (1991). Four further books are soon to be published. Other publications include two standard anthologies on poetry, an autobiography, a historical novel, a history of piracy and a biography of Joan of Arc. Edward Lucie-Smith has curated exhibitions, lectured and broadcast all over the world.
Photograph by Michael Leonard

DAVID HOCKNEY ▼

Apart from the traditional tools of the artist, David Hockney harnesses the more technical instruments of modern life to interpret his art – the camera, the laser copier, computer and the fax machine are all put to work to this end. Born in Bradford and educated at the Bradford School of Art and the Royal College of Art. He went to Los Angeles in 1963, at the age of 26, and moved there permanently in 1964. He has held teaching posts at the universities of Iowa, Colorado and California (Los Angeles and Berkeley) and at the Maidstone College of Art. One man shows include: Kasim Ltd, London (1963, 1965, 1966, 1968, 1969, 1970, 1972); Alan Gallery, NY (1964-67); Museum of Modern Art, NY (1964-68); Stedlijk Museum, Amsterdam (1966); the Louvre, Paris (1974); Galerie Claude Bernard, Paris (1975, 1985); Knoedler Gallery (1979-84, 1986, 1988); Andre Emmerich Gallery (1979-80, 1982-annually); Tate Gallery (1986, 1988) and Hayward Gallery (1983, 1985). His exhibitions of paintings, drawings, prints and photographs have toured the world. He has edited and illustrated several books and designed for inter alia, La Scala, Glyndebourne, Covent Garden, Los Angeles and the Metropolitan Opera, NY. He is currently designing for the Royal Opera. David Hockney was elected to the Royal Academy in 1991.

LUCIAN FREUD ➡

Lucian Freud, grandson of Sigmund, was born in Berlin in 1920. Ten years later his father moved the family to England because of the growing persecution of the Jews. Lucian was educated at the Central School of Art and the East Anglian School of Painting and Drawing. He joined the Merchant Navy in 1942, as an ordinary seaman and was invalided out after five months. There followed several years in London, working on near-surrealist autobiographical paintings and drawings. From 1946 to 1948 he painted in France and Greece and from 1948 to 1958 he taught at the Slade School of Art. He has had two retrospectives at the Hayward Gallery, in 1974 and 1988, the latter of which toured the USA. Freud's works are on permanent exhibition at the Tate and National Portrait Galleries, the V&A, British Museum, the Arts and British Councils and the Department of the Environment in London and in all the leading galleries throughout the UK and worldwide. Lucian Freud was created a Companion of Honour in 1983.
Photograph by Michael Todd-White
Portrait by Zsuzsi Roboz

BRIAN SEWELL ▼

Brian Sewell is art historian and art critic for The London Evening Standard.

RICHARD AND DUNCAN HISLOP ➡

In 1968 Richard Hislop and his wife Bridget started a company to process and disseminate information on auction sale results. Richard, a founder member and Fellow of the British Computer Society, introduced computer typesetting for all publications in 1970 and, from there, the Art Sales Index databank of sale results began. The Hislops have developed a company whose products are used by art establishments throughout the world – not only the National Galleries in London and New York, but the IRS and the Inland Revenue. In 1983 ArtQuest, the international on-line service was introduced and, in the mid-1980s, Duncan Hislop joined ASI Ltd, after a career at ICI and Shell. He has reprogrammed ArtQuest into a simple, menu-driven service giving instant international access 24 hours a day to the 1.4 million sale results of the 120,000 artists now held on the databank.

SCULPTORS

GRENVILLE DAVEY ▼

Allusive in association, Grenville Davey's abstractions are an examination of geometric forms – often the circle. His most recent work, "objects with purpose" like Mideget Satire, Commonground and HAL, has become an examination not only of the form but of the functionality of objects. Grenville's first one-man show was at the Lisson Gallery in London in 1987; he had three shows in 1992: at the Kunsthalle für die Rheinlande und Wesfalen, Düsseldorf, at the Galleria Franz Paludetto in Turin and at the Chisenhale Gallery in London. His work has been included in group shows in Europe, America and Japan – most recently at the Whitechapel Open and in the finalists' show for the Turner Prize – both in 1992. Born in Launceston, Cornwall, in 1961, he studied at Exeter College of Art and Design and is a Fine Art graduate of Goldsmiths College. Grenville Davey won the Turner Pirze in 1992; he lives and works in London.

SIR EDUARDO PAOLOZZI ➤

Eduardo Paolozzi's signature is unmistakeable in the rich diversity of forms and materials that is his art. He has worked in figurative and abstract styles, in great differing scales and with various materials – including bronze, aluminium, cast iron, fibreglass and found objects. Professor of Ceramics at the Fachhochschule in Cologne, he studied at the Edinburgh College of Art and the Slade School of Art. There have been major retrospectives of Paolozzi's work at the Venice Biennale in 1960, the Tate Gallery in 1971, the Nationalgalerie, Berlin, in 1975 and the Royal Scottish Academy in 1984. Works-in-progress include a commission for a 12ft high figure of Issac Newton for the forecourt of the new British Library in London. A Royal Academician and a Trustee of the National Portrait Gallery, Eduardo Paolozzi has been Her Majesty's Sculptor-in-Ordinary for Scotland since 1986 and a Knight Bachelor since 1988. He was born in 1924.

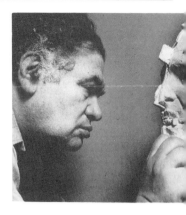

GLYNN WILLIAMS ▼

Professor of Sculpture at the Royal College of Art, Glynn Williams has work in more than 30 public collections in the UK and abroad, including the Tate Gallery in London. His work was included in a group exhibition in Rome as early as 1961 and he had his first one-man show at the ICA six years later; his most recent exhibition was at the Margam County Park in West Glamorgan in 1992. A distinguished lecturer, he has been teaching since the early 1960s. Glyn Williams is also a respected critic and writer with many publications to his credit; an authority on sculpture, he has acted as a consultant to numerous civic authorities and television production companies. He studied at Wolverhampton College of Art between 1955 and 1961 and was a Rome Scholar in Sculpture at the British School between 1961 and 1963. An Honorary Fellow of Wolverhampton University, Glynn Williams is also a Fellow of the Royal College of Art and of the Royal Society of British Sculptors.

ANDY GOLDSWORTHY

Andy Goldsworthy's work, usually made outside and with his hands, is an intimate response to light, colour and weather: "the atmosphere of a place". He studied at the Bradford College of Art between 1974 and 1978 and at the Lancaster Annex of Preston Polytechnic between 1975 and 1978. His earliest works, Seven Spires and Sidewinder, made between 1984 and 1985, were commissions at the Grisedale Forest in Cumbria. His more recent work includes Touchstone North in Dunfriesshire and Enclosure at the Royal Botanic Gardens. The subject of several television documentaries, Andy Goldsworthy has worked and exhibited in Europe, America and Japan. His latest work, Black Spring, is a commission for the Botanic Gardens in Adelaide, Australia.

ANISH KAPOOR ⬆

Of his sculpture Anish Kapoor has said: "It is not made, it is just there." Abstract in form, but with multiple geometric and organic references, the works are usually covered in pigment and have a profoundly spiritual aura. Anish, who was born in Bombay in 1954, studied at the Hornsey College of Art between 1973 and 1977 and at the Chelsea School of Art between 1977 and 1978. He taught briefly at Wolverhampton Polytechnic and was Artist in Residence at the Walker Gallery in Liverpool in 1982. From large installations to arrangements of unusually formed objects, Anish is now making large-scale sculptures. With numerous group shows since 1974, and some 15 one-man shows since 1980, Anish Kapoor's work has been seen most recently at the San Diego Museum of Contemporary Art in La Jolla and at the Stuart Regen Gallery in Los Angeles. Voted the Best Artist Under 35 at the Venice Biennale in 1990, he won the Turner Prize in 1991.

LYNN RUSSEL CHADWICK ⬆

Lynn Russel Chadwick, who was born in 1914, was educated at the Merchant Taylors' School, as an architectural draughtsman, between 1933 and 1939. A pilot in the Fleet Air Arm between 1941 and 1944, he has been a sculptor since 1948. His work won the International Sculpture Prize when it was shown at the Venice Biennale in 1956. Lynn's sculpture is in many public galleries in the UK, including the Tate Gallery and the Victoria and Albert Museum in London, Pembroke College, Oxford, and the Whitworth Art Gallery at the University of Manchester. Exhibitions of his work have been organised by the Arts Council and the British Council in several London galleries. Lynn Chadwick's sculpture is also highly respected in Europe, the Americas and Australia; his work has been acquired by public galleries from the Musée Nation D'Art Moderne in Paris to the Institute de Artes Contemporaneas in Lima. He was made a Companion of the British Empire in 1964 and Officer des Arts et des Lettres in 1986.

DONALD McINTYRE

Born in Yorkshire of Scottish parents Donald McIntyre spent his formative years in Scotland. He studied painting under James Wright, RSW, at Garelochlead but qualified as a dentist in Glasgow, remaining in the profession until the age of 40. Donald is a member of the Royal Institute of Painters In Watercolours, the Royal Society of Marine Artists and the Pastel Society. He has exhibited at the Royal Academy, the Royal Scottish Academy, the Royal Society of Marine Artists, the Royal Institute of Painters in Watercolours, Millioud Gallery, Houston, Sweden and the Bahamas, had one-man exhibitions at, among other galleries, the Thackeray, the Bohun, the Howard Roberts, Cardiff and the Racinée in Brussels. His work is in the private collections of, among others, HRH The Duke of Edinburgh and the Rt Hon James Callaghan and in public collections such as the DoE, London; Williamson Art Gallery, Birkenhead; Newport Art Gallery and the Welsh Arts Council.

HARRY HOLLAND

Harry Holland studied at St Martin's from 1965 until 1969. Among the galleries at which he has had one-man exhibitions are the Jill George, Thumb, Bohun, the Roundhouse, Robin Garton and Ian Birksted. Group exhibitions in which he has participated include the National Eisteddfod of Wales, where he was a prizewinner, Art of the Eighties at the Walker (1981), The Male Nude (1983), selected by Edward Lucie-Smith at the Ebury and the International Contemporary Art Fair, Los Angeles (1986, 87, 88, 89). In 1992 his work was once again on show at the Jill George.

KEN KIFF ➤

After leaving Hornsey School of Art Ken Kiff taught at comprehensives and ESN schools and subsequently at Chelsea School of Art and the Royal College of Art. In 1977 he worked on the Illustrated Folk Tales of the British Isles (edited by Michael Foss, Macmillan). He began working on woodcuts with Jo Briggs in 1991 and a year later worked on lithography with Erik Holgersson in Sweden. His work on drypoints with Mark Balakjian at Studio Prints began in 1990. He has had numerous one-man exhibitions, at the Gardner Centre Gallery, University of Sussex, the Nicola Jacobs Gallery, Fischer Fine Art and the Serpentine Gallery, to name a few. Ken Kiff Monotypes was shown at the Pamela Auchinloss Gallery in New York in 1990 and an exhibition of Kiff's prints was held in 1991 at Marlborough Graphics Ltd.

DONALD HAMILTON ▼ FRASER

Donald Hamilton Fraser studied at St Martin's and in Paris on a French government scholarship. He was a tutor at the Royal College of Art from 1958 to 1983, made an Hon Fellow of the Royal College of Art in 1984 and a member of the Royal Fine Art Commission in 1986. He has had 60 one-man exhibitions in Britain, Europe, North America and Japan. His work is in several public collections in the US and in many private and corporate collections in Britain, including the DoE and the Arts Council. He designed the Commonwealth Day issue of postage stamps in 1983. He was vice-president of the Artists General Benevolent Fund in 1981 and its chairman until 1987.

COLIN SMITH ▼

Colin Smith attended Falmouth School of Art and the Royal College of Art. His first solo exhibition was at the Nicola Jacobs Gallery in 1982. Since then he has also exhibited at Ruth Siegal in New York, in Kunst Europa, Kuntsverein, Freiburg, Germany, and at the Anderson O'Day Gallery in London. He was awarded a Greater London Arts Association Award in 1982, a Harkness Fellowship (For 1983-85) and was joint prizewinner at the Royal Overseas League Annual Exhibition in 1987. His work is in the Galerie de Beerenburght, Holland, the Royal College of Art, the Arts Council of Great Britain, and at Unilever, Prudential and Pepsi Cola (London).

JOHN HOUSTON ▲

John Houston studied at Edinburgh College of Art where he is currently deputy head of painting. He was elected academician of the Royal Scottish Academy in 1972. He is a member of the Society of Scottish Artists, the Royal Glasgow Institute and the Royal Scottish Society of Painters in Watercolour, Royal West of Engalnd Academy. He was awarded the OBE in 1990. He exhibits with the Scottish Gallery in Edinburgh and the Mercury Gallery in London. His work is in numerous public collections in Europe, the US and Canada and in Aberdeen Art Gallery, Bradford Art Gallery, Edinburgh City Art Gallery, Glasgow Art Gallery and Museum, the Walker Art Gallery, Liverpool, Middlesbrough Art Gallery, Robert Fleming Holdings Ltd, Portsmouth City Art Gallery, the Scottish National Gallery, the Scottish Naitonal Gallery of Modern Art, the Scottish Arts Council, the Scottish National Gallery of Modern Art, the Scottish National Portrait Gallery. He is married to the painter Elizabeth Blackadder.

FRANK AUERBACH ▲

One of our most respected contemporary artists, Frank Auerbach was born in Berlin and came to England in 1939 when he was eight years old. He was educated privately before winning places at St Martin's and the Royal College. His work has appeared in one-man exhibitions and group exhibitions of 20th century art all over the world, and he has won, among other awards, the Golden Lion Prize at the Venice Biennale for his work in the British Pavilion in 1986. His work can be seen in Britain at the Arts Council, the British Council, the British Museum, the Tate and the Contemporary Art Society; in the US at the Metropolitan and the Museum of Modern Art (New York) and at the County Museum of LA, the Cleveland Museum in Ohio and the University of Cincinnati; and in Australia at the National Gallery of Victoria, Melbourne, and the National Galleries of Australia, West Australia and New South Wales.

LEONARD ROSOMAN ▲

Born in 1913 Leonard Rosoman studied at Durham University, the Royal Academy School and the Central School of Art. He was official war artist to the Admiralty from 1943 to 1945 and then taught at Camberwell School of Art, Edinburgh College of Art and Chelsea School of Art. He was a tutor at the Royal College of Art in 1957, elected ARA in 1960 and RA in 1969. He was awarded the OBE in 1981. His works have been bought by HM The Quen, the Arts Council, the British Council, the V&A, York City Art Gallery, the Contemporary Art Society, the National Portrait Gallery, the Imperial War Museum, the Chantrey Bequest and the British Museum. He has executed murals for the Festival of Britain (in 1951), the British Pavilion at the Brussels World Fair (in 1958), the Royal Academy (1986) and Lambeth Palace Chapel Ceiling (1988).

Photograph by Richard Faulks

83

PAUL HUXLEY ▲

Paul Huxley studied at Harrow School of Art and the Royal Academy Schools. He was visiting professor at Cooper Union in New York in 1974, a trustee of the Tate Gallery from 1975 to 1982, and a visiting lecturer at the Royal College of Art from 1976 until 1986. He was elected ARA in 1987. His awards include first prize at The New Generation, Whitechapel Art Gallery (1964), a Bourse de Séjour at the Paris Biennale in 1965, and a Harkness Fellowship to the US in 1965. He was awarded a Linbury Trust Award in 1977 and won equal first prize at the Tolly Cobbold/Eastern Arts Fourth National Exhibition in 1983 and equal first prize at the Athena Arts Awards in 1985. His commissions include King's Cross Station (1984), the Royal Academy poster design for the Summer Show in 1991 and the Rambert Dance Company sets and costumes for Cat's Eye in 1992. He has had solo exhibitions and participated in group exhibitions all over the world. His work is in a number of corporate collections including, in London, the Chase Manhatten Bank, ICI and Arthur Anderson & Co, and in public collections such as the Museum of Modern Art and the Albright-Knox Gallery in New York; the Centro Cultural Arte Contemporaneo, Mexico City; the Art Gallery of Ontario, Toronto; and the V&A, the Tate, the Royal College of Art and the British Council in London.

MICK ROONEY ▲

Mick Rooney studied at Wimbledon School of Art, the Royal College of Art and the British School at Rome. He taught part-time at various art colleges before becoming artist-in-residence at Towner Art Gallery, Eastbourne, in 1983. In 1988 the Financial Times commissioned a painting from him to celebrate the centenary of the paper and in 1990 London Underground commissioned him for the poster A Windy Day, Brick Lane. In 1991 he was elected RA and became a lecturer in painting at the Royal Academy Schools. That year he also won a tapestry commission from TSB and a ceramic plate commission for RA Enterprises. He has won numerous awards and prizes including the Austin Abbey Scholarship, the British School of Rome, the Calouste Gulbenkian Printmakers Award (1984), the John Player Portrait Award, National Portrait Gallery (1985) and the Korn/Ferry "International" Premier Award, Royal Academy Summer Exhibition in 1989. He has had one-man exhibitions at, among other galleries, the Mercury; Patrick Seale; Galerie Petit, Amsterdam; Rye Art Gallery; and Metropole Arts Centre, Folkestone, Towner Art Gallery, Eastbourne, Cleveland Bridge Gallery, Bath, with Still Memories, 1978-88 (a retrospective touring exhibition). His work is in public collections around the world including Museo Ralli, Punta del Este, Uruguay, and in Britain the South East Arts Collection, Prudential, TSB Group and Bolton Museum and Art Gallery.

MICHAEL LEONARD ▲

Born in Bangalore Michael Leonard studied graphic design and illustration at St Martin's and then worked as a freelance illustrator for ten years before turning to painting as a full time occupation. In 1972 he began to exhibit with Fischer Fine Art, where he has since held five one-man exhibitions. In 1984 he was commissioned by Reader's Digest to paint a portrait of HM The Queen, to celebrate her 60th birthday. The portrait now hangs in the National Portrait Gallery. Leonard's work also hangs in the V&A; De Beers, CSO; the Ferens Art Gallery, Hull; the New Orleans Museum of Art; and the Museum Boymans-van Beuningen in Rotterdam. He has been the subject of several monographs, and has featured in countless anthologies, catalogues, articles and reviews.

HUMPHREY OCEAN ⬆

Humphrey Ocean was a bass guitarist with Kilburn and the Highroads in the early 1970s before being chosen as artist-in-residence on Paul McCartney's Wings tour in 1976. His work for this was published by Plexus as The Ocean View in 1982. That year he also won The Imperial tobacco Portrait Award. He went to Northern Brazil in 1988 to make drawings for Big Mouth: The Amazon Speaks by Stephen Nugent, which was published by Fourth Estate in 1990. Since this time he has done several important portrait commissions including Paul McCartney, Philip Larkin, A J Ayer, and most recently, Lord Whitelaw, all for the National Portrait Gallery. Other portraits include Lord Callaghan, Maureen Lipman and Sir Claus Moser, as well as Graham Greene for the Royal Library, Windsor, and Danny McGrain and Ralph Glasser for the Scottish National Portrait Gallery.

PETER BLAKE ⬆

Peter Blake studied at the Gravesend School of Art and the Royal College of Art, where he gained a first class diploma in 1956. In 1957 he received a Leverhulme Research Award to study popular art in Europe and in 1958 he won a Guggenheim Painting Award at the Whitechapel Art Gallery in London. He followed this with the junior prize at the John Moores Liverpool Exhibition in 1961, the same year in which he was featured in Ken Russell's BBC film Pop Goes The Easel. In 1963 he visited Los Angeles to do a portfolio of drawings for the Sunday Times. He taught at St Martin's and Walthamstow School of Art in the early 1960s, and began teaching at the Royal College in 1964 where he remained until 1976. He was a founder member of the Brotherhood of Ruralists in 1975. The group exhibited at the Royal Summer Academy Exhibition in 1976 and had a major exhibition at the Arnolfini Gallery in Bristol in 1981. In 1985 Peter designed the poster for Live Aid. He was one one of three judges for the Arts Festival, London, in 1990. He has featured in numerous television and radio programmes and been the subject of a monograph by Marina Vaizey (published in 1986). He has also illustrated several editions of Shakespeare plays. His work is on permanent display at, among other institutions, the Tate, the V&A, the Thyssen Bornemisza, the Museum of Modern Art in New York and the Royal College of Art. He was elected RA in 1981 and appointed CBE in 1983.

LIN JAMMET ⬇

Lin Jammet was educated at Millfield School and Chelsea Art College. He formed a rock group in 1977 which released two singles and an album before beginning a freelance career in illustration in 1980. He started working for women's magazines and doing story boards for pop promos and TV ads and went on to book sleeve illustration. He had his first one-man show of mixed media at St Jude's Gallery in London in 1990. That year he was also commissioned for the book sleeve illustration of Jump, a collection of short stories by Nadine Gordimer, winner of the Nobel Prize for Literature. In 1991 he had a one-man show at the Contemporary Fine Art Gallery in Eton and won Just Art '91 in association With Prisoners Abroad. In 1992 he had a one-man show at Beaux Arts, Bath, and exhibited at Just Art '91 Award Winners Show for Prisoners Abroad at the Barbican Centre. 1993 sees him at the Islington Art Fair (Beaux Arts Stand), at the Philip Graham Gallery and at the CFA Gallery in Eton (both one-man shows).

DAVID REMFRY

David Remfry was born in Sussex in 1942. He studied at Hull College of Art from 1959 to 1964. He was elected a member of the Royal Watercolour Society in 1987. His work is in the V&A, the National Portrait Gallery, Middlesbrough Art Gallery, Hove Museum and Art Gallery, Towner Art Gallery, Eastbourne, Minneapolis Museum of Art, Swarthmore College, Pennsylvania and the Museo Rayo, Columbia. He has had numerous solo exhibitions in London (eight times at the Mercury), Holland, Edinburgh (at the Mercury), and in America at the Ankrum Gallery in Los Angeles and Florida.

NICK BALLANTINE ▼

Furniture designer, graphic artist and art director Nick Ballantine's first published work was a drawing of a Simca car for an article in TV Times when he was eight years old. Cars and toys have inspired him, he says, since he could walk. An interest in America led to a photographic project on American muscle cars and American sports played in London. It resulted in a broken nose from photographing street hockey while lying on his stomach in the road. Painful, but rewarding, as the pictures were used by The Face for their main colour story. A design travel bursary from Thames Television took Nick to Southern Africa to take pictures of witch doctors before he headed for New York to freelance for Cosmopolitan, Village Voice and W magazine. He became deputy art director at Cosmo in London and then worked at the Evening Standard magazine, where he rose to become art director in three years. He has designed everything from filofaxes to baseball caps and a range of furniture based on car parts and street signs as well as The Room restaurant at the Halcyon. He is currently redesigning Arts Review for relaunch this spring and will also be designing for Slush Puppie, "an all time hero".

PETER CHANG ▼

Peter Chang studied at Liverpool College of Art and the Slade where he took a postgraduate diploma in printmaking and sculpture. After college he lived in Liverpool for several years, pursuing his interests in sculpture, jewellery and silversmithing, designing and model-making for TV and graphic design agencies, and working in interior design and garden design. During this time he evolved objects in many materials which are "both sculpture and jewellery and can exist purely as objects on their own or be worn". He now works almost exclusively in plastic and silver, but his work is distinctly organic in feel, its inspiration drawn directly from nature, rather than from multiple sources. His work is on permanent show at many prestigious museums and collections, including the V&A, the British Council Collection in Prague, Kelvingrove and the National Museum of Scotland. His exhibitions worldwide enter the hundreds; in 1992 he showed at Triennale du Bijou, the Musee des Arts Decoratifs in Paris and had a one-man show at the Helen Drutt Collection in Helsinki.

CRAIG MORRISON ▼

Twenty-eight year old Craig Morrison was born in Scotland and graduated in Theatre Design from Wimbledon School of Art. Searching for a medium that was strong and malleable led him to try out liquid latex. Taking the technology several steps further he invented an advanced HS Dipcoat method using natural latex "farmed" from the heavea or latex tree. This fabric, with its tactile surfaces, was ideal for his accessories and furniture designs. In October 1991 he was the British nominee for the Accessory Designer at Premier Class in Paris and in 1992 he was elected by the Chartered Society of Designers as Best of British Designers to show his furniture at Earls Court. His work has been commissioned by TV companies and for many videos, including Seal, Soul II Soul and Brian Adams.
Photograph by Michael Donovan

RICHARD LA TROBE-BATEMAN

Richard La Trobe-Bateman studied sculpture under Sir Anthony Caro at St Martins and furniture design under David Pye at the Royal College of Art. Today he has his own workshop in Somerset where he designs and makes furniture, bridges and other lightweight structures, using oak, ash and elm. His commissions include a child's high chair cleft from Longleat oak, presented to HRH the Prince of Wales by the Crafts Council in 1982, and the high table at Pembroke College, Oxford, made from a single 7m long oak plank, which won a national competition in 1983. Richard's work is in many private and public collections including the V&A and the Crafts Council. He has exhibited and lectured worldwide and in 1986-87 was visiting professor of furniture design at San Diego State University.

ANDREW LOGAN

Our best known sculptor-jeweller Andrew Logan is Britain's first living artist to have a museum dedicated entirely to his work. The Andrew Logan Museum in Wales opened in 1991 with an archive which holds a copy of every piece Andrew Logan has done in his 24 years as an artist. He is also famed as the man behind the Alternative Miss World, which took shape in 1972 with 100 people crammed into a tiny studio, the event is now televised all over the world. A feature film has been made about it and the last one made the headlines in the Bangkok Post! Andrew studied architecture at Oxford before turning his talents to jewellery and sculpture. Since then he has collaborated with the likes of Zandra Rhodes and Norman Parkinson – the fruits of their work together can be seen in the Metropolitan Museum of Art in New York and at the V&A in London.

DAVID WATKINS

David Watkins is best known for his experimental and innovative modernist jewellery in a wide variety of traditional and contemporary materials. He achieved recognition soon after finishing his fine art degree at Reading University in 1963 and by 1968 was exhibiting worldwide. Today he is represented in many international collections including the V&A, the Royal Scottish Museum, Edinburgh, the Museum fur Kunst und Gewerbe in Hamburg, the National Museum of Modern Art, Kyoto, and the Australian National Gallery in Canberra. David is a Fellow of the Chartered Society of Designers, the Royal Society of Arts and the Royal College of Arts.

DEREK FROST

Furniture designer Derek Frost set up his own design company eight years ago, having trained and worked with David Hicks and Mary Fox Linton, where he was chief designer and director. He has exhibited since 1987 at Leighton House, the British Interior Design Exhibition in 1989 and 1990 and at Bonhams in 1992. He lectures at various design schools, reviews books on his subject for Books magazine and has been asked to write a book on Contemporary Detail and Finish for Mitchell Beazley. Derek Frost Associates recently executed commissions for Nash House, Edward Heath's Queen Anne house in Wiltshire, a 17th century farmhouse in Umbria, a 40 metre super-yacht in Thailand and a hotel in Swaziland.

ASHLEY CARTWRIGHT

Ashley Cartwright studied furniture design at Kingston College of Art and the Royal College of Art before joining John Makepeace as a designer and maker in 1973. In 1976 he opened his own workshop and a year later was invited to join the Crafts Council Index and given a New Craftsman grant. He teaches in the UK, Ireland and USA and has been designer/craftsman-in-residence in Australia. In 1992 he exhibited at Oxford Gallery, Bonhams (Decorative Arts Today) and the Royal Festival Gallery (Arts and Crafts to Avant Garde). He owns and runs a furniture design and workshop (Cartwright Designs), based in Northamptonshire.

FRED BAIER

Trained at Canterbury College of Art, Birmingham College of Art and the Royal College of Art, Fred Baier has been recognised as a major force in furniture design since the 1970s. His extraordinary furniture shows "structural bravura and illusionist finish which marries well with a flamboyant use of colour". His awards include a Northern Arts Fellowship, a Royal Society of Arts Bursary and a major award from the Crafts Advisory Committee. He has done consultancy work for the Design Council, the Crafts Council and such prestigious architects as Terry Farrell Partnership. He has exhibited widely in the USA and Britain and his work has appeared in countless publications. His commissions include a Star Wars table for Birmingham Museum and Art Gallery, a conference table for Templeton College, Oxford, and coffee bar stools for the Crafts Council Gallery.

PIERS HART ▲

Branded rebellious by his headmaster Piers Hart was rejected from 18 universities before studying philosophy, politics and economics at Lausanne University. Finally deciding that "conventional academics were not for him" he found his way into cabinet making. Bred in an era when "made in England" meant the best, he has striven to maintain a quality of craftsmanship which he believes is still part of our heritage. Today his luxuriously finished range of cases and trays are sold worldwide. He lives above his shop in Suffolk with his opera singer wife, their three young children, numerous cats and a clutch of vintage motors.

JOHN MAKEPEACE ▼

John Makepeace, founder and director of The Parnham Trust and the driving force behind both the School for Craftsmen in Wood and Hooke Park College, is best known as a furniture designer. He has been designing finely crafted furniture since 1961. He has carried out furniture commissions for, among others, Kodak, the Royal Society of Arts and Lambeth Palace. His work is displayed in public collections around the world, from the Royal Museum of Scotland to the Chicago Art Institute. A founder member of the Crafts Council, he is consultant to the EEC and the Commonwealth Secretariat, a Freeman of the City of London and Liveryman of The Worshipful Company of Furniture Makers. He received an OBE for services to furniture design in January 1988.

DAVID LINLEY ▲

David Linley, son of Princess Margaret and Lord Snowdon, went to school at Bedales, which is known for its emphasis on arts and crafts. He then studied under John Makepeace at Parnham House School for Craftsmen in Wood. He set up David Linley Furniture Ltd in 1985 after three years designing and making his own furniture in his workshop in Dorking. The company produce a wide range of furniture, most "contemporary classics" from consoles, screens and desks to bookcases and cabinets, designed for museums or retail. Commissions have ranged from modest domestic furniture for private houses to items such as the 60ft table for the Metropolitan Museum of Art in New York.

RICHARD DAVIDSON

Working for Sotheby's and a West End antique dealer gave Richard Davidson the knowledge and experience to set up his own dealership in 1974, when he was 26 years old. He became a member of the British Antique Dealers Association in 1977. In 1988, with his wife Deidre, he set up R. & D. Davidson, designing and manufacturing fine furniture, inspired by the antique, but with a flavour of the 1990s. The business, run alongside Davidson Antiques, has met with tremendous success and fitted furniture for domestic and commercial clients is now being manufactured as well as individual items.

CRAFTSMEN

JOHN BATCHELOR ▶

Gilbert's have been making footballs since before William Webb Ellis invented rugby, and rugby balls as well ever since. John Batchelor started work for Gilbert's in 1949 as an apprentice and rejoined the company in 1964 after 12 years military service. He is now the company's senior craftsman, and in his time has made in excess of 60,000 balls.

ROBBIE LITTLE ▼

Robbie Little is the master of the stickmaker's art. He lives and farms in one of the most unspoiled areas of Cumbria, and he raises black-faced sheep and Galloway cattle native to the area. Robbie began shepherding straight from school and cut his first stick at the age of 15, for practical purposes, and his philosophy remains that his sticks should be used and are not for decoration. On 18 occasions Robbie has brought home the Royal Highland Trophy, and he has won the Great Yorkshire Show 14 times. Robbie has won all 22 stickmaking competitions and is the only man to have won all nine classes at the Royal Highland Show. His sticks are sought out by people from all over the world, and in 1992 he became the British Champion of Crookmakers.
Photograph by Cumberland News Carlisle

PETER COATES ▼

Peter Coates is the Best of British Cooper's Apprentice. This may have something to do with the fact that, according to Clive Hollis, the Cooper to whom he is apprenticed at Theakston's Masham Brewery, he is the only one. When 18 year old Peter qualifies after four years, 57 year old Clive intends to retire, leaving Peter as one of only ten Coopers nationwide still making barrels in the traditional way. It looks as if when Peter qualifies, he will be the last man to be subjected to "trussing out", the traditional ceremony where a barrel is built around the new Cooper, and he is rolled around the yard, showered with beer dregs and wood shavings. When Clive was "trussed out", at 21, 120 Coopers worked at his Derbyshire brewery.

MARC AND TONY STEVENSON ▲

Stevenson Brothers of Bethersden, Kent, are craftsmen in rocking horses. Carving rocking horses has been a family tradition for over 50 years. In 1982 Tony began making horses with his uncle, James Bosworthick who, for 40 years, had been making them as a hobby. Meanwhile, twin brother Marc was studying graphic design and the development of educational aids for children. The coming together of craftsmanship and education led to the founding of the partnership. Besides the traditional range of horses, they also make horses to commission, two recent ones being a 12 horse carousel for Brunei and a magnificent life-size stallion, now a permanent feature of Harrods equestrian department. Restoration is an important part of the business, and the Stevensons provide an impressive service; they will collect the stricken animal, identify, date and value it and give an estimate for restoration, free of charge. They also make other animals in wood, and there is a limited edition of teddy bears stuffed with rocking horse shavings!

← ROBERT ELDERTON

Robert Elderton is the medallic sculptor still resident at the Royal Mint in London. Born in the East End, it was at Lister Technical School in Plaistow where signs of artistic talent started to show. In 1964 he was accepted into an apprenticeship at the Royal Mint, the first year of which was spent at the Central School of Art and Design. Subsequently, he took a day release course, and gained City & Guilds certificates in Silversmithing and Allied Crafts. He went to work in the engraving department, and now believes that he must have modelled more coins and medals than any other living artist. He has been elected an Associate of the Royal Society of British Sculptors and a Fellow of the Institute of Goldsmiths, has gained the Freedom of the Goldsmiths Company, and is a Freeman of the City of London. In 1991 he won the Jacques Cartier Memorial Award and made Michael Clark memorial medal for the Royal Society of British Sculptors.

STEPHEN CLEEVE AND ← MATTHEW HOLT

Stephen Cleeve and Matthew Holt are the first winners of "The Best Thatched House Award", awarded by the National Society of Master Thatchers, for their work on Bluebell Cottage, Micheldever, Hants. Both Stephen and Matthew served apprenticeships under Stephen's father, Bill Cleve, a past chairman of the National Society although, after Bill's death, Matthew continued his pupilage under Stephen. Stephen took over the family thatching business in 1981, the fifth generation of the family to be in thatching. At present, Stephen and Matthew employ three people, all serving their full five year apprenticeship, and their business takes them all over the South, and as far as Jersey. Their aim is to encourage and promote thatch as environmentally friendly for buildings of real character to be lived in and enjoyed.

PETER STOCKEN ▼

Peter Stocken was born in 1940, and educated at Winchester, Oxford and Trinity College, Dublin. From 1967-72 he worked for the Thomson organisation, and travelled widely in Europe and the Far East. In 1972 he set up his company, Puzzleplex, to cut hand-made jigsaws, and devised his own type of three-dimensional puzzle in 1973, and has been cutting these in exotic wood ever since, designing over 1,500 different shapes. He specialises in individual commissions, and his puzzles are in the hands of "princes, premiers and prelates, not to mention a pop star or two". Married to a judge, Peter is a Bridge Life Master, and lives in a farmhouse that he built himself from a ruin.

GORDON WILTON ▼

Gordon Wilton is the best competitive dry-stone waller in Britain, having won the 1992 DSWA Grand Prix. Born in 1947, he learned the art working on a local farm at his home town of Biggin in Derbyshire for 20 years. In 1985 he decided to make dry-stone walling his full-time profession, and became Derbyshire limestone champion in 1989.

DICK TUTTON ▼

A beekeeper for many years Dick Tutton decided to make skeps (domed shaped hives made of straw) in order to keep the craft alive – they were the only type of hive in use in Britain for over 2,000 years until the end of the 19th century. He learnt the craft from an old forester and skep beekeeper and now makes skeps for the Weald and Downland

DAVE FOX ▲

Trained as a bricklayer Dave Fox started building flint walls 35 years ago, continuing a tradition that dates back at least to the 16th century. Dave gathers his flints from fields or takes them from old walls and shapes and naps (puts a face on them) the stones himself, using lime as a binder instead of modern day cement. He works almost exclusively in Dorset, building and repairing garden walls. He recently demonstrated flint wall building on TVS Country Ways.

PETER KINGDOM ▲

Peter Kingdom's work in leather ranges from saddles to music cases to revolver holsters to fire bellows. He entered the saddlery trade in 1950 and is now a member of the National Saddlery Training Committee, is the National Examiner for the Society of Master Saddlers and a saddlery instructor with the Council for Small Industries in rural areas, a post he has held for 20 years. He does specialist work for Riding for the Disabled and recently designed a "shoe stirrup" for young children.

JOHN CARNELL ▼

John has worked with wood ever since he was a boy. Fifteen years ago he started making trug baskets (a craft which all but died out during the Agricultural Revolution) prompted by a visit from an aunt who wanted to take one back with her to America. Panels made from white willow are split and shaved into shape using very sharp draw knives. The handle and frame are then shaped from sweet chestnut. John can be seen demonstrating trug making at Singleton museum and agricultural shows throughout the year.

TOM SHEPPARD ▲

Tom Sheppard was offered a job on the railways when he was injured at 16 in a train crash. He has spent his life on the railways, continuing with his woodworking hobby until this turned into a business. He and his wife, Molly, whom he has known all his life, now make around 45 items – everything from tapestry frames to rocking horses, for which Molly makes the manes. Molly is also an enthusiastic embroiderer, wood carver and watercolourist. Their work has been featured on TVS Country Ways.

Museum as well as beekeepers all over the country. To make a traditional hive Dick uses blackberry briar split cane (modern skep makers use chairmakers' cane) using a curl, made from a turkey or goose leg bone and a girth, fashioned out of a cow horn. He demonstrates the technique at county fairs countrywide.

◄ ARTHUR NASH

Arthur Nash's family have been making bissum brooms for the last 300 years. Today Arthur and his son and daughter are some of the few people left practising the craft. From start to finish a bissum takes a year to produce; six months are spent collecting and then storing the necessary materials. Arthur cuts all his own wood, using birch twigs for the brush and hazel for the handles. Bissums are still much in demand – from private individuals who order bissums beautifully decorated with dried flowers to those who just want brooms made from natural materials that are good for their ground. The family supplies Buckingham Palace, the Royal parks and London Zoo.

BRIAN JOHN ►

Brian John runs Cilgwyn Candles, an Aladdin's Cave of candles and related paraphernalia in Wales, as a family business with his wife Inger. A geographer by training Brian has an MA and DPhil from Oxford and worked in the Antarctic as a research scientist before becoming a lecturer at Durham University. Cilgwyn Candles has been going for 17 years, with Inger on the production side and Brian involved with product design, marketing and financial control. Cilgwyn's main products are hand-dipped tapers with graded colours as well as scented candle-pots, and water, sand and flower candles. Some of the output goes to the craft and gift trade but most is sold from the premises to the 12,000 or so visitors who call each year. As well as to buy the products, they come to see candles hand-dipped; in the workshop and the mini-museum are, among other items, candlesticks, snuffers and lanterns from around the world.

KEN GALTON ▼

Ken Galton is one of the few people in Britain plying the difficult craft of weaving wood. He began working with wood at 15, and is now 42. These days he works alone, cutting his own hazel, on a good day finishing about 24ft of 6 x 6 hurdles. He sells his work to the Weald and Downland Open Air Museum and to those who see his fences at agricultural shows. He was recently on TV (TVS Country Ways) demonstrating his rare skills.
Photograph by Hampshire Chronicle

PETER INGRAM ▼

Peter Ingram bought his first gypsy van when he was 15 for just £8 and ten shillings. At the time he was working as an apprentice carpenter, joiner and coachbuilder. He became a journeyman van builder and painter and travelled with a horse and van and motor and trailer van until 1974 when he settled in Selbourne. It was here that he opened the first working museum of Romany Folklore two years later. He still restores and decorates gypsy vans and his work is now on show in several museums and private collections around the country. He has done vans for the film Danny the Champion of the World as well as for Alan Tichmarsh and David Gilmore.

GALLERY OWNERS

BERNARD JACOBSON ▼

Bernard Jacobson's career as an independent art dealer began in 1969, after several years in journalism, and working at the Everyman Gallery in New York. He started by selling Hockney prints as a bet. From then on, Bernard Jacobson established himself publishing prints by artists such as Rusche, Hodgkin, Freud, Tillyer, Abrahams and Maclean, selling through his galleries in London, New York and Los Angeles. During the 1980s he began to focus on acquiring his now pre-eminent collection of works by modern British painters, including Nicholson, Hitchens, Spencer, Sutherland, Lanyon, Bomberg and Scott. He opened his Clifford Street Gallery in 1989 and continues to be market leader in modern British painting. In addition, he represents Glynn Williams, Ivor Abrahams, William Tillyer, Maurice Cockrill, Maggi Hambling, Stephen Finer and Wendy Connely.

GODFREY PILKINGTON ▲

Following school, university and six years in the Army, Godfrey Pilkington joined the art dealers Frost and Reed (his mother was a Frost) in 1947. His inclination, however, was for a more modern kind of art and, in 1953, he opened, on a shoestring, the Piccadilly Gallery. By about 1960 his tastes and those of his wife, Eve, had crystallised – they knew what they liked, and began to show it. Subject matter is all-important, and Godfrey Pilkington has always been aware of the importance of symbolism and allegory. No abstract or descriptive art here!
Photograph by Dick Scott Stewart

REG SINGH ▲

Reg Singh was born in 1939 in London, and educated in Manchester, where his first job was in an advertising agency. He did his art gallery training with Andras Kalman, who left him to run his Manchester gallery when he moved to London. There followed extensive travel for several years until 1970 when he and his wife, Patricia, took over the Wills Lane Gallery in St. Ives, where he became known for dealing in the works of artists of the St. Ives School. In 1980 they moved to Bath and opened the Beaux Arts, dealing in modern British painting, sculpture and ceramics, including such artists as Michael Ayrton, Lynn Chadwick, Elizabeth Frink, John Bellany, John Piper, William Scott and Keith Vaughan. They hold up to 20 exhibitions a year, and attend art fairs in the UK, Europe and the USA.
Photograph by Ray Williams

DAVID BINGHAM ▼

David Bingham's love of the country was in perfect accord with the merchandise of Tryon's Gallery, which he joined in 1960, and of which he is now chairman. The gallery merged with the Moorland Gallery in 1972 and moved to Cork Street. The subject matter is still sporting and natural history pictures, prints, bronzes and books, and exhibitions for contemporary artists.

GORDON SAMUEL ▲

Gordon Samuel is, with Margaret Thornton, joint managing director of the Redfern Gallery, a position which he has held since 1989. Born in Rangoon in 1951 and educated in London, he joined the gallery in 1970. His areas of particular expertise include 20th century British and European prints, Modern and Contemporary British Paintings and Drawings. He is married with two children.
Photograph by R. J. Selby

ANDRAS KALMAN ▲

Born to a wealthy Hungarian family, Andras Kalman was sent to England at the age of 17 to study leather chemistry. The outbreak of war interrupted his studies, however, and there followed several frustrating years when, unable to join the armed forces, and out of touch with his family who were, in fact, killed by the Germans, Andras finally began work labouring in a Leeds factory. He opened his first gallery in a Manchester air-raid shelter, and subsidised his early struggles by giving tennis lessons, went on to play at Wimbledon, and still plays regularly. He bought his London gallery in 1957, and success has followed him ever since. He has trusted his own judgement and remained faithful to a comparatively small group of artists throughout his career as a dealer and collector, Nicholson, Lowry, Moore, Christopher Wood, Alfred Wallis and two people he feels are greatly underrated, Ruskin Spear and Duncan Grant. "I don't find a new genius every six months," he says.

THE DUKE OF BEAUFORT

The Duke of Beaufort is the chairman of Marlborough Fine Art (London) Ltd, holding six to eight exhibitions a year and dealing in selected Old Masters, Fine Impressionists and 20th century paintings, drawings, watercolours and sculpture. They are the agents for numerous famous artists, including the Estates of Graham Sutherland, Barbara Hepworth, Henry Moore and Francis Bacon, Modecai Ardon, Christopher Bamham, Stephen Conroy, Lynn Chadwick, Ken Kiff, Celia Paul and John Piper.

THOMAS GIBSON ▼

Thomas Gibson was born in Buenos Aires in 1943 and educated at Eton. He started his career as a painter, studying briefly at the Ontario College of Art. In 1962/63 he joined a group of Oxbridge graduates as gallery manager of Editions Alecto, who were responsible for the commissioning of David Hockney's "The Rake's Progress". Subsequently, he was employed at the Carnegie Museum in Pittsburgh as special sales representative for Carnegie International. He worked for the Marlborough Galleries in London, and Marlborough Gerson Galleries in New York, where he had special responsibility for Henry Moore and Francis Bacon. In 1969 Gibson decided to return to London and start his own business where, from 1974-79, he was joined by his old friend, the Earl of Gowrie. Thomas Gibson Fine Art Limited is now considered to be one of the top ten galleries world-wide, dealing in 19th and 20th century paintings, as well as selected Old Masters.

WILLIAM JACKSON ▼

William Jackson was born in Sheffield in 1943, and educated at Bedales and Perugia University, where he studied Italian language and culture, and travelled extensively throughout Italy. In 1963 he joined fine art dealers J. Davey & Son, as PA to the managing director and, in 1968, moved to Aitken Dott Ltd in Edinburgh, initially as PA to the owner, but in 1984 as managing director in Scotland and, from 1988 to 1990, as managing director in Edinburgh and London. In 1990 he opened the William Jackson Gallery in Cork Street.

ROY BUTLER ▼

Roy Butler was a departmental administrator at Hawker Aircraft from 1940-42 and served in the RA ordnance corps from 1942-47, three years of which were spent in the Middle East. He became a partner in Wallis & Wallis, the Military Arms and Armour Auctioneers in 1962 and a director of Arms Fairs Ltd in 1967. He was a founder of the Military History Museum in Lewes in 1977. He has appeared on Going For A Song and the Antiques Roadshow as arms and military expert, ITV's Herlooms and the BBC's Heirs and Graces. He was consultant editor on Miller's Annual Antiques Guide, is president of the Lewes division of the St John Ambulance, a benefactor and life member of the Society fo Friends of RN Museum and a life member of HMS Warrior Association. He is also a Freeman of the City of London and a member of the Worshipful Company of Pipemakers.

MICHAEL TURNER ▲

Michael Turner began collecting and repairing clocks and watches when he was only 12 years old. He spent eight uneventful years at a minor public school where he excelled at nothing but was encouraged in his horological interests by his tutor. At the age of 18 he joined the prestigious Camerer Cuss & Co, specifically to work with antique clocks. After a number of years he moved to the antique dealer John Neil to expand his knowledge of English furniture and to buy clocks which would compliment his stock of fine furniture. After two years he left to set up his own business restoring clocks and selling clocks and watches at Portobello Market. In 1978 he applied to Sotheby's and was taken on in an administrative position, but moved in a short time to the clock department as a junior cataloguer, later becoming senior clock cataloguer and auctioneer for the department.

◄ HENRY SANDON

After army service Henry Sandon gained a scholarship to the Guildhall School of Music. He then worked as a lay clerk in the Cathedral Choir of Worcester, music master of the Royal Grammar School, conductor of local choirs, and singer and broadcaster. The chance to live in a medieval house and an interest in archaeology led to a series of excavations in his garden and other parts of Worcester, and when he found early pottery and porcelain his latent interest in ceramics was aroused. He was appointed curator of the Worcester Royal Porcelain Company and the Dyson Perrins Museum, a position he held for 17 years. He carried out a series of major archaeological digs on the original site of the Worcester porcelain company which dramatically increased our knowledge of 18th century English porcelain and led to the first of an outstanding series of books. His friendship with Arthur Negus led to his appearance on Going For A Song, Collectors' World, Arthur Negus Enjoys and the highly popular Antiques Roadshow. He has made many lecture tours of the US and is an honorary curator of the Cheekwood collection of Worcester porcelain in Nashville, Tennessee.

ANTHONY BUSH

Although he was keen to work in the antiques trade, having been a fanatical collector from an early age, Anthony was discouraged from becoming an antiques dealer by his parents. He became a junior litigation clerk in the West End in 1964 and studied English and Law at night school. Four years later he decided to dispense with Law and set himself up as a dealer with a £60 van and £200 in savings. He moved his business to St Albans but returned to London seven years later to set up shop in Islington. He now deals from one of the largest showrooms in London, handling both domestic and foreign trade in 18th and 19th century furniture and works of art. He has been established in Islington for over 14 years.

DEREK ROBERTS ➡

Derek Roberts has been involved in the world of horology for some 25 years, running an internationally based business in Tonbridge, Kent, where he advises on, buys, researches, restores and sells fine antique clocks. He also makes, in conjunction with John Martin, fine precision weight driven wall regulators to order, building them to the same standards as the best clockmakers of previous centuries. He gained his Freedom of the Worshipful company of Clockmamers in 1977 and was elected to the Livery the following year. He has held several major exhibitions, probably the most important being Precision Pendulum Clocks, in which he displayed examples of all the major advances in precision timekeeping. He has written several books on horology, mostly with the aim of providing a definitive work on one particular type of clock. These are British Skeleton Clocks, Continental and American Skeleton Clocks, The British Longcase Clock, Carriage and Other Travelling Clocks and A Collector's Guide to Clocks.

DAVID BATTIE ▼

David Battie left art school and became a graphic designer before starting a new career as a porter at Sotheby's in 1967. He worked in several departments and headed the ceramics and Oriental works of art department at Sotheby's, Belgravia, when it was set up in 1971. He became a director in 1976. He has written price guides to both 19th Century British Pottery and Porcelain, is the editor of Sotheby's Encyclopedia of Porcelain and has contributed articles and chapters to various other publications. He has made numerous radio and TV programmes and has appeared on the Antiques Roadshow since the first series in 1979. He lectures on a wide range of topics in this country and abroad to NADFAS, antique societies, business executives and other groups.

NICHOLAS NORTON

Nicholas Norton has spent practically all his working life at S J Phillips Ltd, which was founded by his great grandfather in 1869. He is involved with the work of various committees within the antique world and his appointments to date are Council Member of the BADA since 1981, Member of the Executive Committe since 1984 and Member of the Antique Plate Committee at Goldsmiths Hall for five years. He served on the Minister of National Heritage's 1992 Committee for the harmonisation of VAT and the coming of the free market. He is a Member of the Working Party for the Export of Works of Art and an executive member of the Grosvenor House Antiques Fair Committee. He is also chairman of BADA Reed Ltd.

ANTHONY FOSTER ▼

Born in London in 1924 Anthony Foster was educated at London University. He joined the army in 1942 and took part in the Normandy campaign. After the war he worked for the civil engineer Sir Alexander Gibb on the Owen Falls dam in Uganda. In 1952 he enrolled as a full time painting student at High Wycombe College of Art where he met his future wife, Elinor. On leaving art school he worked as a film art director and, in 1956, joined the BBC where, in 1970, he became head of graphic design. During this time Elinor set up a small antiques business, specialising in treen – small domestic wooden objects. In 1974, aged 50, Anthony left the BBC to join Elinor, and the firm A & E Foster was born. Since then Anthony and Elinor's interest in treen has become an obsession: their particular passion is for wooden objects from the 16th and 17th centuries. They became members of the British Antiques Dealers' Association in 1975 and exhibit each year at the major London antiques fairs.

JOHN BLY ▲

Journalist and television and radio presenter, John Bly worked for Sotheby's before joining his family's firm, dealers in Tring since the early 19th century. He presents his own programme, Heirloom, on ITV, is a regular contributor to the BBC's Antiques Roadshow and is resident furniture expert on the BBC series Heirs and Graces. He lectures extensively in Britian and America and writes for Antique Dealer, Collectors Guide and other specialist magazines, with a monthly article in The Lady and a weekly column in The Daily Telegraph. His books include Discovering English Furniture, Discovering Hallmarks on English Silver, and he was editor and contributor to Is It Genuine? and chief consultant editor or The Antiques Directory of Furniture and The Field Guide to Antique Furniture. He was also consultant editor of the Antiques Roadshow Book and Treasures in Your Home, to be published by Readers Digest in 1993. In Tring, John runs showrooms and workshops in cabinet making and restoration work. He is responsible for the furniture at Burghley House among other major collections. In 1991 he opened showrooms in Bury Street, St James's, where he holds lecture courses and study groups. He is a Fellow of the Royal Society of Arts and a Liveryman of The Worshipful Company of Goldsmiths.

MARK RASMUSSEN ▼

Born in Derbyshire in 1950, the eldest of five children, Mark was educated at various schools around the country from which he emerged knowing he wanted to pursue a career in the arts. He was offered an unconditional place at Bideford College of Art, but because of his interest in coins joined Spink & Son in 1967. He has been there ever since. Currently departmental director, he specialises in British milled coins, post Oliver Cromwell to the present day, in gold, silver and bronze. He has also dealt in other areas of numismatics, such as banknotes and world coins. Over the last ten years Spink & Son have sold a number of very important coins, including the unique 1954 penny (for £23,000 in 1989), the last 1933 penny (£15,000 in 1985), the gold penny of Edward III (£100,000 in 1988) and the Gothic crown of 1847, struck in gold (sold at a Spink Taisei sale in Tokyo for a world record price of £124,000).

MARTIN DEARDEN

After graduating from Cambridge, where he won an exhibition, Martin Dearden spent five years as a tour guide specialising in Europe. In 1969 he joined Malletts of Bond Street and worked for them in London, Geneva and New York. In 1972 he opened the Hay Galleries in Hay-on-Wye, specialising in period pine furniture. Six years later he opened a new shop in Bath, his current premises from where he deals in pine and French fruitwood furniture to clients throughout the world.

PHILIP COLLINS ▼

At secondary school Philip Collins excelled in maths and technical drawing. He left at the age of 16 with seven O levels and started work at NatWest. He moved to a leading computer firm in London before moving to Devon where he set up his present business in 1979. In 1990 he opened new premises in converted derelict buildings especially adapted for barometer work. He has received recommendations from many leading auction houses, is a member of BAFRA and is listed by the UKIC Museum and Galleries commission. He has produced the largest catalogue of barometer spare parts available and is the author of Care and Restoration of Barometers.

ERIC KNOWLES ▲

Eric is best known to the general public as a member of the BBC's Antiques Roadshow team, for whom he has appeared for the last 12 years. He embarked on his career in antiques at Bonhams in 1976 as a porter responsible for ceramics and works of art. Three years later he became a cataloguer in the department working on sales of modern decorative arts and eventually he became head of the department. In 1985 he was appointed to the board of directors. His expertise covers a wide range of subjects including English, European and Oriental ceramics, Art Nouveau and Art Deco, Bronzes, Metalwork and Curiosities and Bygones. In January 1992 he opened Bonham's regional office in Bristol. Over the past two years he has written three books covering Victoriana, Art Nouveau and Art Deco while contributing to several other books and magazines, including the Radio Times. As well as his television appearances, Eric describes stolen property on the BBC programme Crimewatch UK and in the past few months he has become Jimmy Young's antique expert on Radio 2.

CHRISTOPHER WOOD ▼

Britain's leading writer and broadcaster on Victorian art, Christopher Wood was educated at Sedburgh and St John's College, Cambridge. From 1963 to 1976 he worked for Christie's where he rose to become director of 19th century paintings. In 1971 he published The Dictionary of Victorian Painters, which is still considered as the standard work of reference on the subject. His other books include Victorian Panorama, Olympian Dreamers, Paradise Lost and The Pre-Raphaelites, which has been translated into Japanese. Since 1977 he has run his own gallery in London, specialising in Pre-Raphaelite and Victorian art. In 1988 the gallery was acquired by Mallett, the well-known furniture dealer. The Christopher Wood gallery is now located in the Mallet building at 141 New Bond Street. In 1990 Christopher wrote and presented a TV series for Channel 4 entitled Painters to the People.

◄ RICHARD MARCHANT

Richard joined S Marchant & Son, his family's firm of Oriental Art Dealers (founded by Sydney Marchant in 1925) in 1953. Richard's speciality is Chinese taste Ming and Qing porcelains but he is generally recognised as one of the world's leading experts in all types of Chinese ceramics. He travels worldwide, advising on forming collections and attending auctions. The arrival in the business of his son Stuart ensures its continuance through the third generation.

JONATHAN HORNE ►

Jonathan Horne's interest in archaeology dates back to his childhood when he used to camp out in the woods in Kent to help with excavations at the Roman villa at Lullingstone. On leaving school in 1958 he began work as a floor manager at Selfridges, but continued to dig in his spare time. In 1968 he decided to become a dealer and found the stock he needed to set himself up in his father's enormous cellar. It was always his ambition to specialise in English pottery, which he prefers to porcelain. "Porcelain is too delicate. With pottery you can feel the fingermarks of the person who made it, and no two pieces are alike." He has ventured into publishing, both with his own, academically research catalogues on his subject and with his book on William Greatbatch, published in 1991.

◄ IAN HARRIS

Ian Harris joined the family firm of N Bloom & Son, formed by his maternal grandfather in 1912, when he left school in 1953 aged 16. At the time the firm dealt principally in antique silver, restoring and exporting quantities to the US, where they had a showroom. Towards the end of the 1950s they opened a shop in the West End, and in the late 1960s, following Ian's suggestion, they started dealing in antique jewellery. Ian also pioneered the Blooms advertisements and instigated the mailing of colour catalogues worldwide, both moves which greatly increased the company's clientele. In the 1970s he became a Freeman of The Worshipful Company of Goldsmiths and of The City of London, and started broadcasting for the BBC in Going For A Song with Arthur Negus. He has also appeared on the Antiques Roadshow since its inception ten years ago. He has written two books, The Price Guide to Antique Silver in 1969 and The Price Guide to Victorian Silver in 1971, both commissioned by the Antiques Collector's Club, together with countless articles for leading publications.

DAVID LAVENDER ▲

An antiques dealer for the past 46 years, David Lavender is a leading expert in the field of 16th to early 19th century portrait miniatures. He also specialises in antique jewellery, snuff boxes and small works of art of historical importance. He always buys pieces that are in perfect condition and sells to private collectors and museums all over the world.

JULIAN THOMPSON ▶

Julian Thompson has been described as "among the most respected connoisseurs of Chinese art to be found today in either East or West". Julian's interest in Oriental art was sparked off by his uncle, Richard de la Mare, chairman of the publishers, Faber, and a renowned collector of porcelain. He joined Sotheby's Chinese and European ceramic department in 1963, after leaving Cambridge. He managed to teach himself to read Chinese in four years and he has also learned to speak some Cantonese. He was responsible for the success of Sotheby's sales of Chinese works of art in Hong Kong, which he began in 1973. Before then the market in such pieces had been small and run by a very few discreet dealers. Under Julian's influence a major market in the Far East, spanning Hong Kong, Singapore, Taiwan, Korea and Japan has been successfully developed. The first sales ever held by Western auctioneers were pioneered by Sotheby's in Tokyo in 1969 and the company now holds two sales a year there. In 1991 Julian oversaw the launch of Sotheby's India Pvt Ltd, a joint venture company of which he is a director. His most recent initiative in Asia was setting up auctions in Taipei.

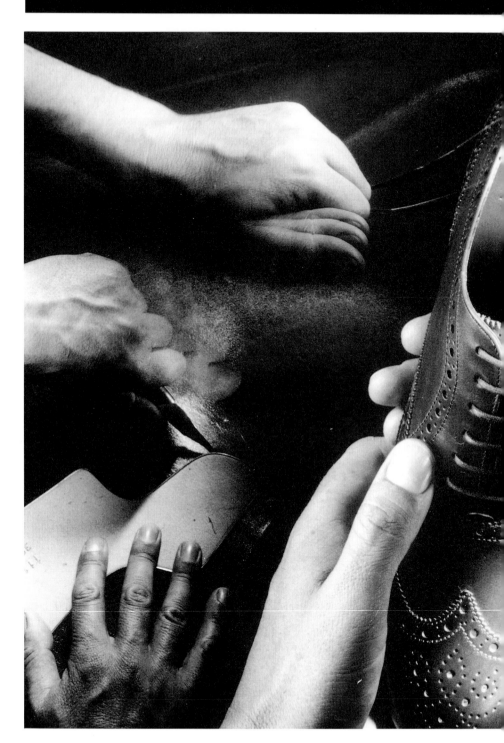

Herbert Johnson Limited,

30, New Bond Street, London W1Y 9HD. Tel: (071) 408 1174. Fax: (071) 495 3655.

JOHN ROBERTS ▲

John Roberts is the managing director of Dents, the Master Glovers of Worcester. Leaving Simpsons, Piccadilly, in his 20s he joined Aquascutum and served as PA to the president of Aquascutum Canada, and later as general manager in New York and in the UK. He joined R J Pullman in 1976 as main board director and Dents in 1990 who won the British Knitting Clothing and Export Council Export Award for 1992.

EDDY ROWLAND ▲

Eddy Rowland trained at the London College of Fashion in the early 1960s. He was apprenticed to Tommy Nutter, and worked up and down Savile Row, until renting his own table in a shop and then buying Redwood & Feller Ltd in the 1970s. He is now the holder of the Royal Warrant – one of the few cockneys to boast this.

FRANK KAHOUT ➡

Frank Kahout is the manager of the Asprey Leather Workshop, a position which he has occupied since 1976. He began his trade in Vienna at the age of 14, and came to England just after the war, teaching refugees. In 1967 he joined Aspreys, happy to return to the craftsman's bench. He may be the last great craftsman in all forms of leatherwork.

GERALD BODMER ▲

Gerald Bodmer acquired S. Launer & Co Ltd of Croydon in 1981. Unheard of then, under Bodmer's direction and with his designs of understated elegance, classic, sleek shapes and form and functionality, Launer is now the holder of the Royal Warrant as handbag manufacturer to Her Majesty the Queen.

JOHN DAVIES ▼

Firmin and Sons plc have been manufacturers of uniforms, regalia and accoutrements since 1677. John Davies has been a craftsman here since 1967 making buttons and hand embroideries for which the firm holds the Royal Warrant.

ERIC LOBB ▲

Eric Lobb is the fourth generation of Lobb's to have shod the rich and famous since John Lobb walked from Cornwall to London to set himself up in St. James's. From Queen Victoria to Queen Elizabeth II, the craftsmanship has hardly changed, and the wait is still worthwhile. Royal Warrant holder.

BRONISLAW LUBOWICKI "RONY"

Mr Rony (as he calls himself) came to London from Poland in 1941 and joined the RAF. After the war he joined Elizabeth Winter, the top belt-maker in London, and 10 years later set up on his own. For 20 years he has presented two collections a year and is the holder of the Royal Warrant, having made belts for the Queen for 20 years. He operates with his wife, Elizabeth, in Bond Street.

SIR HARDY AMIES, KCVO

Born in London in 1909, Hardy Amies has had a remarkable career. Spending much of his post-school formative life in Germany, his war service with the SOE culminated in him being honoured with the Ordre de la Couronne. For 28 years he has held the appointment of Dressmaker to Her Majesty Queen Elizabeth II. A great patron and lover of the arts, society and culture in all its forms.

DOUGLAS KINLOCH ANDERSON

Douglas Kinloch Anderson is the fifth generation chairman and managing director of Kinloch Anderson, the Edinburgh firm that holds Royal Warrants as Tailors and Kiltmakers to Queen Elizabeth II, Prince Philip and the Prince of Wales.

JOHN RICHMOND ▲

John Richmond is a top call designer for both men's and women's wear. He is very forward thinking and combines his creativity in fashion with an acute business sense.

PAUL COSTELLOE ▼

Born in Dublin to an Irish father and American mother, Paul Costelloe found at school that all he was good at was art. After leaving school he went to Paris, Milan and Manhattan before landing in London where his beautifully designed and manufactured collections have attracted Woman Magazine Designer of the Year (1989), Saltzenbrau Designer of the Year (1991) and F'll D'Or Awards (1986, 1988 and 1990).

JASPER CONRAN ▲

The famous son of famous parents. After his return to the UK from Parsons School of Art and Design, New York in 1977 he had his first independent collection in 1978. In 1979 he was elected to the London Designer Collections, in 1988 produced his first menswear collection, in 1989 opened shops throughout Japan and in SW3. He produced hosiery, sunglasses and glasses, organised the charity Fashion-Aid in 1985, and has won awards too numerous to mention in full but which include Fashion Group of America Award 1987, F'il D'Or Awards (1982 and 1983), Laurence Olivier Award for the Best Costume Designer 1991 and "British Collections" Award 1991.

JOE CASELY-HAYFORD ▶

Combining a broad-minded approach with a strong personal identity and direction, Joe Casely-Hayford has always been at the forefront of fashion. Born in Kent in 1956 of renowned Ghanaian ancestory, he is a firm favourite of the music industry and, amongst other awards, was nominated Innovative Designer of the Year.

DAVID FIELDEN ▶

Since making the transition from dancer/choreographer to fashion designer, David has created some of the most beautiful and directional evening wear and bridal wear in the country.

GRAHAM FRASER AND ▼ RICHARD NOTT

Richard Nott trained in fashion at Kingston Polytechnic and returned there as principal lecturer in fashion after assisting Valentino in Rome. Graham Fraser trained in accountancy and became fashion merchandising manager at Liberty's. In 1985 they opened the doors of Workers for Freedom, which now exports worldwide. Awarded the British Fashion Council's Designer of the Year Awards 1989.

JOSEPH ETTEDGGUI ▼

Born in Casablanca and trained as a hairdresser, Joseph is "the man who brought black to the High Street", and undoubtedly one of the great retail barons of the past decade, whose ever-burgeoning fashion empire spreads across London to Paris, Cannes and New York. Sixty per cent of the merchandise in his shops is his own label Tricot, his knitwear range (Designer of the Year 1990) and Joseph (British Classics Award 1990).

BEN DE LISI ▲

American born Ben de Lisi arrived in London in 1982 and opened Ciboure the restaurant. Its success allowed him to concentrate on fashion, and promoting British fashion as a viable international alternative. In October 1990 he was nominated as one of Britain's six most innovative designers, and in January 1992 for an export achievement award by the British Knitting and Clothing Export Council.

TERENCE NOLDER ▲

Born in 1946, Terence Nolder was an itinerant singer in heavy rock bands before attending Chelsea School of Art 1973-75 (first prize National Bridal Competition) and Harrow School of Art and Design (first prize In-Flight uniforms, Modern Menswear, Knitwear). He then became Terence Nolder at Quorum, before setting up on his own after winning British Designer of the Year in 1981.

BENNY ONG ▼

Benny Ong graduated from St. Martin's School of Art and Design in 1977 and in the same year formed his own company and became a member of London Designer Collections. He has lectured at St. Martin's and spoken at many fashion forums. Not only does he produce prestigious clothes for the Princess of Wales, but he has also prepared unbranded collections for C&A.

105

◄ BRUCE OLDFIELD

His instictive understanding of how to make a woman look and feel her best has taken Bruce Oldfield to the top of his profession, despite an inauspicious start as a Barnardo's child. Immediately on finishing his studies at St. Martin's School of Art in 1973 Bruce's outstanding design skills brought him important commissions, along with his first show in the USA. He set up his own company in London in 1975 and three years later added to his already successful ready-to-wear collections a couture division that attracted a sophisticated international clientele. Bruce has gone on to develop both aspects of his business in his Beauchamp Place shop, opened in 1984, producing his first diffusion collection in 1992. On top of numerous academic honours he was, in 1990, awarded the OBE.

DOUG HAYWARD ▲

From the Mount Street, Mayfair, premises where he has worked for over 25 years, Doug Hayward dresses English aristocrats, film and television personalities and British and American business leaders. Throughout the 1970s he ran the successful restaurant and club Burkes. Doug spends his weekends at his country home, reading, enjoying sport and being with Bert, his much-photographed Jack Russell.

TOMASZ STARZEWSKI ▶

A unique gift for pleating and draping and the use of an extraordinary colour palette are Tomasz Starzewski's signature. His sophisticated clothes, ranging from witty day wear, through sexy cocktail dresses, to grand evening gowns, grace social events throughout Europe and the USA. Born in 1961 of Polish lineage, Tomasz sees it as his task to bring out the beauty that every woman possesses. He was nominated in the prestigious couture category in the British Fashion Awards for 1990. The following year the House of Tomasz Starzewski was opened in Pont Street, Knightsbridge – a luxurious salon featuring both the couture collection and the ready-to-wear range.

MARK POWELL

Classic bespoke touches like the Edwardian velvet collar and fabric buttons are the signature of Mark Powell who, in the 1980s, helped put high-quality men's tailoring back on the fashion agenda. Self-taught, he started tailoring at 14, his career taking off in the early 1980s when, with partner Nick Tentis, he ran Soho's influential men's outfitters Powell & Co. Nowadays, based in D'Arblay Street, he numbers Jonathan Ross and Vic Reeves among his discerning customers from the worlds of entertainment, the media and business.

DAVID EMANUEL ➤

Building on 13 years' experience in the fashion business, in 1990 David Emanuel formed David Emanuel Couture, based in London's Regents Park Terrace. Offering personal attention, from the concept stage to the final creation of the garment, he follows this, where appropriate, with advice on the client's total look. After leaving the Royal College of Art in 1977 David founded, with his now estranged wife Elizabeth, Emanuel Designs, a partnership embracing haute coutre, ready-to-wear and designs for the opera, theatre and ballet. Having designed Lady Diana Spencer's wedding dress, the couple went on to style many other outfits worn by the Princess of Wales on official engagements. They also dressed the Duchess of Kent, Elizabeth Taylor and Jane Seymour.

PHILIP TREACY

Twenty-five year old Philip Treacy and his downstairs cluttered studio off Eaton Square has become a millinery designing cult since his graduation from the RCA in 1990. His international success and acclaim emerge from his pure talent and skill. Of him, Shirley Hex, the legendary teacher, says: "He's a Rembrandt of Millinery, and how often do we get one of those?"

DAVID SHILLING ▼

David Shilling's famous Ascot designs for his mother have, perhaps, put his other achievements in the shade. Since the 1970s he has changed attitudes to headwear worldwide. A recent exhibition entitled "David Shilling, a Decade of Design" at Chester museum included hats, men's and women's clothes, ceramics, wallpapers, fabrics, tiles, sketches, photographs and paintings.

JIMMY CHOO ▲

Jimmy Choo's father was a shoe designer in Malaysia. Jimmy set up on his own after studying at Cordwainer's College, inspired by London street fashions. He set up his company in 1986 in North London and in 1988 was exhibited at the British Designer Show. Initially he worked with Anouska Hempel, and now he works with many of the great couturiers.

ROGER SAUL (MULBERRY) ▼

Born in Somerset in 1950, Roger Saul graduated in Business Studies from Westminster College in 1969, and joined John Michael. He formed Mulberry in 1971, and designed his first handbag collection in 1973, and luggage collection in 1976. 1978 sees the first Ladies RTW Collection, and 1979 the "Queen's Award to Industry". Numerous awards have followed for this, now international, company.

WAYNE HEMMINGWAY

With his wife Geraldine, Wayne Hemmingway started a Camden market stall in 1982. In 10 years their label, Red or Dead, has become internationally known, and their extensive wholesale network sells worldwide. Their range of footwear and clothing is mail-ordered through Miss Selfridge in a biannual catalogue. One of the most innovative design teams in Europe.

◀ TERRY PURSLOW

Terry Purslow owns not only the Grenson Shoe Company, England's master shoemakers since 1866, but also Herbert Johnson Hatters since 1989 to such unlikely bedfellows as Czar Nicholas II, Kaiser Wilhelm, Batman and Inspector Clouseau. Obviously attracted by long-standing businesses of quality, Mr Parslow sits on the Councils of the British Footwear Manufacturers Federation and the British Knitwear and Clothing Export Council.

◄ GRAHAM SMITH (KANGOL)

After being design director at Kangol from 1981, in 1992 Graham Smith established his own design studio/workroom and shop for his model collection in the West End. However, he continues to act as consultant design director for Kangol, and the label "Graham Smith at Kangol" lives on.

Educated at Bromley College of Art and the Royal College, Graham worked for a year with Lanvin in Paris and seven years with Michael at Carlos Place, where his hats were seen by Fortnum & Masons, who became the first people to market them. His industrial work has included stewardess' hats for BA, and are in the possession of the V&A, who invited him to speak at their Celebration of Fashion in 1990.

PHILIP SOMERVILLE ▲

Philip Somerville started his career in corsetry in his native New Zealand at 21, but developed a passion for millinery, came to London in his mid-20s, and stayed. He worked for Otto Lucas in the mid-1960s and, after Lucas's death, set up on his own in Islington. His Mayfair shop presents quintessentially English fashions, but his easy going manner does not belie his roots.

NICK RAYNE ▯►

The Rayne family has long been associated with quality footwear. Nick Rayne began working in the family shop after leaving Oxford in 1979. After a spell at Charles Jourdan, he became assistant managing director of the Rayne Company before leaving in 1989 to set up "Buckle my Shoe", the highly successful children's shoe business, with his wife Lulu.

Photograph by Desmond Neill

The companion volume to Best of British Men
is also available either direct from
Best of British Publications or from any
good bookseller.

THE BEST
of British
WOMEN

1993
EDITION

OUT
NOW!

EVERYONE
SNOGS IN JOE BLOGGS

NIGEL HAYTER-PRESTON ↑

Born in 1946, Nigel Hayter-Preston studied fine art and graphics in Ealing and began making clothes for himself. He opened Maxfield Parish, his first shop in 1976, selling suede, leather and sheepskin, and the business immediately took off. He cuts all his own patterns, and is renowned for his technical expertise. He has wholesaled men's and women's clothes since 1978. The Maxfield Parish clientele includes such names as Suzy Quatro, Queen and Robert Palmer.

OLIVER SWEENEY ↑

Oliver Sweeney makes shoes in the time-honoured traditional way. His shoe style names are a clue to the timeless elegance of the product – "The Barrymore, The Coward, The Gielgud, The Guinness, The Redgrave, The Olivier, The Rattigan and The Richardson". It is the "old money" look of quality shoes that fascinates him, and led him to his apprenticeship at the age of 15 with shoemaker McAfee. Twenty years on, he works from a converted chapel in Devon and his shoes are stocked by the most exclusive international store, Harrods in the UK. There is a women's range planned for 1993.

NICK COLEMAN ▼

In 1984 Nick Coleman left St. Martin's College of Art (BA Hons) and started work at Burberry's as a designer/merchandiser on menswear. By 1985 he had established his own label, and by October had shown his first collection which was featured on

the cover of Harpers & Queen. In 1989 he started designing a cheaper line of T-shirts and jerseys, started Solaris nightclub and Nick Coleman Ltd, which opened its first retail outlet in Covent Garden in 1992.
Photograph by Jason Bell

SHAMI AHMED (JOE BLOGGS)

Born in Pakistan in 1963, Shami came to England with his family when he was one year old. The family started its fashion business from market stalls and opened its first shop in Burnley selling jeans and casual wear. At the age of 14 Shami was fashion buyer for the family cash and carry. Pennywise, he believes he was born with a flair for fashion, and is now recognised as one of the leading authorities on the British fashion scene. The famous Joe Bloggs denim label is in demand all over the world, and its latest creation, the most expensive pair of jeans in the world, studded with real diamonds, has proved a crowd stopper wherever it is shown.

MALCOLM LEVENE ▼

The son of a master tailor, Malcolm Levene learned the secret and mystique of formal English dressing in Savile Row. He then took his talents to Jon Michael, Washington Tremblett and Aquascutum, where he was design and merchandise director before opening his own West End business in 1982. He has lived and worked in Italy, France and America. You see the Levene influence on clients such as Tom Cruise, Tom Stoppard, Bill Wyman, Eric Idle and Cliff Richard.

STEPHEN KING ▼

Stephen King was born in 1948 and graduated from the Royal College of Art in 1971. From 1971-72 he worked for Tom Gilbey, and then started, with a partner, a company called "Otto" selling a design package of men's clothes to "all the best stores". His concept of producing men's collections in a similar way to women's and with a sporty feel was much imitated. In 1982 he "did his own thing" and moved to the King's Road, where he continues to sell Avante Garde clothes to popstars, media figures, aristocrats, royalty and the simply rich.

NICKY BUTLER AND SIMON WILSON ▲

Nicky Butler and Simon Wilson, who own the glamorous costume jewellery boutiques Butler and Wilson, met in the 1960s and began by dealing in Art Deco and Art Nouveau pieces. They now design some of their own pieces and have two shops in London, one in Los Angeles and one in Glasgow as well as a duty free outlet at Heathrow and other outlets in internationally famous department stores. Their jewellery is renowned for being unashamedly and outrageously fake. Inspired by earlier creations, Butler and Wilson originals are totally modern and in tune with today's and tomorrow's fashions.

MARCO CAIRNS, EDDY PRENDERGAST, ◄ BARRY SHARPE

Marco, Eddy and Barry are "The Duffer" of St. George, which started in 1984 and has become one of Britain's most influential menswear labels. Recently, they have opened a flagship store in Covent Garden, and added bench-made shoes to their classic menswear themes. They have a truly international clientele.

WILLIAM HUNT ▲

William Hunt, at 23, began designing, manufacturing and selling his own line of menswear in 1983, and now supplies over 50 outlets in the UK. Until 1988 he was running every aspect of the business himself. In 1991, with a view to launching his products worldwide, he opened his showcase shop in Neal Street and is now exporting 70 per cent of his produce to Europe, America and Japan.

NICHOLAS GRANGER ↑

Nick Granger runs the family business of Walter Norton and Sons in Savile Row. Born in 1962 he left school at 16 to join the company, left after two years and rejoined after ten, with a lot of experience and a pilot's licence. He specialises in the unique "Field Jacket" and says "You've got a one way ticket through life, make sure it's First Class".

RODERICK MACKRILL ↓

Rod Mackrill has spent his working life within the quality sector of the British textile industry. He believes passionately in the opportunities that remain for the very finest of British garment manufacturers. As managing director of John Scott-Nichol he has succeeded in proving that making men's socks of traditional quality can be a thriving business.

TOM GILBEY ↑

Tom Gilbey makes waistcoats – in fact Tom Gilbey *is* waistcoats. Cut from silks, rayons, wool and anything else, paisley, floral, check, waterproof, reversible – one side for the races and the other for dinner – or customised to your own design. He has been going for ages and will go on.

J. A. de C. HILL ⬆

Of partly French/Swiss descent, John Hill speaks four languages and is conversant with several others. Having been foreign correspondent for the *Daily Mail* and managing director of an insulation company in Italy, he joined the family business (Sunspel, formerly T. A. Hill and Co) in 1968. Sunspel Boxer makes quality boxer shorts in Long Eaton for sale all over the world.

THEO FENNELL ⬇

In 1989 Theo Fennell was invited by Harrods to participate in their Fine Jewellery Hall, placing him alongside Cartier and Garrards. Since his Fulham Road business started in 1982, this was no mean achievement. Fennell has franchises in Tokyo and Osaka and sells his individual jewellery, tableware and fine watches in exclusive stores and from his own premises.

MICHAEL BOOTH ⬆

Hilditch and Key has two outlets in Jermyn Street, one on the Rue de Rivoli and 150 quality outlets worldwide. As its chairman, Michael Booth continues the policy of offering a wide range of shirts of exclusive designs, all made in the factory in Scotland.

MATTHEW CAMBERY ⬇

Matthew Cambery studied design and manufacture at Sir John Cass School of Art and went on to a five year apprenticeship where he developed his fascination for jewellery. In 1992 he was invited to exhibit by the Worshipful Company of Goldsmiths "British Goldsmiths of Today". He was tutor for "Diamonds by Design", organised by De Beers, for the innovation of new diamond jewellery. Cambery Designs Ltd is in New Bond Street.

WARREN LEVY ⬆

Warren Levy took over the Loughborough company of Whyte and Smith in 1991, forming Hall Class Ltd. The Company has been manufacturing men's hosiery since 1861, and the spokesman states that "the difference between what we do and what other hosiery manufacturers do is that we make hosiery which is a high quality fashion accessory NOT an item of underwear".

DAVID DEAKIN ⬆

The great, great nephew of the founder of Deakin's and Francis Ltd, David Deakin is managing director of the famous Birmingham jewellers who, these days, specialise in gentlemen's accoutrements, especially cuff-links and tie-pins as well as manufacturing modern and reproduction jewellery.

PETER GEESON ⬇

Peter Geeson's objective is to be acknowledged as the finest 30 gauge manufacturer in the world. The company, Peter Geeson of England, is based in Long Eaton and manufactures fully fashioned knitwear to the highest standards, trading with 20 countries and supplying Harrods, Calvin Klein, Saks 5th Avenue, Dunhill and Burberry.

JOHN PEARSE ➤

As a Savile Row apprentice in the 1960s, John Pearse would rather have been turning out Mod suits in mohair. In 1966 he left to set up Granny Takes a Trip, making clothes for the Stones, Cream and Jimi Hendrix. After a lengthy break, in 1986 he returned to tailoring, blending 1960s influences with classic elegance. Nowadays, in his Soho shop, he enjoys the custom of, among others, clients who go back a couple of decades.

DAVID SASSOON ▲

Fresh from the Royal College of Art, David Sassoon joined Belinda Bellville, and their elegant clothes have graced a prestigious clientele for over 25 years. Belinda has now retired but acts as consultant to the company which David runs, with Lorcan Mullany as designer for the ready-to-wear collection. This they show each season in London, Paris, Milan, New York, Munich and Düsseldorf, selling to leading stores in Britain and the USA, and in their own shop in Chelsea. Most famous, however, for its romantic evening wear, Bellville Sassoon numbers among its clients the Princess of Wales, the Duchess of York and other members of the Royal Family, actresses including Candice Bergen, Julie Andrews and Barbara Streisand, as well as countless ambassadresses and members of the international jet-set.

ANTONY PRICE ▲

Antony Price states simply that his dresses, worn by clients like Melanie Griffith, Iman, Countess Deborah von Bismarck, Shakira Caine, Steffi Graf and Naomi Campbell, enhance a woman's form, making her feel desirable. Antony first enjoyed success with Stirling Cooper. But his name became far more widely known when he masterminded the album covers and outfits for Roxy Music, as well as creating suits for the stylish lead singer Bryan Ferry. Commissions for the Rolling Stones and Duran Duran were to follow. In 1977 Antony began to design for his own label, Plaza, and opened his first shop, in the King's Road, with a second, in South Molton Street, following in 1986. From here he sold wholesale to prestigious stores in London and New York.

← TIMOTHY EVEREST

After three-and-a-half-years with the late Tommy Nutter in Savile Row, and then running Malcolm Leven's Chiltern Street shop, Timothy Everest set up in business on his own. In the 17th century house in Spitalfields that he is gradually restoring to its former elegance, he translates his thorough grasp of traditional bespoke methods into a modern idiom, describing himself as a craftsman rather than a designer.

VICTOR EDELSTEIN ➤

Having learnt the craft of dressmaking with various British and French companies, Victor Edelstein became assistant to the influential Barbara Hulanicki at Biba in 1967, at the age of 21. After three years in which he built up a considerable following, he had his own business for a similar period, dressing, among others, rock groups, before joining Salvador and then Christian Dior London. Victor launched his own ready-to-wear collection in 1978, but four years later decided to concentrate exclusively on haute couture. The simple lines and individuality of his designs have won him a huge clientele which includes the Princess of Wales and international royalty, Isobel Goldsmith, Mrs Robert Sangster, Victoria Tennant, Lady Solti and numerous influential American customers.

SAM McKNIGHT ⬆

Scottish born Sam McKnight has been in the hair world for 18 years. He was a teacher, before deciding that hairdressing would better suit his creative and artistic talents. He joined Molton Brown's creative team, working with the most sought after photographers and models, and moved to New York to exploit his abilities. His first job in New York was for American Vogue Beauty, and his second an advertising trip with Bruce Webber, after which there was no looking back. Sam is now responsible for the most glamorous heads in the world: Linda Evangelista, Cindy Crawford, Christy Turlingham, Naomi Campbell, Claudia Schiffer, Talisa Soto, Christine Brinkley, HRH the Princess of Wales, Lisa Stansfield and Kylie Minogue, all find him indispensable. Top photographers vie for Sam's expertise at their sessions and in 1992 he was awarded the title Session Hairdresser of the Year for the second year running.

CHRISTOPHER DOVE

With his wife Sonya, Christopher Dove opened his salon, Sophisticut, in Paignton, Devon, immediately after leaving college at the age of 19. Studying in the evenings, he gained his Advanced Hairdessing/Master Craftsman and Teacher Certificates within two years, at the same time as competing internationally with the British World Cup team, winning the Welsh, Scottish and International Euromas Trophies. In 1983 he was presented with the Gilbert Pearse Award, for Most Outstanding Young Hairdresser. Not only have Christopher and Sonya competed and performed successfully throughout the world, they have also built up an enormously successful salon business at home, where they have placed great emphasis on the training and education of stylists. Christopher Dove's dedication and talent are evident in his immaculate shows, inspiring seminars and beautiful photographs.

GARY HOOKER

Gary Hooker owns two Saks hairdressing salons in Newcastle-upon-Tyne. He has been a franchisee with the Saks group for 12 years and, in 1991, was appointed Artistic Director for the group's artistic team.

◀ TIM HARTLEY

Tim Hartley joined Vidal Sassoon as a barber in Manchester in 1974. He was made Art Director of the Barber Shop in 1978, before transferring to the Leeds Ladies Salon to take up the position of Art Director. By 1981 Tim was Art Director of both the Leeds and Manchester salons and, in 1983, he moved to London to become UK Creative Director. Three years later he was appointed European Creative Director, and now holds the post of International Creative Director, responsible for the artistic direction of the Vidal Sassoon salons and academies worldwide.

TOM MULRINE ⬆

Born in Belfast in 1950, and started his hairdressing career at the age of 16, training at the Brenda Gaile Salon, one of Northern Ireland's top salons. Tom won his first All-Ireland title when he was 17. In the late 1960s and early 1970s he trained extensively at Vidal Sassoon in London and at a top salon on the outskirts of Toronto, before returning to Bangor in 1974 to open Gatsby International Salon, in partnership with Brenda Keys, the former Brenda Gaile. The design team which they formed has since won innumerable awards, featured in magazines and on television and styled models for designers' collections. Tom Mulrine is currently Northern Ireland Hairdresser of the Year.

RICHARD STEPNEY ⬇

From 1976 to 1985 Richard Stepney was employed by Vidal Sassoon, working in their salons and schools in England and abroad, rising to the position of Artistic Director of the school. In 1985 he joined Atlas Associates as a partner, extensively involved in fashion photography and show work. Atlas Associates was disbanded in 1990, and Richard opened his own salon, the 4th Floor, in Northington Street, London, where he employs five stylists, and concentrates on providing a discreet salon service for a clientele built entirely on recommendation.

TERRY JACQUES

Terry Jacques has three times been an award winner at the British Hairdressing Awards, which are seen as the Oscars of the British hairdressing calendar and, in 1992, he received the ultimate accolade when he was elected to their Hall of Fame. Terry is the first Afro hair artist to receive this honour. He received his formal training at the London College of Fashion & Complexion International, and worked in various fashionable London salons before opening his own premises in Clapham. During 1992 he has undertaken hair and make-up projects for video sessions and magazine features for such publications as Vogue, Cosmopolitan, Marie Claire, Black Hair & Beauty as well as many trade magazines. He has also made frequent and regular TV appearances, and his clientele has increased all the time, and now includes such people as Lenny Henry, Mica Paris and Kim Appleby.

NICKY CLARKE

Nicky Clarke is the man of the moment in the hairdressing world; according to The Times: "The emerging Crown Prince of the starry snippers. . . Nicky is your traditional megastar hairdresser." Nicky began his hairdressing career with Leonard in the 1970s, and was the creative force behind John Frieda in the 1980s. Amongst his famous clientele are the Duchess of York and Selina Scott, whose images he transformed when he changed their hair from long to short, Yasmin le Bon, Paula Yates, Isabella Rosellini, George Harrison, Paul and Linda McCartney, Jerry Hall, Queen Noor of Jordan and the cream of the world's models and supermodels. In 1991 the first Nicky Clarke Salon opened to great acclaim. Although famous for his royal and cover-girl clients – and his two month waiting list – Nicky aims to make every one of his clients look and feel like royalty.

MICHAEL "ROCKY" EGGISON

Born in 1958, Rocky entered the hairdressing profession when he joined Vidal Sassoon at the age of 19. He started as a junior, but quickly rose to Assistant Art Director, working for Sassoon doing hair and fashion shows, seminars and teach-ins. He cut Sassoon's hair when he was in London. In 1989 he opened his own salon, Eggison Daniel, in Lansdowne House, where he employs seven stylists.

PERSONAL TRAINERS

RALIE JOSEPH ▼

Ralie Joseph founded Body Flex, a personal training consultancy based in Surrey and Hampshire, in 1986, after training at London's Pineapple Studios and Energy Unlimited. For ten years he was principal fitness director at the University of Surrey, coaching many athletes to international competition standard. At the same time he was a world-class judo competitor. With a training system combining mind and body, Ralie holds master classes and workshops throughout Britain and has provided videos and training techniques for the Open University. In addition to starring in Carolan Brown's Shape, Tone, Pump and Funk video, he has appeared on television and featured in magazines.

JERRY POWELL ▼

The holder of the American Council on Exercise's gold certificate for personal training, Jerry Powell has worked full-time in the field of one-to-one training since 1987. Bod-iwerk, Jerry's personal training system, staffed by trainers and a sports injury specialist, is a friendly yet professional programme aimed at ensuring his clients' progress towards a healthier lifestyle. To this end, Jerry recently attended a major international forum on personal training staged in Las Vegas by the International Dance Exercise Association.

NICK PHIPPS ▲

Nick Phipps represented Britain as a decathlete in 14 international competitions between 1971 and 1979, before becoming a key member of the national bobsleigh team for ten years. His last championship appearance in this sport was in the Olympic Games at Albertville, France, in 1992. That year Nick set up a training studio in London's Battersea where, with a growing reputation for dedication and enthusiasm, he trains a large clientele on a one-to-one basis, as well as working with other clients in their own homes.

FLOYD BROWN ▼

The personal trainer and self-defence instructor Floyd Brown is co-director, with Carol Hampton, of Energy Unlimited. This organisation provides corporate and personal fitness training programmes and workshop presentations on one-to-one fitness training. Additionally it maintains the National Register of Personal Trainers, which lists Britain's finest fitness teachers and gym instructors offering one-to-one tuition. Floyd also presents, in London and Europe, workshops on self-defence training for women and manages the Monkhon Dam Muay Thai Boxing Club in London's Victoria.

BOB SAWHNEY ▲

Certified as a fitness instructor by the Hong Kong Sports Institute and as a personal trainer by the influential American Council on Exercise, Bob Sawhney ran a sports centre in Hong Kong. During his time there Bob also became the Hong Kong Goju-Kai Junior Karate Champion. Now based in London, and working in gyms in Earls Court and Regent's Park, Bob trains a wide spectrum of people, from pregnant women to bodybuilders.

ANDY JACKSON ▲

Andy Jackson is a leading authority on children's fitness in addition to having expertise in anatomy, physiology, kinesiology and related disciplines. As Course Director for London Central YMCA's Training and Development team, he has trained thousands of exercise-to-music teachers and fitness trainers from all over Britain. Renowned for his motivating, high-energy master classes, Andy has taught and lectured throughout Britain, in Europe and in the Middle East, and was the first British man to present fitness in the USA. He is a director of the Exercise Company, a merchandising concern specialising in leisurewear and fitness.

◄ SIMON HALL

Edinburgh-based Simon Hall first encountered fitness as a way of life when he served in the Parachute Regiment for three years. In 1989, after spells in security work and modelling, he became a full-time personal trainer, working with both companies and individual clients. Simon is involved in nutrition, programmes to help stop smoking and reducing the risk of heart disease, and company PR, as well as helping Cala Homes Scotland win the BUPA Scotland Health Award for 1992.

CLAYTON MARSHALL ▼

Trained in classical ballet, and having danced extensively in Britian and Europe, Clayton Marshall now exploits the disciplines of dance to train an international clientele of non-dancers in London and New York. Clayton has devised fitness projects, including workshops and audiotapes for Cosmopolitan, had his work featured in the world's leading magazines, and acts as a consultant to journalists in the field of physical therapy. In April 1992, in association with the Royal Marsden Hospital Cancer Appeal, Clayton led 13,222 people in the Boots Aerobathon at London's Earls Court, the largest aerobics event in the world. Later that year he began to appear regularly on BBC 1's Good Morning.

ROBERT SMITH ▲

Based at Loughbrough University, from which he holds a Master's Degree, Bob Smith specialises in the teaching of gymnastics and fitness training, as well as being responsible for postgraduate courses and teacher training. As an internationally acclaimed trainer of fitness instructors, personal trainers and the general public, his guiding principle is that exercise should be safe, effective and enjoyable for all. He also trains a few select athletes and aerobics champions. In 1992 Bob received the Award for Education of the National Association of Exercise Teachers and was the only British fitness specialist to speak at the International Dance Exercise Association's International Convention in Las Vegas.

JAMIE ADDICOAT ▲

Known for his straight-talking approach to fitness regimes like his infamous "Fatbusters" class, Jamie Addicoat is justly known as the Beastmaster by his clients, who include Jonathan Ross, Boy George, Betty Boo and Ellen Barkin, as well as sporting celebrities. Australian-born, but now a UK passport holder, Jamie published his first book, Fatbusters, in 1992, along with a video of the same title and Grunt, Britain's first workout for children. The "baddest boy of fitness", whose philosophy is that fitness helps you enjoy your vices but should never become a vice itself, has also made many television appearances.

MODELS

RICK GILES ➤

Rick was talent spotted by a Select
photographer when he was 18.
Now just 23 he already has an
impressive list of assignments to his
credit, working with photographers
such as Michael Roberts, Robert
Erdmann and the late Stevie
Hughes. He was the OXO boy for
TV commercials and posters and
has done campaigns for, among
others, Joseph Tricot and L'Oreal.
Photograph by Anthony Edwin

JOHN RAWLINSON ▲

John Rawlinson spent a year in
Oxford "failing his 'A' levels"
before working on and off as a
despatch rider and guitar player in a
rock band. He says he stumbled
into modelling and in the last six
years has worked at Nevs with,
among others, Magnus Marding,
Bruce Weber and Nadir. His
campaigns include Ralph Lauren
and Burberry and he has appeared
in "every glossy magazine there is".
He plays the guitar, regularly goes
flyfishing and is mad about
motorbikes – he actually has a bike
stationed in every city he works in.
*Photograph by Bruce Weber for Ralph
Lauren*

GARY ALEXANDER ➤

Twenty-eight year old Gary
Alexander has been modelling for
five years. He works with Nevs
and agencies in New York, Paris,
Milan and all over Europe for
photographers of such international
renown as Wes Bell, Mario
Testino, Bob Frame and Klaus
Wickrath. Gary has just finished his
degree in economics. When he
isn't modelling or studying he finds
time to write short stories, take
photos, play his double bass and go
running.
*Photograph by Sheila Rock for London
Fashion Forecast*

GARY GREENWOOD ▼

Twenty-eight year old Gary Greenwood worked in property maintenance until a friend suggested he try modelling. He joined Nevs and soon enjoyed success with campaigns all over Europe and in New York, Sydney and Tokyo for the likes of Speedo, Issey Miyake, Ferre and Armani.

He collects cars and motorbikes but his abiding passion is surfing – he was the English South Coast Surfing Champion four years ago. He now works in Sydney, Milan, Hamburg and London, and anywhere, he says, where there is good surf.

Photograph courtesy of Moda Men (Photographer: Jonathan Bookalil)

ROBBIE ▼

Twenty-seven year old Robbie was born in Birmingham. He was set to pursue a career in football for Leicester City when an injury forced him out of the game. At college he studied tool-making and worked in this field before moving to London in 1985. He was working in a pub when a model friend introduced him to Annette Russell, of SoDamtuFF. Within months of joining the agency he was travelling to Paris, Milan, Barcelona and Tokyo, a chance, he says, he would never have had had he remained in Birmingham.

Photograph by Gerald Fraser for GQ

CASSIUS ↥

Top model and teen idol, Cassius left school with a handful of 'O' levels and no idea of what he wanted to do. He tried several jobs becoming becoming a messenger with ambitions to become a copywriter at Ogilvy & Mather. It was at the ad agency that he was talent spotted, in the lift, by film and commercial director Marek Keniesvska. His first job was a Bovril commercial with Jerry Hall which earned him more in two days than he had in a year at the agency. Cassius joined SoDamtuFF a couple of years ago and since then he has worked all over the world. Much of his spare time is spent writing poetry.
Photograph by Christopher Griffiths for Menswear

ROGER COOK ▶

Roger Cook graduated with distinction from the Slade and entered the art world in the heyday of the "Swinging 60s", during which time he was photographed by Snowdon for his book on the London art world. A Stuyvesant Foundation scholarship took him to New York after which he started teaching in art schools. The 1970s saw him writing a book on the symbolism of the tree, still in print. His modelling career began in 1985 when he was scouted for Yohji Yamamoto's catwalk show in Paris.
Photograph by Julian Broad

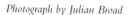

JOHN PEARSON ▶

John Pearson has been modelling since he was 18. He was working in a jeans shop in Hull when an enterprising friend took a photo of him and sent it to Look In. The magazine immediately saw he had potential and shot him for their cover. Since then John has done campaigns with Elite Premier for Valentino, Ralph Lauren and Perry Ellis and appeared in videos for, among others, Banana Republic and George Michael. Last year he did his first film in Hollywood, co-starring with Drew Barrymore. He has just bought a house in Los Angeles and plans to live there full time.
Photograph by Walter Chin

GIAN CARLO ▾

Gian was working on the Stock Exchange when photographer Nick Clements asked if he could take his picture. Nick took it to Select and the agency immediately signed him. That was three years ago. For a while Gian continued his City job while modelling, pretending he was ill when an assignment came up, but soon the modelling snowballed and he left the 9 to 5 for a life of airports and exotic locations – in any one year he takes around a hundred flights. John is this year's Hermes man, photographed by Walter Chin. *Photograph by James Martin*

MOOSE ▾

Twenty-six year old Moose was set to become a pharmacist when he was asked to join in a shoot by a friend of his brother. Moose and Chazz were then cast by Mark Ascoli for the Yohji Yamamoto press show in Paris. With SoDamtuFF work for Martin Brading, Iain R. Webb and Ray Petri and campaigns for Betty Jackson and Katharine Hamnett soon followed. Moose became the Jean Paul Gaultier man and in the mid-1980s he started wearing tailored clothing for the major designers worldwide (a breakthrough for an ethnic male model). *Photograph courtesy of Elle (Photographer: Nick Briggs)*

PETER HOWELL

Peter Howell started his acting career under the name of Alan Troy and, 13 years ago, with a partner, set up "Bovver Boots" agency, satisfying the demand for Streetwise personnel – bikers, punks, skinheads, etc. On the death of his partner, Peter had to take over the administration of this burgeoning business, as demand from casting directors for his Bovver Boys and Girls precluded any acting of his own. He expanded into Europe, by amalgamating with a compatible Dutch agency, and formed United Agents – Europe, and now commutes back and forth, speaks Dutch and is once again finding time for some acting.

GAVIN ROBINSON ▼

Gavin L. B. Robinson, the managing director and founder of Gavin's Models, moved to London from South Africa in 1961 and worked as a model and classical dance instructor. He became responsible for the girls section at Jabies, and was persuaded by the girls to set up on his own. He opened Gavin's in Old Bond Street in 1964, and moved it to Old Burlington Street in 1988. Gavin's work is commercial fashion and print and amongst the models it has represented are Shakira Caine, Victoria Principal, Kate Rabett, David Clay and Nick Kamen. Gavin is a founder member and continuing Main Council member of the Association of Model Agents, the steering association of the industry.

STEPHEN PENN ▼

Born in Scotland, Stephen Penn studied illustration and printmaking at Glasgow School of Art before emigrating to London to work in advertising and film animation. In the early 1980s, with wife, Janis, he set up "Scalliwags", the children's agency, which they have built up through the past decade to the thriving business it is today. Stephen and Janis live in Essex with their two sons.

TOM SHERIDAN ▲

Tom Sheridan was born in 1935, and started his career as an actor, appearing in various TV shows. After a West End production ended in chaos, with Tom bringing the leading man to his knees by tripping over his cloak, he found himself out of work, and took a position with a theatrical agent. When his boss decided to give up the business, Tom struck out on his own. A chance meeting with a model agent, who was looking for a partner, led Tom's career in that direction, and to the foundation of the International Model Agency, one of the most successful in the Capital.

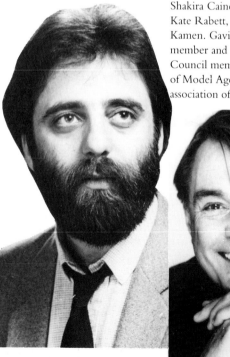

JULIAN CRADER ▼

Julia Crader is known professionally as Julian Barry, to avoid, he says, rather cryptically, confusion with his wife. Julian's wife set up the Norrie Carr Model Agency 27 years ago, and he supported her initially morally, and then administratively and finally as a full-time partner. Over the years, they have built up a highly successful business specialising in providing child and teenage models, and complete families for advertising throughout the world – even in Japan. Julian describes the business as exciting and exacting, with long hours that do not allow him as much sailing as he would like, but happy and successful.

EDWARD MITCHELL ▼

Edward Mitchell was born a Capricorn in 1956, and lives in London. He worked in PR and advertising for two years and, he says, fell into the model agency business by accident, at NEVS Agency, 16 years ago. He has been the overall director of the agency for the last eight years, and represents 60 men and 50 girls in this country, and 100 men and 30 girls in companion agencies worldwide. Amongst his clients in New York is Hoyt Richards, the "first male Supermodel". For relaxation, Edward races motorbikes.

HUGH GALLOWAY ▲

Hugh Galloway has been an established London agent for the last 18 years. "Galloways One" was originally started by his mother, Joy, in 1971, and is still very much a family business. In 1979, he took a sabbatical to work as an agent in Los Angeles for a year and, on his return, set up a division of the agency to represent actors for "walk on" and "extra" work with his sister Jill. More recently, he has gone further and started a theatrical, film and television division. From its successful beginnings in commercials, Galloways can now supply virtually any type of actor in the industry, and has a large clientele in the UK and throughout Europe.

PHOTOGRAPHERS

ANTHONY CRICKMAY ▼

Anthony Crickmay started out in the Bond Street studio of the great portrait photographer Lotte Meitner Graf. He claims she sparked his interest in music and the arts, but it was Ivor Newton, the talented soprano accompanist who introduced him to the world of Covent Garden. His first pictures were for Franco Zeffirelli's Cavalleria Rusticana taken, he says, "with much more luck than judgement". This was the beginning of a 30 year collaboration with the Royal Ballet. An internationally renowned photographer working in portraits, fashion and dance, Crickmay has had five books of his pictures published, and has done portraits of hundreds of famous figures: his pictures of the Royal Family include the 90th birthday portrait of the Queen Mother, and portraits of Princess Margaret, Princess Alexandra and the Prince and Princess Michael of Kent.
Photograph by Everton Waugh

BOB CARLOS CLARKE ▲

A graduate of the Royal College of Art (with an MA in photography) Bob Carlos Clarke worked on book jackets and magazines before photographing the first Janet Reger catalogue, which later became the subject of the book Chastity in Focus. His first book The Illustrated Delta of Venus was published with text by Anais Nin in 1980. Obsession and The Dark Summer soon followed, the first a collection of early commercial and personal work and the second described as "a twilight and sometimes morbid world of sexuality". His black and white portraits are still much in demand – many have appeared on posters and postcards. He has photographed countless personalities including Marco Pierre White for the book White Heat.
Photograph courtesy of Sasha at Hamiltons

EAMONN McCABE ▼

Sports Photographer of the Year for four years and News Photographer of the Year in 1985, Eamonn McCabe is one of our most respected photographers. A Fellow of the Royal Photographic Society, he is on the Arts Council Advisory Panel of Photography and the CNAA Committee on Photography. Eamonn studied film in San Francisco before working for The Guardian and The Observer as a photographer, and as picture editor for Sportsweek and The Guardian. He was the official photographer for the Pope's visit to Britain in 1982 and published a book of the tour. He has had two other books published: Eamonn McCabe – Sports Photographer (1981) and Eamonn McCabe – Photographer (1984). He has exhibited widely in Britain and abroad: in this country at the Photographers Gallery, the Barbican, the Liverpool Art Gallery and the National Museum of Photography, Film and Television.

◄ CHARLIE WAITE

Britain's most gifted landscape photographer, Charlie Waite took up professional photography after 11 years spent acting for theatre, TV and film. He took a course in photographic theory at Salisbury College of Art before rejoining the theatre to take pictures of actors and theatrical productions. His break into landscape photography came in 1981, with the commission for the book of photography The National Trust Book of Long Walks. Since then he has produced 21 books, for which he has taken 70 trips abroad, and travelled half a million miles.
Photograph courtesy of The Special Photographers Company

TERRY O'NEILL ⬆

Terry O'Neill is the most published photographer in the world, averaging 500 covers a year, worldwide. In his time he has photographed the world's leading film, rock and pop stars, as well as sportsmen, business tycoons, world politicians and British and foreign royalty. He began his working career as a professional jazz drummer at the age of thirteen and a half. After completing his National Service he took up photography and became the youngest professional photographer in Fleet Street. The leading photographic biographer of the 1960s Terry took the first internationally published photographs of the Beatles and the Rolling Stones. He describes the highlight of his career as being invited by the Queen to take her official portrait to celebrate the 40th anniversary of her accession to the throne. He has been married twice, to actresses Vera Day and Faye Dunaway and has three children, Keegan, Liam and Sarah.

ANDREW LAWSON ⬇

A keen gardener and accomplished painter Andrew Lawson brings a specialist eye to garden photography. He is a frequent contributor to magazines such as Country Life, Sunday Times Magazine, House & Garden and Country Living, but his main body of work is for books. He took the pictures for Rosemary Verey's Good Planting, Roy Strong's Royal Gardens, Stephen Lacey's Scent In Your Garden and was a major contributor to the RHS Encyclopedia of Garden Plants.

JOHN SWANNELL ➡

John Swannell left school at 16 to work as an assistant at Vogue Studios, before being taken on by David Bailey as his assistant. He stayed with the maestro for four years before leaving to set up his own studio. The next ten years were spent working and travelling for magazines such as Vogue and Harpers & Queen and The Sunday Times. Exhibitions of his work in London and Europe confirmed his reputation as a world class photographer. The National Portrait Gallery in London now have 25 of his photographs in their permanent collection, while 21 were donated to The National Portrait Gallery in Scotland. In 1984 John began directing commercials. The first, for Boots No. 7, won a Gold Award in New York for best commercial of the year. Since then he has directed over 50 commercials, including one for Rimmel cosmetics, which collected a silver at Cannes.
Photograph courtesy of David Burnham

ANDREW AND STUART DOUGLAS ⬆

Andrew and Stuart Douglas launched themselves as the Douglas Brothers in 1990. Andrew, who is ten years older than Stuart, took a degree in fine art at Sunderland Polytechnic and assisted several photographers in London, including Snowdon, before setting up his own studio. During the 1970s he began to photograph punk bands and Stuart went on to do a photography course and to work for Olympus Cameras before joining Andrew full time. They are well known for video production and album artwork.

MARTIN BRIGDALE ▲

Martin Brigdale comes from a family of artists, photographers and designers. He graduated as top student from the London College of Printing in 1978, and trained as assistant to a leading London Food Photographer for two years, where his love of cooking and food blossomed. In 1980 he went freelance, and has worked mainly on editorial projects, his work appearing in such magazines as The Sunday Times, A La Carte, Taste, Good Food, Good Housekeeping, House & Gardens, Homes & Gardens, Cosmopolitan, Woman's Journal and many others. He has photographed more than 30 cookery books, including the Illustrated Escoffier, Great British Chefs, Great European Chefs and the Roux Brothers French Country Cooking. He has just finished a two year location project entitled The Foods of Greece. A food lover and enthusiastic amateur cook, Martin's future plans are to explore the relationship of food, people and places.
Photograph by The Special Photographers Company

LORENTZ GULLACHSEN ▼

Lorentz Gullachsen is a third generation Norwegian, born in West Bromwich to a Geordie father and a Black Country mother. He started work in an advertising agency, but realised that suits didn't suit, and left to study photography at college. He graduated in 1973, and in 1974 established his own studio working in the commercial/advertising field. In the mid-1980s he moved to London and, with agent Peter Bailey, began to specialise in large format landscape photography on such accounts as Rolls Royce, Land Rover, Gallo Wines, Abbey National, Milton Keynes Development Corp., GKN, Powergen and various tourist boards. Lorentz has received many awards, including the B&H Photographer of the Year 1990, several Association of Photographers Gold Awards, and Design and Art Directors Association Awards.
Photograph by Peter Bailey Company

◄ SIMON BROWN

Simon Brown is an interiors photographer whose work appears internationally in a wide range of advertising campaigns and magazines, including the World of Interiors, House & Garden, Architectural Digest, Marie Claire, Vogue and Vanity Fair. Based in his own large London studio, Simon moves easily from sets for Laura Ashley and Sanderson to computers for Hewlett Packard and coffee for Nescafé. More recently, his advertising assignments have taken him on location to Italy for furniture manufacturer B&B Italia.
Photograph by Roger Eaton

SIMON LARBALESTIER ▼

Thirty-year old Simon Larbalestier trained in graphic design in Newcastle-upon-Tyne and in illustration at the Royal College of Art. His fine art work was exhibited while he was still at the Royal College, with shows in London and Japan. His association with The Special Photographers Company began in 1988, with group and joint shows in 1988, 1989, 1991 and 1992. He is currently working on a book about photographic montage – "The Art and Craft of Montage" – to be published by Mitchell Beazley in 1993, while continuing to work very successfully in the fields of record design and advertising.
Photograph by The Special Photographers Company

NICOLAS GEORGHIOU

Born in Burnley in 1958, Nicolas Georghiou's training was as a furniture craftsman, until he took an art foundation course at Burnley College of Art and Technology in 1980. He studied photography at the Royal College of Art from 1984-86, and was awarded the Vogue Award for Photography in his final year. Nick began his association with The Special Photographers Company in 1987, and this association resulted in exhibitions of his fine art work in the UK, Europe, the USA and Japan. Commercially, he is at the cutting edge of creative photography, and because of this, he is commissioned by some of the best art directors.
Photograph by The Special Photographers Company

STEVE ORINO ▲

Steve Orino was 19, living at home in Bracknell and bored with working as a graphic designer in a small advertising agency, when he applied for and was accepted on a photography course at the Bournemouth College of Art and Design. A decade later, Steve is a well-respected professional, with a portfolio of Celebrity Portraits to rank with any of his peers. His subjects include such eclectic fare as Joan Armatrading, Sir John Harvey-Jones, Linda Lusardi (clothed) and Clive Anderson. Amongst his clients he numbers Esquire, Harpers & Queen, GQ, The Architects Journal, The Designers Journal, The Sunday Times, Management Today and The Saturday Review. Steve particularly enjoys the travelling inherent in his professional life.

MICHAEL KENNA ▼

Born and educated in England, landscape photographer Michael Kenna has lived in San Francisco for the past 15 years. Born in 1953, Michael trained at the London College of Printing, where he received a distinction in his photography HND in 1976. His early work, given his North of England location, tended to be of the "Dark Satanic Mills", and his landscapes since, whilst never depicting people, are always redolent of their presence. Michael has won many awards, the most notable of which have been, in 1981, the Imogen Cunningham Award and the Zellerbach Award, both in San Francisco, in 1987, the Art in Public Buildings Award in Sacramento and, in 1989, the Institute for Aesthetic Development Award, in Pasadena. He has had over 60 one man shows since 1978, all over the world, and has permanent collections in Canberra, Paris, Prague, San Francisco and at the V&A in London, and has published several books.
Photograph by Nicole Katano, courtesy of Sasha at Hamiltons

MICHAEL ROBERTS ▼

Michael Roberts is a former fashion editor of the Sunday Times, style director and art director of Tatler and design director of British Vogue, Paris editor of Vanity Fair, and contributing editor of Conde Nast Traveller. An acknowledged illustrator and film maker, he has received an MTV Award for Breakthrough Video in 1988. For six years Michael has been a contributing photographer to Manner Vogue, L'Uomo Vogue, British Vogue, French Vogue, Vogue Hombress, Vogue Espana, GQ, Vanity Fair, the Sunday Times, the Independent on Sunday, Interview, Harpers & Queen and Esquire.
Photograph courtesy of Sasha of Hamiltons

NEIL THOMAS

Neil Thomas is Great Britain's most successful male gymnast, and reigning British Champion. He has represented his country in the Commonwealth Games, three European Championships, two World Championships and the Barcelona Olympics, and holds Commonwealth silver and gold medals, and a European bronze. The great USSR coach, Vladimir Zaglada, spotted Neil in 1988, when he was training in Moscow, and requested that Neil be left with him, stating "I will make him the Olympic gold medallist in floor exercises". It will be possible to monitor his progress in the Individual World Championships in Birmingham in April 1993, and in the Commonwealth Games in 1994, when he will compete for a possible eight gold medals.
Photograph by Alan Edwards

SPORTING MEN

If the father and son three-legged race was introduced as an Olympic sport, then there would be no doubt in the mind of every Briton that this country would win the gold medal. We see ourselves as amateurs in a world of ever-encroaching professionalism and never believe that our young men and women have the back-up and support provided for those, probably less talented, competitors from other countries. We therefore tend to accept defeat with a good grace, knowing as we do that the game is the thing and it is, after all, only a game. Against this background of what often amounts to superior indifference, the achievements of the men on the following pages shine like a beacon.

SEAN KERLY

Sean Kerly is Great Britain's first hockey superstar, winning bronze and gold Olympic medals (1984 and 1988) and a World Cup silver (1986). He has done more than anyone to popularise the sport. In an international career which started in 1981, against Poland, he went on to score 65 times for Great Britain and 45 times for England in some 270 internationals. Although he chose the Barcelona Olympics as a fitting time to retire from the international team, he still plays for Canterbury in the National League.

COLIN CLARKE ▲

Colin Clarke wrote himself into the record books when he became Northern Ireland's all-time leading goal scorer, scoring his 13th goal in 36 matches against Albania in September 1992. Born in 1962, Colin played for Peterborough, Tranmere and Bournemouth before making his First Division debut for Southampton with a hat-trick against QPR. He was Southampton's top scorer for two years, before moving to QPR in 1989 for a club record £800,000. In 1990 Colin moved back to the South Coast, joining Portsmouth.

ALLY McCOIST ▲

Ally McCoist, the Rangers and Scotland striker and hero, is now, incredibly, 30 years old. He first sprang to prominence at 18, when he was transferred to Sunderland from St. Johnstone for £400,000. Returning to Scotland and Rangers after two years, his career blossomed, and in 1991 he was Europe's most prolific goal scorer. In 1992 his striking rate has been almost a goal a match, and he has now won over 45 Scottish caps, recently as vice-captain. A great character, and a man who transcends the Glasgow religious divide, Ally's pastimes are golf, horse racing and tardiness.

GARY LINEKER ⟶

Gary Lineker is one of the best known and most highly respected footballers in the world and second highest scorer for England of all time, behind Bobby Charlton, with 48 goals. From 1976 to 1985 he played for Leicester City, scoring 103 times in 209 League and Cup appearances. He transferred to Everton in 1985/86 (40 goals, 56 appearances). Going to play for European clubs has always been problematic for British players, with language, culture and homesickness problems, but when Gary moved to Barcelona in 1986, he and his wife, Michelle, learned the language and immersed themselves in the culture, and his stay from 1986-89 was an unqualified success. Gary returned to England in 1989, to Tottenham, and is now moving to Nagoya Grampus, in Japan. An accomplished cricketer and golfer, Gary is well known as a TV presenter and commentator, and was the 1992 Football Writers Association Footballer of the Year.
Photograph by BBC Photo Library

ALAN SHEARER ▼

Alan Shearer was born in Newcastle in 1970, and developed his love of football on the terraces of St. James's Park. After trials with Newcastle United, he joined Southampton, and became the youngest player to score a League hat-trick in his debut against Arsenal. After 13 games and 13 goals for England Under 21s, Alan was called up for the England team, and at the time of writing has five caps. He transferred to Blackburn Rovers in 1992, for a British record fee of £3.3m, and is currently the leading scorer in the, League with 16 goals in 17 matches.

IAN RUSH ▲

Liverpool's Ian Rush became the club's record goal scorer when he scored his 287th against Manchester United in 1992, passing Roger Hunt's long-standing record. Ian was born in St Astaph, Denbighshire in 1961, and started his playing career as an apprentice with Chester. He turned professional in 1979/80, and in 1980 transferred to Liverpool for £300,000. In 1986, his transfer to Juventus was agreed for £3.2m, and he stayed there for the 1987/88 season, scoring seven goals in 24 appearances, before returning to Anfield. An automatic choice for Wales, latterly he has been reproducing his club form for his country.

RUGBY UNION

GAVIN HASTINGS →

Gavin Hastings was educated in Edinburgh, and went on to study land economy at Cambridge, where he won two rugby blues, and was captain in 1985. In 1986 he won his first cap for Scotland against France, and kicked six penalty goals in the 18–17 victory. Gavin's rugby career spans both the 1987 and 1991 World Cups, and he was a member of the British Lions team that so successfully toured Australia in 1989. He has captained the Barbarians in the Hong Kong Sevens and has played for them in end of tour matches against Australia and New Zealand. A seven handicap golfer, and keen squash and tennis player, Gavin Hastings is Scotland's all time record rugby points scorer.

WILL CARLING →

A controversial choice as England captain when he was appointed at only 22, Will Carling has been not only England's youngest captain but also its most successful. Born in 1965 and educated at Durham University he has represented and captained England Schoolboys (1982-84), Durham University (1986-89), Harlequins and England, and taken England to back-to-back Grand Slam titles in 1991 and 1992 and so nearly the World Cup. He has a degree in psychology and, in 1990, he founded Inspirational Horizons Ltd and in 1991 became managing director of Insights Ltd, presenting motivational seminars to captains of industry and sport. He was appointed OBE in 1991. In 1992 Will Carling was voted Player of the Year at the Whitbread Rugby World Awards.

PETER WINTERBOTTOM →

Peter Winterbottom arrived in international rugby in 1982 as an explosive and destructive flank forward, and since then has probably done as much to promote his country's cause as anyone else in history. An enormous amount has been expected of Peter, as a No. 7 – to be on the ball when England are in possession, to range far and wide when they are not, and to draw the opposition in on the fringes. His tackling is always deadly, and his all round expertise makes him clinical as well as heroic. England's most capped flanker, with 53 caps at the time of writing, and more to come in 1993.

RUGBY UNION

◄ BRIAN ROBINSON

Number 8 for Ulster, London Irish and Ireland, Britain Robinson made his debut in the full international season of 1991. Born in 1966, Brian works for the Belfast Royal Academy teaching physical education and health education, he is a house teacher and coaches the 1st XV. He toured New Zealand in 1992 and, at November 1992, had received 15 caps and scored five tries.

EMYR LEWIS ▼

Born in 1968 in Camarthen, Emyr Lewis plays flanker for Llanelli and for Wales. At 6ft 4in and weighing 16½ stone, he is also a county shot-putt champion and has represented his county at football. Nicknamed "Tarw", which is Welsh for "bull", because of his head down charging. He made his international debut in 1991 and was Welsh Player of the Year for 1991-92. Emyr Lewis is a policeman and a famous critic of foul and dangerous play.

RORY UNDERWOOD ▼

Rory Underwood is the most capped England rugby player, and Britain's highest ever try scorer. A pivotal player in England's relentless surge to the top of world rugby, Rory has been a spectacular scorer of crucial points. Born in 1963, Rory made his debut for Middlesbrough RFC in 1979, for Durham County and England Under 23s in 1981/82, for Leicester RFC in 1983, and for England in 1984. A pilot in the RAF, his service has prevented him taking part in various tours which would further have stretched his lead in the record books. With the debut of brother Tony, on the opposite wing, England have two brothers in the national team for the first time since 1938.

SHAUN EDWARDS ▼

Twenty-six year old Shaun Edwards is a household name in Rugby League, having signed as a professional for Wigan on his 17th birthday. He has been a focal point of their astonishing success ever since. An automatic choice for Great Britain, Shaun topped the try scoring charts in 1991/92 with an impressive 40 tries, as Wigan captured almost all the trophies on offer. Shaun made his Great Britain debut at only 18 against France, and has since led his country out against them. His ability not only in play, but in bringing out the best in his team-mates, is invaluable.

JONATHAN DAVIES ▼

Jonathan Davies, the great fly-half, has captained Wales at Rugby Union and Rugby League. Born in South Wales in 1962 he was a schoolboy athlete, but regarded as being too delicate for rugby. His career with Neath and Llanelli disproved this theory as did 27 Welsh caps and the title World Player of the Year in 1988 and 1989. He turned professional in January 1989 when he joined Widnes for a World Record fee and has continued to be one of the best backs in the game.

DENIS BETTS ▼

Denis Betts was born in 1969, and burst into the Rugby League scene as an 18 year old, signing with Wigan from Leigh Rangers. A powerful forward, and Great Britain star, Denis was nominated Young Player of the Year in 1989 and 1990. A fine all round sportsman, Denis Betts was once on the books of Manchester United FC.

GARRY SCHOFIELD ▶

Garry Schofield is the current captain of Great Britain's Rugby League team and, to many, the complete Rugby League player. He is fearless, an expert kicker and has a combination of tactical awareness, speed and strength which can exploit any opportunity. Garry moved from Hull to Leeds in 1987, for a then World Record fee of £155,000, and has proved an invaluable asset to them both on and off the field. His play has won him awards and admirers, and his half-back position is ideal for displaying his running and kicking skills. A clear communicator and born leader, Garry conducts coaching clinics for youngsters in and around the Leeds area, and has been instrumental in bringing many young players into the game.

ANDY PLATT ▼

Born in 1964, Rugby League forward Andy Platt joined Wigan from St. Helens in 1988, for what was then the club record fee of £140,000, and has helped them to the First Division Championship and the Challenge Cup for the past four years. A Great Britain star and a relentless tackler, Andy is a fine clubman and his coach's ideal player.

MARTIN OFFIAH ▼

In 1991 Martin Offiah captured sporting headlines around the country when he moved from Widnes to Wigan for the World Record sum of £440,000. Brought up in Stoke Newington, and educated in Suffolk, Martin played Rugby Union for Rosslyn Park before turning professional with Widnes in 1987. For the next four seasons his try scoring exploits kept him constantly in the record books. A dispute with the club kept him out of the game for five months, but he came bouncing back for Wigan with undiminished power. Now 27, Martin Offiah is popularly regarded by experts as the best Rugby League player in the world.

GRAHAM STEADMAN ▲

Graham Steadman plays at full-back for Castleford RLFC in the town where he was born in 1961. At the time of writing he has scored 538 points for Castleford in 95 games, originally as stand-off, the position in which he started his career in York in 1982, moving to Featherstone in 1986 and Castleford in 1989 for a then world record fee of £170,000. He was voted The Stones Bitter First Division Player of the Year at the 1992 Man of Steel Awards.
Photograph by Andy Howard

CHRIS WILKINSON ▲

Coached by ex-Davis Cup player Jonathon Smith, Chris Wilkinson is Britain's fast improving No. 2 tennis player. He left school in Southampton in 1986, and turned professional in 1988, and was ranked 365 in the world in 1990, 202 in 1991 and 140 in 1992. He represented Britain at the Olympics, and in the Davis Cup where, against India, he was the only team member to win a match. Chris and Paul Hand won the doubles in the British National Championships and, also in 1992, he came second in the British Satellite Circuit, beating Jeremy Bates in the process.

JEREMY BATES ▼

Jeremy Bates, Britain's leading tennis player, has enjoyed considerable success on both the Tour and Challenger Circuits. A serve and volley specialist, most of his notable titles have come in doubles competitions, including the 1987 Wimbledon Mixed Doubles title, with Jo Durie in 1987. In 1992 Jeremy's world ranking rose by 60 places to 106, based very largely on his performance in the Wimbledon Singles, when it seemed that, for once, the Wimbledon crowd actually lifted "their" player, instead of putting him off, and in a series of sterling matches, Jeremy showed his true class, and reached the last 16, before being narrowly beaten by Guy Forget. Jeremy is the reigning British champion.

PETER MARSHALL ▼

Ranked No. 1 in Britain, and No. 7 in the world, Peter Marshall is a truly unique squash player. As a youngster he developed a double handed grip, and has retained it, the only top-flight player to do so. After an illustrious Junior career, Peter took the National title in 1992, and proceeded with excellent performances in International competitions, culminating in reaching the quarter finals of the World Championships. A Leicestershire lad, Peter looks Britain's best bet for a major world title in 1993.
Photograph by Stephen Line

PETER NICOL ▲

Peter Nicol, aged 19, comes from the Scottish mountains around Aberdeen – not a traditional heartland of squash. In November 1991 he was selected for the Scottish Senior team in the World Team Championships, and in spring 1992, proceeded to win the British Junior Championships. Also in that year, Peter was instrumental in enabling the Scottish team to win the European Team Championship for the first time. Edging towards the world's top 50, Peter is poised to become a major force in world squash.
Photograph by Stephen Line

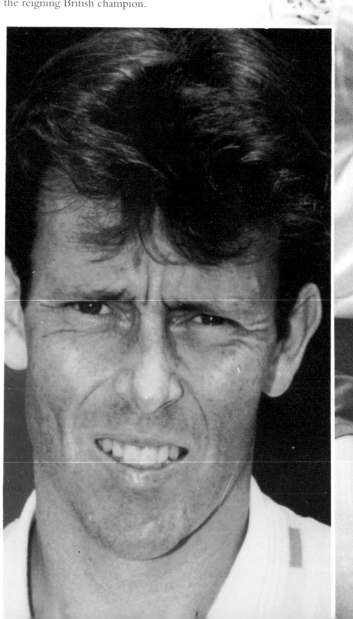

DARREN HALL ▼

Darren Hall was born in 1965, and lives in Essex, for whom he plays county badminton. Darren and his uncle and coach Ray Stevens share the record for the most English National Championship wins, both having won the title five times. Darren just failed to make it six straight wins when he was beaten by Anders Nielson in 1992. Currently ranked No. 1, Darren has represented his country since 1985. He won the bronze in the singles at the 1990 Commonwealth Games, and the gold in the team event. In 1992 he won the men's singles in the Wimbledon Open and the Danish Open, the first Englishman to win this title for 50 years. Darren represented Britain at the 1992 Olympics. He likes golf and fast cars.

Photograph by Peter Richardson

CHEN XINHUA ▲

Chen Xinhua, aged 32, from Rotherham, is the current Table Tennis English National Champion, the English No. 1 and the world ranked No. 12. In 1985 he won the World Cup and reached the final of the World Championships. He reached the final of the 1990 English International Open, and was part of the team which won the bronze in the 1990 World Team Cup, and the silver in the 1992 European Championships. He also won the 1992 Italian International Open. One of the great entertainers of the game, he currently plays for a German club.

Photograph courtesy of English Table Tennis Association

CARL PREAN ▼

Carl Prean, the 1991 English Men's Singles Table Tennis Champion, was competing and winning in the junior circuit by the time he was 11 years old. In 1982 he won the European Under 14s singles, the first of five gold medals won in these Championships over three years. He ended his Junior career as English Boys Singles Champion. At Senior level, Carl won the 1986 Belgian International Open, and has won many team medals for England. Capable of beating any player in the world, Carl's world ranking is 20th. Now aged 25, Carl lives on the Isle of Wight.

Photograph courtesy of English Table Tennis Association

ANDERS NIELSEN ▲

Anders Nielsen was born in Cape Town in 1967, the son of Heather (nee Ward), the 1959 All England Badminton Champion. Anders lives in and plays for Surrey, and is currently ranked No. 2 for England, which he first represented in 1985. He is the European Badminton Union Champion, 1992, and the holder of the English Men's Singles title. Also in 1992 he won the bronze medal in the European Championships, and represented Britain in the Barcelona Olympics. In his spare time, Anders plays golf off a descending 13 handicap.

Photograph by Peter Richardson

ATHLETICS

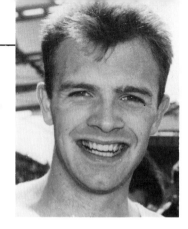

LINFORD CHRISTIE ▼

Britain's finest ever 100 metre
runner, Linford Christie has
competed 48 times for Britain and
won more medals than any other
British male athlete. He was born
in Jamaica and came to Britain
when he was six. Britain's team
captain in the 1992 Olympics, his
gold medal added to the European
and Commonwealth golds which
he won in 1990. The only
European to have run the 100
metres in under 10 seconds, he has
remained unbeaten by a Briton in
six years. He is the first man to
have won the 100 metre World
Cup twice.

JOHN REGIS ▼

Twenty-seven year old John Regis
has been Britain's top 200m runner
since 1989, the year in which he
became the first and so far the only
world indoor champion. He won a
record four medals at the 1990
European Championships when he
first made an impact as a 4 x 400
metre relay runner. He ran below
his best in Tokyo and Barcelona
yet equalled Christie's record on
the way to becoming first
European finisher at the Olympics.
*Photograph courtesy of British Olympic
Association Photography Library*

CURTIS ROBB ▲

Born in 1972, Curtis Robb won
the English Schools' Championship
1500m in 1989 and 1990, and the
AAA 1500m in 1990. He won the
European Championship at 800m
in 1991, and was a silver medallist
in the World Student Games. At
senior level he went on to win the
UK and AAA Championships in
1992. He qualified for the final of
the Barcelona Olympics, the only
British middle distance runner to
do so.

COLIN JACKSON ▼

Aged 25, Colin Jackson is the
reigning Commonwealth and
European Champion at 110 metre
hurdles. He is among the world's
top three since 1987. He has set six
European records and his personal
best of 13.04 places him fourth on
the world all time list. World
No. 1 in 1990, he was injured in
1991 but came back in 1992 to
clock the world's sixth fastest time.
Twice a winner of the European
Cup, last year he won the World
Cup in Havana.

KRISS AKABUSI ▲

Kriss Akabusi's commitment and dedication to his work is legendary. Born in 1958 in London, he joined the Army in 1975, and left as a sergeant in 1990. He is British record holder at 400 metre hurdles, and holds eight gold medals at 400 metres and 400 metre hurdles, including 1990 European Championships at 400 metres and the hurdles. A dedicated Christian and family man, he is also a seasoned speaker and performer and regular contributor writing on sporting matters, to all national papers.

ROGER BLACK ▼

Twenty-seven year old Roger Black rescinded the place he had won at Southampton University, reading medicine, to concentrate on his athletics. He has won six gold medals and was Britain's first 400 metre runner to retain gold European medals in 1990. In 1991 he took the silver in the World Championships in Tokyo and won the Gran Prix final in Barcelona. In 1992 he made the Olympic semi-final, running 44.72 despite injury problems.
Photograph by BBC Photo Library

STEVEN SMITH ▼

Steven Smith ended the 1992 season as world No. 1 high jumper, a considerable achievement for anyone and remarkable for a junior – he is only 19. Steven is world junior champion and British and Commonwealth record holder. He qualified for the finals of the 1992 Olympics and was the youngest member of the athletics Olympic team.

JON RIDGEON ▼

A fine all round athlete, Jon Ridgeon represented Suffolk Schools at swimming, rugby, cross country and athletics. Specialising in 110 metres hurdles, he was European Junior Champion in 1985 and won the World Student Games in 1987. In the last three years he underwent major surgery on his achilles tendon, and successfully emerged as a 400 metre hurdles contender in 1992, coming second in the World Cup. Between sporting activities, Jon is a reporter for the BBC Radio.

CITY OF CARDIFF

STEVE BACKLEY ▲

Currently the world record holder Steve Backley's progress as a javelin thrower has been awesome. Born in 1969 in Northumberland, his father was a county champion runner. Steve won the European Junior Championship in 1987, with a world record for his age. In 1990 he won gold at both the Commonwealth Games and European Championships and Olympic bronze in 1992. He is studying sports science at Loughborough University and works in all areas of the media.

DAVID GRINDLEY ▼

Born in Lancashire, 20 year old David Grindley has had a brilliant junior career, the highlight of which was when he broke the British 400 metre record in 1992, making him the second fastest European runner ever in this category. It ensured he qualified for the final of the Olympics, in which he came sixth. He also took the bronze in the 4 x 400. 1992 also saw him win the Europa Cup under 23 championships and a bronze medal at the European Indoor Championships in Italy.

GOLF

IAN WOOSNAM ▼

Born in 1958, Ian Woosnam is a 5ft 4in golfer of amazing power. Whilst 1992 may not have been his best year, he retained the Monte Carlo Open title in July, and his performance in the opening rounds of the Toyota World Matchplay Championship will not be forgotten – at one stage seven successive birdies, and none on a par-5. By the end of 1991 Ian's career winnings since 1976 topped $7 million. He was No. 1 in the Order of Merit in 1987 and 1990 and has been in the top ten since 1981. He won the US Masters in 1991.

Photograph courtesy of IMG

STEVEN RICHARDSON, DAVID GILFORD AND JAMES SPENCE ▲

Born in 1966, 1965 and 1963 respectively, Steven Richardson, David Gilford and Jamie Spence are the vanguard of the new breed of British golfer, and formed the team which won the Dunhill Cup for England in 1992, by defeating Scotland 2–0 in the final. Son of Club professional John Richardson, Steven announced his arrival on the golf scene by winning the English Amateur Championship in 1989, and turning professional for the 1990 season. A massive hitter, seemingly with nerves of steel, Steven's placings in the Volvo Order of Merit have been 29th in 1990, 2nd 1991 and 19th in 1992. In 1991 Steven won the Girona Open and the Portuguese Open. David Gilford has been on the Professional circuit since 1986, and celebrated his best year so far in 1991, when he won the English Open, and came ninth in the Order of Merit. In 1992 he won the Moroccan Open Championship. Jamie Spence's first season on the tour was 1990, when he had an excellent Open, for which he had to qualify, and finished 51st in the Order of Merit. He has followed this with 29th in 1991, and 10th in 1992. He won the European Masters in 1992, with a last round 60, but is probably better characterised, at the moment, by the consistency of his top ten finishing.

Photograph courtesy of Alfred Dunhill Ltd

NICK FALDO ▼

Nick Faldo, MBE, is currently the world's No. 1 golfer. His golf seems to go from strength to strength and, in 1992, he won the Irish Open, the Open Championship, the Scandinavian Masters, the European Open and the Toyota Matchplay Championship. In pursuit of perfection, Nick spent 1985/86 distmantling and rebuilding his swing, since when he has won the Open Championship in 1987, 1990 and 1992, and the 1989 and 1990 US Masters titles as well as a host of other events. In 1983 he won three events in succession, the first time anyone has achieved this since Peter Alliss in 1958. When he won the Heritage Classic in 1984, Nick became the first British professional to win in America since Tony Jacklin's US Open victory in 1970. He is the only English golfer ever to have won three Open Championship titles.

Photograph courtesy of IMG

COLIN MONTGOMERIE ▼

Born in Troon in 1963, Colin Montgomerie became "Rookie of the Year" in his first season on the tour, 1988. Since then he has had 25 top ten finishes on the European tour. 1992 was a great year for him, and at one stage he looked certain to win the US Masters at Pebble Beach, playing a great final round in windy conditions, but the wind died, Tom Kite won and Colin was third.
Photograph courtesy of IMG

◄ SANDY LYLE

A colossus amongst British golfers, Sandy Lyle turned professional in 1977, after an impressive array of Junior and Schoolboy victories. In 1978 he was Rookie of the Year, and won his first Open Championship in Nigeria. He was first in the European Order of Merit in the next two years and, in 1985, when he won the Open at Royal St. George's – the first Briton to do so for 16 years and, as one journalist wrote: "It couldn't happen to a nicer guy." In 1988 Sandy became the first Briton ever to win the US Masters at Augusta, clinching the victory with a seven-iron from the bunker on the 18th, which no-one who saw it will ever forget. Sandy has always been a great team player and an integral part of the victorious 1985 and 1987 Ryder Cup teams. He suffered a loss of form in the late 1980s to the distress of his many friends and admirers, but his form returned during 1991, and continued in 1992, culminating in a magnificent victory in the Volvo Masters and his finishing eighth in the Order of Merit, with much more promised in 1993.
Photograph courtesy of IMG

STEPHEN DUNDAS ▲

Born in 1973 Stephen Dundas was the winner of the 1992 British Amateur Championship at Carnoustie. Stephen has been playing golf since he was five years old, and has represented Scotland at every level. In September 1992 he won the High Country Open in New Mexico by eight shots with rounds of 70,65,68. His 65 broke the course record hitherto held by an American professional. Stephen is at college in Texas.

BARRY LANE ▲

1992 saw Barry Lane at his best, playing consistently well with 13 top ten finishes. He has been runner up twice and won the German Masters with 16 under par total of 272. Since acquiring his tour card in 1981, 32-year-old Barry has been consistently amongst the prizes, even after having to return to Tour School after contracting a debilitating tropical disease in 1985. He requalified and went on to win the 1988 Scottish Open.
Photograph courtesy of IMG

Alec Stewart is an attractive and aggressive right-handed batsman with a full range of shots, but particularly strong on the off-side and the front foot. He topped the England averages in the 1992 series against Pakistan with 56.71, and made a magnificent 190 in the first Test at Edgbaston. Son of recently retired team manager Mickey Stewart, Alec is captain of Surrey and heir apparent to Graham Gooch as captain of England.

DAVID GOWER ▲

David Gower is the best left-handed batsman to come out of England since the War, and perhaps ever. The effortless style of his batting, his superb timing and the way he can make the fastest bowlers seem leisurely have formed a two-edged sword throughout his career, at his best he is peerless, when he gets out, he appears careless. Gower is the highest run scorer in England's Test history, with an average of 44.25 and, in the 1992 series against Pakistan, when he averaged 50, perhaps his most important innings was a painstaking 31 not out, which saw England to victory in the Fourth Test. David left University before the completion of his Law degree to concentrate on cricket, and played for Leicestershire for 15 years before moving to Hampshire in 1990. He was captain of Leicestershire for three years and captained Hampshire, in Mark Nicholas' absence, to victory in the 1991 Nat-West final. During one of his spells as captain of England, David became one of only three England captains to win a series in India. A witty commentator and fluent journalist, David Gower was appointed OBE in 1992.

ROBIN SMITH ▼

Born in Durban in 1963, Robin Smith's arrival at Hampshire was eagerly awaited, heralded as it was by elder brother Chris, who was already doing great things for the County, and who said that Robin was even better. So far, all the early promise has been fulfilled. Since his County debut in 1982 he scored 33 first-class hundreds and more than 70 fifties. Probably the hardest hitting batsman in the world, Robin is devastating anywhere square either side of the wicket. His performances for England, starting in 1988, have made the No. 4 position his own, and his average after 33 Test Matches is still in excess of 50. 1992 was not the best of seasons by Robin's exacting standards, but he crowned it with a wonderful innings of 90 (run out) in the Benson & Hedges final which effectively won the match, and won him the Man of the Match Award.

PHIL TUFNELL

Born in 1966, Phil Tufnell is a slow left-arm bowler in the Middlesex tradition, a tradition unfortunately not favoured by covered wickets and three-day County matches. Unfortunately 1992 was a season marred by illness and injury for Phil. However, up until the end of 1991, his 306 wickets in 93 matches, on almost always unfavourable surfaces, show how devastating Phil Tufnell ("The Cat") can be. Phil is currently ranked ninth in the Coopers & Lybrand world ratings for bowlers.

GRAHAM GOOCH

Graham Gooch originally played for Essex in 1973, he was a reserve wicket-keeper and No. 11 batsman. Since those days, his direction has changed radically, and he has become one of the truly great forces in post-war cricket. Gooch has been so dominant in the England side since he assumed the role of captain in 1988, that his dismissal, which is unusual, is a major psychological boost to the opposition. It is probably true to say of him, as they did of Bradman, that the opposing side would be happy to give him 70 runs to stay in the pavilion. In 1989/90 he led England to their first victory over the West Indies for 16 years, and his 333 against India in 1990, followed by 123 in the second innings represents the highest Test Match aggregate in hisotry. A great accumulator of runs on "flat" wickets, one of his best innings was in 1992 in the 4th Test against Pakistan at Headingly, when his first innings 135 on a technically poor wicket effectively won the match for England. A dedicated believer in application, Gooch has also had unparalleled success as captain of Essex.

MIKE GATTING

Mike Gatting is the captain of Middlesex CCC, and was the captain of the England team which, in 1986/87, won the Ashes, the Perth Challenge Cup and the World Series Cup. Gatting made his County debut in 1975, and has scored 28,512 first-class runs, at an average of over 50. He has scored 1,000+ runs for 14 seasons and, in 1992, scored 2,000 runs (av. 73.46), and led Middlesex to the Sunday League title. Mike is also a very useful medium-paced bowler and a specialist slip-fielder.

PHILLIP DeFREITAS

Phil DeFreitas was born in 1966, and made his Test debut at the age of 19, following a spell on the MCC ground staff from the age of 16. Originally picked as an all-rounder, with an emphasis on his strike bowling, Phil was one of the many people pencilled in to fill the yawning gap left by Ian Botham. A fixture in the England side, by the close of the 1992 season, Phil had played in 34 Tests and 78 one-day internationals. He has taken 93 Test wickets at an average of 32.44. Originally with Leicestershire, Phil moved to Lancashire in 1989.

ROBERT CHARLES "JACK" RUSSELL

Jack Russell is the latest in a tradition of great English wicket keepers, the natural successor to Bob Taylor and Alan Knott. Spotted by the Gloucestershire coach at the age of nine, Jack holds the record for the most dismissals in a first-class debut with seven caught and one stumped for Gloucestershire against Sri Lanka in 1981. Jack has toured all the cricketing countries with England and, as a batsman, has made 869 runs (av. 26.33) with a memorable 128 not out against Australia in 1989. Jack Russell's other career is as an accomplished and highly regarded professional artist. He started sketching on rainy days on the County circuit, but his strong and highly atmospheric style has led to commissions on many subjects outside cricket, including one to commemorate the 50th anniversary of the commando raid on St. Nazaire, an artist's proof of which hangs in St. Nazaire Town Hall.

Photograph by James Ruston

HORSE RACING

GEORGE DUFFIELD ▼

The son of a Yorkshire miner, George Duffield has been retained as a jockey by Sir Mark Prescott since 1973, a partnership which may become the longest in racing history. George rode his first winner in 1967 and, in 1992, reached a hundred winners in a season for the first time. Over the years, George has gained the respect of owners, trainers, punters and fellow jockeys, and the joy he exhibited on winning the 1992 Epsom Oaks on User Friendly – his first classic win – was a delight to all. George is in the Guiness Book of Records for winning 11 consecutive races on the Prescott trained Spindrifter, the only jockey this century to perform such a feat.
Photograph by Edward Whitaker and The Sporting Post

RICHARD HANNON ▼

Richard Hannon first held a trainer's licence in 1970, following in his father's footsteps. In 1992 he became champion trainer for the first time, both in prize money and number of winners. He has won the 2000 Guineas three times, the Irish 2000 Guineas twice and many other Group 1 races ranging from the Prix de l'Abbaye and Nunthorpe Stakes to the French St Leger. His ability to produce outstanding racehorses from comparatively cheaply bought yearlings is legendary.

MARTIN PIPE ▼

Martin Pipe's unique training methods have enabled him to break every record in the training books. He started training with his father's handful of horses on a derelict pig farm in Somerset and, over 20 years, has developed it into the most envied training centre in the West Country. Uncluttered by generations of handed down methods, Martin has developed a unique interval training system on a hilly half-mile all-weather artificial gallop. The only time his horses touch turf is when schooling over jumps or while actually racing. He has a lab for instant blood test results, an equine swimming pool, a treadmill, automatic exercisers and every possible medical facility. Martin trained his first winner in 1974/75 and took ten years to reach 50, but only two more to reach a 100. He has sent out over 200 winners in each of the last four seasons, and most of the major races have fallen to the stable.
Photograph by R. H. White

PETER SCUDAMORE

Peter Scudamore has been champion jockey in 1981/82, 1985/86, 1986/87, 1987/88, 1988/89, 1989/90, 1990/91 and 1991/92. In the 1988/89 season he rode the fastest 100 winners in a season and became the first National Hunt jockey to exceed 200 winners in a season, finishing with 221. He rode his 1500th winner in 1992. He has won the Champion Hurdle, The Sun Alliance Hurdle, the Welsh Grand National (four times), the sun Alliance Chase (twice), the Hennessey Gold Cup and the John P. Harty Memorial Handicap Chase. He has ridden winners in France, Ireland, Norway, Germany, Switzerland, Belgium, Australia, New Zealand and America. He has won The Sportsman National Hunt Jockey Award four times. He was appointed MBE in 1990 and received the Variety Club of Great Britain Award for helping deprived and handicapped children.
Photograph by R. H. Wright

RICHARD DUNWOODY ▼

Born in 1964, Richard Dunwoody rode his first winner in May 1983. Since then his career has been phenominally successful, including wins in the Mackeson Gold Cup, Tote Gold Cup, Breeders Cup Chase, Christmas Hurdle (twice), King George VI Chase (twice), Champion Hurdle, John Hughes Memorial Handicap Chase (twice), Arkle Challenge Trophy Chase (twice), the Jameson Irish. In 1986, on West Tip, he won the Aintree Grand National. He has partnered Desert Orchid on many of his outstanding achievements. Richard kicked off the 1992/93 season with five winners in five rides on a card of six. He is retained by David Nicholson and Nicky Henderson.

PHILIP BLACKER ▲

Philip Blacker turned to full time sculpture in 1982, having spent the previous 12 years as a successful steeplechase jockey. He rode 300 winners and won, inter alia, the Whitbread Gold Cup. Philip has now completed four life-sized portraits of legendary thoroughbreds, an unprecedented achievement for a sculptor. In 1985 Seagram UK commissioned him to produce a statue of Red Rum to stand at Aintree. the next commission was from the Marquis and Marchioness of Tavistock, and the statue of Mrs Moss now stands in front of Woburn Abbey. Desert Orchid followed, for Kempton Racecourse, and Northern Dancer, whose image now stands at Woodbine Racetrack, Ontario, near where the great stallion was born. Philip is now working on the statue of the St Leger winner, Snurge.
Photograph by Mark Cranham

PETER O'SULLEVAN ▼

Peter O'Sullevan is the voice of racing, and a wonderfully mellifluous voice it is. From his slow build-up at the start to his 220-words-a-minute at the finish he never stumbles and manages to observe, effortlessly, the rules of syntax and elocution. A true lover of horses and horse-racing, he started with the Press Association in 1944, and joined the Daily Express in 1950, making it required. reading for race goers for the next 35 years. His last column was mounted in his racing colours of yellow and black, and the letters bidding him farewell came from everywhere, "from the workhouse to Clarence House". The 1993 Grand National will be his 46th commentary, 12 on radio and all the televised races since the inception of TV coverage in 1960. As an owner he has been notably successful with Attivo and Be Friendly – and remarkably cool when commentating their races. Peter O'Sullevan's autobiography, Calling the Horses, was published in 1989. He was appointed OBE in 1977 and CBE in 1991.

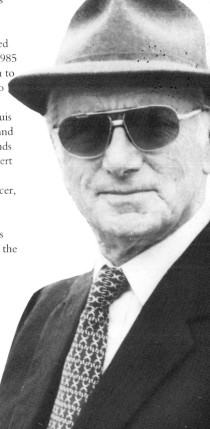

EQUESTRIAN

DEREK FRANCIS ⬆

At the age of 45 Derek Francis was a successful businessman, chairman of his family business. He decided to learn to ride one weekend and seven years later he took up endurance riding. Now 68 he is probably the oldest endurance rider in Europe, but he's also one of the best. He holds four BHS gold and two silver medals and has competed in all the major competitions in Europe. In 1992 he won the Ardennaise 75 mile race in Belgium, setting a new course record, came second in the Scottish championship and won the Berkshire Downs 100 mile CTR. Despite his outstanding successes Francis modestly describes himself as "chronically short-sighted and well known for getting lost in races".
Photograph by Mike Phimister

IAN STARK ➡

Ten years ago Ian Stark gave up his clerical job to concentrate on riding and running his own livery yard. He was then 28 and had been riding for 17 years. In 1984 he earned a place on the Olympic short list after coming third and sixth at his first Badminton. At Los Angeles he came ninth and the team took the silver. In 1988 he won both first and second places at Badminton, the only rider ever to do so, a success followed by the team silver and second place at the Seoul Olympics. In 1992 he won at Belton Park, Savernake and Brigstock but was unlucky at the Barcelona Olympics when, doing well in fourth place after the cross country, he was forced to leave the competition because his horse was injured. Ian has held the MBE for services to eventing since 1989.

HOWARD HIPWOOD ⬆

Captain of the English team and easily our most outstanding polo player, Howard Hipwood is also the highest rated player in Europe. Now 42, he started playing polo at his local pony club when he was just ten. He progressed quickly through the ranks and, at 18, he was put up to four goals after winning the Cupa de Presidente in Argentina. From 1979 and for six years he played in America during the winter, on the winning World Cup team for four of them. Howard won the British Open in 1990, and the New Zealand Open in 1991. In 1992 his team were narrowly beaten in the Westchester Cup, forcing the very strong American side into two overtime periods. For that game Howard was named Most Valuable Player. Although he has been nine goals for 11 years, Howard would still like to reach ten, something no Englishman has done since before the war.
Photograph by David Lominska

DAVID BROOME ▲

Our most famous showjumper David Broome has been competing at the top of the sport for over 30 years, but he has actually been riding since he was two. By the age of 19 (in 1959) he was earning more than any other showjumper in Britain. Between 1960 and 1972 Broome rode in four Olympic Games and he is the only showjumper to have won the men's individual European Championship three times, the King George V Gold Cup six times and the British National Championship six times. He received an OBE for services to showjumping in 1970. A member of the British team at the Olympics, David won the A3 competition at Kapellen and the A4 at Wolfsburg. He was on the winning Nations Cup team at Hickstead and won the International competition at Millstreet.
Photograph by Kit Houghton

GEORGE BOWMAN ▼

Ranked in the top five drivers in the world George Bowman is our most successful competitive carriage driver. He used to be a rodeo rider but was forced to give it up after a serious injury. He took up carriage driving in 1973. He has been national four-in-hand horse driving champion 15 times and has won silver and bronze individual and team gold, silver and bronze team medals in world driving championships. In 1980 he won the individual silver and, along with HRH the Duke of Edinburgh, took the team gold medal in the World Championships. In 1992 he came seventh in the World Championships and, at the time of writing, had already won eight titles: The National Championships for the 14th time, Sandringham, Brighton, St. Fort, Dunlarigg, Castle Howard, Lowther and Streatland Park.
Photograph by Fred Wilson

◄ JOHN WHITAKER

John Whitaker has partnered many excellent horses, the most famous of which is Milton. But he first captured the hearts of the public when he was 18 on Ryans Son. It had just 50p on its card at the time. John's trophies with Ryans Son include the team silver medal at the Los Angeles Olympic Games, and an individual silver medal at the Rotterdam Compensatory Olympic Games in 1980. Henderson Milton became John's partner in 1987. This soon proved to be a winning combination. At the European Championships in 1989 they won both the individual and team gold medals. 1992 was a brilliant year for John. He won five major classes at the Horse of the Year Show as well as Grand Prix at Antwerp, Calgary and Wolfsburg. He was also a member of the British showjumping team in Barcelona.

CARL HESTER ▼

Twenty-five-year-old Carl Hester is the current national dressage champion. He spent his childhood in the Channel Islands where he had his first major win – the Sark Bareback Derby. He became Britain's under 21 champion in 1984, and was runner-up in 1987 and 1988. He combined these successes with an event career, winning the Jumping National Championships in 1989. He was the youngest person to represent Britain at a major championship at the 1990 World Championships in Stockholm in 1990. In 1992 he won the final Olympic trial and at Barcelona was the highest placed British rider, finishing 15th overall.

NIGEL IRENS ▲

In 1972 Nigel Irens and a partner set up Bristol Sailing School, which Nigel ran until he joined Paul Weychan's multi-hull building yard in 1975. Three years later Nigel and Mark Pridie sailed the American-designed racing trimaran Jan of Santa Cruz to a class victory in the Round Britain Race. The experience led Nigel, in 1980, to design and build his first racing trimaran, Gordano Goose. Throughout the 1980s Nigel crafted a series of internationally successful trimarans and catamarans. Among his other recent achievements, his Ilan Voyager set a new Round Britain power boat record, without refuelling, in 1989, while in 1991 Fuji II captured the Trophée des Multicoques and the following year won the Europe 1 Single Handed Race and took second place in the Haute Normandie.
Photograph by Paula Gardiner

IAIN PERCY ▼

Iain Percy has been involved in the RYA Youth Racing Programme since 1987, through both the Optimist Race Training Scheme and the Laser Radical and Laser I, representing Britain internationally in all three classes. At the 1992 World Youth Championship he was, at 16, one of the youngest sailors ever to represent his country.
Photograph by Peter Bentley

ED DUBOIS ↱

Borsalino III, the first yacht Ed Dubois designed, won the British Three Quarter Ton Cup trials in 1976, the year it was launched. Three years later the two-tonner Police Car captured the Champagne Mumm Admiral's Cup. Since then Dubois Naval Architects, the company Ed founded in 1977 in Lymington, has enjoyed success year after year with yachts, raceboats, production cruisers, multi-hulls, motor yachts and sailing super yachts. Recent triumphs for Ed, who trained at Southampton College of Technology, include Full Pelt, which won the 1989 Lake Garda Regatta; Gefion, four-times winner of the International Eight Metre Class championship and the 37.4m performance ketch Taramber, which took the 1991 Showboats Award for best sailing yacht over 35m.

ROB WILSON AND SIMON TEMPLEMAN ▲

Both still under 20, Rob Wilson and Simon Templeman first met while competing against each other in the popular International Optimist dinghy. Subsequently teaming up, with Rob the helmsman and Simon the crew, they went on to achieve local victories and, in 1992, to represent their country in Portugal in the 420 World Youth Championship and in Israel in the World Championship. The same year they achieved fourth place in the National Open Championship.

BARRIE EDGINGTON

Barrie started windsurfing in 1979 at the age of 12. He won hist first national title at the age of 14. Since then he has won every national title from team racing to funboarding. On the international scene he won the much publicised Bic Thousand Kilometre Race. Since then he has concentrated on the Olympic Class including winning the World Championship in January 1992 and representing England in Barcelona at the Olympic Games.
Photograph by Roger Lean-Vercoe

KEVIN CURTIS ▲

Kevin Curtis is the current holder of the Silk Cut Helmsman of the Year Award. Kevin was injured in an industrial accident in 1978, and has been confined to a wheelchair since then. Although he had sailed from the age of 12, he only returned to sailing when introduced to the prototype Challenger Trimaran by Douglas Hurndall, some 18 months after his accident. In 1992, sailing one of the original Challengers, Ken won the Scottish Challenger Championships, the UK National Challenger Championships and the Irish Disabled Sailing Regatta. He was an obvious choice for the British team for the World Disabled Sailing Championships, in the Olympic harbour at Barcelona where, in a Raucho three-man dinghy, a boat that neither he nor his crew had seen before, Kevin won the gold for the team event, and reached the final of the match racing, where he came third.

BEN VINES ▼

Already crewing in cadet dinghies at seven, helmsman Ben Vines moved on to the 420 and joined the National Youth squad. In 1991 he won the National Youth Championship with his crew Eddie Low, with whom, later in the year, he came fifth in the IYRU Youth Championship in Scotland. The following year Ben and crew Eddie Low and Matthew Peregrine Jones won the RYA National Youth Match Racing Championship, earning themselves the chance to represent Britain in 1992's World Youth Match Racing Championship in Auckland, New Zealand.

NIK BAKER ▲

Since winning the Youth Championships in 1987, Nik Baker's career as a professional windsurfer has gone from strength to strength. He is ranked in the world's top ten, and excels at all three of the disciplines of the World Cup Grand Prix Circuit. Nik is the No. 1 sailor for Rushwind sails, and sails in the Mistral team alongside Robby Naish. In a sport in which height and weight mean extra leverage and, therefore, speed, he is remarkable in competing against and beating men often 6in taller and 10-20kg heavier than himself. How he does it, nobody knows.
Photograph by Darrel Wong

LAWRIE SMITH ▲

Lawrie Smith began sailing dinghies at the age of 6 and at 20 was European Champion in the Fireball Class. The titles of British and World Fireball Class Champion followed in 1977 and 1978. Two years later he skippered Britain's America's Cup challenger Lionheart in the first of three such competitions in which he has participated. A string of further successes followed, including being the six metre world champion in 1981 and the six metre European champion the following year. In 1988 Lawrie was placed fourth in the highly competitive Soling Class in the Olympic Games and took the bronze medal in the same event in the 1992 Olympics in Barcelona. Earlier that year he took the Lymington Cup Match Racing title and retained the Ultra 30 National Championship title, having won it in 1991.
Photograph by Colin Taylor Productions

STEPHEN HENDRY ▼

Stephen Hendry, the world's No. 1 snooker player since 1990, became a professional in 1985 – at the age of 16 the youngest player ever to be accepted by the sport's World Governing Body. The same organisation made him its Player of the Year in 1990, 1991 and 1992. In 1990 the Scot became the youngest ever winner of the World Championship – at 21 years and three months – and took the title again in 1992. He has also scooped 36 major titles, a tally second only to that of Steve Davis. In 1991 he equalled the highest number of titles won in a season (eight), a total previously achieved by Davis, and the following season set a new record by going one better. Stephen was voted Sports Personality of the Year in 1989 by viewers of BBC Scotland.

ROSS McINNES ▼

As a part-time professional Ross McInnes won the UK Suzuki Masters Championship in 1983 and the first UK Superleague Professional Championship in 1986, as well as holding the World Speed Pool Record for seven years. In addition, from 1987 to 1990, he was ranked Britain's No. 1 pool professional. Since becoming a full-time professional in 1988, Glasgow-based Ross has travelled all over the world, competing and giving exhibitions – some of the latter to raise money for the treatment of cystic fibrosis, from which his daughter, Laura, suffers.

◄ JIMMY WHITE

Jimmy White turned professional in 1980, since when he has become one of snooker's best known names, both in Britain and abroad. Ranked No. 3 in the world in 1992, Jimmy was the youngest ever Amateur British Champion when, in 1979, he scooped the title at the age of 17. He has competed in four World Championship Finals, narrowly missing taking the title each time. In a consistently successful career, the "Whirlwind's" most recent victories include winning the Rothmans Grand Prix in 1990, the Mercantile Credit Classic in 1991 and, in 1992, the Pearl Assurance British Open, the European Open and the Rothmans Grand Prix for the second time.

JOHN PARROTT ▲

John Parrott and Phil Miller, who recognised the Liverpudlian's outstanding ability when he was 15 years old, have enjoyed a 12 year player-manager partnership, the second longest in snooker. John achieved amateur success by winning the Pontins Junior Championship in 1981, the Pontins Open Championship in 1982 and the BBC's Junior Pot Black in 1982 and 1983. In his final year as an amateur he won a record 14 tournaments. Among his other major successes, the "Entertainer" was the European Open Champion in 1989 and 1990 and, in 1991, won the Embassy World and the UK Championships. The following year he took the China Kent Classic and the Dubai Duty Free Classic, both for the second time.

DENNIS PRIESTLEY ▼

Like many others, England international Dennis Priestley began playing darts at the start of the sport's television boom in the mid-1970s. Picked to play for Yorkshire in 1983, he won his first Open Championship, the McEwans, the same year, and two years later took the Dunlop Classic Singles Championship title. Spurred on by reaching the final of the 1988 International Open Tournament while on holiday in Dalls, Dennis returned to the USA the following year to win the Los Angeles Open Championship. In 1990 Dennis plucked the Embassy World Championship title from the legendary Eric Bristow, consolidating his world supremacy three months later by winning the coveted World Champions Challenge in 1991. Among his British successes in 1991 were winning both the Matchplay and the Gold Cup Championships.

◄┐ KEITH BREWER

Manchester-based Keith Brewer, who started playing pool at the age of 17 and first entered competitions two years later, has enjoyed a consistency which over the past decade has made him the most feared of opponents. Keith's first major amateur win was in the North West Open Championship in 1981. Three times UK Champion – in 1985, 1988 and 1991 – and British Open Champion in both years the event was held, 1987 and 1990, he turned professional in 1990. An England international since 1984, he took the Bronze Medal in the European Nine-Ball Championship in 1988. In 1992 Keith scored around 150 major wins, including the UK Tour Grand Finals. As well as the British game, he is heavily involved in American eight-ball and nine-ball pool, and in that same year competed in a major eight-ball competition, the Three Nations World Cup, in Australia.

PHILIP TAYLOR ▲

Shortly after being made redundant from his job as an engineer in 1990, Philip Taylor won the Embassy World Professional Championship, beating his famous mentor, Eric Bristow, in the final. Ranked Britain's No. 1 in 1990, 1991 and 1992, and a regular competitor for his country, Philip regained the Embassy World Professional Championship title in 1992. To date the winner of more than 50 championship events, in the 1991-92 season he won 23 of the 27 events in which he competed.

TOMMY DONLON ▲

First involved in pool tournaments at the age of 15, Tommy Donlon scored his first major victory the following year, in the Metropole Masters, and soon afterwards joined the Professional Pool Players Organisation. Among Tommy's most notable tournament successes are the Daily Star Win a Car Competition in 1989 and the UK Masters in 1991, in addition to four PPPO tournament wins. Ranked No. 1 by the PPPO in 1992, he was that year Haydock Open Champion, Websters National Champion, UK Nine-Ball Champion and European Eight-Ball Singles Champion, as well as UK Masters Champion for the second time.

MIKE GREGORY ▲

Lucky enough to have a half-brother who played darts for England, Mike Gregory was only four years old when he was first smitten by the sport. His first big break was winning the Finnish Open Singles in 1983. That same year he competed in the finals of both the World Masters and the British Open Tournament, and played for England. Mike turned professional after scooping the British Professional, the British Matchplay and the Butlin's Grandmasters Championships – all in 1984. In 1987 came the News of the World Championship title, which he retained the following year. His most recent victory was in the 1992 Lada UK Masters.

NOMINATION FORM

I would like to nominate the following person for inclusion in the Best of British Guides 1994.

Name _____

Address _____

_____ Postcode _____

Tel No. (Home) _____ Tel No. (Work) _____

Occupation _____

Category of Nomination

Reason for Nomination

Proposer's Name _____

Address _____

_____ Postcode _____

Tel No. (Home) _____ Tel No. (Work) _____

Occupation _____

Signature _____

Would like to congratulate

Tony Hand

on his nomination in the

Skiing and Skating Category

of

The Best of British Awards

MARK TOUT AND LENNY PAUL

Mark Tout is the driver and Lenny Paul the brakeman of Britain's two and four man bobsleigh. Representing Britain in the Olympics in 1992, they achieved creditable placings of sixth in the two man and seventh in the four. Their overall placings in the 1991 World Cup were sixth in the two man and third in the four, with a combined placing of fourth. Mark is a corporal in the 2nd Royal Tank Regiment, and has been an Army decathlete for many years. Lenny was a sergeant in the Royal Anglian Regiment until October 1992, and has been a world-class sprinter.

Photograph by Richard Francis – Action Plus

STEVEN COUSINS

In November 1992 Steven Cousins won his fourth consecutive British Senior Championship. Now aged 21, Steven started skating at the age of six, and at 14 he won the British Primary and British Junior Championships within four months of each other. He was sent to various junior competitions, coming third in Czechoslovakia, second in Bulgaria and first in Poland. Steven is currently ranked seventh in Europe, and represented Great Britain in the 1992 Olympic Games, coming 12th. Steven is currently being coached in the USA by Alex McGowan, coach of world champion Debi Thomas.

ANTHONY HAND

Tony Hand started playing ice-hockey at 11 years old for Murrayfield Ravens. Born in 1967 he has now been playing professionally for seven years, and has played for Great Britain at junior and senior levels. Tony is the all-time top scorer in the Heineken Premier League, and has twice been voted Heineken Player of the Year. Perhaps his greatest accolade came when he became the only British born and bred player ever to be drafted by an NHL ice-hockey team, when he joined the Edmonton Oilers, at that time the best team in the world.

STEPHEN COOPER

Born in Co. Durham in 1966, Stephen Cooper started playing ice-hockey at the age of ten for Durham's junior team. His parents took him to the ice-rink seven days a week and, at the age of 14, he was selected for the Durham Wasps. He played for the Wasps until 1988, with a four month break to gain experience in Canada. In 1988 he signed a two year contract with Cardiff, when they won the League and Wembley Championships and, in 1990, he returned to the Wasps and was in the League and Wembley Championship team again for 1991 and 1992. He has just signed a new contract to rejoin Cardiff, and hopes to help Britain qualify for the 1994 Olympics.

ROLAND DUNCAN ▼

Roland Duncan is Britain's best downhill skier, currently ranked 35th in the world. Educated at Cambridge, where he acquired an MA in physics and theoretical physics, Roland was also a rugby league half Blue. He has been three times British downhill champion, twice British Giant Slalom champion and twice British champion at skiing and, in the 1991/92 season, won the Chilian Downhill Championships and the Kandahar de los Andes Downhill (coming fourth in the Super Giant Slalom). Roland is a multi-lingual, and works as a journalist for the Telegraph, local papers and Skier Magazine.

MICHAEL DIXON ▶

Michael Dixon, BEM, was born in Scotland in 1962, and joined the Army at 17. He took up cross-country skiing at 19 and, two years later, represented Britain in the Nordic skiing event at the Olympic Games, the first Briton to compete at this level without at least six seasons experience. He was British champion in 1985 and 1986, when he changed to the biathlon, becoming national champion in 1987, 1989, 1990 and 1991. He represented Britain in the 1988 Olympics and has achieved by far the best results by a Briton in World Championship events. Only three people have ever shot perfectly in the Olympic 20km since small bore was introduced in 1976, and Michael Dixon is one of them.

RICHARD COBBING ▼

In 1989, having won three world records, and the World Games Championships at trampolining, Richard Cobbing changed sport and took up freestyle skiing. He applied his acrobatic skills to aerials and turned his first successful somersault on skis in December 1989. In 1990 he won the British Championships, only the second competition he had entered. In 1991 Richard was selected for the British team and became the first Briton to jump a triple somersault with three twists. Richard came 11th in the 1992 Olympics and in 1992 was voted Britain's Most Improved Skier.
Photograph by British Ski Federation

CYCLING

GETHIN BUTLER ▼

Sussex-born Gethin Butler, currently a post-graduate student in Lancaster, started cycling in 1980 and began racing seriously in 1986, at 17, when he won the Surrey Junior Road Race Championship. The following year he took the event's senior title, and in 1990 joined the British squad. His achievements since then have included riding the fastest 100 miles (160km) in 1991, the fastest 50 miles (80km) and 100 miles in 1992, and in the same year winning both the National 100-mile Championship and the National 12-hour Championship.

ROGER HAMMOND ▲

Roger Hammond, at the age of 11, became the English Schools under 13 cyclo-cross and time-trials champion, going on to be the national juvenile (under 16) cyclo-cross champion in 1989 and 1990. He also won the National Junior Championship in 1990, 1991 and 1992, this hat-trick setting a new British cyclo-cross record. In 1992, at 18, Roger won the World Junior Cyclo-Cross Championship, held in Leeds – only the second win by a British competitor in the history of the World Championships. Currently studying materials technology at Brunel University, Roger finds time to be a member of the National Road Race and Team Time Trial squads and has represented Britain on many occasions.

CHRIS BOARDMAN ▼

Riding an ultralight track bike with a revolutionary design by Lotus which stunned and aroused the envy of the world of international competitive cycling, in the summer of 1992, Chris Boardman set a new 5,000 metres world record. Six-times British pursuit champion (1986-89, 1991 and 1992), Chris is a frame-design consultant and a qualified cabinet-maker, and cites his parents and first coach, Eddie Soens, as the original inspiration behind his ambition to race. Among Chris's other achievements on the track in 1992 are setting a world record for the 4,000 metres as well as a British record for the 4,000 metres. He was also the British team pursuit champion in 1991 and the 4,000 metres pursuit champion in the 1992 Olympics.

ROBERT MILLAR ↟

Now in his 14th season as a professional cyclist, Glasgow-born Robert Millar, now based in France, has been the highest ranked Briton in the field since 1982. With the gift of a light build, he is above all known the world over as one of the sport's great climbers. Robert finished fourth in the 1984 Tour de France, winning a stage and becoming the first Briton to win the coveted King of the Mountains jersey. He finished second in the 1987 Tour, again winning the best climber's prize, and second in the Tour of Spain in both 1985 and 1986 – performances unequalled by a Briton. Among Robert's other achievements are victory in the 1989 Tour of Britain and, in 1990, in France's Dauphiné Libéré. In 1989 he was voted British Cycling Personality of the 1980s by Britain's cyclists.

KEVIN DAWSON ↟

Britain's Best All Rounder of 1992 – at 22 the youngest since Phil Griffiths in 1971 – Kevin Dawson is by profession a laboratory technician. Riding distances of 50 miles (80km) and 100 miles (160km) and 12-hour events, during the season he improved most of his 1991 qualifying times, and in the North Midlands event covered the second greatest distance for a 12-hour ride.

SHAUN WALLACE ↓

A track and short-distance road specialist, since 1984 Shaun Wallace has raced all summer in the USA and trained and raced during the winter in Australia or on the European Six-Day circuit. After taking the silver medal in the professional 5,000m pursuit at the 1991 World Championship – which he again won in 1992 – Shaun was invited to take part in 1992 in Japan's 1981-established International Keirin Series, the first ever Briton to receive the honour. Shaun competed in the 1984 Olympic Games, the following year he set the amateur world record for the flying start kilometre and in 1986 set the corresponding professional world record.

DAVID BAKER ↟

Multi-talented Yorkshireman David Baker's first specialisation was cyclo-cross, in which he was national champion in 1990 and again in 1992. He first tried mountain bike racing in 1988, when he won the Shimano MTB Series. The following year he was placed second in the European World MTB event in Belgium and third overall in the prestigious Grundig World Cup Series. After concentrating on city centre road racing in 1990, David returned to mountain biking in 1991, becoming the overall winner of the 7-Up/British Mountain Bike Federation National Points Series. In cyclo-cross he finished the 1991-92 season by taking ninth place in the World Cyclo-Cross Championship in Leeds – the highest-ever placing for a Briton in that competition. Also in 1992, he was the National Mountain Bike Champion and won the silver medal in the National Criterium Championship.

TIM GOULD ↓

Tim Gould, who began cycle racing at the age of 11, competed in the 1982 World Junior Cyclo-Cross Chamionship, finishing seventh as a member of the victorious British team. Six years later he came a creditable ninth in the World Amateur Cyclo-Cross Championship. Switching to mountain bike racing in 1988, Tim came third in the World Championship of that year, and in 1989 and 1990 was World Uphill Champion. British Champion in 1990 and 1991 and placed second in the event in 1992, he was also the winner of the World Cup in Italy in 1991 and in Switzerland the same year.

TONY ALLCOCK ➤

Born in 1955, Tony Allcock is Britain's World Outdoor Singles Champion, a title which he holds until 1996. His achievements are numerous and include, at Outdoor, three times England Junior Champion, twice England Open Champion, British Singles Champion, English Singles Champion of Champions 1988-91-92, World Triples and Team Winner 1980, World Fours Winner 1984, and World Team Winner 1988. Indoors, he has won the English Junior Championship, the Champion of Champions, National Singles Title (twice), Triples (twice) and Fours. In 1992 he won the World Pairs title for the sixth time. He has played for England continually since 1976. A keen charity supporter, he is a Patron of the Society of English Visually Handicapped Bowlers. He was appointed MBE in 1989 for services to the sport.
Photograph by Martyn Green

ANDY THOMSON ➤

Born in St. Andrews in 1955, Andy Thomson is currently No. 1 in the UK Indoor rankings. He started bowling in 1973 in Fife, and in 1975 won the Fife County Junior Championships. In 1977 he won the Scottish Junior Indoor title, and in 1979 became a full Scottish international. 1979 was also the year in which he moved to England, and since then he has won the following National Championships: at Indoor, England Singles, 89, 90, 91, England Pairs, 86, 91, England Triples, 81, England Fours 83, 84, 88, 89, 90, British Singles 91, 92, British Pairs 87, 92, British Fours 89, 90, 91, UK Singles 91, 92, England Players Assoc. 91. At Outdoor he has been England Singles Champion 81, England Pairs Champion 92, and has represented England in the 1986 and 1990 Commonwealth Games. He is married with two children, and works as a sales representative.

BRIAN DUNCAN ▼

Brian Duncan was born in Wigan in 1943, and was introduced to bowls by his father when he was eight. In the 1960s he was a member of the Lancashire Professional Bowling Association, and won his first major tournament, the Lancashire Merit, in 1964. He won the BBC Top Crown Tournament in 1973 and 1974 and the Talbot Trophy in 1974. Amongst many other trophies, he has won the Granada Television Bass Masters in 1984, 1990 and 1992, the Waterloo Handicap in 1979, 1986, 1987 and 1989, and made it five wins in the Mecca Tournament in 1992. He has won seven Warrington Charities, seven Burnley St. Andrews, four Patriots and five Whitbread Black Horse Trophies. In 1992 he became Champion of Champions for the first time.
Photograph by John Lomas

SIMON TERRY ▲

Now aged 19, Simon Terry took up archery when he was eight, coached by his father. He achieved his first success in 1984, becoming EFAC Champion, and then in 1985 he became European EFAC World Club Champion. His perseverance and dedication, and that of his father, have achieved outstanding results, culminating in his winning a bronze medal at the Barcelona Olympics in 1992. He is the first British archer to win an individual medal for 80 years, and also won a team bronze. Simon holds the record for three consecutive UK Junior Championships.

JOHNNY DAVIS ►

Johnny Davis was born in Northern Ireland, and still considers Belfast his home. He moved to London to study and to develop his fencing skills. He made the British foil team in 1985, and has been in it ever since. He competed in the Olympics at Seoul and Barcelona, where he came 19th. He believes that the levels of sacrifice and dedication required to compete at the highest level are immense, but are more than compensated by the adrenalin rush which accompanies competing and, particularly, winning. He is a partner in a music and sports promotion company based in London.

STEPHEN MULLINER

Aged 39, Stephen Mulliner, an investment banker, is currently ranked No. 2 amongst British croquet players. He has represented England since 1980, and Great Britain since 1982, and was chairman of the Croquet Association Council 1990-92. He is the holder of the President's Cup, which he has won on five occasions, was golf croquet champion in 1991, and was ranked No. 1 in the UK from 1986-1990.

◄ ROBERT FULFORD

Robert Fulford is Great Britain's world No. 1 croquet player. He started playing croquet in 1985, aged 16, at Colchester, and was clearly a natural with a fluent hard-hitting style which contrasts strongly with other, more mechanical, players. By 1990 Robert had been dominant in England all season, and he picked up his first world title without any real challenge. 1991 was a rather lean year for him, although he won the British Open title, but in 1992 he swept all before him, retaining his Open title, as well as winning the World Championship for the second time. He is a member of Britain's strongest doubles team, with Chris Clarke. Robert is currently trying to find a full-time coaching post in the USA.
Photograph by Picturelink

KIRK ZAVIEH ▼

Kirk Zavieh was public schools sabre fencing champion at the age of 15. He trained intensively in Budapest, under Peter Frölich, the Hungarian national coach, before taking up his place at Cambridge, where he was a full Blue, Universities champion and competed in the World Student Games. While studying at Law College, he trained in Hungary whenever possible and, in 1992, qualified for the British Olympic team, where he succeeded in defeating the eventual gold medallist, only to be eliminated later.

FITZLLOYD "FITZ" WALKER

Fitz was born in Jamaica in 1957, and is probably the best known freestyle amateur wrestler in Britain. As the eldest and most experienced member of the Great Britain wrestling squad, he commands the respect of the young wrestlers who join each year. Fitz also excels as a coach, both for the Northern England Senior squad, and for his own club, based at the Manchester YMCA. With two Olympic Games behind him, Fitz continues to defy all expectations by winning British titles. In 1992 he won his 14th consecutive title at welterweight, gaining a place in the Guinness Book of Records, at the expense of Ken Richmond, the man who struck the gong at the start of Rank movies.

TICKY DONOVAN

Ticky Donovan, OBE, became England national team karate squad in 1976. In the following year he fought the last time internationally when he represented Britain in the Tokyo World Championships. At the previous World Championships in 1975 he had been a member of Britain's winning team and, in 1982, 1984, 1986, 1988 and 1990, he has been team manager and coach to the world beating British squad, the only team to have won the World Championship more than once. Ticky has always been a winner, at first in association events and eventually in the British Karate Control Commission Championships, where his team won victory after victory. His book Winning Karate is published by Pelham Books.

RAY STEVENS

Ray Stevens is Britain's judo Olympic silver medallist and double Commonwealth champion. Born in Camberly in 1963, Ray was raised in High Wycombe, where he started judo at the age of ten. Leaving school at 16, he acquired a City & Guilds qualification in rooftiling. At the age of 19 he moved to London to pursue his judo career with Neil Adams in Fulham, where he still trains. He became a full international competitor at 17 and is Grade Black Belt 3rd Dan. Ray works full-time as a personal fitness trainer, and is a part-time model. He lives in Kennington with his girlfriend, Deborah, and their son Louis.

SHIRLEY CRABTREE "BIG DADDY"

Big Daddy, the famous Brobdingnagian wrestler, was born in Halifax to a wrestler father, and has been active in the sport since he was six years old. He has been a Coldstream Guardsman and a Blackpool lifeguard, where he won several life-saving commendations. His 58 inch chest once earned him an entry in the Guinness Book of Records, and he has been featured on This is Your Life. During his thousands of fights he has become the "kiddies favourite", an opinion not shared by the recipients of the "Big Daddy Splash".

CHRIS EUBANK ▲

Christopher Livingston Eubank was born in London in 1966 and educated in the UK and at Morris High School in New York. He signed as a professional boxer under the New York State Athletic Commission in 1984, and has so far had 33 fights at various weights – and 33 wins. Chris is the former undefeated WBC International Middleweight Champion, the former Undefeated WBO Middleweight Champion of the World, and the current WBO Super Middleweight Champion of the World, a title which he won by defeating Michael Watson in a famous fight in 1991, which left Watson in a coma. At first Eubank's apparent arrogance, and his expressed distaste for boxing did not endear him to his home crowds, but as his career has progressed, the public's attitute has changed, as Chris has continued to prove that he is, as he says, "Simply the Best".

LENNOX LEWIS ▲

Lennox Claudius Lewis produced the most stunning finish seen by a British heavyweight boxer at world level when he knocked out the highly fancied Donovan Razor Ruddock in the second round at Earl's Court in the early hours of November 1st, 1992. Within a month he became WBC World Heavyweight Champion when Riddick Bowe lost the title, and no-one who witnessed the demolition of Ruddock could have doubted that Lewis deserved to be the first Briton to become World Heavyweight Boxing Champion since Bob Fitzsimmons won the crown in 1897. Lennox Lewis was born in London and brought up by his mother, Violet, in Canada. Fighting for Canada in the 1988 Olympic Games, he won the super heavyweight gold medal by stopping every opponent within the distance (including Riddick Bowe, who would figure so crucially later). Returning to England, and under the management of Frank Maloney, Lennox made his professional debut in 1989, and since then has won all 22 of his professional fights, 19 inside the distance. Lennox Lewis styles himself "A Man On A Mission", and the Mission is to win the world title – watch this space!

TIM STEPHENS ▼

Tim Stephens is the most successful lightweight fighter in the history of world karate, and one of Britain's most successful fighters of all time. Now aged 31, and a full-time karate instructor, Tim began fighting for England as a Junior in 1981, and has competed in every major event since 1983. Individually he has won the World Championship, two World Cups, European Cups at two weights, Dutch, Finnish, Italian and Belgian titles, six English titles, two British titles, ten British Grand Prix and numerous Open titles.

TONY MOORE ▼

Tony Moore is the most highly qualified instructor in Thai Boxing in Great Britain. He is the only Briton ever to achieve the White Mongkon (Sacred Headband), the highest award in the sport, which was awarded to him in 1991. On being elected British team coach in 1991, Tony retired, undefeated, as British Thai Boxing Champion (1985-91) and British All-Styles Champion (1987-91). He is the first Westerner ever to win an Eastern title (Champion of Champions, Hong Kong, 1988) and the first Briton qualified to instruct in the Siamese warrior art of Krabi Krabong. Now aged 37, Tony lives with his family in Manchester.

GREG AND JONNY SEARLE, AND GARRY HERBERT ⬆

Oarsmen Greg and Jonny Searle, and cox Garry Herbert, are the reigning British Olympic champions in the coxed pairs, winning the title in Barcelona in 1992. Jonny is ex-President of the Oxford University Boat Club, and rowed in the boat race winning crew for three years. He holds a gold and a silver medal at junior World Championship level, and two bronzes at senior. He has won five Henley medals, including the Stewards and the Grand Challenge. At the age of 18 Greg Searle was the first British oarsman to compete at both Junior and Senior World Championships in the same year. Greater things followed, and in 1989 and 1990, Greg became only the second Briton to win back-to-back gold medals in the Junior World Championship coxless fours. He joined the National Eight in 1990. Garry Herbert took up coxing in 1984 and from 1985 to 1987, coxed at the Thames Rowing Club. In 1987 he coxed the fourth placed eight at the Junior World Championships. In 1988 he joined Leander, and in 1990, made his senior international debut coxing the National Eight to victory in the Grand Challenge Cup, and a bronze medal at the World Championships.

ANTHONY DEAN ➡

Anthony Dean is Britain's 550 limited world champion jet-skier. Born in 1970 Anthony started jet-skiing when he was 13 years old, and entered his first race before his 14th birthday. He has won many championships at various levels on his way to the top, and has been British overall champion for the last two years. He hopes that by winning the World 550 Championships, that he will attract sponsorship to compete in the US Pro National Tour in 1993, for the most prestigious title in jet-skiing.

JOHN BATTLEDAY ➡

John Battleday's name is inextricably linked with the world of international waterskiing. He has been a member of the British team for 20 years, has won the European title for the last four years, and the European tour for the last two. In World Championships John has won two bronze medals, a silver and, in 1985, the gold. He has been British track record holder since 1978. Australian born 35 year old John is the resident professional at Kirsten's Farm Hotel and Country Club in Berkshire, recognised as the foremost waterskiing venue in Europe, where he operates a ski school and corporate activity centre.

MATTHEW PINSENT ▲

Steve Redgrave's partner in the 1992 Olympics, Matthew Pinsent won the coxless pairs gold medal, following the World Championship which they won in Vienna in 1991, when they set the world record. Matthew had a distinguished junior career, winning the world gold medal in the coxless pairs in 1988, and has been a member of the victorious Oxford crews in the 1990 and 1991 boat races. Also in 1990 he was in the coxless fours which won the Stewards' Cup at Henley. At 22 years old, Matthew is looking forward to another gold in Atlanta 1996, and more thereafter.
Photograph by Peter Spurrier, Sports Photographer

NICK GILLINGHAM ▼

Double Olympic medallist Nick Gillingham began his senior international career in 1984, and in 1986 won a bronze medal in the 200m breaststroke at the Commonwealth Games. In 1987 he entered the world top ten for the first time, and in 1988 won the Olympic silver medal, and broke the British record. In 1989 he broke his first world record, and collected gold and bronze at the European Championships. In 1990 he became European champion and, in 1991, won a bronze in the World Championships, and broke the world record twice. In 1992 he won the Olympic bronze.

STEVEN REDGRAVE ▶

Steve Redgrave, 30, has proved himself to be one of the greatest athletes Britain has ever produced. He has won gold medals in rowing at three consecutive Olympic Games – for the coxed fours in 1984, and the coxless pairs in 1988 (with Andy Holmes) and 1992 (with Matthew Pinsent). In addition to these, Steve has won three World Championship golds, was a triple Commonwealth gold medallist (1986), has won the Diamond Sculls at Henley twice, the "Goblets" four times and has been five times winner of the Wingfield Sculls. He holds the world and Olympic records in the coxless pairs, with Pinsent, and was indoor world rowing champion in 1990. Steve was appointed MBE in 1986, and was the British flagbearer in 1992 at Barcelona. His sights are set on a fourth gold in 1996.
Photograph by Peter Spurrier, Sports Photographer

SPENCER HARGRAVES ▼

Spencer Hargraves started surfing at the age of seven in his native Cornwall, and now 19 years old, the sport takes him all over the world. At the age of 14 he won the prestigious Pro-Junior Tracks Cup in Sydney, and is now a world pro-junior champion. He has recently retained his European Professional Championship for the third year in succession. Spencer covers about 60,000 miles a year in the pursuit of excellence.

ADRIAN MOORHOUSE ▼

Adrian Moorhouse is the most successful and distinguished British swimmer of recent years. He has been captain of the British team since 1985, and has competed in three Olympic Games, winning the gold medal in the 100m breaststroke in 1988. Born in 1964, and educated at Bradford Grammar School and the University of California, and first swam for the British senior team at the age of 15. Since then Adrian has won gold medals in three consecutive Commonwealth Games, one of only two people to achieve this, has one four consecutive European Championships, again, one of only two, has been ranked in the top three in the world at either 100m or 200m every year since 1981, and was ranked No. 1 in the 100m from 1986-90. Adrian was appointed MBE in 1987, and was awarded an Honorary MA from Bradford University in 1991. Adrian is a member of MENSA.

GEORGE DIGWEED

Twenty-nine year old butcher, George Digweed, started shooting at the age of 13, with his mother's old 20 bore rook gun. He won a few junior titles and moved on to a Miroku sporting gun, which helped him make the giant step from junior to senior level. Having achieved near perfection in skeet shooting, he graduated to sporting shooting and has not looked back. He won the British and English titles in 1989, and the English, Dutch, Belgian, Swiss and EEC Grand Prix events in 1990. In 1991 he won the American Sporting Championship in San Antonio, Texas. 1992 was a phenomenal year for George. He started by winning the CPSA Centenary Shoot, the European Championship and the World Championship, in Vermont, with a record breaking score of 191/200. To conclude this dream year, George won the World Cup in Cyprus, achieving the ultimate treble. His next target is the Olympic Games in 1996, for which he is changing disciplines to Olympic Trap – look out, Atlanta!

ALAN ROSE ↑

Alan Rose followed his two brothers to the West London Sporting Grounds after working for a year in a wallpaper factory. He spent nine years as a trapper and also went loading in shoots, particularly for Lord Hambledon. Alan learnt gun-fitting and instruction from the late Percy Stanbury, and started instructing under him. In 1986 he was made head instructor, in succession to his brother and amongst his pupils he numbers members of the Royal Family, Tom Selleck, Max Hastings, Rocco Forte, Wilbur Smith and a wide cross-section of the aristocracy. Alan has shot, loaded and instructed on many famous moors and shoots, including Castle Hill, Wemergill, Invercauld, Gurston Down and Helmsley. When not shooting, loading and instructing, Alan works and breeds labradors, rears game and is a keen fisherman.

◄ JOHN PUGLSEY

Veterinary surgeon John Pugsley, 43, lists his hobbies as shooting, shooting and shooting. He shoots target pistol, small bore rifle, shotgun, match rifle and full bore rifle. He also builds and maintains rifles for himself, his wife and selected friends. John took up target shooting at university, as an antidote to athletics, and has shot for Devon for over 16 years and represented Great Britain on four tours of Canada and one of Australia. In 1992 he coached for England in the National Match and shot for England in the Mackinnon. John has won most major competitions, notably: the Grand Aggregate in Canada (1985), the St George (1989), the Queen's Prize (1988) and the Prince of Wales (1992). His ambition is to win the Grand Aggregate at Bisley, the only major trophy so far to have eluded him.

Photograph by Peter Hicks

DAVID HITCHINGS ↑

Farmer and farmer's son, David Hitchings was born in 1928 at Knapp Farm, Broad Chalke, near Salisbury. After doing his national service, he started up his poultry business, which has grown into a large pullet rearing enterprise, a high proportion of which is free range. His interest in shooting saw him initially develop the deep valleys at the top of the farm into a shoot for his friends but, with spiralling costs, he started to sell days in 1973 and, over the next few years, his skill in making both pheasant and partridge cross the deep valleys made Gurston Down famous as a quality shoot. In 1992 he published his book, Showing High Pheasants and Partridges, which he is marketing from home, celebrating the first 25 years of the Gurston Down Shoot.

◀ ANTONY RINGER

Having captained his school team and the GB Under 19 team at full-bore rifle shooting, Antony "Ant" Ringer first represented Great Britain in 1988, at the age of 21. He took two years off from competitive shooting and returned in 1990 to win the St George's at Bisley, and to finish in the top ten of the Grand Aggregate. In 1991, having spent time in Australia and New Zealand gaining experience, Ant won the St George's for the second consecutive year – a unique achievement – and came third in the most prestigious competition, the Queen's Prize. He also represented Great Britain in Canada. In 1992 Ant won major competitions in five countries, New Zealand, South Africa, England, Canada and the USA. He won the Queen's Prize at Bisley and, in the USA, achieved the record World Championship score of 440/450. By winning the Fulton Prize, Antony is now recognised as the best full-bore shot in the world.

HIS GRACE THE DUKE OF WESTMINSTER ▶

Although he was brought to the public attention as a shooter of clay pigeons in the famous Jackie Stewart team, the Duke of Westminster does not consider himself a clay pigeon shot and agreed to join as a favour, in the interests of charity and for fun. He is predominantly a grouse and pheasant man and all his shooting these days takes place on his 22,000 acres at Abbeystead, near Lancaster, where he shoots as often as his other commitments allow. Aside from his stewardship of Grosvenor Estates, with property and investment in the UK, Canada, Australia and the USA, the Duke is a director of Business in the Community, for whom he chairs the Rural Target Scheme, chairman of the North West Business Leadership Team and chairman of the Manchester Olympic Bid 2000 committee. He is also a Lieutenant Colonel in the Territorial Army and the Commanding Officer of the Queen's Own Yeomanry. With extensive farming enterprises in both Cheshire and Lancashire, the Duke enjoys the outdoors and is committed to the conservation of the countryside and rural life. Amongst the 60 odd charitable organisations of which he is president are the British Association for Shooting and Conservation and the Game Conservancy Board.

DAVID GROVE ▼

Born in Essex in 1955, by the time David Grove was 14 years old he had won all the county's junior fly-fishing competitions. On leaving school he moved to Dartmoor, where he went on to complete a nine year apprenticeship in mechanical engineering, achieving the highest qualifications in the trade. He now runs the family business, which allows him to enter all the international fly-fishing competitions. Among his formidable list of successes are: the South-West England Fly-Fishing competition; the South-West Television Championship; the National River Championship; places in the England Loch Style teams; and the European Championship 1991 and 1992. David is captain of the English River team for 1993 and will be representing England in the Commonwealth Championship in Canada.

BOB NUDD ▲

In 1991 Bob Nudd became world angling champion for the second year in succession and was listed by Ladbrokes as third favourite for the BBC Sports Personality of the Year Award. He didn't win (some fishermen believe he would have done had the BBC had any footage of him!) but was voted BBC Radio Essex Sports Personality of the Year a few weeks later. Britain's only professional angler, Bob was born in Norfolk in 1944 and only started fishing when he was 26 years old. He rose to prominence in 1978, when he came within 2oz of breaking the world five hour match fishing record, with a catch of 498 fish, totalling 166lb 9oz 8dr. He was picked to fish for England in 1984 and has been a member of the team ever since. During that time England have been world champions four times and are acknowledged as the best side in the world. Bob was the first person to win back-to-back World Championships since 1959-60. On average he fishes four days a week, his responsibilities as director of a groundbait company preventing his going more often. In 1993 Bob Nudd wrote his fishing autobiography, How to Become the World's Best Fisherman.

◀ ROY LEWIS

On October 26th, 1992, 38-year-old electronics engineer Roy Lewis landed a 46lb 13oz record breaking pike from the Welsh Llandegfedd reservoir. In the noble tradition of anglers, Roy who has been fishing since he was eight, put the fish back in the water after it had been weighed and witnessed. The pike was caught on a Creek Chubb Pikie lure and must have put even Welsh fishing stories to shame for a day or two.

STEPHEN MILLS

Stephen Mills was born in East Africa in 1952, the son of a colonial policeman. He came to England in 1956 and, from an early age, evinced a strong interest in sea angling, forming an angling society at school. He joined the Gosport & District Angling Club and has won their boat championship 11 times, graduating through the committee to become first chairman and now president of the club. He has won around 30 open championship titles at all levels, most recently successfully defending his title at the Rosslare small boats festival in Ireland in September 1992. In 1991 he was selected to represent England when they won the World Championship, also in Ireland. Stephen is the holder of the British record for a thresher shark, landing a 323lb monster in his 17ft boat off the Hampshire coast, in 1982 – when he was Daily Mirror Angler of the Year.

ALAN YATES ▼

Born near Dover in 1945, Alan Yates took up sea angling at the age of five, with his father, Charles. By the age of 12 he had moved on to competitive fishing, winning school championships. He won the News of the World National Award at the age of 16 and, since then, he has won over 1,000 open competitions worldwide, including World, European and British titles, a unique feat by a British angler. Alan has been England's national team captain since 1978, with over 50 caps. He is the founder of the Sea Anglers' Match Federation and the National Sea League and is currently treasurer for the National Federation for Sea Anglers' South-East Division and an NFSA

National Standing Committee member. Alan started writing about sea angling in 1965 and has written various books and made several videos on the subject. His most recent book is The Complete Book of Sea Fishing, written jointly with boat angler Ted Entwhistle. He took up full-time journalism in 1978 and has written a weekly column for the Angling Times for 16 years. He now writes for various publications as well as being the "Agony Aunt" (Ask Alan) for Sea Angler magazine and a consultant to the EMAP Pursuit Publishing company. The biggest fish which Alan has caught from the shore was a 167lb Bronze Whaler Shark, caught in competition in Namibia.

◀ STEVE POPE

Born in 1956, the son of the landlord of the Plume of Feathers in Rickford, Steve Pope started his fishing as a child, using maggots and worms. At the age of nine he had his first opportunity to fly-fish at the Blagdon and Char Valley lakes, near Bristol. Over the next few years Steve demonstrated the stoical fatalism for which fishermen are famous for, although at one stage he only caught two fish in two years, he was determined to master the art. He became more and more successful throughout his early teens and, in 1984, had his first opportunity to enter an England eliminator, which he won convincingly, thus becoming, at the age of 18, the youngest fly-fisherman ever to represent his country. Since 1984 Steve has been a member of the winning team in the Benson & Hedges Fly-Fishing competition three times, second once and third once. 1992 was a particularly successful year when, out of a field of 50 teams, he eventually won the final over a two day event at Rutland Water.

KEITH GREGORY ▼

Colliery deputy Keith Gregory is the Division 1 National Angling Champion for 1992, with a catch of 17.35kg, on the River Trent. He is the only angler to have achieved two individual and two section winner's medals in the 1st Division. Keith won his first match at Cadnor Park reservoir in 1969 and has won over 100 matches in the ensuing 23 years, some on the open circuit and some at club level. He has been team captain and vice-president of the Ripley & District Angling Club for the last 12 years, and has won around £50,000 in his angling career to date.

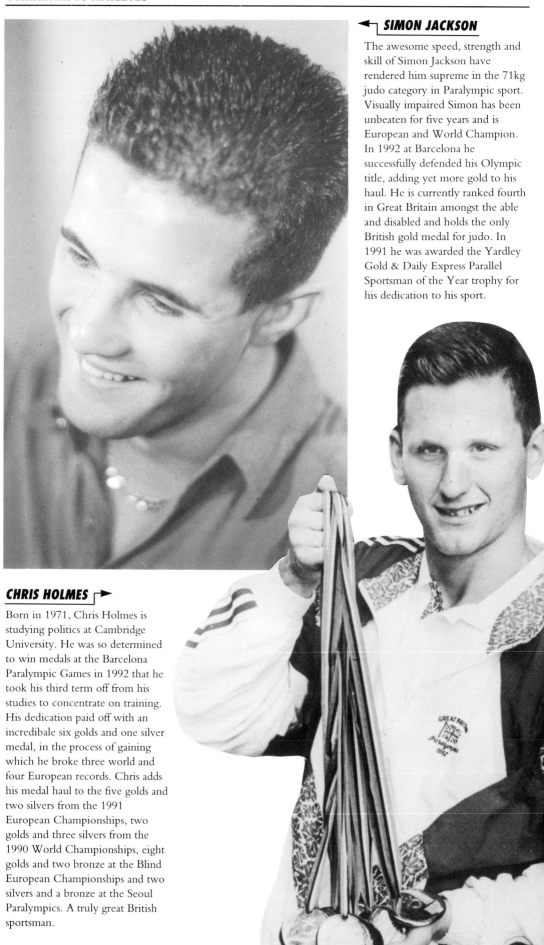

SIMON JACKSON

The awesome speed, strength and skill of Simon Jackson have rendered him supreme in the 71kg judo category in Paralympic sport. Visually impaired Simon has been unbeaten for five years and is European and World Champion. In 1992 at Barcelona he successfully defended his Olympic title, adding yet more gold to his haul. He is currently ranked fourth in Great Britain amongst the able and disabled and holds the only British gold medal for judo. In 1991 he was awarded the Yardley Gold & Daily Express Parallel Sportsman of the Year trophy for his dedication to his sport.

CHRIS HOLMES

Born in 1971, Chris Holmes is studying politics at Cambridge University. He was so determined to win medals at the Barcelona Paralympic Games in 1992 that he took his third term off from his studies to concentrate on training. His dedication paid off with an incredibale six golds and one silver medal, in the process of gaining which he broke three world and four European records. Chris adds his medal haul to the five golds and two silvers from the 1991 European Championships, two golds and three silvers from the 1990 World Championships, eight golds and two bronze at the Blind European Championships and two silvers and a bronze at the Seoul Paralympics. A truly great British sportsman.

◄ ROBERT MATTHEWS

Bob Matthews, MBE, is a runner of the highest class. He is a true inspiration to other blind athletes and his role in Paralympic sport and its development cannot be overestimated. Born in 1961 and already a gold medallist in the 1984 and 1988 Paralympics, Bob's determination to retain his titles at Barcelona had him and his guide runner training for 35 hours a week in 1992. Once again the training paid off. Bob won the gold medal in the 5000m, in a new Paralympic record time, the silver in the 800m and a bronze in the 1500m. When not competing or training, Bob is studying to be a sports physiotherapist.

PETER HULL ▼

Peter Hull, MBE, is a well-known, experienced media personality, having competed in the London Marathon many times and been a regular guest on regional and national sports programmes. He has competed for Britain's swimming squad in Sweden, Holland, Korea and Spain, is a fine team member and a brilliant example to aspiring young athletes. Born in 1965, Peter is an administration officer at the Ministry of Defence. His finest hour came in the Barcelona Paralympics in 1992, when he won three gold medals in the 50m backstroke and the 50m and 100m freestyle. Whatever leisure time is available to him when not training or competing in marathons, he spends compiling access guides for the disabled.

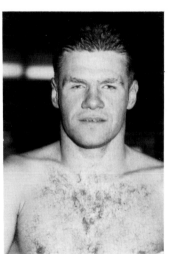

◄ DAVID MORETON

As a youngster at the New York Amputee Games, David Moreton broke five world records. In Miami he took four junior world records and in the Holland World Championships he broke a further seven. In the 1988 Paralympics, he won two gold, three silver and two bronze medals and, in 1990, became the first disabled swimmer to complete the 100m freestyle in under a minute. Great hopes rested on him for the Barcelona Paralympics, and he did not disappoint, with gold in the 100m butterfly and the 400m freestyle, and bronze in the 100m freestyle.

PAUL WILLIAMS ▾

A member of Nottingham Athletics Club, Paul Williams is a great all-rounder. In the 1988 Paralympics he set world records in the javelin, shot and discus. He is a martial arts black belt and goalkeeper for the English soccer team. He won a silver medal in an international cerebral palsy soccer tournament in 1991. The javelin is a particularly tough and popular event at the Paralympics and, once again, at Barcelona 1992, Paul showed his mettle by winning the gold, and breaking his own world record.

◀ STEPHEN BRUNT

Marathon runner Steve Brunt suffered what must be the nightmare of all visually handicapped runners when training in 1990. A car hit him, rendering him unconscious and fracturing his pelvis and leg and necessitating the removal of nerve endings to his knee, thigh and shoulder. Less than a year later he was back at the peak of his form running 100 miles a week. In 1992 he went with the British team to the Barcelona Paralympics to defend the gold medal which he had won at Seoul four years previously and did so successfuly in extremely hot and adverse conditions, also taking fifth place in the 5000m with a personal best time. Steve is now pounding the roads of Bristol, training for the 1996 Atlanta Paralympics.

NOEL THATCHER ▾

Noel Thatcher is unquestionably one of the stars of the British Paralympic team. He is immensely popular in the squad and has appeared many times as a guest on television. Noel has held records for visually handicapped running at all distances from 400m to 5000m and at his club, the Newham and Essex Beagles, regularly competes in able-bodied races where he finishes, if not first, then well up the field. A senior hospital physiotherapist, in 1991 Noel was voted Royal Mail Paralympic Sportsman of the Year. He went on to justify this honour at Barcelona in 1992, winning the gold in the 1500m, a new games record, with silver in the 4 x 400m and the bronze in the 800m.

JOHN NETHERCOTT ↱

Cerebral pasly sufferer John Nethercott won the cross country gold medal at the 1992 Paralympic Games in the new world record time of 4mins 30.15secs. Student John also won the CP National Cross Country 5000m Championship in 1992 and, in 1989, the 1500m gold and 4000m silver in the 1989 Paralympic Youth Games in Miami. He maintains a demanding training schedule of long distance running at his club in Penarth, South Glamorgan. Now 21 years old, John is determined to retain his position as best in the world.

PAUL NOBLE ↑

Scotsman Paul Noble is a swimmer with a very large trophy cabinet. In Paralympic games he won a silver and bronze medal in 1984, three golds and four silvers in 1988 and, in Barcelona 1992, he took the gold in the 200m Individual Medley in a new world record time and two further silvers and a bronze. An amputee, Paul was British team captain at the 1990 World Championships and has been Scottish captain since 1986. In 1991 his team won the BSAD National Trophy. Paul is also a keen golfer and ten-pin bowler, and a champion at Trivial Pursuits.

INDUSTRIALISTS

LORD YOUNG ▼

Former government minister Lord Young of Graffham, at present executive chairman of Cable and Wireless, was born in 1932. He graduated from University College, London, and practised law for a short time before joining Great Universal Stores. He went on to form an industrial construction group and a British subsidiary of Manufacturers Hanover Trust Company. Following the General Election in 1979, Lord Young acted as adviser to the then Secretaries of State for Industry and for Education and Science. A former member of the National Economic Development Council and chairman of the Manpower Service Commission, he became minister without portfolio in 1984. Appointed Secretary of State for Employment in 1985 and for Trade and Industry in 1987, Lord Young was the deputy chairman of the Conservative Party from 1989-90. Married with two daughters, he has been chief executive of Cable and Wireless since 1990 and is a director of Salomon Inc and Salomon Brothers International, as well as being the president of Jewish Care.

LORD WEINSTOCK ▲

Lord Weinstock, managing director of the General Electric Company since 1963, was born in 1924. He graduated from the University of London and joined the Admiralty as a junior administrative officer in 1944, leaving in 1947 to work in finance and property development. Lord Weinstock, appointed managing director of Radio and Allied Industries Ltd in 1954, became a director of the General Electric Company in 1961 and was director of Rolls-Royce from 1971-73. A trustee of the British Museum and the Royal Philharmonic Society, he has honorary degrees from many universities including Salford, Aston, Bath, Reading and Ulster. He is an Honorary Fellow of Peterhouse, Cambridge, and the London School of Economics, and an Honorable Bencher of Gray's Inn. A member of the Jockey Club, Lord Weinstock's recreations include horse racing and music. Knighted in 1970, he was elevated to the Peerage in 1980.

LORD HANSON ▼

Lord Hanson is chairman of the Anglo-American industrial management group Hanson plc, one of the UK's top ten companies. In 1946, after serving in the Duke of Wellington's Regiment during the war, he joined the transport and distribution business founded by his great-great-grandmother. The business expanded into Canada until its trucking interests were sold in 1963. Lord Hanson then became chairman of Oswald Tillotson, a UK commercial vehicle sales company and, in 1965, chairman of what is now Hanson plc. He has been chairman of Trident Television and is currently chairman of London's Melody Radio. A Freeman of the City of London and an Honorary Liveryman of the Worshipful Company of Sadlers, with honorary degrees from the universities of Leeds and Huddersfield, he is also a Fellow of the Royal Society of Arts. Married with two sons and a daughter, he was knighted in 1976 and became a Peer in 1983.

SIR ERNEST HARRISON ▲

A chartered accountant, Sir Ernest Harrison joined Racal (of which he is now executive chairman) as secretary and chief accountant in 1951. He became deputy managing director of the electronics and telecommunications group in 1961 and chairman and managing director in 1966. Architect of Racal's acquisition of the Chubb Security Group, he is executive chairman of the group and chairman of Vodafone Group plc. Knighted in 1981, he has honorary doctorates from the universities of Surrey and Edinburgh, City University, London and the Cranfield Institute of Technology. He has received numerous industry awards including the Hambro Businessman of the Year and the Aims of Industry National Free Enterprise Award. An owner and breeder, he enjoys horse racing and was elected a member of the Jockey Club in 1990. Married with five children, he is chairman of the Ronald Raven Chair of the Clinical Oncology Trust at the Royal Free Hospital, London.

SIR DENYS HENDERSON ▲

Appointed chairman of Imperial Chemical Industries in 1987, Sir Denys Henderson is married with two daughters. A former solicitor, he was born in 1932. He joined ICI in 1957 after serving as a staff captain with the Army Legal Services. With wide international business experience, particularly in the chemical industry, he became a member of the main Board in 1980 and deputy chairman six years later. He is a Companion of the British Institute of Management and a non-executive director of Barclays Bank and the RTZ Corporation. A trustee of the Natural History Museum, member of the President's Committee of the Confederation of British Industry and of the Save the Children Fund, Sir Denys is also a Fellow of the Royal Society of Arts and holds honorary doctorates from the universities of Aberdeen, Brunel, Manchester, Nottingham and from the Cranfield Institute of Technology. President of the Society of Business Economists, he was knighted in the 1989 Birthday Honours List.

◀ SIR CHRISTOPHER HOGG

A graduate of Trinity College, Oxford, Sir Christopher Hogg, chairman of Reuters Holdings, Courtaulds and Courtaulds Textiles, was born in 1936. He earned an MBA from Harvard in 1962 and in 1980 he became chairman of the Courtaulds Group and non-executive chairman of Reuters in 1985. A director of the Bank of England, Sir Denys is an Honorary Fellow of Trinity College, Oxford, the Chartered Society of Designers and a Foreign Honorary Member of the American Academy of Arts and Sciences. He retired as Courtaulds' chief executive in 1991.

FRANK WILLIAMS ▲

Born in 1942, Frank Williams became really hooked on motor racing watching the 1958 British Grand Prix at Silverstone. In the mid-1960s he raced an Austin A40 and a Formula 3 Brabham but, although not unsuccessful, he soon realised that his real talents lay in preparing and running cars for other people. Formula 1 was always Frank's ambition and he realised it in 1969 with his friend Piers Courage driving a private Brabham. Their efforts were rewarded with second placings at Monaco and Watkins Glen, and eighth overall in the championship. Piers was tragically killed in the 1970 Dutch Grand Prix, but Frank struggled on, usually with hopelessly inadequate budgets, until 1976, when an unsatisfactory partnership led to the loss of all the teams assets and he had to start again from scratch. The new team, Williams Grand Prix Engineering, incorporated a promising racing car engineer called Patrick Head. In 1978 Head designed his first GP car, and since then the Frank Williams team has won eight World Championships, including the 1992 drivers' and constructors' trophies. Frank suffered a serious car crash in 1986, which has left him paralysed below the neck, but was there to witness his team winning the drivers' and the constructors' trophies in 1987, and has been present at every race since. In 1982 the team received the Queen's Award for Export Achievement and, in 1986, Frank Williams was made a CBE in recognition of his services to motor racing.

CARL FOGARTY ▶

Carl Fogarty is Britain's 1992 Endurance World Champion in international motorcycle road-racing. He adds this title to the three Formula 1 World Championships which he won in 1988, 1989 and 1990. Carl is arguably the most versatile rider in the world. Whether riding on roads or short circuits and no matter what the machinery, his talent and determination have brought him constant success. Three times an Isle of Man TT winner, Carl currently holds the outright lap record for the course.

NIGEL MANSELL ▶

Unlike most motor racing champions, Nigel Mansell was forced to spend many years of his career at the wheel of uncompetitive cars. He was unable to secure a drive worthy of his talents until 1985 – 13 years after he had begun racing. Born in 1953, Nigel first drove a Grand Prix car in 1979, testing a Lotus 79 at the Paul Ricard circuit in France. He had his first Grand Prix win in 1985, driving for Williams-Honda in the Grand Prix of Europe and immediately followed this with another win in South Africa. In 1986 a puncture at Adelaide famously robbed him of the World Championship despite his five GP wins but, as some compensation, he was voted BBC Sports Personality of the Year. 1987 again saw him as runner-up for the championship, despite winning six GPs against team-mate Piquet, the eventual champion there. 1988 was not a happy season for Williams, and in 1989, Nigel moved to Ferrari, where he had two unsatisfactory seasons by his standards, culminating in his announcing his retirement from the sport. The Williams team persuaded him to rescind this decision and there followed two magical seasons for them, as runner-up in 1991, for the third time and, finally, in 1992, as champion, with a record five successive GP wins and a record total of wins in a season. Mansell won the BBC Sports Personality of the Year Award for the second time in 1992.

MAX MOSLEY ▼

Born in London in 1940, Max Mosley obtained a physics degree from Oxford University and was called to the Bar in 1964. For the next five years he practised as a barrister, while indulging his hobby of motor racing at club and

international Formula 2 level. In 1969 he became founder director of March Engineering and, until 1978, was involved in all aspects of building and racing cars at international level, including jointly representing the Formula 1 constructors at the CSI. From 1978 until 1983, Max was a member of the FISA Formula 1 commission and a deputy member of the executive committee, involved in the organisational promotion of many Grand Prix races and in the negotations which led to the Concorde Agreement. From 1983 to 1986 he continued to act as a consultant, while pursuing his own interests. In 1986 he returned as president of the FISA Manufacturers' Commission and, in 1991, became president of the FISA.

◄ KURT NICOLL

The 1992 500cc motocross season finished with Kurt Nicoll as British champion for the fourth time in five years and as runner-up in the World Championship, only two points behind the winner. Born in 1964, Kurt started racing in 1979, in the schoolboy class and became national champion in 1980. He started adult racing in 1981 and by 1982 had won the British Support Championship. A serious leg injury put him out of the 1991 season in June but, that year apart, he has not been out of the top ten in the World Championship since 1985 and was runner-up in 1987, 1988 and 1990 as well as 1992.

DEREK WARWICK ▲

Born in 1954, Derek Warwick began his career in motor sport at the age of 12 in go-karts and progressed to his first season in Formula Fords in 1975. In 1976 he won the European Formula Ford Championship and, the following year, graduated to Formula 3. In 1980, he came second in the European Formula 2 Championships to Toleman team-mate Brian Henton. Derek Warwick's Formula 1 career started in 1981 with Toleman, when the team was not really competitive and, although he finished seventh in the World Championship with Arrow in 1988 and tenth in 1989, his Formula 1 career has been a history of uncompetitive cars and inadequate finance, which have never allowed his great talent full rein. In 1986, lacking a competitive Formula 1 drive, he joined the Jaguar team, and was placed second in the World Sportscar Championship. In 1991, having won Monza and Nurburgring, only a technical disqualification cost him the championship which he won in 1992, driving for Peugeot.

◄ COLIN McCRAE

The most exciting young British driver to arrive on the international rallying scene in recent years, Colin McCrae has, in 1992, underlined his potential to become a future world champion with a second place in the Swedish Rally and strong finishes in the Acropolis and the Thousand Lakes. A strong drive into sixth place in the 1990 Lombard RAC Rally convinced Dave Richards to give Colin a professional contract in a Prodrive-prepared Subaru Legacy RS in the 1991 season, which finished with him producing a sensational drive in the Lombard RAC Rally.

ENVIRONMENTALISTS

JONATHON PORRITT ▼

Probably the best known "green" in Britain today Jonathon Porritt was voted "most impressive environmentalist" in a 1991 MORI survey of environment journalists. He transformed Friends of the Earth from an organisation with ten staff and 15,000 members to a staff of 80 and a membership of 200,000. His book, Seeing Green, is one of the most important ground-breaking expositions of green thought to have appeared in the UK. Much of his work in 1992 centred around the UN Conference on Environment and Development in Brazil for which he spearheaded an initiative, the Tree of Life Project, whereby non-government organisations and concerned individuals could make their voices heard at the summit. His latest TV series How To Save the Earth features 12 "green warriors" from around the world and discusses different ways of saving the planet. As an ex-teacher he has continually presented a vision of a sustainable world for the younger generation and is known to children as presenter of BBC TV's Going Live! His latest book, Save The Earth, brings together contributions from some of the most eminent environmentalists and ecologists in the world. *Photograph by Phillip Cam*

SIR DAVID ▼ ATTENBOROUGH

Sir David Attenborough's distinguished career in broadcasting spans some 40 years. In 1954 he launched the first of his famous Zoo Quest series which took him, over the next ten years, to all parts of the tropics. In 1965 he was made controller of BBC 2, then less than a year old, and in 1969 he became director of programmes for both the BBC networks. In 1973 he returned to programme making with Eastwards With Attenborough, a natural history series set in SE Asia and The Tribal Eye which examined tribal art worldwide. In 1979 he began writing and presenting Life On Earth, the most ambitious series the BBC Natural History Unit had ever produced. This was followed by The Living Planet series five years later and The Trials of Life in 1990. He was knighted in 1985 and has received honorary degrees from many universities and awards which include the CBE for work in conservation, an International Emmy Award in 1985 and a gold medal from the Royal Geographical Society. He is a Fellow of BAFTA and the Royal Society. In 1991 he received the Royal Television Society's gold medal and was made President of the British Association for the Advancement of Science.

JOHN RICHARD-SANDBROOK ▲

It was while working for the chartered accountants Arthur Anderson and Company that John Richard-Sandbrook founded Friends of the Earth with colleagues from the world of student politics. He had previously studied Biological Sciences at the University of East Anglia, staying on after completion of his degree for another year as the first Sabbatical President of the Students' Union. By 1974, the year John became Director of Friends of the Earth, the organisation was firmly established with local groups targeting key campaigns around the country. In 1976 he was asked to join the staff of the International Institute for Environment and Development, to assist with marine environmental issues. He was soon drawn into general management and is now ILED's executive director. John remains a member of FoE Trust and is involved in the work of many other environment and development organisations.

ROBIN GROVE-WHITE

Robin Grove-White studied PPE at Oxford before becoming a comedy script writer. He was drawn to environmental issues in the early 1970s, becoming director of the Council for the Protection of Rural England (between 1981 and 1987), as well as chairman of Countryside Link and vice-chairman of the European Environmental Bureau and the Council for National Parks. He is currently director of the Centre for the Study at Lancaster University, a fast-developing inter-disciplinary research centre on environment, science and culture.

DAVID SHEPHERD →

David Shepherd describes his early career as a "series of disasters". After failing to be a game warden in Africa he turned to painting – and was turned down as "not worth training" by the first art school he tried to enter. He says he owes his subsequent success to Robin Goodwin, the man who taught him, and the Royal Air Force who flew him all over the world to paint aircraft pictures and commissioned his first elephant painting. Now regarded as one of the world's leading wildlife and landscape artists he is also known internationally as a leading conservationist. His paintings have raised over £2.5 million through the David Shepherd Conservation Foundation, he has been awarded the Order of the Golden Ark by Prince Bernhard of the Netherlands and the OBE for services to conservation. He is a member of honour of the World Wide Fund for Nature and holds an honorary doctorate of Fine Arts at the Pratt Institute in New York. A BBC documentary has been made about him and he has been a subject of This Is Your Life. He has written six books and is chairman and founder of the East Somerset Railway, a registered charity raising money for our steam railway heritage and wildlife.

EDWARD GOLDSMITH →

Born in Paris in 1928 Edward Goldsmith went to school in France, England, the Bahamas and Canada before ending up at Oxford where, he says, the most important thing he learnt was that conventional wisdom on almost every subject was wrong. In 1969 Edward founded the Ecologist, the first magazine to combat the myth that economic development can solve man's problems. Since then he has spent most of his time writing, lecturing and campaigning. Among the books he has written and co-authored are A Blueprint for Survival (1972), The Earth Report and The Great U-Turn (1988).

ENVIRONMENTALISTS

JOHN BRETT ELKINGTON ▼

A co-founder of SustainAbility and one of Europe's leading authorities on environmental strategies for business, John Elkington has worked in the environmental field since 1972. He is the author and co-author of some 30 books and reports, including the best selling Green Consumer Guide, The Green Capitalists, The Green Business Guide, The Corporate Environmentalists and Holidays That Don't Cost The Earth. He is also the editor of Biotechnology Bulletin. Currently the director of the Association of Environmental Consultancies, he is a member of numerous councils and committees including the Council of the World Resources Institute. He sits on the advisory councils of Business in the Environment, the Merlin Ecology Fund and the US Natinal Wildlife Federation's Corporate Conservation Council Environmental Achievement Award. In 1989 he was elected to the UN Global 500 Roll of Honour for outstanding environmental achievements.

PAUL EKINS ▲

Paul Ekins is currently a Research Fellow specialising in environmental economics. Since 1984 he has been director of The Other Economic Summit and director of the New Economics Foundation. He is chairman of the consumer-information company New Consumer Ltd and coordinator of the International Living Economy Network of Economists and Social Scientists. He is also research director of the Right Livelihood Awards. Last year he published three books, A New World Order: Grassroots Movements for Global Change, Real Life Economics and Wealth Beyond Measure: the Gaia Atlas of Green Economics.
Photograph by Hans Knodt

PROFESSOR DAVID BELLAMY ▲

Over the last 20 years the world famous botanist, writer and broadcaster David Bellamy has communicated to thousands of people via television, radio and books his enthusiasm and concern for the natural world. Since his first major TV series and accompanying book Bellamy on Botany in 1972, David has published some 80 papers and 34 books, many for children, with subjects ranging from the boglands of Ireland to the botanical history of America. His programmes have won many national and international awards including the much coveted Richard Dimbleby Award at BAFTA in 1978. President, patron or trustee of numerous conservation and environmental organisations he founded The Conservation Foundation in 1982 and is still its director.

TOM BURKE ▼

Co-author of Green Pages, the Green Capitalists and Ethics, Environment and the Company, Tom Burke has been a professional environmentalist for 19 years. He was executive director of Friends of the Earth and a member of the Executive Committee of the European Environmental Bureau from 1985-91. He served on the Executive Committee of the National Council of Voluntary Organisations from 1984-89 and was a member of the Council of the Royal Society of Arts from 1990-92. In 1992 he became a member of the Overseas Advisory Committee of the Save the Children Fund. He is currently a special adviser to the Secretary of State for the Environment after serving as director of the Green Alliance since 1982. He is a member of the Board of the World Energy Council's Commission, Energy For Tomorrow's World. A Senior Visiting Fellow at Manchester Business School and a Visiting Fellow at the Cranfield Institute of Management he is on the Advisory Committee of the Global Councils of Media Natura and the Earth Centre. Tom was recently invited to become a founding member of the Council of the Institute of Environmental Management.

DAVID PEARCE ▲

Professor of Environmental Economics at University College, London, and Director of the Centre for Social and Economic Research on the Global Environment, David Pearce was educated at Harrow, Oxford (where he read PPE) and LSE. He has lectured in economics at Lancaster and Southampton universities and been Professor of Economics at Aberdeen University. An advisor to several major international companies he has also worked as a consultant all over the world, from the Far East to India, America and Africa and taken part in consulting missions for, among others, the World Bank, the European Commission, the International Union for the Conservation of Nature, date he has written around 200 articles in learned journals and has been editor or co-author of over 30 books.

NIGEL HAIGH ▲

Nigel Haigh studied engineering and practised as a chartered patent agent for ten years before turning to the environment field. He helped to found the European Environment Bureau in 1974, serving as its vice-president from 1975 to 1979. Today he is a director of the Institute for European Environmental Policy, an independent body which informs and guides policy makers and analyses environmental policies in Europe. He is also the author of several books including Manual of Environmental Policy: the EC and Britain, the standard work on the subject. Chairman of the Green Alliance since 1989 he is an Honorary Research Fellow at the Faculty of Law, University College, London and a Visiting Research Fellow at Imperial College Centre for Environmental Technology. He was awarded the OBE in 1992.

◄ HEATHCOTE WILLIAMS

Painter and writer Heathcote Williams is best known for his books, Whale National and Falling For a Dolphin (1988), and Sacred Elephant (1989). With these beautifully written expositions of man's effect on the animal world he reached a huge public and brought much needed media attention to the problems faced by endangered animals. He has several award-winning plays to his credit, has written many screenplays and is also a screen actor.

NOMINATION FORM

I would like to nominate the following person for inclusion in the Best of British Guides 1994.

Name _____

Address _____

_____ Postcode _____

Tel No. (Home) _____ Tel No. (Work) _____

Occupation _____

Category of Nomination

┌────────────────────────────────────┐
│   │
│   │
└────────────────────────────────────┘

Reason for Nomination

Proposer's Name _____

Address _____

_____ Postcode _____

Tel No. (Home) _____ Tel No. (Work) _____

Occupation _____

Signature _____

The area of medicine is a difficult one to research, because of the strictures imposed by the General Medical Council. We feel, however, that there is no reason why the consumer should not be told who is at the top of this or any other field. The people who appear on these pages are not indisputably the best, but their names have been put forward by a broad cross-section of their peers as having achieved a pinnacle of excellence in their chosen areas. The medical profession seems to come in for more and more criticism in the press and in television "insight" programmes, forever pointing out the horrors of medical mistakes and the supposed cover-ups which follow. It is only necessary to look across the Atlantic to see which way this path leads. American medicine is rapidly reaching the stage where every doctor is terrified of taking the smallest risk or performing any experiment for fear of the massive law suit which will inevitably follow and he spends as much of his earnings on professional indemnity insurance as he does with the IRS. Fortunately, we have not yet reached this point in Britain and we hope that common sense will continue to prevail.

There is no doubt, however, that in this as in any other field of endeavour, some people are better than others and here we are pleased to introduced you to some of the best.

OPHTHALMIC SURGEONS (eyes)

Mr Roger Hitchings
Moorfields Eye Hospital
Tel: (0761) 4866987

RHEUMATOLOGISTS

Prof Verna Wright
Leeds University Hospital
Tel: (0532) 431751

ENDOCRINOLOGISTS (glands (pituitary)/hormones)

Prof Howard Jacobs
Middlesex Hospital
Tel: 071- 636 6454

PAEDIATRICS (children)

Prof Albert Aynsley-Green
Newcastle University
Tel: 091-222 6000

CARDIOLOGISTS

Dr Paul Oldershaw
Brompton Chest Hospital
Tel: 071-352 8121

HEART SURGEONS

Sir Magdi Yacoub
Royal Brompton Hospital
Tel: 071-935 3922

GYNAECOLOGISTS

Mr Marcus Setchell
St Bartholomew's Hospital
Tel: 071-601 8888
(Gynaecologist)

Prof Robert Winstone
Hammersmith Hospital
Tel: 081-743 2030
(Infertility Specialists)

NEUROLOGISTS (brain doctors)

Prof C David Marsden
National Hospital of Neurology
Tel: 071-837 3611

BRAIN SURGEONS

Prof Lyndsay Symon
National Hospital of Neurology
Tel: 071-837 3611

LIVER SPECIALISTS

Dr Ronald Zeegan
Westminster Hospital
Tel: 081-746 8106

PSYCHIATRISTS

Sir Michael Rutter
The Maudsley
Tel: 071-703 6333

VASCULAR SURGEONS (veins and arterys)

Prof Roger Greenhalgh
Charing Cross Hospital
Tel: 081-846 1234

DERMATOLOGISTS (skin)

Dr Jeremy Gilkes
Middlesex Hospital
Tel: 071-935 6465

AIDS

Prof Michael Adler
Middlesex Hospital
Tel: 071-935 6465

ENT (ear, nose and throat)

Mr Tony Bull
Ear, Nose and Throat Hospital
Tel: 071-935 3171
(Rhinologist: Nose Reconstruction)

Mr Jonathan Hazell
Middlesex Hospital
Tel: 071-935 0328
(Tinnitus: Ear)

Mr Malcolm Keen
St Bartholomew's Hospital
Tel: 071-224 6249
(Voice)

ORTHOPAEDICS (joints)

Mr Tom Bucknill
St Bartholomew's Hospital
Tel: 071-601 8888
(Knees and Hips)

Mr Jonathon Johnson
Princess Grace Hospital
Tel: 071-486 1234
(Spine)

Mr Paul Aichroth
Wimpole Street
Tel: 071-935 2349
(Knees)

GASTRO-ENTEROLOGISTS (stomach/bowel)

Mr Barry Jackson
St Thomas's Hospital
Tel: 071-928 5485

CANCER

Prof Karol Sikora
Hammersmith Hospital
Tel: 081-743 2030

RE-HAB CLINICS (alcohol and drug addiction)

Robert Lefever
Promis Counselling Centre
Tel: 071-584 6511

THORACIC MEDICINE (chest and lungs)

Prof Peter Barnes
National Heart and Lung Institute
Tel: 071-352 8121
(Asthma)

PLASTIC SURGERY

Mr Freddie Nicolle
Harley Street
Tel: 071-637 9595

TROPICAL DISEASES

Dr Anthony Bryceson
Hospital of Tropical Diseases
Tel: 071-580 2475

KIDNEYS

Dr Laurence Baker
St Bartholomew's Hospital
Tel: 071-580 2475

RAYMOND BROOME ▼

Raymond Broome, who has maintained a private practice in Oxford since 1966, is noted for having developed innovations on peripheral joint technique, a subject on which he has lectured widely in Europe and the USA (he graduated from Palmer College of Chiropractic in Davenport, Iowa, in 1965). He was a part-time lectuer on the Clincial Sciences at the Anglo-European College of Chiropractic from 1967-80, chairman of the Board of Governors 1980-84 and its Clinic Director from 1984-87. He is a member of the British Chiropractic Association, European Chiropractic Union and American Chiropractic Association.

◀ STUART KORTH

The son of Leslie Korth, a well-known pioneer naturopath and osteopath, Stuart graduated from the British School of Osteopathy in 1964 and is in private practice in Tunbridge Wells and London. He was clinic tutor to the British School of Osteopathy from 1972-82 and initiated courses in Applied Technique and Osteopathic Care of Children. He established and directed the Children's Clinic at the European School of Osteopathy and is currently consultant to it. More recently he co-founded the Osteopathic Centre for Children, a revolutionary organisation (and registered charity) which provides subsidised treatment for children, gives post-graduate training to paediatric osteopathy and carries out research into the effectiveness of osteopathy. Since it acquired its own premises in London, the centre has helped to raise public awareness of the broad scope of osteopathy. Married and father of three, Stuart Korth lives in Forest Row, East Sussex.

BRIAN HAMMOND ▼

The letters after Dr Brian Hammond's name reflect his achievements at the Anglo-European College of Chiropractic (DC – winner of Canadian Award for Academic Distinction) and the University of Surrey (PhD for the detection of spondylolysis using lumbar sonography). He has been clinic director of Sutton Chiropractic Clinic in Surrey since 1975 and Governor of the Anglo-European College of Chiropractic from 1976-80, during which time he edited the European Journal of Chiropractic. He has been a member of the BCA since 1975 and the National Back Pain Association since 1977. He is married with three children, lives in Sutton, Surrey, and is a county Master at bridge.

ALAN BREEN ▲

Glasgow-born Alan Breen's early career was destined to be spent in Canada after his parents emigrated there in 1953 when he was nine years old. He graduated from the Canadian Memorial Chiropractic College in Toronto in 1967 and held various clinical posts in Canada, Australia and the UK until 1971. He was senior lecturer in diagnosis, therapeutics and biomechanics at the Anglo-European College of Chiropractic from 1973-82. During that time he conducted epidemiological surveys of chiropractic practice in the UK and initiated a Medical Research Council clinical trial into chiropractic. He has now been Director of Research at the college since 1986 and gained a PhD from the University of Southampton in 1991 for studies into the development of an image-processing radiographic technique for the measurement of vertebral motion in patients. Married with four children, Dr Breen lives in Ringwood, Hampshire.

STEPHEN SANDLER ▶

Stephen Sandler is director of Osteopathic Practice at the British School of Osteopathy, where he is also senior lecturer in Obstetrics and Gynaecology and head of the Expectant Mothers Clinic. He has travelled widely as an authority on these subjects, lecturing in France, Spain, Belgium, Italy, Australia and the former Soviet Union, as well as throughout the UK. He edits the Bodyworks section of the Journal of Alternative and Complementary Medicine, a monthly journal which goes to thousands of practitioners of complementary medicine. Stephen is also tutor of a part-time course for medically qualified doctors. Married with a daughter and two sons, he lives in London.

LAURIE HARTMAN ➤

Laurie Hartman is technique consultant and senior tutor in Osteopathic Technique at the Bristol School of Osteopathy, from which he graduated in 1964. He runs a private practice in Barnet, Hertfordshire, and is the author of The Handbook of Osteopathic Technique (with accompanying video, updated in 1991). He has travelled extensively, teaching "the unique blend of gentle yet specific and effective technique that makes the BSO world-famous". He regularly teaches in Japan, Canada, the USA and Europe and has been visiting lecturer at institutions in France, Belgium, Norway, Denmark and Australia. A martial-arts expert, he teaches (3rd Dan) and is osteopathic consultant to the British Shotokan Karate Association. He is also a consultant to the British Judo Association. Laurie is osteopathic adviser to the International Journal of Alternative and Complementary Medicine. Married and a father of three, he lives in London and manages to find time for hobbies including golf, computers, skiing, flying model helicopters and being a radio ham!

CHRISTOPHER HAYNE ▼

As a chartered physiotherapist specialising in ergonomics and occupational health, Christopher Hayne has been committed for many years to the prevention of injury and disease, particularly of occupational origin. He has worked with the Royal College of Nursing, National Back Pain Association and Prevention Forum. He qualified in 1963 and was awarded a Fellowship of the Chartered Society of Phsyiotherapy in 1977. He became a member of the Ergonomics Soceity the same year and was admitted to the Register of Professional Practitioners in 1985. He is also a member of the Institution of Occupational Safety and Health and the International Commission on Occupational Health. His book, Total Back Care, was published in 1987. For the past two years he has acted as consultant, advising industry and health-care services on current health and safety litigation. He is also visiting lecturer at the Centre for Extension Studies at the University of Loughborough. Married with one daughter, he lives in Beeston, Nottingham.

FRED STREET ▼

Fred Street must be the most familiar face in his profession. When England footballers take their inevitable knocks during international matches, Fred is the man who races on to the field to apply the treatment which commentators insist on reducing to the phrase "the magic sponge". He has clocked up well over 200 games with the England team, including four World Cup campaigns (he is looking forward to a fifth in the USA in 1994). Born in 1933, Fred spent five years in the Royal Air Force as a sergeant physical-training instructor, specialising in the rehabilitation of disabled servicemen. After the RAF he trained as a remedial gymnast and then as a chartered phsyiotherapist, qualifying in 1962. Then came a number of posts in London hospitals, including two years as superintendent at the Medical Rehabilitation Centre. He spent three years as rehabilitation officer at a centre for young epileptics and head-injury victims in Australia. His first job in big-time soccer was as trainer and physiotherapist with Stoke City from 1968-71. He was then "transferred" to Arsenal, where he helped the players through five Cup finals and a European final. It was during his time with the Gunners that he was invited by the Football Association to join the England team staff. A popular character in the game, Fred operates a private practice in Mayfair, London.

NUTRITIONISTS

PROFESSOR ARNOLD BENDER ▲

Professor Arnold Bender gained an honours degree in biochemistry and a PhD at Liverpool and Sheffield Universities, respectively. He is a DSc(Hon) of the University Complutense, Madrid, Hon FRSH, Hon MAPHA and FIFST. Professor Bender spent 20 years in research in the pharmaceutical and food industries and 23 years in academic life. Now retired, he was formerly Professor of Nutrition and Dietetics and Head of the Department of Nutrition at Queen Elizabeth College, University of London. Currently he is MRC Clinical Scientific Staff and Honorary Consultant Physician at Addenbrooke's Hospital, Cambridge.

PROFESSOR IAN ▼ MacDONALD

Professor Ian MacDonald is Emeritus Professor of Applied Physiology at Guy's Hospital, University of London, from which he holds an MD, DSc, PhD, MB, BS and FIBiol. Professor MacDonald has published research on gastric physiology and foetal growth, but his main area of research has been dietary carbohydrate metabolism in humans.

DR JOHN CUMMINGS ▲

After medical studies at the University of Leeds, an MSc in biochemistry at London's Chelsea College and general medical training, Dr John Cummings specialised in gastroenterology, joining the Medical Research Council's Gastroenterology Unit in London in 1970. His early research studies were on prostaglandins and gut functions, followed in 1972 by the start of work on dietary fibre. Dr Cummings transferred to the MRC's Dunn Nutrition Centre in Cambridge in 1975, to continue research on diet and gut diseases.

DR ROBERT GRIMBLE ▲

Having obtained an honours degree in biochemistry and physiology at University College, Cardiff, Dr Robert Grimble was awarded a PhD by the University of Wales for his research into Vitamin C metabolism. After working for the Medical Research Council in Cambridge and Uganda, and doing research at Surrey, he transferred to the University of Southampton, where he is a Senior Lecturer.

DR THOMAS SANDERS ▲

Dr Thomas Sanders graduated in nutrition from Queen Elizabeth College (now King's College), London, in 1971. After voluntary work for UNICEF in Indonesia, he returned to Britain to work as a nutritionist at Kingston Hospital in Surrey. In 1977 he received a PhD from the University of London for research into the health and diet of vegans and vegetarians. In the same year he returned to Queen Elizabeth College as a Rank Prize Funds Fellow, where he became a lecturer in nutrition in 1982. Appointed Reader in Nutrition at King's College in 1991, he continues to teach and carry out research, particularly in the area of diet, fats and cardiovascular disease. Dr Sanders has served on the Council of the Nutrition Society and, among his present offices, he is honorary Nutritional Director of the Family Heart Association. He has co-authored two popular books on diet and published over 100 papers.

PROFESSOR W. P. T. JAMES ▼

Director since 1982 of the Rowett Research Institute, the largest nutritional science institute in the West, Professor W. P. T. James, BSc(Hons), London 1959, MB, BS, MD, was Senior Lecturer in Human Nutrition at the London School of Hygiene and Tropical Medicine before establishing in 1974 the clinical nutrition section of the Medical Research Council's Dunn Nutrition Unit in Cambridge.

PROFESSOR NICHOLAS READ

Following medical studies at Cambridge and London and after general medical training, Professor Nicholas Read, MA, MD, FRCP, became Gastrointestinal Research Fellow in both Sheffield and the USA. In 1978 he joined the University of Sheffield's Department of Physiology, where he has since combined the teaching of physiology, clinical practice as a consultant gastroenterologist and the directorship of an active research programme. Professor Read edits the *Journal of Gastrointestinal Motility,* has edited several books and has written over 250 papers on gastrointestinal physiology and pathophysiology, half of which relate to nutrition.

DR MARTIN WISEMAN

After completing his medical studies at London's Guy's Hospital Medical School in 1975, Dr Martin Wiseman held clinical medical posts in Southampton, Guildford, Bournemouth, Sheffield and the Westminster Hospital until 1980. He was then Research Fellow in Diabetes at Guy's Medical School from 1981 to 1986, and since 1981 has been Clinical Assistant in Diabetes at Croydon's Mayday Hospital. Dr Wiseman is currently Head of the Department of Health's Nutrition Unit. In 1991 he won the Caroline Walker award.

DR DAVID BUSS

Dr David Buss received his BSc and PhD in chemistry from the University of Bristol. He then held two research fellowships in the USA, before working from 1965 to 1971 for the Southwest Research Foundation of San Antonio, Texas, researching into lactation and infant growth in non-human primates. Since 1971 he has been Head of the Nutrition Branch of the Ministry of Agriculture, Fisheries and Food in London. Dr Buss is concerned with nutritional aspects of food policy in Britain and Europe; the nutritional value of food; dietary habits in Britain and factors that affect them; and the provision of scientific advice to government, non-government organisations and consumers. He has published over 100 papers on human nutrition, the British diet and the nutritional value of food, as well as number of books.

DR ROGER WHITEHEAD

Director of the Medical Research Council's Dunn Nutrition Unit, in Cambridge, Dr Roger Whitehead, CBE, is also the Vice-Master and a Fellow of Darwin College, University of Cambridge. He is the immediate past President of the Nutrition Society and is a member of various government committees, including the Food Advisory Committee, which advises the Ministry of Agriculture, Fisheries and Food. He was also chairman of a 1991 panel forming part of the Committee on Medical Aspects of Food Policy (COMA). Dr Whitehead has received a number of honours and prizes, including the 1983 UNESCO Science Prize for outstanding contributions to scientific and technical development in developing countries, and the 1990 British Nutrition Foundation Prize. He is also an Honorary Member of the Royal College of Physicians and the British Paediatric Association, and a Fellow of the Institute of Biology. In 1992 he was awarded the CBE.

ALTERNATIVE THERAPY

LEON CHAITOW ▼

Born in South Africa Leon Chaitow came to the UK in 1956 after matriculation. He graduated from the British College of Naturopathy and Osteopathy in 1960 and set up a private practice in Worthing in 1966 which he ran until 1983. He studied acupuncture under Dr Jacques Lavier of Paris in 1963 and cranial osteopathy with Denis Brookes from 1969 to 1978. He was a founder member of the Cranial Osteopathic Association and a director of post-graduate studies at the British Naturopathic and Osteopathic Association from 1980 to 1983. He became the first director of the Thera Trust in 1989. He was a visiting scholar at the Los Angeles College of Chiropractic between 1985 and 1988 and a visiting lecturer at the National College of Chiropractic, Chicago, the Palmer College of Chiropractice, Iowa, the Israeli College of Natural Health Sciences, Tel Aviv. He is a member of the Israeli College and the advisory board of the Bastyr College of Natural Health Sciences, in Seattle.

HARALD GAIER ▶

Harald Gaier has a DO from the International College of Osteopathy, an ND from the Naturopathic College of SA, and an MD (Hon) from the SA Faculty of Homoeopathy Medicine. He became a state-registered practitioner in SA and in 1985 was awarded a fellowship by the SA Homoeopathic Association for outstanding achievements in homoeopathy. In January 1987 he was invited to address the Royal Society of Medicine. He is currently a director of professional education at the Letchworth Centre for Homoeopathy and Complementary Medicine, and editor of the Journal of Alternative and Complementary Medicine. He has a private osteopathic and naturopathic practice at the Hale Clinic.

JAN DE VRIES ▲

After leaving pharmacy, in which he qualified in Holland in 1959, Jan de Vries studied homoeopathy in Switzerland where he met his future partner Alfred Vogel, the world famous nature cure practitioner. Together they set up the first nature cure clinic in Holland. From Switzerland he moved to Germany to study osteopathy, then back to Holland to study naturopathy and then to China to learn about acupuncture. He holds diplomas in all these therapies. Today Jan has seven clinics, two in London, one in Newcastle, one in Preston, one in Belfast, one in Holland and one in Troon, Scotland, where he now lives.

◄ ROBERT TISSERAND

Robert Tisserand has been a lifelong student of essential oils and a pioneer in the work of training aromatherapists. His book, The Art of Aromatherapy, published in 1977, was the first book on aromatherapy in the English language and has become a definitive work, reprinted 12 times and translated into seven languages. Robert trained himself in the use of essential oils, studying massage and then gleaning knowledge from books, courses and seminars on how to combine the oils with massage techniques. The Tisserand Institute, of which he is head, is now a leading training establishment for aromatherapists and is a member of the Aromatherapy Organisations Council. Essential oils and proudcts carrying the Tisserand name are marketed by Aromatherapy Products Ltd, with Robert as consultant. With the boom in interest in essential oils turnover now tops £1 million. Editor of the International Journal of Aromatherapy Robert is founder of The Aromatic Oil Company.

PROFESSOR (DR) HARRY ▼ HOWELL

Harry Howell began his professional career as a hypnotherapist. He continued formal training in psychology and psychotherapy. He took training in biochemistry and clinical nutrition at St Bartholomew's Hospital and a doctorate in Health Education at Harley University, London. Since then he has studied homoeopathy, acupuncture, colon therapies, manual lymph drainage, kinesiology, lasertherapy, tropical medicine, mycology and Ayurvedic. He set up the first Candida Clinic in the world in 1982, and has worked in hospitals in the Indian sub-continent and lectured in hospitals and countries worldwide. Until 1991 he practised in London at the Hale Clinic and in Harley Street. He is currently president of the National Guild of Clinical Nutritionists, president of the British Association of Lymph and Colon Therapists and Dean of the British Academy of Tropical Medicine. Last year he was elected Physician Of The Year by the IMC and received the Dag Hammarsjold Award.

ALTERNATIVE THERAPY

◄ JAMES SNEDDON

After leaving school James Sneddon trained at the Glasgow School of Natural Therapeutics before joining his father, the famous naturopath James Russell Sneddon at his practice, The Buckingham Clinic in Glasgow. Since his father's death in 1974 James has been principal of The Buckingham, one of the longest established clinics in Britain, where he is head of a team of practitioners covering a wide range of complementary therapies from osteopathy and naturopathy to acupuncture, phsyiotherapy, herbalism and homoeopathy. In treating patients practitioners use the full range of these therapies as well as the latest in electro-medical technology.

DR SIR PETER GUY MANNERS ▲

Dr Sir Peter Guy Manners qualified in England and Germany with medical degrees specialising in osteopathy and natural and electro-magnetic medicines. He has been researching the use of cymatics and bio-magnetics for medical diagnosis and treatment for some 30 years, studying the healing effects of sound vibrations and harmonies on the structure and chemistry of the human body, and the importance of sound and light in our environment as principles of periodicity in the human organism. He has lectured at the World Health Organisation worldwide. He holds the Dag Hammarskjold Merit of Excellence from the Academie Diplomatique, De La Paix, and the Diploma of Honour in bio-energetic medicine, Moscow. He is currently director of Bretforton Hall Clinic in Worcestershire.

DR ROYSTON LOW ▼

Dr Low is one of the leading lights in acupuncture in Britain. He has practised as a registered ostepath for over 40 years and, originally studying with Dr Lavier, has practised as an acupuncturist for over 30 years. He was one of a small group of eminent practitioners who were invited to study acupuncture in China as guests of the Chinese government in 1975. He is a past president of the British Acupuncture Association, Dean of the British College of Acupuncture, founding governor and senior lectuer of the Anglo-Dutch College of Acupuncture, Dean of the National College of Acupuncture of Ireland and chairman of the Acupuncture Research Association. In 1982 he was awarded the certificate of Most Outstanding Teacher of Traditional Chinese Acupuncture by the Academy of Oriental Heritage in Vancouver. He is the author of numerous articles and seven seminal text books on acupuncture.

PETER MOLE ▼

Peter Mole read modern history at Oxford and became a licentiate of acupuncture at the College of Traditional Acupuncture, Leamington Spa, in 1978. He set up a private practice at the Oxford Acupuncture Centre in 1978 and became a bachelor of acupuncture at Leamington Spa in 1981. From 1983 to 1986 he was a faculty member at the College, becoming a master of acupuncture in 1984 and a senior faculty member from 1986 to 1992. A member of the Steering Committee of the Council of Complementary and Alternative Medicine from 1986 to 1991 he is currently a member of the Steering Committee of the Council for Acupuncture. He was a member of the Scientific Sub-Committee Research Council of Complementary Medicine from 1988 to 1990, a member of the Executive Council of the British Holistic Medical Association from 1989 to 1990, and president of the Traditional Acupuncture Society from 1989 to 1992. He is currently vice-chairman of the Traditional Acupuncture Society and Dean of Studies at the College of Integrated Chineses Medicine in Reading. He published Acupuncture: Energy Balancing For Body, Mind and Spirit in 1992.

PETER FIREBRACE ▼

Peter Firebrace, BAc, MIROM, studied homoeopathy and herbal medicine before going on to study acupuncture at the International College of Oriental Medicine. He taught at the College from 1983 and was it s principal from 1985 to 1990, instigating extensive curriculum development. During this time he set up the International Register of Oriental Medicine (UK), and became its first chairman. He was a founder member of the British Acupuncture Accreditation Board, helping to formulate a common core curriculum for acupuncture colleges. Since 1985 he has organised eminars in London on Chinese Medicine from the Classics with the Ricci Institute and European School of Acupuncture (Paris), and in 1989 he co-founded Monkey Press to publish the transcripts of this series. In 1988 he co-authored New Ways to Health: A Guide To Acupuncture (Hamlyn). IN 1991 he co-founded the Orientation Oriental Medicine Clinic and workshop programme in London. He has made extensive studies of classical Chinese concepts and terminology with a particular interest in their application to alternative perceptions of health and disease.

MICHAEL McINTYRE ▲

Michael McIntyre completed a four-year training in herbal medicine with the National Institute of Medical Herbalists in 1980 and the following year went to Nanjing to study acupuncture. In 1985 he completed another course in Chinese herbal medicine and returned to Nanjing in 1987 to study herbal medicine. He is co-founder and principal of the School of Chinese Herbal Medicine and president of the National Institute of Medical Herbalists. He is also a member of the Register of Chinese Herbal Medicine and the Register of Traditional Chinese Medicine. He is the author of two books on herbal medicine and, together with his wife, runs a busy herbal and acupuncture practice.

JONATHAN MONCKTON ▼

After a short spell in the army Jonathan Monckton worked with an international medical charity, spending a year at their headquarters in Rome. In 1975 he returned to England to the Benedictine monastery at Worth where he trained to be a Catholic priest. He spent four years studying philosphy and theology at Allen Hall before becoming ordained in 1980. For seven years he was active in the school, spending four years as head teacher in the junior school. He then worked in London for two years before deciding to leave the priesthood. In 1989 he was appointed director of the Research Council For Complementary Medicine.

KEN SHIFRIN ▲

Ken Shifrin emigrated from the US to Britain in 1970. He graduated from the College of Traditional Acupuncture in Leamington Spa in 1977 and received his master of Acupuncture qualification in 1981. He then joined the College as a faculty member and began his political work. He was closely involved in creating the Council For Acupuncture and had a major role in developing the Codes of Ethics and Practice. He has held the posts of chairman and president of the Traditional Acupuncture Society and was a founding member of the Council For Complementary and Alternative Medicine. He has been the Council's chairman since 1988. He helped initiate the formation of the British Acupuncture Accreditation Board.

DAVID LORIMER ▼

David Lorimer was born in Scotland and educated at St Andrew's and Cambridge universities. He became director of the educational charity Scientific and Medical Network in 1986 – an informal international group consisting mainly of qualified scientists and doctors concerned with widening the horizons of science and medicine beyond a materialistic and reductionist approach. David published Survival? Body Mind And Death In The Light Of Psychic Experience in 1989 and Whole In One – The Near Death Experience and the Ethic of Interconnectedness in 1990.

GIOVANNI MACIOCIA ▼

Giovanni Maciocia studied economics at Naples University before coming to England to take a degree in acupuncture at the International College of Oriental Medicine in East Grinstead. He received a herbalism diploma at the National Institute of Medical Herbalists in 1977 and followed this trainig with several courses in traditional Chinese medicine and advanced acupuncture in Nanjing. Since the mid-1970s he has been in private practice as an acupuncturist and Chinese herbalist. He is also an acupuncturist at the Imperial College of Science and Technology Health Centre in London and an honorary lecturer at the Nanjing College of Traditional Chinese medicine. He has lectured worldwide and presented hundreds of seminars on acupuncture and Chinese methods of treating illness. He taught himself Chinese in order to read ancient and modern Chinese medical books and articles. He has published several books: Tongue Diagnosis in Chinese Medicine (1987, East Press (USA)); The Foundations of Chinese Medicine (1989, Churchill Livingstone, Edinburgh), now a textbook used by all the major acupuncture colleges in England, the US, Belgium, Holland Norway, Chinese Medicine: The Treatment of Diseases With Acupuncture and Chinese Herbs comes out this year.

ALTERNATIVE THERAPY

DR PETER MANSFIELD ▲

Peter Mansfield graduated in medicine from Cambridge and London in 1968. After a research fellowship in community medicine at University College Hospital Medical School he chose general practice as the best opportunity to study people and cultivate health. He founded a practice in London's East End before settling in Lincolnshire in 1976, where he founded an NHS practice based on nutrition, homoeopathy, osteopathy and counselling in which pharmaceutical costs declined drastically. In 1980 he founded Templegarth Trust, a charity devoted to researching the nature of health and developing a true health service. This led to Good Healthkeeping, in 1990, a prototype health service still doing extremely well despite recession. The Trust is beginning a four-year research programme entitled Gold Standards For Health, to identify and evaluate quantifiable measures of personal health. Dr Mansfield is the author of several books including Chemical Children (with Dr Jean Monro) and The Good Health Handbook. He was adviser to New Health and Living magazines and presented the ITV series The Health Experiment. he was founding president (now vice-president) of Doctors In Britain Against Animal Experiments and is president of the National Pure Water Association.

DR ANDREW H LOCKIE ▲

Born in Glasgow and brought up in the countryside of the central Lowlands of Scotland Andrew Lockie graduated in medicine from Aberdeen University before moving to London and gaining his membership to the Faculty of Homoeopathy after studying at the Royal London Homoeopathic Hospital. After a short spell in practice he gained his MRCGP, Dip Obst RCOG and Family Planning Certificate working in the Oxford region and the New Forest. In 1978 he started his first homoeopathic practice in Ealing before moving to Guildford where he still practises. He is the author of the best-selling The Family Guide To Homoeopathy and co-author of the recently published The Women's Guide To Homoeopathy, both published by Hamish Hamilton. He is currently information officer for the Faculty of Homoeopathy and a regular broadcaster on radio and TV.

DR BARRY ROSE ▲

Dr Rose has practised homoeopathy for more than 20 years. After training at Manchester University Medical School he won a Nuffield Practitioner Award which enabled him to gain further experience in gynaecology, obstetrics and paediatrics. He qualified as a doctor in 1959. In 1981 he was elected president of The Faculty of Homoeopathy of Great Britain and appointed executive Dean in 1986, a post that he still holds and in which he oversees the training of conventionally trained doctors in homoeopathic medicine. He is a Fellow of the Faculty of Homoeopathy, and in addition to teaching homoeopathy he acts as an examiner for the Faculty's Membership examination, one of the few world-recognised post-graduate qualifications in homoeopathic medicine. Dr Rose is the National vice-president for the UK on the International Homoeopathic League. Since 1964 he has worked in a general practice in Cheshire, treating patients with both conventional and homoeopathic medicine.

STEPHEN GORDON

Born in Cornwall in 1949 Stephen emigrated to New Zealand when he was ten years old and returned to the UK in 1972. He gained a diploma in osteopathy at the College of Osteopaths in 1978 and then enrolled to study homoeopathy at the pioneering College of Homoeopathy. Following graduation and entry to the Society of Homoeopaths' register he moved to East Anglia and has practised homoeopathy full-time ever since.

DR D K OWEN

D K Owen qualified from the Royal London Medical School in 1982 and since 1983 has been working full-time in complementary health care with a special interest in homoeopathy, nutrition and allergies, magnetic therapy and acupuncture. He has his own practice, which brings together a skilled team of therapists treating a huge variety of patients and illnesses.

DR PETER FISHER ▼

Dr Fisher is a consultant physician at the Royal London Homoeopathic Hospital and a lecturer in rheumatology and complementary medicine at St Bartholomew's Hospital Medical College, London, the first such appointment at a British medical school. He is also editor of the British Homoeopathic Journal, the leading international journal of homoeopathy. He became interested in homoeopathy early in his medical career, attending the Faculty of Homoeopathy's six month full-time course in homoeopathy soon after graduating in medicine from Cambridge, and passing the MFHom (member of the Faculty of Homoeopathy) exam in 1976. He has published a number of scientific papers in leading journals, including the British Medical Journal and regularly lectures at both medical and public meetings.

DR PETER DAVIES ▼

Before becoming a student of homoeopathy in London in 1981 Peter Davies studied engineering at Cambridge, and then took a PhD in biomedical engineering at McGill University. He was information manager at the Institute for Complementary Medicine from 1982 to 1987, a senior research Fellow at St Mary's Hospital Medical School from 1987 to 1989. He is currently research director of Clinical Audit and chairman of the Management Committee at the Marylebone Centre Trust, Regent's College, London. He is consultant to and a member of AAH Meditel's Design Advisory Group, trustee and vice-chairman of the Research Council for Complementary Medicine and a member of the Scientific Committee of Blackie Foundation.

DR ROGER LICHY ▲

Dr Lichy held various hospital posts in obstetrics, neonatology and paediatrics and was an NHS general practitioner for six years until, frustrated by not being able to help people sufficiently with conventional medicine he turned to homoeopathy in 1981. He became a classical homoeopath and studied at Cornwall College from 1982-84 for a Diploma in Humanistic Psychology. He was a co-founder of the Penzance Natural Health Centre and the Truro Natural Health Centre in 1984. From 1984-85 he worked as a medical officer at the Bristol Cancer Help Centre. He has a special interest in childbirth and uses homoeopathy as an effective alternative to hospital obstetric intervention, enabling many women to deliver safely at home. He encourages waterbirth as a method of relieving labour pain and is currently writing a book on the subject.

DR FRANCIS TREUHERZ

Director of the Society of Homoeopaths Dr Treuherz also edits the Society's journal. He lectures in London, Manchester and Helsinki, and is an avid collector of information relating to homoeopathy.

DR PATRICK C PIETRONI ▼

Dr Pietroni is an associate regional adviser with the British Postgraduate medical Federation, a council member of the Royal College of General Practitioners and a member of the Medicines Commission. He is a founder member and past chairman of the British Holistic Medical Association, set up in 1983, and is a practising Jungian analyst. He is principal of an NHS health centre which, as part of a research project, incorporates complementary therapies, audit, community outreach and education and self-help programmes. As a result of this research work the Marylebone Centre Trust was set up in 1988 to promote and develop the experimental work of the health centre with education and training programmes, the aim being to encourage similar models of health care within the NHS.

◀ DR DAVID PETERS

David Peters graduated from Manchester University in 1972 and then trained in homoeopathic medicine at Glasgow Homoeopathic Hospital before becoming medical officer at Camphill Rudolph Steiner School in Aberdeen in 1976. In the late 1970s he trained as a GP and in 1982 joined an NHS family practice which used complementary therapies. He became a GP trainer, then lecturer in general practice at St Mary's Medical School, London. In 1986 he qualified as an osteopath and joined the clinical team in the experimental Marylebone Health Centre as senior research fellow to research and develop osteopathic and stress management programmes for NHS practice. he is currently chair of the British Holistic Medical Association. He has written widely on the application of holistic approaches in medical education, patient care, staff support and organisational health. He lives on a houseboat in West London with his wife and three young sons.

DR JULIAN JESSEL-KENYON ▶

Dr Julian Jessel-Kenyon is co-director of the Centre for the Study of Complementary Medicine in Southampton and London, and director of the Dove Healing Trust, a project through which he is researching the scientific basis of subtle energies believed to underlie many traditional forms of healing. The team involved in this work is drawn from the disciplines of biology, electronics, physics and mathematics. The first part of Julian's career was in ENT surgery and he completed an MD on the development of the human typanum, awarded from Liverpool University in 1978. After a short period as a principal in general practice he went into full-time complementary medical private practice. He has published 12 books, some medical text books and some written for the lay public. He has edited several books and has written many scientific papers on complementary medicine

WILLIAM CASH ▶

The Conservative MP for Stafford since 1984 and a solicitor since 1967, William Cash is also legal adviser to the Council on Complementary and Alternative Medicine and joint chairman of the Parliamentary Group for Complementary and Alternative Medicine. He was vice-chairman of the Conservative Small Business Bureau (1984-89) and the Conservative Constitutional Committee on Financial Services (1985-87). He was a member of the Standing Committee on Financial Services (1985-86), on Banking (1986-87) and Broadcasting (1989). He is currently chairman of the Backbench Committee on European Affairs and the All Party Committee on European Legislation and the Select Committee on Employment. He has been director of the Ironbridge Gorge Museum Trust since 1980. *Photograph by Peter Rogers.*

and on the scientific bases of subtle energies. he was the founder chairman of the British Medical Acupuncture Society in 1980.

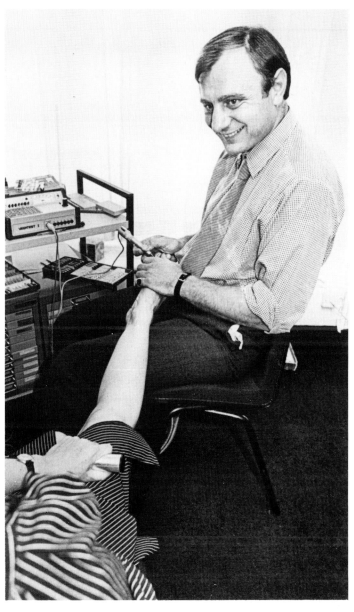

DR GEORGE LEWITH ▶

George Lewith qualified in medicine in 1974, having trained at Trinity College, Cambridge, where he took a biochemistry degree and at Westminster Hospital, London. He became a member of the Royal College of Physicians in 1977 and a member of the Royal College of General Practitioners in 1980. After several jobs as a senior house officer and registrar in general medicine, he entered general practice and became a lecturer in primary medical care at the University of Southampton in 1979. Two years previously he had taken a three-month course in acupuncture at the Nanjing College of Traditional Chinese Medicine. In 1982, with Julian Kenyon, he established the Centre For The Study of Complementary Medicine in Southampton with the aim of providing a clinical service, a research base and a teaching institution. Dr Lewith has been involved in many areas of research, the most important of which is the development of clinical trial methodology for complementary medicine, a research endeavour which has resulted in over 50 publications. He has also written and edited a number of books on acupuncture, clinical ecology, clinical research methods and homoepathy.

CANON CHRISTOPHER PILKINGTON ▶

Canon Pilkington and his wife Pat set up the Cancer Help Centre in Bristol in 1980 with Penny Brohn. Penny has now retired from the Centre to pursue her career in teaching and writing, but Pat and Christopher are still there, working in an honorary capacity. Before working at the Centre Canon Pilkington served in several parishes in Worcestershire and at Bristol Parish Church. It was his profound belief in the ministry of healing that led to his becoming involved in the Centre.

BRUCE WOLF ▼

Bruce Wolf owns and runs the Oasis Fitness Centre, probably the country's leading health and fitness club, with 25,000 sq ft, and 2,500 members. Born in 1949, Bruce started in the music industry and built up the Rock Dreams chain of record shops. He established Rumours Cocktail Bar in 1978, and expanded it by opening a private squash club. The study of health and fitness trends in America led him to convert this into the Oasis. It is his aim to expand this business, promoting his ideas of preventative health care, and to raise the awareness of people to the benefits of health and fitness.

◄ JOHN TREHARNE

Born in 1954, and a qualified accountant, John Treharne represented England and Sussex at squash, and was the British racketball champion for three years. With these combined talents, John joined the Coral Leisure Group as an area manager, with specific responsibility for the development of commercial squash clubs. Whilst the business was very successful, John became frustrated by the limited market targeted by squash – largely male 20-35 – and set up his own consultancy company to develop the other aspects of fitness and leisure as well as squash. The expansion of the target markets of his client clubs was dramatic and, in 1988, John bought a run down squash and tennis club in Hove, which in January 1990, he launched as the Dragon Health & Leisure Club. The club has been extremely successful, and in 1992, a second was opened near Guildford. A third club is scheduled for 1993.

GEORGE EVANS ▲

George Cameron Evans is arguably Scotland's most highly respected leisure professional. After five years as a PE teacher, he moved into Leisure Management in 1983, and was immediately involved in the design and launch of a £5.5m Galleon Leisure Centre, the first of its kind in Scotland. In 1989 George was headhunted to set up what has become Scotland's most prestigious Leisure Club, Parklands, catering to top professional sportsmen and women as well as lesser mortals. George plays squash, golf off a single figure handicap and is a scuba instructor. A man who truly preaches what he practises.

GORDON THOMSON

Gordon Thomson joined the Ballet Rambert in 1970, and studied there for three years, followed by a further year at the London Contemporary Dance Theatre. In 1974 he danced in the opera ballet at Glyndebourne. In the late 1970s, he enrolled as sports and pilates trainer on a cruise liner, and the pilates technique has dominated his career ever since. In 1979 he opened his own pilates studio within the London Contemporary Dance Theatre School and, in 1981, his own studio at the Urdary Academy School of Dance. Ten years after opening at the Urdary, he moved into his own independent premises in South Kensington, serving a wide range of devoted clients. He has recently opened a new studio off Sloane Square. Gordon sees the future in adapting and combining the Finnish Mekostenon technique with pilates.

IAN MAHONEY

Heading the management team at the prestigious Cannon Sports Club is director Ian Mahoney After acquiring a PE degree, Ian became a further education lecturer in physical and health education, but later decided on a career in the leisure industry. He joined Australian Olympian athlete Ron Clark, the managing director of Cannon Sports Clubs, in 1983. Ian is a keen and accomplished sportsman, a triathlete, Channel relay swimmer and marathon runner, and still acts as an aerobics instructor at his club.

BRYCE TAYLOR

Bryce Taylor is the founder director of the Oasis Fitness Centre in Marlow, Bucks, one of the largest and most successful health and fitness clubs in Britain. In 1989 he launched LA Fitness plc, to develop a chain of distinctively branded health and fitness clubs in the UK. Bryce started as a professional squash player, rising to be junior champion in his native New Zealand. In 1981 he became coach/manager to Phil Kenyon, who became British champion, and to Susan Devoy, from 1982-89. Under his tutelage Sue won six consecutive British and two world titles.

PETER HARRISON

Peter Harrison graduated BEd(Hons) from Exeter University in 1983, and spent 1½ years teaching French and PE before moving to be manager of a luxury health club in London and, three years later, to be in charge of overall company development within the group. He set up his own consultancy company, Lifestyle, initially involved in the design, building and operation of health and leisure clubs, expanding into corporate hospitality, leisure recruitment and customer service training. In 1991 he fulfilled his major ambition by opening his own club, the Presidents Health & Fitness Club, in Taunton, which he operates alongside Lifestyle.

PETER RAINSFORD ▼

Born in Liverpool in 1952, Peter Rainsford studied piano at the Royal Northern College of Music. He is an examiner at the Guildhall School of Music, Chairman of the Liverpool branch of the Incorporated Society of Musicians and currently holds the position of Director of the Wirral School of Music. In 1979, inspired by a tour of Russian schools, Peter set up the Tafelmusik organisation, specialising in teaching musical skills to children between the ages of one and nine. Various games and activities are specifically designed to enable a child to understand and enjoy the language of music and, over the years, thousands of children have benefited from the Tafelmusik approach. Peter spends much of his time training teachers in the Tafelmusik approach, visiting schools and giving concerts.

DAVID CADOGAN ▼

After completing a degree course in visual studies, David Cadogan determined to enter the commercial art world as a children's muralist. The main attraction of this medium was the chance to use colour on a large "canvas" and to be able to transform a child's room into something special and unique. Having completed commissions in America, David spent six months in Japan, where he studied traditional art techniques, though these influences rarely enter his work today. Instead, he is usually asked to produce popular children's characters and is noted for his ability to copy detail and colour. In recent years he has also started using a smaller "canvas", painting designs on children's furniture, and now offers the full "room service". This combination has attracted a great deal of attention at exhibitions and fairs.

DAVID GODFREY-FAUSSET ▲

After many years spent farming in both Devon and Cornwall, David Godfrey-Fausset and his family moved to France, where he divided his time between restoring and letting property and photography. On returning to Devon in the mid-1980s, David opened his first studio in Exeter, swiftly followed by a second in Truro. In the studios a cross-section of people were photographed, with no particular bias to any age group. However, children began to dominate more and more his photography and, during the last few years, he has specialised in classical black and white child photography, now printed closely to resemble drawings. David photographs all his child portraits in the home, using the same equipment as in the studio, but giving the child the benefit of being in his or her house.

PETER MEADOWS

While travelling through India and Pakistan in the early 1980s, Peter Meadows and his wife Lotte were overwhelmed by the beauty of the Hunza Valley and, on their return, named their high fashion children's clothing business after it. Peter started Hunza from a basement in London in 1983. The company became a massive success within two years and now 80 per cent of its output is exported throughout Europe. He travels widely in India and Bali, gaining inspiration for his highly individual ranges, of which over 50 per cent are manufactured in the UK. He also played an important role in the development of the fabric Lycra, which is now used extensively worldwide.

PHILIP DAVIES AND NIGEL RAGG

Philip Davies and Nigel Ragg met in 1982, when they were both working for Club Mark Warner in the French Alps. In the following year they founded Quest Adventure, a schools travel company specialising in ski courses and outdoor adventure. They built Quest into a highly successful school travel company before selling to the Granada group in 1987. In 1990 Philip and Nigel left Granada to start Crechendo which, in just two years, has become the leading activity programme in London for the under fives, providing play gyms and children's parties for pre-school children at 15 centres across London. The company now caters for over 1,200 children a week and has more than 3,000 members.

BILL COSGRAVE

The founder of and technical consultant to Tumble Tots, Bill Cosgrave started life as an orphaned war baby. He served in the Army Physical Training Corps and, for 12 years, was an Olympic gymnastics coach. He spent two years working in the Middle East to earn the money to start Tumble Tots, and opened his first gym with sunken foam pits in 1979. In 1982 he redesigned the equipment for portable use in village halls and, in 1984, sold the company to the Jack Chia Group. Today, Tumble Tots has over 100 franchisees in the UK alone, and caters for over 60,000 children from crawling to school age. Bill has trained well over 2,000 Tumble Tots leaders and conducts regular national technical workshops. He defines the activities of Tumble Tots as "building children from the inside".

DAVID GRAFF

David Charles Children's Wear was founded by David Graff and his wife Susan in 1970 and has become one of England's leading children's outfitters. Exports now account for 75 per cent of the turnover and, in 1990, the company won the British Apparel Export Award. David is a keen traveller and his conservation interests have taken him trekking into the high Himalayas, through the rain forests of Brazil and across Patagonia. Other interests include sculpture and classic cars and he is currently working on a new travelogue.

RICHARD HAYES

The Society of Motor Manufacturers and Traders' first award for furthering the cause of road safety for children was presented to Richard Hayes at the 1992 Motor Show. As Road Safety Officer for Southend Borough Council, Richard encourages schools to instigate experiments so that children can learn good practice for themselves. A salesman from the age of 15, Richard's philosophy in road safety is "if you can't interest them, you can't sell it to them". Among the equipment he uses in his lectures are wooden cars. The children have to design and make seats and seat belts for the cars which are strong enough to stop eggs from breaking.

LESLIE HAYTER

Although 72 years old and having to use an invalid chair to get around, Leslie Hayter can often be seen in Spalding with his litter bag and litter picking stick. This year, for the first time, Leslie was able to take part in the National Spring Clean, spending all day picking up litter, in his chair, on 20 acres of land in the centre of Spalding. Leslie received a National Commendation Certificate in the 1992 Queen Mother's Birthday Awards – the premier award programme of Tidy Britain Group.
Photograph by Lincolnshire Free Press

GEORGE WINGFIELD

1992 was the first year of the Britain's Favourite Plumber competition. Nominations from the Institute of Plumbing requested the public to list the attributes they felt to be most important in a true professional plumber and then say why they felt their plumber should be nominated. The six regional winners were picked on their technical knowledge, their business approach and their customer care policies. George Wingfield was the overall winner. He began his plumbing career in 1963, serving a five year apprenticeship, before undertaking research work for the Electricity Council Research Centre and working as a marine plumber for P&O. He set up his own company in 1973. He received the award for his outstanding domestic, commercial and industrial work.

USHI VITHANI ➡

Ushi and his cousin Varsha Vithani won Britain's Newsagent of the Year award for 1992, sponsored by the Daily Mail in association with Retail Newsagent. Ushi was born in Kenya and came to England when he was 16 years old. He trained as an accountant and worked in the field until the desire to be his own boss led to the purchase of a lease on a shop in Thamesmead, London. The Front Page opened in 1986. A philosophy of personal service, a spotless environment and products constantly updated to current trends, all have helped bring about its great success.

COLIN DEAN ▼

Fifty-four year old Colin Dean from Brotherton in West Yorkshire has been a milkman for 17 years. He was awarded Britain's Best Milkman for 1992 by Me magazine for services to the community. A tireless organiser who is "always ready to help anyone with anything", Colin organises luncheon clubs, pantomimes and transport to functions for the elderly and disabled, is a church warden and serves on the parish hall committee. He also produces theatrical shows for kids and organises sequence dancing. "This is a lucky village to have such a friend," said his nominator.

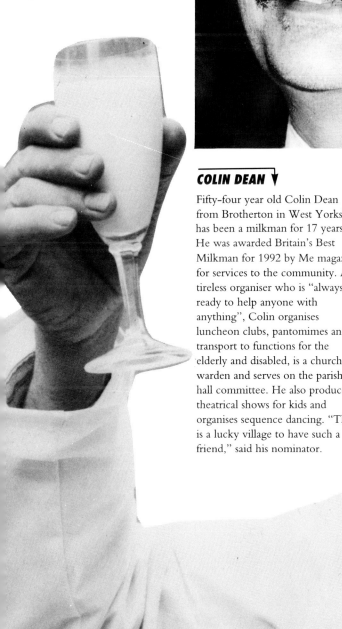

THOMAS WHELAN

Firefighter Thomas Whelan, who is based at Whitechapel Fire Station in London's East End, showed exceptional bravery when called to an incident at nearby Watney Street. Two workmen were trapped, unconscious, in black slurry at the bottom of a four metre deep manhole. Despite severely cramped conditions Thomas, who was at that time a probationary firefighter with only nine months' service, extricated the first. However, as he was attaching the other workman to a line he discovered a third, completely submerged. Acting rapidly, he freed the man's upper torso from the slurry, and secured both men to lines so that they could be pulled out. Finally, he searched for more bodies before emerging. Sadly, despite his prompt action and the efforts of on-site medical teams, none of the rescued men survived their ordeal.

ALAN THOMAS

Alan Thomas, coxswain of the Tenby lifeboat was awarded the RNLI's silver medal for bravery following a dramatic resuce of three fishermen. Said Mike Vlasto, inspector of lifeboats for the West Division: "It required considerable courage, determination and exceptional boat handling ability to carry out this service. The coxswain's quick thinking when Silver Stream was virtually capsized undoubtedly saved the skipper's life." It was thanks to Alan's boat handling skill, in a force 9 gale and 30ft breaking seas, that the rescue team managed to get close enough to pluck the skipper to safety through the wheelhouse window where he was trapped by loose gear on deck.

Photograph courtesy of the RNLI

STEVE BROOK

Good samaritan taxi driver Steve Brook was presented with the Courtesy Award at Motorshow 92, an award which is in recognition of the most outstanding service to the public by an employee of an acknowledged motoring organisation. Prestigious though this award undoubtedly is, it is of scant comfort to Steve who, while going to the aid of a woman motorist whose car had broken down, was ploughed into by a drunken driver and will remain in a wheelchair for the rest of his life. Despite the fact that, at the time of writing, Steve has been unable to work and has received no compensation, he is remarkable for his lack of bitterness.

JAMES DOUGAL ▼

For his iniative, skill and bravery in a rescue carried out in a hurricane off the Scottish coast, James Dougal received the RNLI's silver medal, the second highest award for bravery bestowed on a lifeboatman. James, assistant mechanic at Eyemouth lifeboat, took command of the lifeboat in the absence of the coxswain and second coxswain. He controlled it at some of the most critical moments of the mission: leaving Eyemouth harbour where 20ft seas met the team head on, keeping the boat in position while the survivors were pulled to safety and bringing the lifeboat safely to Burnmouth during a power cut.
Photograph courtesy of the RNLI

◀ JEFFREY SIMPSON

A nine-year-old boy fell through the ice into the Thames at London's Shadwell Basin while trying to rescue his dog. He was clinging to a small boat moored some 30 metres from the Basin's wall when a fire crew from Shadwell arrived on the scene with a pump ladder. One of the crew, firefighter Jeffrey Simpson, volunteered to attempt to rescue the boy unaided. Despite crashing through the ice, he extricated himself and pressed on undeterred. At length he was able to help the boy into the safety of the boat, which was then towed to the edge of the Basin. For his courage, determination and professionalism, which almost certainly saved the boy's life, Jeffrey was awarded a Certificate of Commendation by the Chief Officer.

ROSS KELLY ▼

Twelve-year-old Ross Kelly and his ten-year-old sister Hannah were the joint recipients of the Public Bravery Award, presented at a VIP lunch at Motorshow 92 at the NEC Birmingham. Ross was riding in the back seat of his father's car and Hannah in the front passenger seat on a trip down the M1, when their father, Ted, suddenly collapsed over the wheel as they were travelling in the fast lane at some 70mph. Immediately, Ross pushed his 15 stone father out of the way and, grabbing the steering wheel, succeeded in negotiating his way through the traffic and on to the grass verge, where he told Hannah to apply the handbrake. What would unquestionably have been a fatal accident was averted. Ross is a pupil at the Henry Box Comprehensive School in Witney, Oxfordshire, and his hobbies are Nintendo, flying and, thankfully, driving.

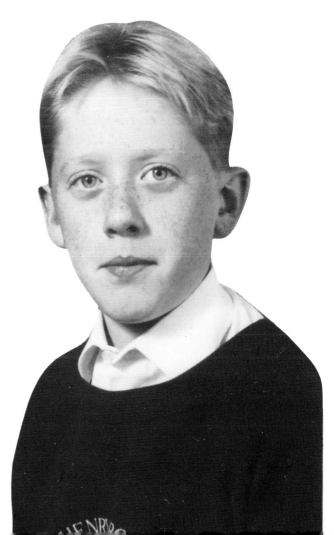

MICHAEL WHITLAM

Michael Whitlam has been Director General of the British Red Cross Society since January 1991, having previously been Chief Executive of the Royal National Institute for the Deaf since mid-1986. He has a lively, entrepreneurial style and has encouraged good management in the voluntary sector. Born in 1947, he first qualified as an Assistant Governor of HM Prison Department in 1970, at the same time studying at Manchester Business School and completing an advanced management course for directors of voluntary organisations. After service with the National Association for the Care and Resettlement of Offenders, he became Deputy Director, UK Child Care and Director, UK Operations of Save the Children, leaving in 1986 to join RNID. He has written numerous papers on juvenile delinquency and charity management. In 1986 he was awarded an MPhil Social Policy (Management Voluntary Sector).

JOHN MAYO

John Mayo became Director General of Help the Aged in 1983 after a 30 year military career. He served in Malta, Cyprus, North Africa, Malaya and Germany and, as a Colonel on the General Staff, was Head of Public Relations for the British Army on the Rhine and Northern Army Group. Since joining Help the Aged, he has raised the charity's profile considerably. It is now seen as a leader in the field of working with older people and, during John's period of office, its income has increased from £9 million to an impressive £34 million a year. He has also been the guiding force in establishing HelpAge International, confirming the charity's leading role in organisations in 19 countries worldwide. His work has earned him wide recognition, notably the award of the OBE.

IAN VENTHAM

When the Royal National Lifeboat Institution was looking for a Head of Fundraising in 1990, it found the perfect candidate in Ian Ventham, a former Army officer with a brilliant track record with other major charities. He is now responsible for all fundraising for the RNLI, which has an income budget of about £50 million a year. After service in Germany, Northern Ireland and the Sultanate of Oman, he left in 1977 to pursue a career in industry. Returning to the UK from his Cyprus base in 1983, he joined Help the Aged the following year, becoming Co-ordinator for that charity's Jubilee Appeal. In 1986 he joined the NSPCC as National Appeals Manager, responsible for all regional fundraising through a network of branches and committees. In addition to his position with the RNLI, he is chairman of the Institute of Charity Fundraising Managers.

PATRICK HUNTER MURPHY ▲

As Executive Director of Starlight Foundation, Patrick Hunter Murphy helps to make dreams come true for seriously and terminally-ill children. Co-founded in 1982 by actress Emma Samms, the organisation has had a UK branch since 1987, granting wishes for more than 750 British children since then. Youngsters may ask for anything from a meeting with a celebrity to a drive in a racing car. The seemingly impossible takes a little longer – one child who wanted to walk on the Moon was taken to the NASA Centre in Florida to simulate the experience. Born in New Zealand in 1958 and educated in Bournemouth and at the University of London, Patrick is responsible for the UK operation's fundraising, wish programme and volunteers. His previous experience has been as Director of Fundraising for Homes for Homeless People, and as Information, Education and Research Officer of Population Concern, a charity dealing with child and maternal health projects overseas.

NICHOLAS HINTON ▶

Nicholas Hinton has been Director General of Save The Children since 1985. With political turmoil and famine still dominating world events, the charity is guaranteed a high profile and is clearly one of the most vital in modern times. Born in 1942, Nicholas was educated at Marlborough College and at Cambridge University, where he gained an MA. While still in his early 20s, he was Assistant Director of the Northorpe Hall Trust, later serving as Director of the National Association for Care and Resettlement of Offenders. He has served on the Council of VSO since 1981, on the Executive Committee of Business in the Community, and was a

SIR JAMES SAVILE ▶

One of the most instantly-recognisable characters at charity events is Sir James (Jimmy) Savile, the disc jockey whose work on behalf of Stoke Mandeville, Leeds and Broadmoor hospitals over the past quarter of a century has brought him many honours culminating in his knighthood in 1990. Born in Leeds in 1926 he left school at the age of 14 to go down the mines as a "Bevin boy". He worked at South Kirby and Waterloo collieries during WWII but a career in the pits was the last thing on his mind. By 1955 he was assistant manager of the Mecca ballroom in Leeds and he joined Radio Luxembourg as a presenter three years later. His "cheeky" persona, flamboyant appearance and ever-present cigar made him a natural for TV and he became a regular on shows like Top of the Pops and Juke Box Jury throughout the 1960s. His career on Radio 1 began in 1965, the year

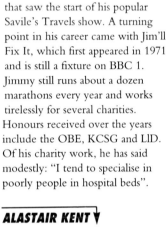

that saw the start of his popular Savile's Travels show. A turning point in his career came with Jim'll Fix It, which first appeared in 1971 and is still a fixture on BBC 1. Jimmy still runs about a dozen marathons every year and works tirelessly for several charities. Honours received over the years include the OBE, KCSG and LlD. Of his charity work, he has said modestly: "I tend to specialise in poorly people in hospital beds".

trustee of Charities Aid Foundation from 1977-84. His main recreation is music and he was Director of the Edington Music Festival from 1965-70. He has flirted with politics, too; he contested the Somerton and Frome seat for the SDP-Liberal Alliance in 1983. He is married with one daughter.

ALASTAIR KENT ▼

Working in the local education career services with school leavers with disabilities and learning problems set Alastair Kent on his own career in the voluntary sector. Since 1989 he has been Director of Action for Blind People. Born in 1952 and educated at Birkenhead School and Cambridge University, Alastair worked in local government until 1981. He then took up the post of Principal at Banstead Place, a residential centre. In 1986 he was appointed Director of Education, Employment and Residential Services at the Royal National Institute for Deaf People.

PR PROFESSIONALS

PETER HEHIR ▼

Peter Hehir, who trained and worked as a journalist and press officer, is the chairman of the Countrywide Communications Group – the consultancy he founded in 1973. With an unusual brief, that extends to the management of reputation, the Countrywide Group has won more awards from the Public Relations Consultants' Association than any other consultancy. Since 1984 the Group has been voted Consultancy of the Year twice and runner-up twice and it is now one of the UK's top ten consultancies. The Countrywide Communications Group is noted for having innovated the use of formal planning practices in the public relations industry; it was also the first UK consultancy to be awarded BS 5750 quality accreditation. Peter Hehir is the UK representative of ICO (the world body for consultancy associations), a Fellow of the Institute of Public Relations and was the chairman of the Public Relations Consultants' Association between 1988 and 1990.

MICHAEL MURPHY ▲

For its innovative client and account management, PR Consultants Scotland was recently voted the UK's top public relations consultancy. Its chairman and managing director, Michael Murphy, specialises in marketing strategy and corporate and financial public relations. A member of the Scottish Young Conservative Business Group, he acted as joint marketing adviser to the Government and to the two Scottish electricity companies during the recent privatisation of the industry. PR Consultants Scotland has been a part of the Shandwick Group since 1979. Michael Murphy is chairman of Shandwick subsidiaries Quorum Graphic Design Consultants Ltd and PR Centre Ltd, he is non-executive director of the Belfast group Causeway Communications Ltd and a former non-executive director of Ship Ltd. He is a member of the West of Scotland Committee of the Institute of Directors and chairman of the Institute's Marketing Committee.

ALAN CAPPER ▼

Alan Capper, chairman of Rowland Worldwide, has worked in the public relations industry for 25 years. A former Fleet Street journalist, he became a PR consultant in the late 1960s – specialising in parliamentary and government affairs. Since then he has worked with a bewildering number of clients, including IBM, Sir Andrew Lloyd Webber and numerous industrial trade associations. A former adviser on fund-raising to the Imperial War Museum and the Victoria and Albert Museum, he is a trustee of the RIBA Awards Committee and a member of the Museum of Modern Art and the Metropolitan Museum in New York.

MARTIN LANGFORD ▼

Martin Langford is the chief executive officer of Burson-Marsteller in the UK. An authority on European crisis management, he has also advised on product liability and extortion. He joined Burson-Marsteller in 1971 and was seconded to the company's Hong Kong office in 1973. Manager of the office for four years, he was involved in many public relations campaigns in Asia – notably, the introduction of McDonald's fast-food to Hong Kong. He returned to London in 1979, managing the central service's department until his appointment to the Board in 1984; he became deputy managing director in 1986 and joint managing director in 1989. Martin is a Member of the Institute of Public Relations and speaks regularly at the International Management Institute in Geneva and the London Business School. He was named Public Relations Professional of the Year by PR Week in 1987 and was appointed chairman of the Public Relations Consultants' Association in 1992.

QUENTIN BELL ▼

Founded when the industry was in its infancy, Quentin Bell's eponymous public relations organisation is now one of the UK's top ten independent PR consultancies. With a brief to offer PR solutions to marketing problems, the consultancy is the fruit of Quentin Bell's varied apprenticeships in journalism, publishing, advertising and marketing. A member of the Institute of Public Relations, vice-chairman of the Public Relations Consultants' Association and chairman of the Association's Development Committee, Quentin Bell is also a member of the Communications Panel of the British Red Cross. Soon to finish his second book, How To Win That Pitch, he is also the author of The PR Business. He is a Friend of the Royal Academy of Arts and a life member of the Glyndebourne Festival Opera.

◀ RODERICK DEWE

With offices in the City of London, and subsidaries in New York and Tokyo, the Dewe Rogerson Group is public relations consultant to the major players in the world's capital markets. The consultancy was founded by chairman Roderick Dewe, an authority on international finance, in 1969. In the late 1950s he worked in the Treasury of the Rhodesian Government and then Nyassaland Government and then for the first public relations consultancy in the City of London to deal exclusively with finance. Involved in the establishment and management of the Wider Share Ownership Council, he worked for the Campaign for Company Pensions in the mid-1970s. An architect of many of the retail strategies used in the privatisation of British Telecom, he was involved in most of the Government's important public share issues in the 1980s.

JIM DUNN ▼

A leading figure in UK and European lesiure PR, Jim Dunn worked as a journalist for the Travel Trade Gazette Group before joining TPS Group Ltd – of which he is now chairman. Managing director of TPS Public Relations, which he founded in 1969, he has played a critical role in the development of the UK travel industry; from the marketing of the first mass-market package holidays to the United States to the introduction of mini-holidays in the UK. Since joining the Shandwick Group with TPS in 1990, he has been instrumental in the development of Shandwick Travel, Transportation and Leisure, now the industry's most comprehensive PR consultancy.

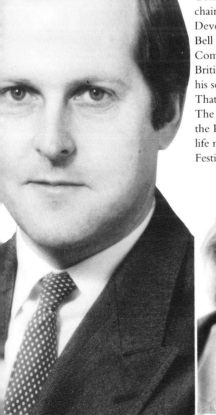

ROBIN WIGHT ▲

Robin Wight set up the first student advertising agency when he was still a Cambridge undergraduate. His career proper began as a copywriter with Robert Sharp and Partners and continued at other agencies including Collett Dickenson Pearce and Partners. He then took over from Charles Saatchi to become creative director of Richard Cope and Partners – and he was still only 23 years old! After a decade with the agency (during which it changed its name to Euro Advertising) he realised there was a gap in the market for a new premium-quality agency in London. In 1979 he helped start Wight Collins Rutherford Scott and in 1982 it went public and built a world advertising, media, PR and sponsor network. Robin Wight is now chairman of WCRS and joint chairman of the network. He served as marketing advisor to Peter Walker when he was Agriculture Minister, and also as a Council Member for Food from Britain.

JOHN HEGARTY ▼

The man behind the celebrated Levi laundrette and Audi Vorsprung Durch Technik campaigns, John Hegarty has collected numerous awards over the years. He started as a junior art director at Benton and Bowles in 1965 and 18 months later his career almost ended where it began – they fired him! He joined a small Soho agency, John Collings and Partners, and in 1967 moved to the Cramer Saatchi consultancy which became Saatchi & Saatchi in 1970. John was a founding shareholder and became deputy creative director a year later. He left in 1973 to co-found TBWA as creative director. The agency was the first to be voted Campaign magazine's Agency of the Year in 1980. He started Bartle Bogle Hegarty two years later and picked up the Campaign award again in 1986. A keen tennis player, golfer and London Marathon competitor, John Hegarty is married with two children, a cat and a mortgage.

◄ MARTIN BOASE

Martin Boase is chairman of Omnicom UK and recently stepped down as chairman of the Advertising Association. Born in 1932, he gained an MA at New College, Oxford, and was with the London Press Exchange from 1958-60. He joined Pritchard Wood and Partners in the early 1960s and in 1968 was a founding partner of the Boase Massimi Pollitt partnership, of which he was chairman from 1977-89. A keen race-goer in his spare time, he is married with four children and lives in London.

JOHN WEBSTER ▲

John Webster joined Mather and Crowther as an art trainee in the late 1950s and, after stints with Hobson Bates & Pritchard Wood, he became a founder member of Boase Massimi Pollitt in 1969. Two years later he took over as creative director and helped to put the agency in the forefront of the advertising boom of the 1970s and 1980s. John has given the world such characters as the Smash instant-potato Martians, the Sugar Puffs Honey Monster and the Hofmeister bear as well as producing successful campaigns for the Guardian, Sony, PG Tips and others. His awards include two Grand Prix at Cannes and the D&AD President's Award in 1982.

RUPERT HOWELL ▼

Born in 1957, Rupert Howell worked for O&M Partners and Grey before joining Young & Rubicam as an account director in 1983. Two years later he was appointed new business director and helped the agency win more than £100 million of new business over the next two years. In late 1987 he started Howell Henry Chaldecott Lury, of which he is managing partner. It now bills more than £50 million and includes Britvic, Indesit, Lego, MTV and Golden Wonder among its clients. HHCL was voted Agency of the Year in 1989, won the Grand Prix at Cannes in 1990 and has collected other major awards in 1992. Married with a daughter, Rupert Howell lives in London.

← TIM DELANEY

Tim Delaney started his career in an advertising agency's mail room at the age of 15 and worked for various companies before founding Leagas Delaney in 1980 when he was 34 years old. Over the years he has built up an impressive list of clients including Harrods, Porsche, Talking Pages, the Nationwide Building Society and the Guardian newspaper. He has won awards in the UK and the USA. In the 1970s he was advisor to Labour Prime Minister James Callaghan and is currently working for the Royal Marsden Hospital Appeal and the Suzy Lamplugh Trust. In 1992 he was President of the Designers and Art Directors Association, the leading awards scheme in this country, and he is in great demand as a speaker at seminars here and abroad.

WINSTON FLETCHER ▼

Winston Fletcher became chairman of the Advertising Association in 1993 and is chairman of Delaney Fletcher Slaymaker Delaney and Bozell, which he helped found in 1985, and Bozell Europe, which has agencies in over 20 countries. He was formerly chairman and managing director of Fletcher Shelton Delaney (1974-83) and chairman/chief executive of Ted Bates UK Group (1983-85). He has written eight books including The Admakers, Teach Yourself Advertising and the novel The Manipulators, as well as over 800 articles in national and trade publications. Winston Fletcher is a Fellow of the Royal Society of Arts and a Visiting Professor at Lancaster University Management School.

GRAHAM FINK ▼

Graham Fink is deputy creative director of Gold Greenless Trott and was formerly Group Head of Saatchi & Saatchi (1987-90). He has won awards with campaigns for Hamlet cigars, Land Rover, British Airways and other clients. Born in 1959 he started with French Gold

Abbott in 1980-81, moving to Collet Dickenson Pearce from 1981-87. He was Head of Art at WCRS before moving to Saatchis. A judge for the Campaign Poster Awards in 1991, he is a member of the Creative Circle of the Design and Art Directors Association.

DAVE DUNAN

Born in 1955, Dave Dunan's first taste of the leisure security industry came at the age of 30 when he attended Showsec International's training school, specialising in security consultancy and close protection. From 1986 to the present, he has provided security services to, amongst others; Madonna, Nenah Cherry, Dire Straits and Gloria Estafan, while between tours he acted as a security consultant to the BBC, Capital Radio and MTV. Dave Dunan's current postiton at Showsec International is that of Advance Tour Security and he is widely regarded as one of the most knowledgeable venue security men in the industry.

MICK UPTON ⬆

Originally trained by the British Army in anti-terrorist skills, Mick Upton has been involved in security work of all types for the last 23 years. Starting in 1964, he worked with the Rolling Stones, The Who, Led Zeppelin and the Bay City Rollers during the height of their success. In 1972 Mick began to specialise in crowd management operations, working all over the world with some of the biggest names in the pop world. He co-founded Showsec International in 1972, the first training school exclusively tailored to the security needs of the leisure industry. Showsec has been a great success, training and advising students and companies from many different countries. As well as working with such national figures as Princess Margaret, Princess Alexandria and Edward Heath, Mick has submitted papers on security studies for the Home Office and the Concert Promoters Association. He is currently working with the Department of Trade and Industry looking into the viability of introducing a system of formal qualifications for leisure security.

ADEN DERVAN ⬆

Thirty-two year old Aden Dervan is joint director of Praetorian Associates, a company he co-founded three years ago. An ex-serviceman, Aden was previously a Jujitsu instructor for 10 years, a communications specialist and a commercial pilot for helicopter and fixed wing aircraft. Following a period as consultant for various security firms, he formed Praetorian and now supplies a range of services according to the particular needs of the client. Employing specialists from the Government and Police servies, as well as ex-Special Forces personnel, the company also provides a flexible training programme both here and abroad.

BARRY MURFETT ▲

Born in Tottenham, London, Barry Murfett started out working in the building industry. After a period as a tour manager, he moved into the then quite new field of tour security, working with the Monkees and on the Beatles' Magical Mystery Tour during the sixties. Since those early days, Barry has been involved with bands and stars too numerous to mention, his most recent engagement being the Dire Straits world tour that took him away from home for some eighteen months. Barry has been married for 32 years and apart from his frequent tours abroad, has lived in London all his life. With such a long career it is perhaps surprising that Barry has never had any serious trouble, employing instead the courteous but firm manner that has led many of his clients to look on him more a PA than a minder.

GERRY SLATER ▼

Starting his career as a partner with Artiste Services in 1967, Gerry Slater soon branched out from straight forward security services to the provision of studio and instrument hire, as well as tour management. Working with acts like, Frank Zappa, the Doors, Leonard Cohen and Sly and The Family Stone during the 1970s, Gerry left Artiste Services in 1980 to open a management company. In 1983 he returned to security work when he became a partner in Showsec International where he co-ordinates the security on all tours booked through the company.

GRAHAM COURT ▼

Graham joined the army after finishing school, leaving in 1983 to spend a year in Australia touring with a stunt show, work that required him to take part in all manner of hair raising activities involving cars, horses and great heights. Returning to England in 1983, Graham met up with Mick Upton who invited him to attend the Showsec training school where his military experience quickly established him as an instructor of high standing. Working with stars like David Bowie, Madonna, Diana Ross and Bruce Willis, Graham is now based in the USA where he is a security consultant and Showsec's North American representative.

TONY BALL ▲

Showsec International's Operations Director, Tony Ball, joined the company in 1988 after seven years of military service. He spent the next couple of years training extensively in crowd management, a field in which he is now an acknowledged expert, working with acts like Elton John, Prince and George Michael. Tony is also widely regarded as an authority on large-scale events, regularly managing concerts with attendance figures from 20,000 to 200,000, such as Madonna's Wembley concert, Michael Jackson's show at Milton Keynes or the U2 concert at Earls Court.

BOB MAXEY ▲

A popular figure in the security industry since 1977, Bob Maxey started his career with the Gentle Giant company, working with them for the next couple of years. Moving on to Artiste Services Limited in 1979, Bob remained with the company until it was brought out by Showsec International and he became Administration Manager for the new operation. With a list of entertainment clients that include Paul Hogan, the Eurythmics, Jerry Lee Lewis and Bryan Adams, Bob has also worked with some of Britain's leading sports personalities such as Jimmy White, Christopher Dean and Gary Linekar.

Mail

DAY

o support

E

st

ITISH

rds

The Mail
ON SUNDAY
NOVEMBER 29, 1992   60p

DELIA SMITH
MORE OF HER COOKERY CARDS IN **YOU**

Dramatic midnight statement from the Chancellor

LAMONT: HOW £4,000 LEGAL BILL WAS PAID

By LORNA DUCKWORTH
Political Reporter

TAXPAYERS helped Chancellor Norman Lamont to pay legal costs after publicity surrounding a tenant at his London home who claimed to be a 'sex therapist.'

Details of the secret deal — prompting a midnight statement from the Chancellor — in which the Treasury agreed to underwrite part of the £23,000 bill, emerged yesterday following revelations about Mr Lamont's credit card account problems.

The legal bill was incurred when he started actions to evict the tenant, who later moved out of his £500,000 house in Notting Hill.

The Treasury paid £4,000 plus VAT

FEE PAID: Chancellor Norman Lamont yesterday

Continued on Page 2

TELEVISION 50-53 ■ JOHN JUNOR 21 ■ VICTOR LEWIS-SMITH 31 ■ NIGEL DEMPSTER 47 ■ PATRIC WALKER 60 ■ MONEY 71-80

The Mail
ON SUNDAY
FEBRUARY 21, 1993   60p

LIFE IN THE SINGLE LANE
HOW KATE MENZIES IS HELPING
DIANA AFTER HER SEPARATION – Page 25

A £100,000 WINNER, AND A NEW GAME TODAY – Page 16

Premier pledges new crackdown on bail offenders who break law again

MAJOR'S CRUSADE ON CRIME

NEW ATTITUDE: John Major's appeal

EXCLUSIVE
By PETER DOBBIE Political Editor

JOHN MAJOR has intervened dramatically in Britain's deepening law and order crisis.

He pledged to tackle the rising crime threatening to engulf society.

In a dramatic appeal, he called on the public to put the victim before the criminal.

And he promised tough new laws to stem the rise in lawlessness.

In a candid interview with The Mail on Sunday, the Prime Minister placed the issue firmly at the top of the Government's agenda.

Calling for a new attitude, Mr Major

BOYS CHARGED WITH JAMES MURDER

TWO boys of ten were charged yesterday with the abduction and murder of two-year-old James Bulger.

They are also accused of attempting to abduct a second two-year-old boy.

The youngsters, from

the Walton area of Liverpool, are due to appear at South Sefton Juvenile Court in Bootle tomorrow.

They had been questioned for three days by detectives investigating the killing of James, freed with multiple injuries beside a

railway line last Sunday.
James disappeared eight days ago while out with his mother at a shopping precinct in Bootle.

A special service was held for James at his local church in Kirkby.

Full interview with the Prime Minister — Pages 8&9

TELEVISION 50-53 ■ JOHN JUNOR 21 ■ VICTOR LEWIS-SMITH 31 ■ NIGEL DEMPSTER 47 ■ PATRIC WALKER 54 ■ MONEY 73-83

Quality on Sunday.

ANDREW NEIL ▼

Andrew Neil graduated from the University of Glasgow in 1971, with an MA (Hons) in politics and economics. His first job was as political adviser to the Secretary of State for the Environment. He became a correspondent for The Economist in 1973 and went on to become The Economist's lobby correspondent in the House of Commons and then Labour editor. Also in the 1970s he presented Tomorrow's World and The Risk Business for the BBC, Look Here for LWT and commented on the news for BBC's Nationwide, Radio 4's Today. He became American correspondent for The Economist in 1979 and spent two and a half years working in New York and Washington, including covering the 1980 presidential campaigns. He also made several documentaries about America for the BBC, returning to Britain to become UK editor of The Economist in 1982. He was appointed editor of the Sunday Times in 1983. In November 1988 he became executive chairman of Sky TV with the job of launching four new satellite TV channels and seeing them through their first year which he did while continuing to edit the Sunday Times. He returned full-time to the paper in 1990. He continues to broadcast regularly on TV and radio, on both sides of the Atlantic, and presents his own two-hour news programme on London radio.

PETER PRESTON ▲

Peter Preston was educated at Loughborough Grammar School and St John's College, Oxford, where he read English. He started off in journalism as a trainee reporter on the Liverpool Post, moving three years later to The Guardian in Manchester where he worked as a political reporter before moving to London in 1964 as education correspondent. He was appointed diary editor in 1966 and then features editor in 1968. During the Indo-Pakistan War, and in Bangladesh and Cyprus, he served as a war correspondent and foreign correspondent. In 1972 he was appointed production director. He took over as editor of The Guardian in 1975 and is now editor and chairman of Guardian Newspapers (since 1988), and a director on the Board of The Guardian and Manchester Evening News. In May 1988 he became chairman of the British Executive of the International Press Institute. He received an Hon DLitt from Loughborough University in 1982.

KEITH McNEILL ▲

Keith McNeill was educated at Slough Grammar School and began his career on the Slough Evening Mail, moving in 1985 to join the launch team of CHAT, the first of the new Euro women's magazines in Britain. He became features editor of CHAT before moving to take up the position of features editor on the relaunch of the London Evening News in 1987. With the paper's close he was made redundant but soon became deputy editor of Woman's Own in April 1988. He took over the editorship of IPC's most prestigious title two and a half years ago and is currently ensuring Woman's Own continues to evolve, remaining not only a top women's weekly, but also making the most of sale or return to grow in circulation and pose an even stronger challenge to the new Euro mags.

RUPERT PENNANT-REA

Rupert Pennant-Rea has degrees in economics from Trinity College, Dublin, and the University of Manchester. Before joining The Economist he worked at the Confederation of Irish Industry, the General and Municipal Workers' Union and the Bank of England. He joined The Economist in 1977, and worked first as economics correspondent and then as economics editor. He was appointed editor in 1986. Between 1980 and 1985 he was regularly seconded to the World Bank to edit its World Development Report.

NICHOLAS COLERIDGE ▾

Nicholas Coleridge was educated at Eton and Trinity College, Cambridge. He was associate editor at Tatler (1979-81), a columnist for the Evening Standard (1981-84), and a war reporter (1984-85). He won Young Journalist of the Year at the British Press Awards in 1983. He became deputy editor of Harpers & Queen in 1985 and was appointed the magazine's editor a year later. In 1989 he became editorial director of The Conde Nast publications Ltd. He has published six books: tunnel Vision, Around The World In 78 Days, Shooting Stars, The Fashion Conspiracy, How I Met My Wife and, most recently, Paper Tigers.

TERRY HORNETT ▾

Terry Hornett started in journalism as a tea boy on the teen weekly Boyfriend in 1960. Three and a half years later he was appointed features editor of IPC's Mirabel. He was promoted to editor and then became editor of Rave, a teen monthly. He launched 19 for IPC in the 1960s and then became editor of Petticoat. In the early 1970s he conceived the men's magazine, Club, which lasted

18 issues before folding. Hornett formed Carlton Publishing as a joint venture with IPC and launched the youth fashion magazine Look Now. Subsequent launches from the company included the teen title OK, Woman's World, Options and Country Homes and Interiors. In 1987 Terry sold his share of Carlton to IPC for £3 million and retired temporarily from magazine publishing. He signed a three-year non-competition clause and spent part of that time exploring publishing opportunities overseas. In 1992 he returned to the UK magazine industry, buying a controlling interest in the London listings weekly City Limits from the TV producer Bernard Clark. He relaunched the magazine as a women's entertainment weekly and is currently working on a plan to increase sales by at least 150 per cent.

DONALD TRELFORD ▾

After two years as a pilot in the RAF Donald Trelford read English at Cambridge. He worked as a reporter and sub-editor on newspapers in Coventry and Sheffield before being sent to Africa by the Thomson organisation at the age of 25 to edit the Nyasaland Times (now The Times of Malawi). He stayed in Africa for three years and while there was also a correspondent for The Observer, The Times and the

BBC. He returned to England in 1966 to join The Observer as deputy news editor. He was appointed assistant managing editor in 1968, deputy editor in 1969 and editor and director in 1975. In 1982 The Observer was named British Newspaper Of The Year and in 1984 Trelford was commended by the World Press Review as International Editor of the Year. He is a regular broadcaster on radio and TV as a panellist, writer and interviewer and has presented TV programmes worldwide. A member of the British Executive Committee of the International Press Institute he also sits on the joint Press-Government D-Notice Committee, a liaison body on publication of defence secrets. He holds an Hon DLitt and is a member of the Board of Trustees at Sheffield University. He is also a fellow of the Royal Society of Arts, a Freeman of the City of London, a Liveryman of the Stationers' Company and a member of the advisory board of the Olivier Theatre Awards Committee. A keen sportsman he has published books on snooker, chess (with Gary Kasparov) and on Len Hutton.

SIR ROGER ELLIOTT ▼

Secretary to the delegates and chief executive of Oxford University Press since 1988, Sir Roger is also professor of Physics at Oxford. He has been a Fellow of New College, Oxford since 1974. He was educated at New College (MA, DPhill). He was a Research Fellow of the University of California, Berkeley (1952-53), a Research Fellow at UKAEA, Harwell, 1953-55), a lecturer at Reading University (1955-57), a Fellow of St John's College, Oxford (1957-74) and Honorary Fellow in 1988. He was a University Reader at Oxford from 1964-74. He was Wykeham Professor of Physics from 1974-89. He was a delegate at Oxford University Press from 1971-88, chairman of the Board for Universities and Research Councils from 1983-87, vice chairman of the Parly Office of Science and Technology 1990-. He is a member of the advisory board for Research Councils (1987-90). He has been vice president of the Royal Society (1984-88), and is currently treasurer of the Publishers Association (1990-). He has been a visiting professor at the University of California, the University of Illinois, and visiting dist. professor at Florida State University. He won the Maxwell Medal in 1968 and the Guthrie Medal in 1990. His publications include Magnetic Properties of Rare Earth Metals, Solid State Physics and its Applications.

ANTHONY CHEETHAM ▲

Educated at Eton and Balliol, Oxford, Anthony Cheetham started in publishing as educational editor at New English Library Ltd. He joined Sphere Books Ltd a year later as paperback editor and was appointed editorial director in 1968. In 1973 he joined BPC as founder and managing director of a new paperback imprint, Futura Publications Ltd. From 1980-81 he was managing director of Macdonald Futura Ltd. He founded Century Publishing in 1982, and his efforts since that date bore one of the great publishing successes of the 1980s. He implemented the merger of Century with Hutchinson in 1985, and then presided over the sale of Century Hutchinson for £64.5 million to Random House in 1989. He was, until 1991, chairman and chief executive of Random Century Group Ltd, consisting of Century, Hutchinson, Arrow, Jonathan Cape, Chatto & Windus and Ebury Press.

RICHARD CHARKIN ▼

Educated at Haileybury, ISC and Trinity College, Cambridge (MA) Richard Charkin became science editor at Harrap & Co in 1972 and senior publishing manager of Pergamon Press a year later. He moved to Oxford University Press where he became medical editor in 1974 and then head of science and medicine, head of reference and managing director of academic. He became executive director of Reed International Books in 1988. He was made a visiting Fellow at Green College, Oxford, in 1987.

TIM HELY-HUTCHINSON ▼

On graduating from University in 1975, the Hon Tim Hely-Hutchinson joined Macmillan where he progressed from a management traineeship to middle-management positions in Australia and Britain. In 1982 he joined Macdonald & Co Ltd a marketing director and shortly thereafter became managing director. During his time in the job, Macdonald's large losses were turned around to substantial profits. He left Macdonald in 1986 to found Headline with three colleagues. He is now the company's managing director. In 1990 he won the British venture Capital Association's inaugural 'Venture of the Year' award. In 1991 Headline was floated on the London Stock Exchange and in 1992 it was voted Publisher of the Year in the British Book Awards.

TREVOR GLOVER ▲

Trevor Glover began his publishing career as a college representative with McGraw-Hill in Sydney in 1964. He moved to McGraw-Hill, UK, two years later, and became College sales manager and then general manager of the Professional Reference Book Division. He joined Penguin UK in 1970 as UK sales manager, rising to become UK sales and marketing director. He then worked briefly with Viking-Penguin, New York, prior to his appointment as managing director of Penguin Australia, a position he held for 11 years, until 1987. He has twice been president of the Australian Book Publishers Association, from 1983-85 and from 1986-87. He was appointed Penguin Group managing director in 1987 and remains chairman of Penguin Books Australia Ltd. He was appointed member of the Publishers Association Council in April last year.

◄ MICHAEL FISHWICK

Michael Fishwick entered publishing in 1982 after completing his postgraduate studies at Oxford. A job as copy editor for Penguin was followed by the position of junior editor at Chatto & Windus and then commissioning editor for Collins. As publishing director of non-fiction he now looks after all the non-fiction published by the Harper Collins Trade list in hardback and paperback, generally regarded as the best non-fiction list in British publishing and one which has featured, over the last few years, such diverse luminaries as the Gorbachevs, Lord Hailsham, General Sir Peter de la Billiere, Jung Chang, and many more.

DUNCAN HEATH →

Duncan Heath was born in 1946 and educated at Wrekin College until 1964. He went on to study Law at the Inner Temple and then travelled for two years in Australia, India, Africa, Cambodia and Vietnam. He was at Dorland Advertising from 1970-71 and left to work at William Morris for a year. He set up his own agency in 1973 and sold Duncan Heath Associates to ICM in 1984. Duncan Heath Associates merged with ICM in 1991 and Duncan became chairman of the joint companies in the same year. He is divorced with two children.

JULIAN BELFRAGE

Son of the well-known wartime newsreader Bruce Belfrage, Julian Belfrage was born in 1934. He was educated at Canford School, after which he did National Service in the Royal Navy. He then spent three years training to be an actor at the Central School of Speech and Drama. After two years in Roar Like A Dove at the Phoenix Theatre, he joined MCA and became an agent. He now runs his own firm, Julian Belfrage Associates, where his clients include Judi Dench, Daniel Day-Lewis, John Hurt, Ian Holm, Geraldine James, Colin Firth and Alan Howard.

ANTONY HARWOOD

Born in 1960, Antony Harwood went into publishing straight from school. He started at Chatto & Windus, working with authors such as Angela Carter, Antony Sher, Howard Jacobson, Dirk Bogarde and A S Byatt. In 1985 he joined Aitken & Stone literary agency as a fledgling agent, became a director of the agency in 1989 and left in 1990 to join the board of directors at Curtis Brown Group Ltd.

MICHAEL SISSONS →

Michael Sissons has been chairman and managing director of the Peter Fraser & Dunlop Group Ltd since 1988. After reading modern history at Oxford, he became a freelance journalist and then joined A. D. Peters as a writer's agent. He became director of the company in 1965 and chairman and managing director eight years later. He has written, broadcast and lectured widely on media topics, in particular on the writer in the marketplace and on the multi-media, and was for three years President of the Association of Authors' Agents. He has been a director of the radio station LBC, a member of the Council of the Consumers' Association, a member of MCC and is now chairman of the Arts and Library Committee of MCC.

STEPHEN DURBRIDGE

Stephen Durbridge started out in the film industry, forming his own company in 1966. He joined London Management as an agent in 1968, before going on to represent writers at Curtis Brown in 1971. Thereafter he ran his own agency until the formation of his own company with Harvey Unna in 1975. His partnership with Sheila Lemmon was formed in 1986. He specialises in the representation of screenwriters for films and television as well as the placing of best-selling novels with international film companies.

CARADOC KING

Caradoc King started his publishing career as a general trainee at Associated Book Publishers after leaving Oxford in 1968. His first job within the group was as a junior editor at Methuen, editing academic books, and in 1970 he was appointed senior editor of Allen Lane, The Penguin Press. He worked at Penguin until 1975, eventually as commissioning editor responsible for plays, film and theatre and joined A. P. Watt in 1976. He became a director of the firm in 1981 and managing director in 1992. He represents a wide range of authors, including the Booker Award winners of 1991 and 1992, Ben Okri and Michael Ondaatje, and Graham Swift, Timothy Mo and Jenny Diski as well as commercial writers Rosie Thomas, Andrea Newman and Stephen Gallagher, biographers Michael Holroyd, Martin Gilbert and Brenda Maddox, and the children's authors Dick King-Smith and Quentin Blake.

ANTHONY JONES

Born in 1940, Anthony Jones went to Marlborough College and then Magdalene College, Cambridge. He worked for the Rights Department of Cassell & Co before becoming London Story Editor at MGM. In 1967 he became an agent at A. D. Peters and Co Ltd, representing top writers and directors.

GILES GORDON

Giles Gordon has been a literary agent with Sheil Land Associates (previously Anthony Sheil Associates) since 1972. He represents around 30 novelists including the 1992 Booker Prize winner Barry Unsworth, Sue Townsend, Fay Weldon, Peter Ackroyd and Michael Moorcock. His non-fiction authors include Hunter Davies, Ben Pimlott, HRH The Prince of Wales, Beth Chatto, Christopher Lloyd, Roy Foster, Richard Ingrams and Nikolai Tolstoy. Before becoming an agent, he was a publisher. His last job (for five years) was editorial director of Victor Gollancz. He has published six novels and three collections of short stories and edited about 25 collections of stories. He has co-edited (with David Hughes) Heinemann's annual Best Short Stories anthology for the last eight years. He has been theatre critic of The Spectator and the London Daily News. Elected a Fellow of the Royal Society of Literature in 1990, he is currently on the RSL's Council. Chatto & Windus will publish his memoirs of a literary and theatrical life, Aren't We Due a Royalty Statement? in October 1993

GILLON AITKEN

Gillon Aitken was born in Calcutta and educated privately at Charterhouse School. During National Service he was taught Russian and served in the Intelligence Corps in Berlin. He was general editor of Chapman & Hall (Evelyn Waugh's publishers) from 1959 to 1966 and spent a year with Hodder & Stoughton before becoming a partner in Anthony Sheil (now Sheil Land) Associates, the literary agency. In 1971 he was appointed managing director of Hamish Hamilton, then owned by the Thomson Organisation, but in 1974 he returned to literary agenting and became co-founder of Wallace, Aitken & Sheil (now the Wallace agency) in New York. He established his own agency in London in 1977 and merged this with Hughes Massie (agents for Agatha Christie) to form Aitken & Stone in 1984. In 1993 the company was renamed Aitken, Stone and Wylie to reflect the close association with Wylie, Aitken & Stone, the New York agency. Gillon has translated several works from Russian including The Complete Prose Tales of Alexandra Segeyevitch Pushkin (1966) and One Day In the Life of Ivan Denisovich by Alexander Solzhenitsyn (1970).

PAUL MULDOON ↑

Paul Muldoon's first book-length poem, Madoo: A Mystery (Faber and Faber) won the Geoffrey Faber Memorial Award in 1991, awarded last spring. Born in County Armagh in 1951 Paul published his first collection of poems while still at university (Queen's in Belfast). He worked as a radio producer for 13 years, but found it claimed too much of the time he wanted to devote to his poetry. Invitations from the creative departments of American universities allowed him to complete Madoo: he worked on it daily for 18 months. The poem's premise is an imagined trip by Coleridge and Southey to America to found a utopian commune by the River susquehana, something they wanted to do in real life; it has elements of logbook, anthology, lyric, epic and riddle, a highly original achievement.

PETER MAYLE ↑

Peter Mayle's A Year in Provence is a publishing phenomenon. Since it came out in 1989 it has sold over 3,000 copies in hardback and 890,000 in paperback. It has been in the UK bestseller list for over two years and has now been televised for the BBC. Peter's first venture into publishing was a book for children explaining the facts of life. This was after 15 years working in advertising in New York. His next book, A Man's Best Friend, was a bestseller in the UK, Italy and Germany. On the royalties Peter moved to Provence to buy the house of his dreams. Letters to a friend detailing life with his wife, the builders, dogs and guests provided the germ for A Year in Provence. The sequel, Toujours Provence, appeared in May 1992. His latest book, Hotel Pastis, concerns the peregrinations of an ad man in the throes of a mid-life crisis who escapes to Provence.

← FERDINAND MOUNT

Of Love and Asthma, Ferdinand Mount's fifth novel and winner of the 1992 Hawthornden Prize (Heinemann), tells the story in fine English comic tradition of a doomed friendship between two men who meet as boys in a sanatorium where they are receiving treatment for asthma. Ferdinand has been much praised as a master of English prose and in this book, in particular, for his ability to combine the serious with the comic to brilliant effect. The editor of the Times Literary Supplement since 1991, he has worked for several newspapers, a political columnist at The Spectator, The Standard and the Daily Telegraph, and was voted Columnist of the Year in 1986. Before this he was a researcher for the Conservative Party and was head of Mrs Thatcher's Downing Street policy unit in 1982.

BARRY UNSWORTH ▶

Joint winner of the 1992 Booker Prize Barry Unsworth is one of our most respected novelists. Sacred Hunger, about the 18th century slave trade, published by Hamish Hamilton, is his tenth novel. He has already been shortlisted once for the Booker Prize for Pascali's Island, made into a film starring Ben Kingsley, Charles Dance and Helen Mirren and won the Heinemann Fiction Prize for Moonraker's Gift in 1973. He has been writer-in-residence at Ambleside in Cumbria in 1979 and at Liverpool University in 1985. Unsworth was born and brought up in Durham. He went to Manchester University which was followed by two years National Service.

ADRIAN DESMOND ▲

Adrian Desmond's biography of Darwin (written with American James Moore), which won the 1991 James Tait Black Memorial Prize for Biography, was described by Stephen Jay Gould as "unqestionably the finest ever written about Darwin". It also went to number one in the Standard's non-fiction best-seller list. His other books are The Hot-Blooded Dinosaurs, The Ape's Reflexion, Archetypes & Ancestors and The Politics of Evolution (1989), a study of the pre-Darwinian generation described by the TLS as intellectual dynamite, and certainly one of the most important books in the history of science published during the past decade. It received the Pfizer Award from the History of Science Society in 1991. Adrian studied at London University and Harvard, has higher degrees in vertebrate palaeontology and history of science and a PhD for his work on Victorian evolution.

NICHOLAS BOYLE ▲

After graduating from Cambridge with a First in Modern and Medieval Languages, Nicholas Boyle became a Research Fellow and then a college lecturer in German at Magdalene and Girton. He is currently tutor and director of studies in Modern Languages at Magdalene and a British Academy research reader in the Humanities. His PhD was on G C Lichtenberg and the French Moralistes. Last year he received the Royal Society of Literature award under the W H Heinemann Bequest for Goethe The Poet and The Age, described by the TLS as "vivid, lucid and pleasurable . . . reads like a fine novel, yet is also quietly encyclopaedic".

THOMAS PAKENHAM ▼

Winner of the 34th W H Smith Annual Award for The Scramble for Africa (Wiedenfeld and Nicolson), awarded in March 1992, Thomas Pakenham received £10,000 for an outstanding contribution to English literature. Born in1933 Thomas is a member of one of our most distinguished literary families. His father, Lord Longford, is the author of some 25 books, his mother is the historian Elizabeth Longford and his sisters are the writers Antonia Fraser and Rachel Billington. Thomas went to Oxford and then became a freelance writer for the Times Educational Supplement, the Sunday Telegraph and the Observer. Before The Scramble for Africa he was best known for The Boer War, a definitive historical work which won him the Cheltenham Prize in 1980. The result of more than ten years work The Scramble for Africa is a detailed account of the period at the turn of the century when five European powers battled for supremacy in the race to colonise Africa. "A thrilling account, fast-moving, imaginative, coherent," John Spurling said of it in the Observer.

ENTREPRENEURS

PETER de SAVARY ▼

Peter de Savary left Charterhouse School at the age of 16 and went to Canada for four years, working in a variety of basic jobs. He returned to England and spent the next five years in manufacturing, based in the south west. His fortunes then took him to West Africa, trading commodities, importing and exporting and running cargo ships. From the early 1970s he was engaged in the trading, refining, transportation and distribution of oil in the Middle East and elsewhere. Peter has been involved in the property and leisure business internationally. He founded the St James's Clubs and has transformed Land's End into one of Britain's major recreational facilities. He has operated and owned commercial shipyards, oil bunkering facilities, refineries, ports, harbours and marinas as well as various manufacturing companies. As an entrepreneur he will take a position, take a risk and deploy his energy and resources to improve the quality and value of assets with the objective of subsequently trading them profitably. Peter de Savary was Britain's challenger for the America's Cup in 1983 and was elected Tourism Personality of the Year in 1989.

SIR TERENCE CONRAN

Terence Conran started his retailing career in 1964, when he founded Habitat, a chain of stores selling modern furniture and furnishing throughout the UK, France, Belgium, Holland, Japan and the USA. He floated the company on the London Stock Exchange in 1981 and in a series of mergers and takeovers, turned it into Storehouse plc, the £1.3 billion retailing empire from which he retired as chairman in 1990. Storehouse incorporated inter alia, Mothercare, Habitat, Heal's, FNAC, Blazer and British Home Stores. Born in 1931 Terence Conran was educated at the Central School of Arts and Crafts in London and was one of the designers involved in the 1951 Festival of Britain. In 1952 he set up as a freelance industrial designer, making furniture from a basement studio and, in 1956, set up the Conran Design Group, which became one of the largest design groups in Europe. In addition to his retail interests in 1983 he set up Conran Octopus Ltd, in association with Octopus Books Ltd, which publishes a range of books, reflecting his style of philosophy. His current interests include a restaurant group including Bibendum, the Blueprint Cafe and le Pont de la Tour, with Quaglinos opening shortly. Terence Conran was knighted in 1983.

RICHARD BRANSON ▼

Founder and chairman of the Virgin Group of companies, Richard Branson was born in 1950. He started Virgin as a mail order record retailer in 1970 and, shortly afterwards, opened a record shop in Oxford Street. During 1972 he built a recording studio in Oxfordshire and, in 1973, the first Virgin record, Tubular Bells, by Mike Oldfield, was released, going on to sell over five million copies. Virgin is now one of the top six record companies in the world. The interests of the Virgin Group include music retailing, book and software publishing, film and video editing and clubs and hotels through over 100 companies in 15 countries. Virgin Atlantic Airways, formed in 1984, is now the second biggest long-haul airline in Britain. In 1991 Virgin Group sales amounted to £1.25 billion. Richard Branson is also trustee of several charities and was responsible for the launch of a health care campaign relating to AIDS in 1987.

DAVID MURRAY ▶

Born in Ayr in 1951, David Murray left Broughton High School with five "O" levels and joined a small company, Scotmet Alloys, before setting up Murray International Metals in 1974. From the early 1970s he was involved in supplying metals for the North Sea industry on a turnkey and urgent basis. From relatively small beginnings he has built the company up to its present level of a £200 million turnover and 2,000 employees, with arms involved not only in metal, but property, office equipment and electronics. He even has a chain of 50 hi-fi shops in New Zealand. The Murray style is to back people of quality in business and, although mistakes have been made – including a disaster with the Sunday Scot newspaper – these have not deterred him. The company is the largest owned by an individual in Scotland and, together with the high profile of owning Glasgow Rangers Football Club, keeps David Murray in the forefront of commerce.

DAVID SULLIVAN ▼

David Sullivan made his first million by the time he was 25 years old, quite soon after leaving Queen Mary's College, London, with a degree in economics. He first worked in advertising and then set up his own mail order business before launching his string of soft-porn magazines. He went into the newspaper business in 1986 and is now publisher of the Sunday Sport, Daily Sport and the News & Echo newspapers. He classes himself as a workaholic and believes firmly in his motto, "perseverance and dedication". Apart from newspapers his business interests are in horses and property.

ROBERT BRAITHWAITE

Yorkshire-born Robert Braithwaite is the managing director of Sunseeker International (Boats) Ltd of Poole in Dorset, one of the world's leading manufacturers and designers of production built luxury powerboats. He joined his father's chandlery company in 1964 and, in 1969, it built its first powerboat. That year the company's turnover was £129,358; in 1992 it had increased to £35 million. A former chairman of the British Marine Industries Federation and of National Boat Shows Ltd, Robert Braithwaite was awarded the MBE in 1992.

DAVID BRUCE

Since he had failed "O" level maths five times, when he left school in 1966, career opportunities for David Bruce were somewhat limited. He became a management trainee at Courage Brewery, before joining Theakston's Brewery in Yorkshire, as sales manager and brewer of the notorious Old Peculiar. He spent the next six years operating a wide variety of leisure outlets throughout the UK. In 1979 David borrowed £10,000 and started Bruce's Brewery at the Goose & Firkin in London. During the next seven years he opened 12 Firkin pubs and breweries. In 1988 he sold his pubs and breweries for £6.6 million. He spent £80,000 on a specially designed boat for disabled people to enjoy cruising holidays.

LORD WAKEHAM ▼

Lord Wakeham, Lord Privvy Seal and Leader of the House of Lords, was born in 1932. A chartered accountant, he was the director of many public and private companies before becoming an MP – representing Maldon and Rochford from 1974 and Colchester and Maldon from 1983. In 1979 Lord Wakeham was appointed Assistant Government Whip. He acted as Lord Commissioner of Her Majesty's Treasury (Government Whip) for a short time before becoming Parliamentary Under-Secretary of State at the Department of Industry in 1981. A Minister of State at the Treasury in 1982, he was appointed Parliamentary Secretary to the Treasury (Chief Whip) in 1983. Lord Privvy Seal and Leader of the House of Commons in 1987, he became Lord President of the Council in 1988 and Secretary of State for Energy in 1989. Lord Wakeham, married with three sons, retired from the Commons in 1992. Following that year's General Election he was elevated to the Peerage and appointed Leader of the House of Lords.

ROBERT SMITH ▼

A chartered accountant and specialist in funding businesses with equity capital, Robert Smith is chairman and chief executive of Morgan Grenfell Capital Development Limited. Between 1983 and 1985 he was the general manager of the Corporate Finance Division of the Royal Bank of Scotland and the managing director of National Commercial and Glyns. Managing director of Charterhouse Development Ltd and executive director of Charterhouse Bank Ltd between 1985 and 1989, he is director of Morgan Grenfell, MFI Furniture Group Ltd, Tip Europe Ltd and Bristow Helicopter Group Ltd. Robert Smith has also held a number of public appointments, including Commissioner of the Museums and Galleries Commission and deputy chairman of the National Museums of Scotland. Born in 1944 and married with two daughters, he is a Freeman of the City of London.

Photograph by Granville Fox

DAVID TWEEDIE ▼

Since 1987 Professor David Tweedie has been the national technical partner of KPMG Peat Marwick. A former national technical partner of Thomas McLintock and Company, he was the UK and Irish representative of the International Auditing Practices Committee between 1983 and 1988. Its chairman between 1989 and 1990, he had been the vice-chairman of the CCAB's Auditing Practices Committee since 1986. A former technical director of the Institute of Chartered Accountants of Scotland, he is a visiting professor of accounting at the University of Bristol and was visiting professor of accounting at the International Centre for Research in Accounting at the University of Lancaster for ten years. He has written or co-authored many books and articles. In 1990 Professor Tweedie became full-time chairman of the newly-formed Accounting Standards Board, a committee responsible for producing the UK's accounting standards.

SIR BRYAN CARSBERG ▼

Sir Bryan Carsberg, Director General of the Office of Fair Trading, is a graduate of the London School of Economics. A Professor of Accounting and Business Finance at the University of Manchester between 1969 and 1981, he was appointed Dean of the Faculty of Economic and Social Studies in 1978. A visiting professor at the University of California (Berkeley) in 1974, he went on to advise the Secretary of State for Trade and Industry on the privatisation of British Telecom. Sir Bryan was first Director General of Telecommunications until 1992, when he was appointed Director General of Fair Trading. A Fellow of the Institute of Chartered Accountants of England and Wales since 1970, he has written or co-written a number of books on economics. Born in 1939, Sir Bryan is married with two daughters. He was presented with the Founding Societies Centenary Award in 1988 for his work with OFTEL, the telecommunications watchdog, and knighted in 1989.

◄ WILLIAM MORRISON

William Morrison, born in 1938, is UK deputy senior partner of KPMG Peat Marwick. He qualified as a chartered accountant in 1961 and became joint senior partner of Thomas McLintock, Glasgow and Edinburgh, in 1974. Since the merger of Thomas McLintock with Peat Marwick in 1987, he has been deputy senior partner. He has served on the boards of many companies, including Thomas Cook and Scottish Telecommunications. Between 1989 and 1990 he chaired a Department of Trade and Industry committee examining auditor's and reporting accountant's liability. A former president of the Institute of Chartered Accountants of Scotland, he has been visiting professor in accountancy at the University of Strathclyde since 1983 and vice-president of the Scottish Council (Development and Industry) since 1982. Governor between 1977 and 1980, he was chairman of Kelvinside Academy from 1975-80. He was elected a Fellow of the Royal Society of Arts in 1990.

ELWYN EILLEDGE ▼

Senior partner of Ernst and Young UK, Elwyn Eilledge is also co-chairman of Ernst and Young International. A philosophy, politics and economics graduate of Oxford, he joined Ernst and Whinny in 1966. Immediately seconded to Liberia, he led a review of government bureaucracy, then went to Hamburg with responsibility for major clients. A partner in the London Audit Department, he was appointed managing partner of the London office in 1983. He became the deputy senior partner of Ernst and Whinny UK in 1985 and senior partner a year later. On the merger with Arthur Young in 1989, he became the senior partner of Ernst and Young UK.

LORD YOUNGER →

Son and heir of the 3rd Viscount Younger of Leckie Lord Younger read modern history at Cambridge. Prior to entering politics he worked for the family brewing firm where he was a director for ten years, until 1968. He was also a director of Tennent Caledonian Breweries Ltd from 1977-79. At the 1964 general election he was elected member for Ayr and held the seat until resigning at the 1992 election. In 1989 he resigned as Secretary of State for Defence to return to business, joining the board of The Royal Bank of Scotland. He is currently chairman of The Royal Bank of Scotland Group plc. He is deputy chairman of four Murray Johnstone Investment Trusts and on the board of Scottish Equitable Life Assurance Society, Siemens Plessey Electronic Systems Ltd, BCH Property Ltd, Banco de Santander SA, Ayrshire Community Airport Project Ltd (ACAP) and Scottish Partnership in Electronics for Effective Distribution Ltd (SPEED). He is also chairman of the Edinburgh Festival Theatre Trust and a Fellow of the Royal Society of Arts in Scotland. Last year he received honorary degrees from Glasgow, Edinburgh and Napier universities.
Photograph by Antonia Reeve

THE RT HON ROBIN ▼ LEIGH-PEMBERTON

Robin Leigh-Pemberton has been the governor of the Bank of England since 1983. After military service with the Grenadier Guards he read Classics at Oxford and then studied Law. He was called to the Bar in 1954. After practising Law he went into industry serving on the Boards of Birmid-Qualcast Ltd, Redland Ltd and the Equitable Life Assurance Society. In 1972 he joined the Board of National Westminster Bank, where he became chairman in 1977.

WILLIAM PURVES ▼

After serving with the King's Own Scottish Borderers, with whom he won a DSO, William Purves worked for the National Bank of Scotland from 1948 to 1954. He then joined the Hong Kong and Shanghai Banking Corporation and in 1966 was seconded to Morgan Guaranty Trust Company of New York. In 1979 he was appointed general manager International and, in 1982, executive director Banking. He became deputy chairman in 1984, chief executive in 1986 and chairman in 1986. He was appointed a member of the Executive Council (the Hong Kong government's highest policy making body) in 1987. He is an honorary doctor of Stirling University, a fellow and vice-president of the Chartered Institute of Bankers and a member of the Exchange Fund Advisory Committee. He is also deputy chairman of the Royal Hong Kong Jockey Club and chairman of the Sports Development Board. In June 1988 he was made a CBE.

SIR NICHOLAS GOODISON

Sir Nicholas Goodison was appointed chairman of the TSB Group in January 1989. He was chairman of the Stock Exchange from 1976 to 1988 and during this term also served as president of the International Federation of Stock Exchanges from 1985-86. He is president of the British Bankers' Association and a director of British Steel plc and General Accident plc. He is also chairman of the National Art Collections Fund and the Courtauld Institute of Art, a trustee of the National Heritage Memorial Fund and vice-chairman of the English National Opera.

SIR CHRISTOPHER TUGENDHAT

Sir Christopher joined the Board of Abbey National plc as non-executive deputy chairman in June 1991 and was appointed chairman a month later. Prior to this appointment he served as chairman of the Civil Aviation Authority (1986-91). His previous directorships include deputy chairman, National Westminster Bank plc and director, Commercial Union Assurance Company. From 1981 to 1985 he served as a vice-president of the Commission of the European Communities and from 1977 until 1981 as a member of the Commission. Prior to this he served as the Conservative member of Parliament for the City of London and Westminster South from 1970 to 1976. Before entering Parliament he worked as a leader and feature writer on the Financial Times. His books include Oil – The Biggest Business; The Multinationals, which won the McKinsey Foundation Book Award in the US; Making Sense of Europe; and Options for British Foreign Policy in the 1990s. His current non-executive directorships include Eurotunnel plc, LWT (Holdings) plc and the BOC Group plc. He is chairman of the Royal Institute of International Affairs, governor and member of the Council of Management of the Ditchley Foundation, vice-president of the Council of the British Lung Foundation and a Freeman of the City of London.

SIR PETER WALTERS

Sir Peter started his business career with BP. From vice-president of BP North America he became regional director for the Western Hemisphere, Australasia and the Far East, then managing director and deputy chairman. He was appointed chairman in 1981 and retired in 1990. He was chairman of the Post Office from 1978-79 and NatWest Bank (1981-89), president of the General Council of British Shipping (1977-78), the

Society of Chemical Industry (1979-80), and the Institute of Manpower Studies (1980-86), a board member and then chairman (1985-87) of the International Management Institute, Geneva. He was also chairman of the governing body of the London Business School and director of the London Business School Trust Company (1987-91). In 1986 he became president of the Institute of Directors and a managing trustee of the Institute of Economic Affairs. He was appointed a non-executive director of Smith Kline Beecham and of Thorn EMI in 1989 and ebcame deputy chairman of Thorn in 1990. He is non-executive chairman of Blue Circle Industries and vice-president of the Chartered Institute of Bankers. He was knighted in the 1984 New Year Honours, holds honorary doctorates at several universities and was awarded the Cadman Medal from the Institute of Petroleum in 1989.

COLIN BROWN, SIMON BROWN AND MICHAEL BROWN ➤

The Brown family has been in the pawnbroking business since 1840 and the current management team of father Colin and sons Simon and Michael has done more than most to update its image. There shop at Castleford, West Yorkshire, is the centre of an impressive empire that includes nine other outlets and an expanding franchise operation with shops in various towns and cities including one in London that is a stone's throw from the Houses of Parliament. Simon, 29, believes the profession's image is changing and that it is no longer just a service for the poor and desperate. Browns' clients include lawyers and restaurateurs who might simply find themselves in need of ready cash. Although watches and jewellery still make up 99 per cent of their business, they have accepted everything from gold teeth to a car, the latter for a businesswoman who wanted to make a quick investment. Another contemporary aspect of the business is the use of computers, although transactions are still entered by hand in a ledger. In the franchise operation, the firm provides expertise and half the necessary funding in return for half the profits. The Browns hope to operate at least 30 franchises in due course and it is hard to disagree with Simon when he says: "Historically, pawnbroking has a bad image – but it's changing fast."

PHILIP MURPHY ▼

Philip (Phil) Murphy has been managing director of Albermarle & Bond Pawnbrokers Ltd since its inception in 1983. From 1962-65 he was pledge manager with E. A. Barker Ltd of London and A. Walker and Sons in the South East. He then became a partner with the latter company in Bromley before acquiring his own jewellery business, Brent Jewellers of Bristol, in 1971 (in partnership with wife Jean). He was managing director of Harvey and Thompson plc in 1979 while retaining involvement in his own business. He is currently responsible for the day-to-day running of a company with 11 pawnbroking and five retail outlets nationwide. Phil and Jean have two grown-up sons.

WARWICK BARTLETT ▼

Warwick Bartlett says he opened Cashline Pawnbrokers, his company in West Bromwich, because he predicted the imminent "credit crunch". He believes the key to success in his profession is training staff in customer service and treating the public with the utmost respect. Contracts are for six months and he writes to customers before and after expiry so they have every chance to avoid losing their valuables. The premises are secured "like a bank" and the firm offers free insurance to the value of twice the loan while goods are in pledge. Many customers find the service preferable to a bank loan because it avoids the inevitable strongly-worded letter! Warwick, 45, was recently asked if he would take a Mercedes 500SL in pawn and had to decline because it would have meant taking possession of the vehicle – but he managed to raise the finance for the customer through a leasing company.

ARCHIBALD CROCKET ⬆

Raised in the East End of Glasgow, Archibald Crocket started work as an auctioneer's clerk with the firm of Arthur E. Collins and Son Ltd in 1971. He became a director of the company nine years later when still only 25 years old. In 1985, along with partners Tom Myles and Margaret Stuart, he took over the Glasgow Pawnbroking Company Ltd in Bath Street, which had been established in 1865. Since 1990 he has been on the council of the National Pawnbrokers Association. He is married with three daughters, aged 14, eight and three.

BARRIE STRONG ⬇

Barrie Strong is the general manager of the pawnbroking section of E. A. Barker Ltd, a firm established more than 250 years ago in the London district of Houndsditch. It remains the only pawnbrokers in the historical square mile of the City of London and maintains the traditional approach of discretion and confidentiality. There are no limits on deposits and the firm specialises in antique jewellery and silver (its main business is as diamond merchants, jewellers, goldsmiths and silversmiths). Barrie is married with three children.

ANDREW BROWN ⬆

As general manager of T. M. Sutton Ltd, Andrew Brown is carrying on a pawnbroking tradition that began when this firm was founded in London's Victoria district in 1776. It moved to its present purpose-built site in 1936, at which time it was a family-run business with agencies in Berlin, Paris and Cannes. These fell foul of the Third Reich. The Garrads/Mappin & Webb group bought it out in 1970 and a more recent change involved a takeover by the Asprey/Mappin & Webb group in 1990. Traditionally, T. M. Sutton Ltd has always attempted to attract the "higher end" of the market and for many years attracted clients from the aristocracy, show business, sport and even politics. More recently, Middle Eastern clients have predominated, with many transactions carried out on a day-to-day basis. There was continuous activity during the Gulf War, when many London-based Arabs suffered a severe shortage of cash and many internationally-known items of jewellery were pledged across Suttons' counter. Married with two children, aged six and three, Andrew Brown lives in Worcester Park, Surrey.

ANTHONY OSBORNE ⬆

Some of Anthony Osborne's earliest memories are of his grandfather's Northampton pawnbroker's shop at a time (the early 1960s) when money was loaned on virtually anything. He recalls a store full of bundles of clothes, shoes, electrical goods and jewellery which was kept in a shoe box under the counter. Anthony left school at the age of 16 and was sent to London to learn the trade with a city firm. After five years he returned to the family business and worked with his father until the elder Osborne's retirement. Now aged 37, and married with two sons, Anthony is an active member of the National Pawnbrokers Association and believes a strong trade association is the best way forward for the profession. He admits, however, that a lot of hard work is still required before pawnbrokers can claim the same "respectable" image as other financial institutions.

ANDREW HOPPER ▼

Born in Poland in 1953, Andrew Hopper moved to England at the age of ten and, in 1974, graduated from the University of Wales with a BSc (1st Class Hons) in computer technology. He went on to receive his Doctorate at Cambridge University in computer science in 1977 and worked at Cambridge as a research assistant from 1977 to 1979. In 1979 he became an assistant lecturer and, from 1983 until 1992, a university lecturer. He is currently Reader in Computer Technology at the University of Cambridge. In 1986 he was asked by Olivetti to start a corporate research laboratory in Cambridge. This involved setting up the research base, the administrative and legal framework and recruiting the research engineers. He is the Director of the Olivetti Research Laboratory (ORL) and currently responsible for the work of 50 researchers. The author of numerous papers and contributor to several books, in 1981 he was elected a Fellow of Corpus Christi College, Cambridge.

STEVE FURBER ▼

Steve Furber is the ICL Professor of Computer Engineering in the Department of Computer Science at Manchester University. Prior to this appointment, he was in charge of the hardware development group within the R&D department at Acorn Computers Ltd. He was a principal designer of the BBC Microcomputer and the Acorn RISC Machine, both of which earned Acorn a Queen's Award for Technology. He led the team which developed the hardware architecture and VSLI components for the Acorn Archimedes. Since moving to Manchester in 1990 he has established a research group with interests in asynchronous logic design and has secured funds from the CEC and the UK government to develop asynchronous logic design methodologies within a range of industrial collaborative projects related to low-power CMOS and high-speed bipolar processor design and portable consumer applications. Steve's first degree at Cambridge was in mathematics and his PhD is in aerodynamics; computing was originally his hobby.

MAURICE V. WILKES ▼

One of the great pioneers of computer technology, Maurice V. Wilkes was for many years head of the computer laboratory of the University of Cambridge. Born in 1913, he graduated with a BA from St John's College, Cambridge, in 1934, an MA in 1936 and acquired his Doctorate in 1937. He spent WWII in radar engineering and operational research. He returned to Cambridge as head of the computer laboratory until 1980. He was Professor of Computer Technology from 1965 to 1980 and is now Emeritus Professor. He has been a Fellow of St John's College, Cambridge, since 1950, a Fellow of the Royal Society since 1956 and was the first President of the British Computer Society, of which he is now a Distinguished Fellow. He is a Foreign Associate of both the US National Academy of Science and of Engineering and was the recipient of the 1992 Kyoto Prize for Advanced Technology. Maurice Wilkes was responsible for the development of the first stored digital computer to be put into regular service, in 1949. Now a consultant for Olivetti, his book, Memoirs of a Computer Pioneer, was published in 1985.

HAROON AHMED ◄

Professor Haroon Ahmed is Professor of Microelectronics and head of the Microelectronics Research Centre of the Cavendish Library at Cambridge University. He graduated from Imperial College, London, in 1958 and received his PhD from Cambridge in 1962. He worked in the Engineering Department of Cambridge University from 1962 to 1984, when he moved to the Physics Department as Reader in Microelectronics. He was elected as a Fellow of Corpus Christi College in 1967 and as a Fellow of the Royal Academy of Engineering in 1990. He is the author of Introduction to Physical Electronics (1968), Electronics (1973) and Analogue and Digital Electronics for Engineers (1984). He is a Fellow of the Institution of Engineers and a Fellow of the Institute of Physics.

ROGER WILSON ▼

A graduate of Selwyn College, Cambridge, Roger Wilson is system design manager at Acorn Computers, a consultant to Advanced RISC Machines Ltd and a non-executive director of Eidos plc, which develops non-linear digital video editing equipment. He designed hardware for Acorn's early ranges before moving into software. He designed and wrote BBC BASIC and designed its operating and dual processor systems. In 1983 he designed the instruction set for the Acorn RISC machine and provided systems design input for the chip set, computer hardware and operating system for the launch of the first personal RISC computer, the Acorn Archimedes. In 1992 he was presented with an award for the development of Acorn Replay.

DAVID MAY ▼

David May graduated from Cambridge University in 1972 with a degree in computer science and went to work at Warwick University on artificial intelligence and robotics. In 1979 he joined Inmos to design microelectronic components for concurrent systems. He is responsible for the architecture of the Inmos transputers and the design of the Occam programming language. Also in 1979 David was appointed a visiting professor at Oxford University. He is currently working at Inmos on the architecture of new products for introduction in 1995. In 1991 he was elected a Fellow of the Royal Society for his contributions to the development of parallel computing.

SIR CLIVE SINCLAIR ▲

Born in London in 1940, inventor Sir Clive Sinclair worked as a technical journalist before founding Sinclair Radionics in 1962. He rapidly developed a reputation as a consumer electronics pioneer, particularly in miniaturisation. In 1972 he produced the world's first truly "pocket" calculator, the Executive. He continued to make developments in digital watches and instruments and, in 1977, developed another world's first with the 2in Microvision. From 1979 onwards, Sir Clive involved himself extensively in pioneering the new era of home computers – initially with the first sub-£100 computer, the ZX80, and later with the ZX81 and the Spectrum, both of which sold over a million worldwide. The flat-screen pocket TV followed in 1983. More recently he has worked on developments from wafer-scale integration through portable computers to satellite receiving dishes. His latest product, the ultra-light Sinclair Zike electric bicycle, was launched in 1992.

BENEDICT FENWICK

After training as a chartered accountant, Benedict Fenwick took the bull by the horns, at the age of 24, and started Investment Intelligence, the first firm of Investment Counsellors in the City. Over the next 20 years the company went from strength to strength before being sold to Bowrings. He then joined a firm of headhunters where he received a thorough training over four years – the only time in his career when he has not been self-employed. Now chairman of David Sheppard and Partners, he joined the firm in 1984 and enjoyed wide-ranging success before buying the company with a colleague. Established in 1967, its reputation is based on a policy of being "professional, human and select". Benedict Fenwick's other business interests include the chairmanship of Family Garden Centre Companies.

SIR ROBIN CHICHESTER-CLARK

The official jargon may be Executive Search and Recruitment Management Consultants but the word most often used is headhunters – and the company that leads the field is the Welbeck Group run by former Government minister Sir Robin Chichester-Clark. He was responsible for what has been described as "the most successful headhunting operation ever" – recruiting Lord King to run British Airways. In recent years he has retired from other business interests to concentrate on Welbeck's activities. Born in 1928, he was educated at the Royal Naval College and Magdalene College, Cambridge. After graduation he worked as a copy boy for Time-Life in New York ("for the dollars"), later being employed as a reporter on the Evening News in Portsmouth and the Hampshire Telegraph. He found "a quieter life" handling public relations for Glyndebourne, where he fell in love with opera and his first wife. He has been an MP, Comptroller of HM Household ("attending the Royal Family at garden parties, diplomatic evenings – that sort of thing"), Opposition spokesman on Northern Ireland while Labour was in power 1964-70, and Minister of State at the Department of Employment 1972-74. He has sat on the Select Committee that considers the Civil List. He has a son and two daughters by his first marriage and two sons by his present one.

IAN ODGERS

South African born Ian Odgers, chairman of Odgers & Co Ltd, made his home in Britain after reading engineering at Cambridge University. After graduating, he indulged his first love – aircraft engineering – by joining the British Aircraft Corporation as an apprentice and subsequently worked on the design and development of electronic systems in Holland and Weybridge, Surrey. In 1965 he studied at Cranfield School of Management, then joined Norton Abrasives until becoming chief executive of Odgers in 1972. His search activities mainly concentrate on plc main board appointments, with particular emphasis on chairman, CEO and non-executive directors. His own non-executive directorship at the City of London Symphonia reflects a lifelong interest in music.

PETER CHALKLEY ▼

Peter Chalkley has been with the same company, Sabre International Search, for 24 years. Now a senior partner, among his responsibilities are operating internationally with EEC and EFTA countries. Prior to Sabre, he was general manager of Associated Foods, having earlier served with the Royal Horse Guards. During his career, Peter has been on a number of committees with various professional bodies including the Confederation of British Industry, the British Institute of Management and the Chartered Institute of Marketing. He is currently serving with the Institute of Directors, having been a member since 1969. He has also been a JP and a school governor.

JOHN STORK ▲

John Stork's early career was in textiles and an interest in fashion and marketing led to appointments in market research with Attwood Statistics and Masius Wynne-Williams (now DMB & B). He was appointed Group Research Director of MWW in 1966, later moving into general management of advertising agencies in the same group. While living in Zurich, Paris and London, he supervised global accounts such as Colgate-Palmolive. In 1974 he founded John Stork International Group which developed into one of the leading European-based executive search firms. It merged with Korn/Ferry in 1988 and John was subsequently appointed chairman and chief executive. He resigned in 1992 to concentrate on international management consultancy.

◀ RODERICK GOW

Roderick Gow, group chief executive of GKR Group Ltd since 1991, spent his early years in the Scots Guards, during which time he held the position of personal staff officer to the chairman of NATO. He then joined Barclays Bank for five years, moving to New York and working as vice-president, Corporate Banking. In 1983 he was headhunted to join a major company of international consultants, taking responsibility for international business development in 1990. Currently heading up GKR's Financial Services Practice, Roderick is a man of many interests: he is an Associate of the Chartered Institute of Bankers, a member of the International Advisory Board of Phillips Fine Art Auctioneers, and a member of the Royal Company of Archers, the Queen's Bodyguard in Scotland.

ANDREW PECK ▼

Newly appointed as managing director of the Richmond Partnership, Andrew Peck moved from Korn/Ferry International where he was a director of the Financial Services Practice in London. Prior to joining Korn/Ferry, he was chief executive of Trinity Insurance Company. During his career he has worked in a variety of roles in the Far East and Australia – he started with the Wharf Company in Hong Kong in 1974 (where he was also manager of the Kidder Peabody & Co office for a number of years) and worked with Merrill Lynch International as an investment banker in both New York and Sydney.

MILES BROADBENT ▼

Chief Executive of Norman, Broadbent International, Miles Broadbent has worked in top-level executive search for 14 years, specialising in recruiting chairmen, chief executives, non-executive board directors and other senior executives for British industrial and commercial companies. He co-founded the company in 1983 with David Norman (chairman), and in his present capacity is responsible for co-ordinating its worldwide reputation. A law and languages graduate from Cambridge (he is now an Advisory Board Member of the University), and with an MBA from Harvard Business School where he specialised in Human Behaviour and International finance, he began his career selling computer systems for IBM. Later he became a director of the brewers Watney Mann and Truman and managing director of Watney's international businesses, as well as chairman of Coca-Cola Southern Bottlers.

◄ BILL HALSON

A graduate in modern languages at Manchester University, Bill Halson also took a degree in business studies while pursuing a successful career in management consultancy. In 1971 Bill set up his own consulting company, PTS Ltd, of which he is still chairman and chief executive, and in 1985 took up an important four-year management contact with Royal Mail Letters. Bill and his wife acquired the Katharine Allen Marriage Bureau, based in London's West End, in 1986 and five years later absorbed their principal competitor, Heather Jenner.

BRUCE BROWN ▼

When Bruce Brown's marriage was destroyed by the restrictions imposed by his multiple sclerosis, conventional introduction agencies proved of little help in finding him a new partner. So in 1981 he founded Disdate, a penfriend and dating agency for lonely disabled people. Understanding the isolation of the disabled and the difficulty they can experience in finding friends and partners, Bruce has been able to bring together many formerly unattached clients. Disdate, run by Bruce from his Bedfordshire home, is a non-profitmaking organisation and a member of the Association of British Introduction Agencies. Its modest registration fee provides three introductions.

ROY GILBERT ▼

After a varied career which included working as an administrator with British Gas and teaching at an adult education institute, Roy Gilbert took early retirement. Not wanting his skill in dealing with people to go to waste, however, he set up the Kent Introduction Service with his partner Ann. A member of the Association of British Introduction Agencies and now in its sixth year, the Tonbridge-based agency has a policy of meeting all members as they join and has made many successful matches, some of them blossoming into marriage.

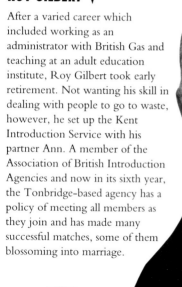

JOHN PATTERSON ▷

While travelling in the USA in 1966 shortly after leaving university, John Patterson saw the potential of the then novel technique of computer dating. Setting up his own company in London, he introduced the idea to Britain. After a slow start Dateline was eventually boosted by full-page advertising in newspapers and magazines and grew rapidly during the early 1970s. Constantly in the forefront of technology, Dateline continued to improve its computer resources and now has a huge VAX machine which is networked between London and Oxford. Employing a staff of 30, the company has a membership of over 40,000 seekers of love and happiness and is the world's largest, longest-established and most successful computer dating agency.

RAMESHWAR BHARGAVA ▲

In 1972, ten years after settling in Britain, Rameshwar Bhargava set up a marriage bureau with the aim of serving the Asian community. Today the Southall-based Suman Marriage Bureau enjoys an international reputation as a matchmaker. Rameshwar's achievement in arranging over 5,000 marriages, saving hundreds of others and keeping Asian traditions alive in foreign countries led to his being honoured in 1990 with the Mother India Award. He has also arranged hundreds of mixed marriages. Rameshwar received the Shiromani Award 1986 from the President of India in person, and his wife Suman was honoured with the same award for 1990. As well as being a partner in the company with his wife, Rameshwar plays an active role in the Asian community and in Anglo-Asian relations, holding a number of important offices.

PETER CHALLENOR ▼

After meeting through a mutual friend, Peter Challenor and his wife Denise decided to help other unattached people by setting up Perfect Partners in 1990. The Preston-based company grew rapidly and in 1991 took over Phoenix Introductions. Having extended its client base to the five north-west counties, the following year it also swallowed up its former rival, the Top People agency. Perfect Partners, which operates a standard and an executive register, aims to help single, divorced, widowed and genuinely separated people find friends and companions. The agency does not regard marriage between partners it has introduced as a primary aim. It also stresses that, because of the imbalance in the birth rates between the sexes, some men under 30 and some women over 50 will be disappointed.

Peter & Denise

SAPHEL ROSE ▲

Aware of a gap in the market for a dating agency using photographs, in 1990 Saphel Rose set up the Picture Dating Agency with Jeremy Wright, with whom he had worked in advertising. Membership of the agency, based just off London's Strand, has grown steadily and now stands at more than 2,000. In addition to its standard introduction service, which is conducted by post, through its Gold Service the agency allows members to attend the office for an interview and subsequently to select partners with the guidance of a consultant. The agency also holds popular drinks parties attended by around 100 members. By combining use of a computer database and manual matching, Saphel and Jeremy have seen the agency forge many successful relationships over the past 12 years.

GEORGE RENWICK ➡

George Renwick has been working in interior design since he left school. He set up his own company in London in 1971. His work ranges from the complete schemes for a 17th century stately home in England to flats and homes in London, Paris, Monaco, New York and Florida. He has designed everything from offices to a car showroom, a private luxury bus and an upmarket delicatessen. He has worked on the interiors of a Chinese junk and modern yachts and is at present recreating the interior for a 100ft 1908 steam yacht. His themes and schemes for parties have included the VIP entertainment tent and Royal Box for the Jean Michel Jarre concert in the Docklands. In 1988 Renwick and Clarke Trading was formed as a company specialising in supplying accessories to other interior designers and top of the range stores. Their range includes hand painted, embossed and gilded leather panels, decorative bronzes, silver, silver plate, pewter, porcelain, hand painted pottery and glass.

SIMON PLAYLE

Simon Playle's first job was with the hand-printed wallpaper company, Coles. From here he went to work for a small interior decorators in Walton Street where he designed, gilded and painted furnitue. In 1970 he joined George Spencer Decorations in Sloane Street where he stayed for ten years as a director decorating and designing as well as buying antiques for the shop. Since then he has been running his own design business, importing and marketing wallpapers and fabrics and marketing his own range of fabrics and carpets. He has exhibited at four British Interior Design Exhibitions winning the award for Best Room in 1989. His commissions range from houses and flats in Britain, New York and Hong Kong to a spa in Germany. Simon is a Fellow of the Interior Decorators and Designers Association and a member of the International Society of Interior Designers.

DAVID LAWS ▼

David Laws has been decorating for over 30 years, 22 of which he was a partner of Colefax & Fowler. He started his own company, David Law Designs Ltd, eight years ago and has been included in the AD100 publication. His commissions have included work for Lady (Oona) Chaplin in New York and Switzerland, the late Earl Spencer and DR Tony O'Reilly in Ireland, USA and the UK. He has worked on the refurbishing of the state rooms at No 10 Downing Street, Wilton's Restaurant in Jermyn Street, the main restaurant at The Berkeley Hotel, many town and country houses and more designing at Claridge's than any other decorator since the 1930s. He has just completed a design for a new dinner service for Royal Crown Derby and is currently working on the refurbishing of the British Embassy in Tehran.

GUY BEDFORD ▲

After leaving Hadlow College of Agriculture and Horticulture with an ONDA Guy Bedford worked on hop, dairy and arable farms and ran an organic farm in Kent. He started japanning antique furniture for export to Europe in 1975 for a local dealer and went freelance supplying outlets such as Harvey Nichols, Liberty and Harrods. During the late 1970s he exported American painted furniture (or Pennsylvanian "Dutch") to the States, all painted by himself, mainly on to pine furniture. 1980 saw the birth of his English Lacquer Shop in Bloomsbury, where he produces and restores modern and traditional furniture. He paints murals, trompe l'oeil and 18th and 19th century animal portraits. He also paints fairground organs, motorcycle and car body parts and has recently started signwriting.

ANTONY LITTLE ▼

Antony Little studied at Flintshire school of Art and then did a degree course at Kingston School of Art which awarded him the National Diploma in Design in 1963. This was followed by five years as a book illustrator and interior designer, producing specialised fabric and wallpaper designs for private clients. In 1968 he founded Osborne & Little, with his brother-in-law Peter Osborne, with a view to putting originality back in to British wallpaper design. They started with a small collection of handprints which earned them Britain's major public design prize, The Council of Industrial Design Award. They won the same prize again, renamed The British Design Award in 1987. Together with Peter, Antony has built up an international company quoted on the London Stock Exchange with divisions in the US and Germany and showrooms in London, Edinburgh, New York, Paris and Munich. Osborne & Little designs are represented in the permanent collection of several museums including the V&A, the Cooper Hewitt in New York, Chicago Institute of Art.

MICHAEL GILES ▼

After leaving school Michael Giles worked as an art tutor before doing his national service in the Royal Marines. He attained the rank of major in the Royal Marines Reserve and was awarded a volunteer reserve decoration in 1968. He then took up a three year apprenticeship as interior designer with Storey's of Kensington, before joining the family practice of Godfrey Giles and Co, founded by his grandfather in 1886, where he is currently managing director. Among his recent design projects was the Grade 1 Wren City Church, St James Garlickhythe, the Grade 1 Wren Building Morden College, Blackheath, the private residence of the Nigerian High Commission in Kensington, the design (won in a competition) of the Grade 1 building, Bridgewater House, St James, SW1. Michael is vice-president of the Chartered Society of Designers, master of the Painter Stationers Company and a brother of the Art Workers Guild. He was a founder member of the Nine Elms Group of Artists in 1987, and has exhibited at, among other venues, the Oval, Lambeth Palace and Painters Hall.

RASSHIED ALI DIN ▼

Rasshied Din is managing director of the design consultancy Din Associates. He set up the company in 1986 when he undertook the design of the Next flagship department store in Kensington Hire Street. Since then he has built up a varied client list ranging from Ralph Lauren to French Connection, Nicole Farhi, Fenwick and BAA. His design for the Dept X store in Oxford Street won the DBA Design Effectiveness Award in 1989, and in 1990 Din Associates collected the D&AD Silver Award for Best Environmental Design for the Nicole Farhi showroom in the West End.

CLIVE RHODES ▼

After five years as an acclaimed restaurateur Clive Rhodes was headhunted by James Lill Interior Decorators Ltd in 1978. He trained under Michael Lill and James Baildom in the traditional domestic interiors market. Five years on, with the retirement of his mentors, he founded Clive Rhodes Interior Design. His favourite era is the Regency for its exuberance and diversity and his specialities include tented rooms and the recolouring of historical wallpapers. His finely detailed curtains, valances, cushions, rondels and tie backs are works of art in themselves.

KENNETH TURNER

Kenneth Turner and his studio produce some of the most coveted decorations to be found in the world of floral design, creating themes and ideas that go to the heart of an occasion, transforming rooms or, even, entire buildings. Kenneth Turner International Ltd has established a trading partnership in Japan, where table linens, kitchen textiles, bed and bathroom accessories, fragrant candles, pot pourries, toiletries and gifts compliment the displays of fresh and dried flowers. The expanding range of products is sold throughout the world. Kenneth Turner's successful TV series Floral Fantasies continues to be networked, and a new book is to be released in 1993.

MYLES CHALLIS

Realising that his flair for laying out and planting "exotic" gardens was unique in Britain, Myles Challis turned his hobby into a business ten years ago. In 1986, at the Chelsea Flower Show, he staged his legendary Neptune Garden, a bust of God emerging from a pool, spurting water and surrounded by exotic vegetation, which was to bring him fame, and lead to the commission of two books to date: The Exotic Garden (1986), and Large Leaved Perennials (1992). Myles is the leader of a movement, now known as the Exoticists, of people specialising in the propagation of exotic looking plants.

RANDAL VAN TWISK

Randal Van Twisk's originality and skill with flowers has brought a large and varied clientele to his London SW1 shop. Local business has been quick to take advantage of his talents, and personal clients use him for special occasions such as weddings and birthdays. Amongst the secrets of the success of Flowers by Van Twisk are employing knowledgeable and helpful staff and buying the best produce daily.

STEPHEN WOODHAMS

Stephen Woodhams started as a horticulturalist, training at the RHS garden at Wisley, and originally went into landscaping design. However, he soon added flowers to his portfolio, and it is here that he has made his name. He has built up an impressive reputation for the flowers he provides for corporate and private clients, and specialises in "theming" an event, taking care of every detail from the tablecloths through to the lighting. Clients include Ralph Lauren, the Royal Opera House and the Waterside Inn at Bray. He is regularly featured in magazines such as House & Garden and Country Homes & Interiors. The landscape division of the company is still based in Surrey, while "Woodhams" is now at Notting Hill Gate.

Photograph by Simon Brown

STEPHEN CRISP

Stephen Crisp is a landscape consultant, garden designer and "Theme Decorator". He qualified in a two year work study course at the Royal Horticulturalist Society in Wisley, and at various training programmes both in the UK and the USA. For six and a half years he was horticulturalist at Leeds Castle in Kent, before moving, in 1987, to his current position, with responsibility for 12 acres of grounds and the theme decoration of a senior diplomatic residence in London. Through his own company, SPC Designs, Stephen practices as a theme decorator for major public and private events, using flowers, fabrics, props, paint effects, light, sound, scent and even fireworks to turn an occasion into a memorable experience. Stephen Crisp is much in demand as a speaker and writer on both sides of the Atlantic.

ALWYN FUNKE

Born in 1951, Alwyn Funke started his horticultural career at the RHS gardens at Wisley. In 1972 the landscaping company the Craigwell group was formed, with Alwyn as managing director. An International Exhibition Division was quickly formed, and soon expanded into Europe, participating in landscaping at such events as the Paris Air Show, Foire de Paris, Telecom in Geneva and industrial exhibitions throughout Germany. Through the 1970s and 1980s Alwyn led the company in the pioneering of shallow-planting in roof garden and atrium projects while still undertaking more conventional gardening, including the restoration of the grounds at Sutton Place. Major construction projects have included a six year contract for a business park at Heathrow, and a landscaping project for the Sultan of Oman's summer palace. Currently, he is working on the restoration of Tittenhurst Park at Sunningdale, and is negotiating projects in France, Germany, Portugal and Spain.

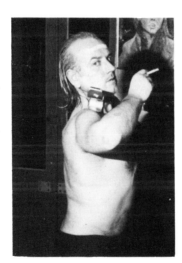

GRAHAM CROAN

Graham Croan recently re-opened his Edinburgh antique shop as a flower shop, also selling modern and antique vases, mirrors, candlesticks and collectables. He supplies hairdressers, restaurants, offices, churches and houses with regular supplies of fresh flowers. Graham is, however, more of a floral decorator than a florist, and works with dried, silk and plastic as well as fresh flowers. He also involves himself with landscape architecture, and has reproduced whole walls of his shop in customers' houses.

ARCHITECTS

TERRY FARRELL ▼

Terry Farrell is rapidly becoming London's landmark architect; his many award-winning designs include Alban Gate in the City, the government buildings for PSA at Vauxhall Cross and the Charing Cross development on the Thames. He graduated from the University of Newcastle School of Architecture, and was a Harkness Fellow at the University of Pennsylvania between 1962 and 1964. Co-ordinating Masterplanner of the Paternoster Square redevelopment at St Paul's, he has also been responsible for several restorations, including Tobacco Dock and work in Covent Garden; he will be co-ordinating the improvement and renovation of the South Bank arts complex. Farrell and Company's work-in-progress includes three major developments in Hong Kong and the restoration of the mediaeval quarter of York. An English Heritage Commissioner, Terry Farrell is a Member of the Royal Institute of British Architects and the Royal Town Planning Institute, and a Fellow of the Chartered Society of Designers.

PETER FOGGO ▶

Peter Foggo is, by his own admission, an architect by accident and not by design. A graduate of Liverpool University, he joined the architecture course in its third year – having studied alone for some time. On graduation he spent two years with Architects Co-Partnership, and joined Ove Arup and Partners in 1959. He worked at Arup for 20 years before establishing his own practice with many of the design group from Arup, in 1989. Peter Foggo Associates is a multi-disciplinary practice, where architects work closely with structural engineers, service engineers and quantity surveyors. Their work includes factories for John Player and Sons in Nottingham and Trebor in Colchester, office developments in Basingstoke for Wiggins Teape and, more recently, Finsbury Avenue phasies 1 to 3 and Broadgate phases 1 to 4 in the City of London. With a brief to design lasting works of architecture, Peter Foggo's work is an outstanding example of his own belief that architecture is an art as well as a science.

PIERS GOUGH ▼

With commissions including Cascades, China Wharf, Wolfe Crescent and The Circle, and with work-in-progress at Metropolitan Wahrf, Piers Gough perhaps qualifies as the architect of London's Docklands. He studied at the Architectural Association and has been a partner in Campbell Zogolovitch Wilkinson and Gough (CZWG) since 1971. CZWG is presently planning the Crown Street Regeneration Project, the redevelopment of a site in the Gorbals, Glasgow. Piers Gough is honorary secretary of the Council of the Architectural Association and a member of the Urban Design Group of the London Docklands Development Corporation. A regular contributor to the art and architectural press, he organised the Lutyens exhibition at the Hayward Gallery in 1982 and the Gilbert exhibition at the Royal Academy in 1985. Visiting professor at the Macintosh School in Glasgow and at the University of Wales Institute of Science and Technology, he has also lectured in Europe, the Americas and Australia.

NIGEL COATES

Nigel Coates, founder of the influential group Narrative Architecture Today (NATO), is noted for examining the dialogue between his designs and the cities in which they will be built. He graduated from the Architectural Association in 1974, became unit master in 1979, and formed NATO in 1983. NATO is the basis of the practice Nigel formed with Doug Branson in 1985 – Branson Coates Architects (BCA). Often working with artists and craftspeople, they were among the first UK designers to work in Japan: Arca di No in Sapporo, BCA's first building in Japan, was completed in 1988. It was soon followed by the Hotel Otaru Marittimo in Sapporo and The Wall in Tokyo; The Penrose Institute, a gallery and museum in the capital is due for completion in 1993. BCA's critically-acclaimed work for commercial clients in London includes shops for Katherine Hamnett and Jigsaw.

JOHN QUINLAN TERRY

Through his early association with Raymond Erith, Quinlan Terry is known for reviving and re-inventing classical architecture. A graduate of the Architectural Association, he joined Erith's practice in 1962. They worked together until the early 1970s on a number of important projects. After Erith's death in 1973, Quinlan Terry continued working in the style of Fundamental Classicism established by the partnership. He has designed new stone and brick country houses, of which Waverton House in Gloucester is a particularly fine example. The practice, still known as Erith and Terry, has a number of commercial schemes in central London to its credit. His most notable public commissions are perhaps the Maitland Robinson Library at Downing College, Cambridge, and the restoration of the Queen's College Chapel, Oxford.

WILLIAM ALSOP ▲

Awarded the William Van Allen Medal for Architecture in New York and the Bernard Webb Scholarship in Rome, architect and painter William Alsop is a graduate of the Architectural Association. He taught sculpture at St Martin's School of Art in London, has been visiting professor at universities in America and Australia and is presently professor of architecture at the Bremen Academy for Fine Art and Music. Notable examples of his recent work include the 125 million pound barrage at Cardiff Bay for the Cardiff Bay Development Corporation, the Tower Project at Caen, the government headquarters for the Department des Bouche du Rhône in Marseille and, in London, the fit-out of the underground station at North Greenwich. Alsop's architecture is intimately related to his painting and he often collaborates with contemporary artists; he worked with Gareth Jones on the Cardiff Bay barrage and with Brian Clarke on the government headquarters in Marseille. His work, both architecture and painting, is often exhibited in Europe – most recently at Aedes Gallery in Berlin.

MICHAEL HAYES ▲

Born in 1945 Michael Hayes started his building career in 1962 as an indentured student with Trollope & Colls, where he spent seven years. He joined Cubitts Ltd as a quantity surveyor, working on their Thamesmead new town project and subsequently in the planning department. He joined Cementation Ltd in 1972 as a quantity surveyor, initially responsible for final account preparation and claims on a project in Bristol, and later as a trouble-shooter on various projects. He moved on to be a site manager, and then a project manager, firstly on the Hilton hotel in Jakarta and later on the Wembley Conference Centre. He joined Norwest Holst Construction Ltd in 1978 as a contracts manager, became divisional director for the Southern Division in 1981, divisional managing director in 1985 and managing director of the company in 1990. In 1992 he was promoted to the group board, responsible for group operations, with an annual turnover of £400 million. Michael Hayes is a member of the Chartered Institute of Building, the Institute of Architects and Surveyors and the Worshipful Company of Joiners and Ceilers. He is married with two daughters and lives in Essex.

JOHN LELLIOT ▼

The founder and chairman of the John Lelliot Construction Group, one of the largest privately owned construction and building specialist groups in the UK, was born in Teddington in 1935. In 1951 he joined Marshall Andrew, a national contractor, as an indentured surveyor/estimator, during which time he took his HNC in building. He spent two years on National Service with the Royal Engineers in Hong Kong, where he took the Institute of Building's final certificate, and rejoined Marshall Andrew for a further two years before starting his own company in 1965. John is a Fellow of the Chartered Institute of Building, a member of the National Children's Home, a committee member of the London City Ballet, vice-president of the St John Ambulance, Prince of Wales district, and holder of the Order of St John, vice-chairman of Wimbledon FC, vice-chairman of the Regional Sports Council, chairman of the London Region Sports Council Finance and Grant Aid Committee and a member of the Institute of Directors. He has been married to Patsy for 33 years.

COLIN PARSONS

Colin Parsons joined Taylor Woodrow in 1959, working with the group's related Canadian company, Monarch. Born in 1934 and a qualified chartered accountant, he worked his way up the corporate ladder to become president of Monarch Development Corporation in 1976. Monarch is Canada's oldest established housebuilder and developer, with activities extending across the whole of North America. In June 1987 Colin Parsons was appointed to the board of Taylor Woodrow plc. He became chairman in 1992. A Welshman by birth he is married with two children.

MARTIN LAING ▼

The chairan of John Laing plc, Martin Laing is the son of the ex-chairman, Sir Kirby Laing and the eldest grandson of the company's founder, Sir John Laing. After reading estate management at Cambridge he spent two years with Jones, Lang and Wootton before joining the Laing group in 1966, working in Yorkshire with the Laing Development Company. He gained valuable experience working overseas for the group, in Canada and the Middle East, before returning to the UK in 1981 to take up the post of group marketing director. He was appointed chairman in 1985. Martin Laing is a past chairman of the executive committee of the BEC's National Contractors Group and, in 1988, was appointed to the NEDO Construction Industry Sector Group as the BEC representative, until the Group was disbanded in 1992. Since 1986 he has been involved with Business in the Community and is currently a member of the Prince of Wales' Urban Villages Group. He was appointed chairman on the CBI Overseas committee in 1989 and is a member of the council. He sits on the UK advisory committee of the British-American Chamber of Commerce and is a director of the UK-Japan 2000 group. A member of the advisory council to the World Economic Forum, he is a governor of its Engineering and Construction forum. Amongst his other many and varied appointments, Martin Laing is the chairman of the World Wide Fund for Nature in the UK and a board member of WWF International. Appointed CBE in 1991, Martin Laing is a deputy lieutenant of Hertfordshire.

BARRY MYERS ▲

Barry Myers started his career in the building industry in 1961, at the age of 17, when he joined the Ideal Building Corporation, working with Carlton Contractors in their scheduling department as a trainee surveyor/draughtsman. The company was subsequently bought by Trafalgar House and Barry Myers worked his way up to become chief surveyor in 1972 and, soon afterwards, a director, at the age of 28. When Willett Ltd was brought into Trafalgar House, Barry Myers joined its board, becoming managing director in 1977 and chairman three years later. In 1982 he moved as managing director to Cementation International Ltd, where his responsibilities rapidly increased to encompass all the Cementation companies, then all the building companies and, in 1986, he was appointed managing director of Trafalgar House Building and Civil Engineering Holdings Ltd, which has increased its activities worldwide, and now become Trafalgar House Construction Ltd, with an annual turnover of £1.3 billion. Barry Myers is married with two children and lives on a farm near Guildford, where he and his wife rear Herefords.

INTERIOR DESIGNERS/DECORATORS

DAVID MLINARIC ▼

One of Britain's most respected interior designers, David Mlinaric is best known for his work on historic buildings. He trained at Bartlett School of Architecture and set up his firm, David Mlinaric Ltd, in 1962. Mlinaric, Henry and Zervudachi Ltd was formed in 1989. They have an office in London in Bourne Street, SW1, and in Paris (54 Galerie de Montpensier, Jardin du Palais Royal). David's commissions have included the faithful restoration of Spencer House, London's only surviving town palace, the National Gallery, the Wellcome Building, Beningborough Hall (for the National Trust), West Dean College and Arundel Castle in Sussex, and numerous private houses in England, France, Italy, Switzerland and the US.
Photograph by Christopher Sykes

DAVID COLLINS ▼

Dublin born David Collins is one of the most innovative restaurant designers working in London today. Each dining room he has created for the capital's most respected chefs is unique and all have received critical acclaim. His work ranges from the 1960s inspired design of The Square which Elle Decoration described as "cool, sleek and decidedly sexy" to the rather more sober but just as distinctive Tante Claire. Marco Pierre White employed him to design Harveys and this success led to his appointment as designer of The Canteen in 1992, White's latest venture and his first collaboration with Michael Caine.

ANTHONY COLLETT AND ▼ DAVID CHAMPION

Anthony Collett and David Champion established Collett-Champion Ltd in 1987. Both men had a fine art and architectural background, with a commitment to historical perspective – David studied fine art at Rhodes University and made his name as an interior designer in Europe and the US, while Anthony studied at the University of Cape Town, Hornsey College and the Royal College of Art before establishing himself in the UK and abroad. Most of the company's briefs include total responsibility for interior design from architecture through to the complete furnishing scheme, with many commissions requiring specially designed furniture, a speciality of the practice.

NICHOLAS HASLAM ⬆

After leaving Eton and working for newspapers and Robert Carrier's PR firm, Nicholas Haslam worked for British Vogue and then for American Vogue, at the same time as Diana Vreeland was made editor, for four years. But it was during his time as ground-breaking art director on Show magazine that he began decorating as a serious hobby. He bought a ranch in Arizona, where between running cattle and breeding Arabian horses, he carried out photographic commissions for Vogue and decorated for a recherché group of clients. He returned to London in 1972 to set up his own practice. Since then his clients have included royalty, rock stars, couturiers, actors and film stars, as well as offices, restaurants and night clubs, both in America and Europe. He now has two showrooms in London, called At Nicholas Haslam. His work is featured regularly in top publications here and abroad, he is a consulting editor to British Vogue and is artistic director of FSI plc, a major design and architectural practice in London.

CHARLES RUTHERFORD ⬆

Charles Rutherford studied architecture at Cambridge and interiors at Kingston. He spent two years designing for Conran Associates, working on projects such as the Whitehall office of the Minister for the Arts. He felt restricted, however, by the constraints of a large organisation and since 1984 has run his own practice. A dedicated modernist whose work is founded in the structural and the sculptural, he achieves the tranquillity that characterises his work through innovative use of texture and rare clarity of detail. He has restructured and furnished (with a collection of his own designs ranging from sofas to bedheads) various listed houses and modern offices in central London. Pictured here with Charles is the model for his latest project, a large new house on a hilltop site in the West Indies. With its natural materials and colours the house literally "grows" out of the landscape.
Photography by Paul Spencer

INVENTORS

RON HICKMAN

Born in South Africa, Ron Hickman came to England in 1955 to pursue his passionate interest in car design. Entirely self-taught, he displayed an exceptional natural gift, and as Design Director of Lotus Cars Ltd was the principal designer of the Lotus Elan, Plus 2 and Europa. The Elan was the world's first car to feature Ron's concepts of body-contoured plastic bumper panels and lowerable headlights, both now commonplace. In 1968 Ron turned his skills to freelance inventing. His first independent invention, the Workmate* portable workbench, was rejected by seven manufacturers, but after four years, during which time it was mainly sold by mail order, it was taken up by Black & Decker. Since then it has earned Ron worldwide fame, with around 30 million units sold and 20 patent infringement cases won. Sadly, Ron's other inventions proved less successful, and he has now retired from inventing and is researching his family's history.

MIKE BURROWS

Mike Burrows went into engineering in 1967, making packaging machines, and eventually designed his own. A keen cycle tourist and racer since his teens, Mike later developed an interest in recumbent cycles, and set about refining their design. The fruit of this decade-long quest is the Windcheetah, better known as the Speedy, a fast, agile tricycle which has been a consistent winner of Practical Vehicle Competitions in Europe, the USA and Canada. More recently, Norfolk-based Mike designed the revolutionary LotusSport track bike on which Chris Boardman took Britain's first gold medal in the 1992 Olympic Games in Barcelona.

NORMAN HOSSACK

Engineer Norman Hossack built cars for Indianapolis and Formula One racing with McLaren before leaving to develop his own ideas, the first fruit of which was a "lobe" engine, first run in 1978, in which a conventional piston and connecting rod were replaced by a single component. That same year Middlesex-based Norman turned his attention to motorcycle suspension systems. His first two motorcycles had won championships by 1983 and the first won the British Single Cylinder Championship in 1986, 1987 and 1988. Hossack single-sided suspension was demonstrated in 1986-87. In 1987 Norman began developing an alternative suspension for road-going BMW motorcycles, and it is now sold in Germany.

DR RIAD ROOMI

A graduate of Baghdad's College of Medicine, Dr Riad Roomi was granted British citizenship in 1984. While working in various NHS hospitals he gained broad surgical experience and developed a particular interest in cosmetic surgery. This led him to invent the Ready-Stitch wound-closure device, an alternative to needle and thread for closing both operative and accidental wounds. Ready-Stitch won for Dr Roomi the SMART Award 1988. That same year he won the Scottish Invention of the Year Award. He is now developing a new anti-ageing cream.

BOB SYMES ▼

Austrian-born Bob Symes was educated in Vienna, Switzerland, and at London's Regent Street Polytechnic, and during WWII served in the British Colonial Service and the Royal Navy. Since then he has been a freelance broadcaster, writer, film director, experimental engineer and lecturer. Best known for his regular appearances since 1986 on BBC television's Tomorrow's World, Bob has presented many other programmes including The Model World of Robert Symes (1979), Bob's Your Uncle (1985-88) and The House that Bob Built, as well as broadcasting on radio. Bob has written several books, including Crikey it Works – Technology for the Young, published in 1992, and many articles on model railways, travel and food. Formerly Chairman of the Institute of Patentees and Inventors, Bob has been its President since 1991. He is a Companion of the Royal Aeronautical Society and holds the Knights Cross (First Class) of the Republic of Austria.

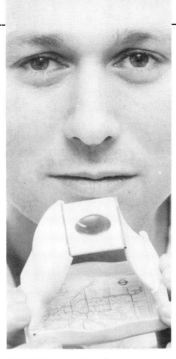

JEFFREY WOOLF ▲

Essentially, maps have not changed since the Egyptians drew them on papyrus: they are cumbersome, fragile and difficult to use in all but ideal conditions. Jeffrey Woolf's MicroMap overcomes the problems of using standard paper maps and has attracted the interest of all outdoor sports markets, the military, major utility companies, leading map producers, tourist organisations and theme parks. Invented in 1990, MicroMap is believed to have won more awards in its first two years than any other invention. These include, in 1991, the BP/Nat-West Award for Technology, the Honeywell/Sunday Times British Innovation Award and the Carlton/Nat-West British Enterprise Award. In 1992 Jeffrey, whose Cascade Corporation is based in London's Golders Green, received the Honeywell/Sunday Times British Innovation Award for Overall Winner of Best Consumer Product of 1991.

LESLIE SELSDON ▲

After learning all about the skills of injection moulding and tool making in his family's plastics business, Leslie Selsdon of Selsdon Filtration Ltd, devoted six years of research and development to a specific project. The end-product was an innovative diesel-engine by-pass filter that has won for him a medal from the Concours Lépine in Paris and the Toshiba Award in London. It has cost benefits but also significant environmental advantages.

MIKE WATSON ▼

Self-styled "inventrepreneur" Mike Watson ran a small electronics business with his partner Gillian in the lounge of a mobile home. But it was not until he wound up the company and started to concentrate on innovations, joining the Institute of Patentees and Inventors, that he hit on the idea of Watsonlinc (cable coupling transformer). It has won, among other awards, the BP/Nat-West Award for Technology in 1991 and the Honeywell/Sunday Times British Innovation Overall Award for Computing and Telecommunication. It is also rated among the top three of its class in the Archimedes Awards. Media coverage, the Design Council's Noticeboard scheme and assistance and advice from the London Enterprise Agency together helped Surrey-based Mike to acquire his first licensee, Oxley Developments, in 1992, while the BP/Nat-West Award continued to help with international patent coverage.

JOHN GRANTHAM ⬆

John Grantham was an aeronautical engineer and helicopter pilot in the Royal Navy before setting up on his own as an engineer in 1979. Technically able but, by his own admission, financially hopeless, he soon went out of business and returned to flying helicopters, first with the Omani Air Force and then with Bristow Helicopters in Aberdeen. On moving to rural Aberdeenshire, John equipped a workshop where he could immerse himself in his hobby of model making and engineering tinkering. Obsessed with solving the problem of uncontrollable supermarket and airport trolleys, he invented a load-activated, locking and steerable castor. The device won John the Scottish Inventor of the Year Award in 1990 and the Honeywell/Sunday Times Innovation Award in 1992.

KEN FIELDING ⬆

Ken Fielding carried on the family tradition of engineering when he left school, and at the age of 22, started working for himself. Building one-off machines, and pursuing a special interest in pneumatics, he built up the business until he was supplying purpose-designed machinery worldwide, to clients ranging from small, start-up companies to multi-nationals. He patented a machine which made the assembly of picture frames much faster and was until recent years used for most of the frames sold in Britain. In 1977 Ken wound up the business and began working independently from his Devon farmhouse, undertaking design and manufacturing jobs. Among his projects is a mooring system, whose development he financed himself and which has recently attracted worldwide interest.

⬅ HUGH FACEY

In 1969, three years after joining Tinsley Wire Industries Ltd as a graduate trainee, Hugh Facey won the British Junior Chamber of Commerce Overseas Travel Award and spent six months in Toronto. His subsequent progress through the company culminated in his becoming Group Sales and Marketing Director in 1979. Hugh formed Estate Wire Ltd in 1984, to manufacture agricultural fencing, barbed wire and staples. Launched four years later, the Gripple joining and tensioning system won France's Grand Prix du Président de la République in 1990 and in 1991 received, on BBC's Tomorrow's World, the Prince of Wales Award for Innovation. Gripple Ltd started trading as a separate company in January 1991.

DAVID TOWNSEND ▼

Born into a family with a history of naval and army service, David Townsend joined the Sea Cadets at the age of 13. Here he learned to sail and later became an instructor in boating, meteorology, radio and seamanship, eventually reaching the rank of Sub-Lieutenant, Sea Cadet Corps/Royal Naval Reserves. David also served for 15 years in the Merchant Navy. He begun inventing in 1991 developing the ideas that he is now building as working prototypes.
His most recent project is an automatic recovery system for marine equipment.

RICHARD TOPPING ▼

After leaving school with no qualifications, Richard Topping completed a five-year apprenticeship in mechanical engineering with the Ministry of Defence, and then gained an engineering degree by day-release and night school. In a career of over 30 years with the MoD he became an expert on ammunition ranging from small arms to anti-aircraft missiles. In 1986 Kent-based Richard was employed by a private company, where he developed an illuminating, long-range mortar bomb. But, despite the success of his innovation, his services were dispensed with in 1990, and he began to develop independently a tracered, 12-bore shotgun cartridge which is soon to go into production. The cartridge will help clay shooters, for theirs is the only participant sport where it is impossible to quantify any improvement – it is a case of either hit or miss.

ALAN BURNS ▲

Buckinghamshire-born Alan Burns' family emigrated to Australia when he was 12 years old, and he now divides his time between Perth, where he is Chairman of AirBoss Limited, and London. In the 1960s, while he was working as a surveyor in the outback, Alan's frustration with the limitations of conventional tyres in difficult terrain led him to develop a system of flexible rubber legs to improve ground engagement. Designed to approximate animal movement, the legs were carried round on a base endless belt, forming a track. He then applied the innovation to a wheel, and after nearly 30 years of development, into which he sank some £4 million of his own money, the AirBoss tyre went into commercial production in 1990, five years after receiving its first patent.

◄ LESLIE CROUCH

When he returned after WWII to a career in the electricity industry, Leslie Crouch also performed as a semi-professional musician for several years, having learned to play the alto saxophone and clarinet while in the Army. At evening classes he gained a distinction in mathematics and electrical engineering and a credit in mechanical engineering, although he did not complete his studies. Before retiring, Leslie obtained the RYA's Ocean Navigating Certificate, and while sailing had an accident which prompted him to think about the use of tidal power. Recently Leslie produced an engineered prototype turbine. He has applied for a patent and is currently seeking backing.

MEDIA

CLIVE WOLMAN ⬆

An expert on City malpractice, who has written countless articles for the Financial Times on a wide range of financial issues, Wolman took the job of city editor of the Mail on Sunday three years ago. This year Wolman and his team (Lawrence Lever, Simon Day, Keith Woolcock, William Lewis, Allan Piper, Anne Ashworth, Susan Gilchrist) were collectively presented with the award for Specialist Writer of the Year. They were praised for the authoritative and compelling style of the section and the way in which they have attracted readers who might not otherwise delve very deeply in newspaper City pages.

JAMES FERGUSON AND ALAN GILLILAND. MATT PRITCHETT ➡

Ferguson and Gilliland were joint winners of the Graphic Artist of the Year Award for 1992. Ferguson of the Financial Times was praised for his "remarkable ability to capture the mood of a story", while Gilliland of the Daily Telegraph "brought clarity and vividness to stories as complicated and diverse as the Gulf War and our continuing obsession with alcohol". Matt Pritchett was voted "What the Papers Say" Cartoonist of the Year 1992. He has been the Daily Telegraph's front page cartoonist since 1988 and is only 27.

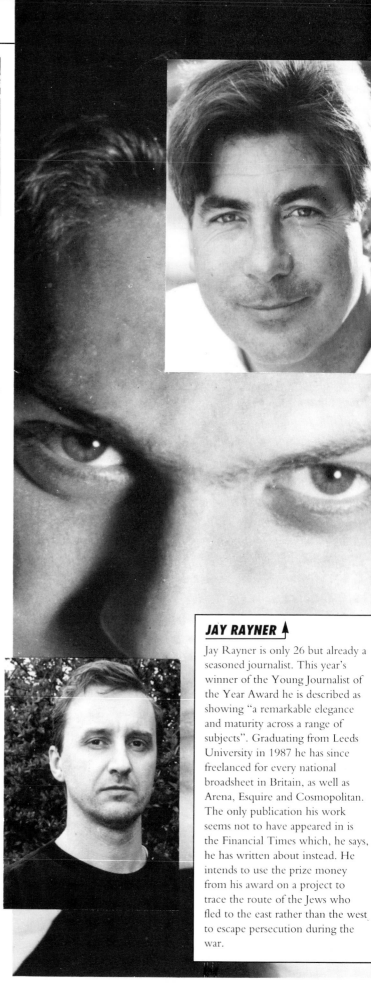

JAY RAYNER ⬆

Jay Rayner is only 26 but already a seasoned journalist. This year's winner of the Young Journalist of the Year Award he is described as showing "a remarkable elegance and maturity across a range of subjects". Graduating from Leeds University in 1987 he has since freelanced for every national broadsheet in Britain, as well as Arena, Esquire and Cosmopolitan. The only publication his work seems not to have appeared in is the Financial Times which, he says, he has written about instead. He intends to use the prize money from his award on a project to trace the route of the Jews who fled to the east rather than the west to escape persecution during the war.

244

◄ STEVE WOOD

Steve Wood ran a photographic business on cruise liners before coming to London to try his luck as a newspaper photographer. In 1973 he joined the staff of the Daily Express. He was the first person into Afghanistan after the invasion and the fall of Kabul and the first journalist to get any pictures or reports out of the country. In 1982 he drove a truck of food into Poland while it was under martial law, and since then he has been back and forth hundreds of times to Israel to cover the war. He has also photographed the Royal Family for many years, often going with them on their visitis abroad. He was responsible for the photo of Princess Diana, taken before her marriage, in which the world saw through her skirt. This year he won the Photographer of the Year Award for the Daily Express.

ROBERT CHESSHYRE ▼

"A superb example of sustained and absorbing in-depth reporting." This is how Robert Chesshyre's work was described by judges of the Magazine Writer of the Year Award for 1992. The Award has traditionally been won by writers rather than reporters but Chesshyre's articles showed, it was thought, just how well magazines can accommodate topical work. The winning articles ranged from a well-judged account of a town where Thatcherism went sour to an excellent piece of reporting on schools in one of Britain's most deprived areas, to which Chesshyre was allowed rare access.
Photograph by Steve Orino

ALEX FRATER ▲

"Colourful, informative and sometimes wildly funny". This is how Alex Frater's writing was described when he was given the Arthur Sandles Award for leisure writing in 1991. He now works for The Observer but has also been a TV presenter – he won a BAFTA for Best Single Documentary in 1990 – and has written four successful travel books. He has received commendations at the British Press Awards twice before.

RICHARD LAMBERT ▲

1992's National Newspaper Editor of the Year Richard Lambert was commended in the award for his leadership and innovative work at the Financial Times. He was made the paper's editor in1991. The judges felt he had improved the overall balance of the FT's news and analysis, developed the authority of the paper overseas and, in particular, its coverage of events in Russia and the reshaping of Europe. Lambert joined the Financial Times in 1966, specialising in company affairs and in 1979 became the paper's first financial editor.

JONATHAN STEELE ▲

A highly respected commentator on Soviet affairs for the past four years Jonathan Steele has, this year, won the International Reporter of the Year Award for his coverage of the last few years in the Soviet Union. The judges mentioned his brilliant coup in talking himself onto the plane bringing Gorbachev back to Moscow from his house arrest in the Crimea, after the failed August coup. Steele has variously been leader writer, chief foreign correspondent and (presently) Moscow correspondent for The Guardian and has been named International Reporter of the Year once before, for his coverage of the Soviet invasion of Afghanistan.

MATTHEW PARRIS ▼

Winner of the Columnist of the Year Award for his work as Parliamentary Sketch Writer for The Times Matthew Parris has a long relationship with journalism and politics. From Cambridge and Yale (studying International Relations) he spent two years in the Foreign Office before joining the staff of Mrs Thatcher's office. MP for West Derbyshire in 1979 he gave up his seat seven years later to present LWT's Weekend World. Parris has led expeditions to Mt. Kilimanjaro, Zaire, Peru and the Sahara and he regularly runs in the London marathon.

JONATHAN POWELL ▾

Until Christmas 1992 Jonathan Powell was Controller of BBC 1 but he began 1993 as Director of Drama and International Development for the new London ITV company Carlton Television. While at the BBC he commissioned a range of comedy, drama and factual programmes that included One Foot in the Grave, Birds of a Feather, Between the Lines, House of Cards, Inside Story, Pole to Pole and Churchill. Born in 1947 he was educated at Sherborne School, Dorset, and at the University of East Anglia. He began his TV career at Granada in 1969, working as a script editor on A Family at War and Country Matters. He spent 18 months as producer of Crown Court, had a huge critical success with The Nearly Man and produced many single plays. In 1977 he joined the BBC and was responsible for all its classic serials until 1984 – a period that took in The Mayor of Casterbridge, Crime and Punishment, Tinker, Taylor, Soldier, Spy and The Barchester Chronicles. He was appointed Head of Drama Series and Serials in 1984 and became Head of Drama Group in 1987. In 1980 he won the Royal Television Society Award for outstanding contribution to television and, in 1983, the American Peabody Award given for the same reason.

MICHAEL WEARING ▴

Award-winning series like The History Man and Boys from the Blackstuff had already made Michael Wearing's name at BBC Birmingham before he was appointed Head of Drama there. In 1989 he became Head of Drama Serials, BBC TV – soon after his five-film series Blind Justice was judged Best Series by the Royal Television Society. His programmes have always been of the highest quality, Blackstuff won Best Series in both the BAFTA and Broadcasting Press Guild awards and his Screen One film First and Last won an Emmy for Outstanding Achievement in Drama Programming and Best Film at the Japan Film Festival. He has also picked up awards at the Edinburgh Film Festival and at Banff, Chicago and Houston.

TOM GUTTERIDGE

In 1984 Tom Gutteridge left his position as Executive Producer of Music and Arts at BBC TV to set up Mentorn Films, now one of the leading independent production companies. In 1983 he masterminded the BBC's General Election coverage. He moved to Arts and Entertainment, ran The Hot Shoe Show and the comedy series A Kick Up The 80s. In 1992 Mentorn produced over 350 hours of programmes for BBC, ITV and Channel 4. Tom is a council member of the Producers Alliance for Cinema and Television and a director of Eastern Arts Board.

MICHAEL JACKSON ▾

Michael Jackson has been Head of Music and Arts for BBC TV since 1991, having joined the department in 1987 and made his name as Editor of the award-winning The Late Show. He was still only 33 years old when he was appointed to his present job – the youngest-ever department head at the Corporation. A former independent producer who launched and edited Channel 4's The Media Show, he made the much acclaimed BBC series Tales from Prague, which won the prestigiuos Grierson Documentary Award. More recent successes have included Moving Pictures and Naked Hollywood. His department is responsible for some 350 hours of music and arts programmes each year.

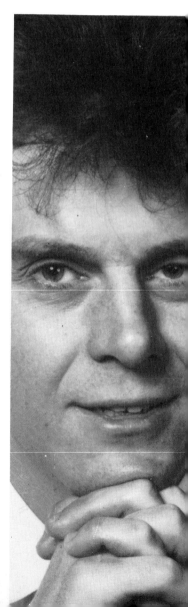

CHARLIE PARSONS ▲

As managing director of Britain's biggest independent production company, Planet 24, Charlie Parsons overseas a wide range of TV programmes including The Big Breakfast and The Word, both on Channel 4 and both created by him. Born in 1958 he joined London Weekend Television straight from Pembroke College, Oxford where he worked on The Six O'Clock Show and The London Programme and produced the first series of Network 7.

WILL WYATT ▼

Will Wyatt has been managing BBC Network Television since April 1991. He trained as a reporter before joining BBC Radio News as a sub-editor in 1965. He moved to TV in 1968 and became Head of Presentation Programmes in 1977, Head of Documentary Features in 1981 and Head of Features and Documentaries Group, Television in 1987. He chaired the group considering violence on television in 1983 and 1987 and their report formed the basis of the BBC's current guidelines on this subject. He is also a director of the Broadcasting Audience Research Board and BBC Subscription TV.

ALAN YENTOB ▼

The man who is Controller of BBC 2 first joined the Corporation as a general trainee in 1968. From 1973-75 he was a producer/director of Omnibus and in 1978 he created Arena, which he edited until 1985, where he became Head of Music and Arts, Television, with overall responsibility for opera, dance and popular culture on BBC TV. Among his awards have been British Academy Awards for Arena (in 1982, 1983 and 1984), and the American Emmy for the Omnibus film The Treble in 1985. Alan is a Director of Riverside Studios, a Director of the British Film Institute Production Board and an Honorary Fellow of the Royal College of Arts. He is on the Advisory Committee of the Institute of Contemporary Arts.

MIKE BOLLAND ▼

Mike Bolland started in TV as an office boy with BBC Scotland. He moved up to film editing and in 1973 helped to set up the BBC's Community Programme Unit. By 1979 he was Senior Producer on the unit. His work caught the eye of Channel 4's Jeremy Isaacs and Mike was hired as Commissioning Editor for Youth Programmes, where he worked on The Tube and The Comic Strip Presents. Moving to Senior Commissioning Editor for Entertainment, he put on Friday Night Live, The Last Resort with Jonathan Ross and After Dark. In 1986 he became Assisistant Director of Programmes and Head of the Arts and Entertainment Group. He then became Channel 4's Controller of Arts and Entertainment and Deputy Director of Programmes. A major coup was stealing Whose Line Is It Anyway? from under the noses of BBC controllers. In 1990 he left Channel 4 to join Initial Film and Television, later joining Jonathan Ross's production company, Channel X, of which he is managing director.

MELVYN BRAGG ▾

Melvyn Bragg went to grammar school in Cumbria before winning an open scholarship to Oxford in 1958 to study modern history. He joined the BBC on a general traineeship in 1961. By the time BBC 2 arrived in 1964 he was producing, directing and writing films. On the new station he edited documentaries, a literary panel game and the arts magazine, New Release, which later became Review and then Arena. The editor and presenter of the South Bank Show from 1978, he became head of arts for LWT in 1982 and Controller of Arts in 1990. He has written several screenplays and the librettos for the musicals Mardi Gras (1976) and The Hired Man (1985), which won the Ivor Novello Award. Melvyn also holds the John Llewellyn-Rhys Memorial Award and PEN awards for his novels and non-fiction. The South Bank Show has won numerous prizes including a record three Prix Italias. Melvyn has presented Radio 4's Start The Week since 1989; it won Programme of the Year in 1990 and 2nd prize in the New York Festival Radio Awards in 1992.

RICHARD BANNERMAN ▸

Richard Bannerman read French and Russian at Cambridge. He joined the publicity department of the BBC in 1969 and began producing Kaleidoscope for Radio 4 in 1978. He has won many awards for his work in radio, including the BP Arts Journalism Radio Prize in 1987 for Thursday the 13th, and in 1988 for Tomticketatom, a programme on Ravel's Bolero which also won a Sony Award for Best Classical Programme and an International Ondas Award. In 1989 he won a Sony Award for Best Magazine Programme as editor of Radio 3's Third Ear, and in 1992 he took a silver Sony Award for Best Magazine Programme for Kaleidoscope. Richard is currently acting editor of Features, Education and Arts Radio.

ALISTAIR COOKE

Alistair Cooke read English at Cambridge and studied in America on an educational grant before landing his first job at the BBC as a film critic. He went on to become a foreign correspondent and in 1946 presented his first Letter From America, one of the BBC's longest running programmes. In 1952 he took his first steps into television and by the 1970s was presenting his own hugely successful series, America, a personal history of his adopted homeland. He has written many acclaimed books, including a study of the Alger Hiss case, A Generation on Trial, published in 1950, and America Observed (1988). In 1973 he was awarded an honorary knighthood and the following year received the ultimate recognition for a journalist in America – being asked to address the United States Congress on its 200th anniversary.

JONATHAN DIMBLEBY

Jonathan Dimbleby began his career in television and radio as a reporter for BBC Bristol. He had previously studied philosophy at University College, London, where he was made a Fellow. He became involved with The World At One and This Week in the early 1970s. Since then he has presented and edited a range of quality programmes from First Tuesday to documentaries such as The Bomb, The Cold War Game and Witness, a documentary series which ran from 1986-88. Writer and presenter on Review of the Year

for the BBC in 1989, 1990 and 1991 he also wrote and presented Russia at the Rubicon in 1990 and interviewed President Gorbachev in the same year. He has been chairman of BBC Radio's Any Questions since 1987 and presenter of Any Answers since 1988. His awards include the Society of Film and Television Arts, and the Richard Dimbleby Award for "the most outstanding contribution to factual television" in 1974. In 1992 he chaired BBC 1/Radio 4's Election Call.

PIERS PLOWRIGHT

Educated at Stowe and then at Christ Church, Oxford, Piers worked for six years in Borneo after university as a DJ and then for the British Council in Iran and The Sudan (where he started a schools' radio and TV service). He joined the BBC in 1968 as a producer in English By Radio, moving in 1974 to the radio drama department, to produce the Radio 2 soap Waggoner's Walk. In 1978 he became a features editor in Radio Drama working for Radios 3 and 4 and since 1990 he has been a senior features producer in the features and arts department. He won the Prix Italia Radio Documentary Prize in 1983 for Nobody Stays In This House Long and again in 1986 (with composer Malcolm Clarke) for Setting Sail, a programme about death and dying. In 1988 he won the RAI prize (at the 40th Prix Italia) with poet Roberta Beake for One Big Kitchen Table, a portrait of a Philadelphia delicatessen. He has also won Sony Awards for documentaries (in 1986 and 1989).

JOHN SESSIONS ▼

Born in Scotland, but brought up in England, John Sessions gained an MA in English from the University of Wales. He went to McMaster University in Hamilton, Ontario, and studied for his PhD, which he didn't complete, but he spent four years teaching undergraduates and travelling extensively in Canada. He returned to England in 1979 and went to RADA. He became a professional actor in January 1982. For five years he acted in rep, television, film bit-parts and one-man shows. In 1987 Porterhouse Blue, for Channel 4, and The Life of Napoleon, for Kenneth Branagh's Renaissance Theatre Company, at the Albery Theatre announced John Sessions arrival, and there have followed, on stage: The Common Pursuit (Phoenix 1988); The American Napoleon (Phoenix 1989) and Tartuffe (Playhouse 1991) and, for television: Spitting Image (1986-); The New Year Shoe (1988); Whose Line is it anyway? (1988); On The Spot (1989); Some Enchanted Evening (1989); Single Voices (1990) and, as writer and performer, Tall Tales and Travelling Tales (1991-92). Now aged 40, John Sessions lives in London.

VIC REEVES AND ▲
BOB MORTIMER ▼

Neither Vic Reeves (Jim Moir) nor Bob Mortimer set out to be comedians, but Vic stepped in one evening to compere at a club, and the Big Night Out was born. Bob, a solicitor, joined in one night and they made each other laugh, and that was that. The Big Night Out was performed to a regular, local and devoted audience at the Albany Empire, Deptford until Jonathan Ross persuaded Michael Grade of Channel 4 to come and see the show. By spring 1990, the first TV series was being broadcast and the second was on the way. In May 1991, they recorded a pilot for a comedy series called Weekenders, which was shown on Channel 4 in June 1992. In autumn 1991, they undertook a 40 date tour which sold out completely. The Newcastle show was recorded and sold 100,000 copies on video. A book, The Big Night In, was published in November and remained in the top three best-sellers until after Christmas. Vic has also pursued a successful recording career, releasing an album, I Will Cure You, from which the single, Dizzy, reached No 1 in the charts.

ROWAN ATKINSON ▲

Born in 1955, Rowan Atkinson has degrees from Newcastle and Oxford universities in Electrical Engineering. After attracting critical acclaim at the 1977 Edinburgh Festival, and mouting his own revue at the Hampstead Theatre in 1978, he became a founder member of the Not The Nine O'Clock News team, on BBC, which won a Silver Rose at the Montreux Festival amongst its host of other accolades. He became BBC Personality of the Year. In 1981 Rowan was the youngest person ever to mount a one-man show in the West End, and won the West End Theatre's Award for Comedy Performance of the Year. In 1983 he embarked, with writer Richard Curtis, on the first Blackadder series. Over the ensuing five years and four series, the situation-tragedy won three British Academy Awards, an International Emmy, three ACE awards and Best Entertainment Performance. Once again, Rowan was voted BBC Personality of the Year. His next major television undertaking was Mr Bean, which has won the Golden Rose at Montreux, an International Emmy and two BANFF Awards and has been sold to over 60 countries. Stage appearances include The Nerd (1985) and The Sneeze (1988). He is currently working on another Mr Bean series.

BILLY CONNOLLY ▼

Born in 1942 in Glasgow, Billy Connolly left school at the age of 15, and worked in a variety of odd-jobs. He learned parachuting in the Territorial Army and, everywhere he went, his guitar and banjo accompanied him. He joined Gerry Rafferty and the Humblebums before embarking on a solo career and, having noticed that he was getting more audience response with his patter than his singing, he refocussed on the humorous side of his act. He became a hero in the Scottish clubs, particularly amongst the CND and anti-apartheid sections of the audience, and became a controversial figure in the religious establishment circles by starting a translation of the story of Moses into Glaswegian, on a BBC Religious Affairs programme with, "Nip hame and get yer peepil . . .". After a performance on the Parkinson Show, where he was unfortunately upstaged by an Emu, Billy Connolly's career took off south of the border, where he became known as Scot of the Antarctic, with his raw-edged humour attacking Margaret Thatcher and the Royal Family, and his frequent references to willies, sanitary towels, haemorrhoids and vomiting. Latterly, Billy Connolly fronted Comic Relief in 1989 and spends much of his time in the USA.

NORMAN WISDOM ▼

A household name for over 40 years, Norman Wisdom broke box-office records and won a British Film Academy Award with his first film, Trouble in Store, in 1952. Born in London in humble circumstances, he joined the army as a 14 year old bandsman. He left the army in 1946 and set about making a career as a professional entertainer. After two years slogging at home and a spell in America, he was offered the starring role in Paris to Piccadilly, at the Prince of Wales Theatre, which ran for 18 months. He signed a film contract with the Rank Organisation and, after Trouble in Store, went on to make a further 15 highly successful films. He appeared in his first Royal Variety Performance in 1952 and has appeared in eight such shows since. He has made other Royal appearances, including a private Christmas concert before the Royal Household at Windsor Castle. His many television appearances are perhaps best characterised by the 1961 Sunday Night at the London Palladium, when industrial action meant that he and Bruce Forsyth had to exercise their versatility, doing the whole show on their own. The winner of a Lifetime Award for Stage and Comedy, Norman Wisdom is guaranteed to fill theatres wherever he appears.

THE SIMMONS BROTHERS ▲

Alan and Keith Simmons are real-life brothers who have a comedy act which is frequently described as being funnier and far more original than those of many of their more illustrious contemporaries. They frequently receive rave reivews as live entertainers and they have written some of TV's top shows, including Cue Gary and Five Alive, which won a gold medal for comedy at the New York TV Festival. Based in Dartford, Kent, where they live a few hundred yards from each other with their respective families, their act is a mixture of manic comedy, clowning and music.

JETHRO ▼

Farmer's son and son of Cornwall, Jethro's talent was discovered when he joined the local operatic society at the age of 18 and people realised that he not only had a bass voice big enough for three, but he could also make them laugh. He started as a touring entertainer around the Cornish pubs, but was soon recognised as Cornwall's top comic. Success and television soon followed.

DAVID WATERHOUSE ▼

David Waterhouse has lived his 37 years in the house where his family has lived for over 80. He trained as a civil engineer, but left the profession to set up his own marketing company. Always having a taste for the unusual and dangerous, David joined the Spice multi-adventure organisation in the late 1980s, and is now available as a fire-eater, sky diver and walker on red-hot coals amongst other unusual pursuits. His most thrilling moment to date came when, after attempting to arrange to be shot out of a cannon at the circus, he was invited instead to try his hand at lion taming. Now, whenever the circus comes to town, David can be found face-to-face with the King of Beasts – unless something more exciting comes along.

◄ DAVE STEVENSON

After the break-up of his marriage several years ago, martial arts enthusiast Dave Stevenson was looking for something to occupy his mind. He found it and now, while retaining his job as manager of a Stoke-on-Trent pottery by day, his free time is taken up flying on planes. Dave does not take the easy option of riding inside the aircraft, he walks the wings of Tiger Moths. Dave has also abseiled 300ft for charity and is an experienced fire-eater, but walking on aircraft is his passion.

◄ KEN BAKER

Born in 1954, Ken Baker's life proceeded quite normally until 1985, when he learned fire-eating and breathing one afternoon while awaiting his turn to go hovercraft racing. He then learned to juggle and, with his fascination with fire, he naturally used fire clubs. Next, he progressed to walking on coals and, ultimately, to being a human torch. He finds the attraction of wearing a coat soaked in petrol and being set alight hard to explain, except to say that it is fun to watch people's reactions. Also very fond of bungee-jumping, climbing, lion-taming and the trapeze, Ken is currently in Ecuador, combining some of his enthusiasms, climbing volcanoes.

NIC PICOT ▼

Magician Nic Picot graduated with an honours degree in physcis from Exeter University and went on to train as a chartered accountant. He later developed his magical skills and became a highly successful after dinner close-up and cabaret magician with clients including Royalty, international corporations and five star hotels. With increasing demand for his services, Nic was able to start his own agency, specialising in supplying magic and novelty acts for private and corporate functions. The agency opened its doors in 1986 and quickly gained a reputation for quality and reliability. Nic's magical skills are still in great demand and the agency has expanded to include all types of entertainment from mix and mingle entertainers and cabaret and function bands to theme evenings and tailor-made shows for sales presentations, conferences and exhibitions.

GRAHAM P JOLLEY ▼

A highly engaging mind-reader psychologist, entertainer and conference performer, Graham P Jolley's appearances on Wogan, Pebble Mill and other television engagements have given him the opportunity of demonstrating his flair for keeping audiences enthralled. Equally at home at The Ritz or at a private party, wherever he performs audiences are never able to explain: The Telephone Book Revelation; Personality Analysis; Dial "M" for Murder; Mind Reading Numbers; The Snooker Ball Experiment or anything from his baffling box of tricks. The razor-sharp wit which accompanies the astonishing demonstrations is guaranteed to keep even the most loquacious in appreciative silence.

DAFT BOB THE SCALLAWAG (HENRY MORGAN)

Seeing a gypsy performing as a fire-eater at Appleby Horse Fair when he was a teenager prompted Henry Morgan to boast to his friends that he could do it. Having his bluff called by the gipsy, he performed so well that he was given ten bob to ". . . bugger off and stop showing me up". This started Henry on his career as Daft Bob, a traditional court jester, fire-eater, conjurer and general scapegoat to whichever king he happens to be working for. In 1990 Daft Bob and 150 pupils staged a mass flame throwing exhibition for Manchester's Olympic Bid Festival – a world first. Bob was later challenged to a flame throwing duel by the then world champion, Pierrot, of the French Archeos Circus, which Bob won in the Frenchman's own Big Top. Bob lives in Manchester and fulfils many feudal and civic duties as Fool and Lord of Misrule.

STEVE RAWLINGS

Specialising in dextrous visual comedy in the Tommy Cooper tradition, Steve Rawlings' show comprises juggling ping pong balls with his mouth, a short demonstration of spontaneous combustion, a combination of balancing bottles and glasses while juggling three fire torches and furniture juggling. Steve's television appearances are frequent and include: Saturday Night Live; Going Live; Daytime Live; It's Wicked; Nothing Like The Royal Variety Performance; Lift Off and Beadle's Box Of Tricks. He appears regularly in the theatre and his credits include Sugar Babies, in 1988, with Mickey Rooney and Ann Miller, and the sole support act in Hale and Pace's sell-out 1991 tour. His recent corporate engagements include Saatchi & Saatchi, Rowntree, IBM and Glaxo.

ERNIE ALMOND

Forty-nine year old Ernie Almond has been entertaining children professionally for 23 years and can expect to perform his act as Smartie Artie in over 400 venues again this year. His act includes comedy magic and ventriloquism, with his puppet fox, Scruffy, as well as balloon modelling and a great deal of audience participation. Ernie also runs the Smartie Artie Children's Entertainment Agency, which was started 38 years ago by his partner. He owns a theatrical shop in Harpenden and is a regular broadcaster. With all the press coverage which he has received for his own performances, whether at the Lord Mayor's annual children's party at the Mansion House, or at parties for various Royal children, Ernie is proudest of a report in a Sunday colour supplement, on an ordinary children's party, which said that his handling of the audience was ". . . like a maestro with a large and delicate orchestra".

BERNI BENNETT

Entertainer Berni Bennett has two professional personae. Firstly, as Super Berni, her emerges from a moving telephone box and defies gravity by wobbling and tripping his way across a tightrope. He balances on a chair on the tightrope, crosses it blindfold and on a unicycle. His other character is Rocky Bennett – the fitness fanatic on stilts. Rocky challenges a ten year old from the audience to box, skip, ride a bicycle and cross a tightrope – and he does it all on stilts. Berni has appeared with Glyndebourne and the English National Operas and his recent television performances include Motormouth and The Noel Edmunds Show.

JOHN STYLES ▼

Gold star member of the Inner Magic Circle and the country's leading expert in Punch and Judy. His work is much admired by fellow performers and he has appeared on children's programmes such as Rainbow, Playschool and The Wide Awake Club. He was the man behind the illusions for Indiana Jones and the Last Crusade and is a favourite entertainer of the younger Royal princes. He provides games, magic, ventriloquism, paper tearing and balloon bending for parties. Punch and Judy is his speciality, ranging from traditional squawk and bash shows to benign stories for younger children. He is one of the few Punch and Judy professors in Britain and performs the show with complete authenticity. His vast collection of booths and puppets includes some that are over 100 years old.

DISC JOCKEYS

JIMMY YOUNG ▼

Jimmy Young served in the RAF and had a successful singing career, with three number ones, before turning to broadcasting. He joined Radio 1 in 1967 and Radio 2 in 1973 where he has stayed ever since, presenting his daily programme, known to its millions of listeners as the JY Prog. Here he has interviewed all the British prime ministers since 1964 as well as the Duke of Edinburgh, Moshe Dayan, the late Princess Grace of Monaco and Lord Snowdon. The programme has been broadcast live from Russia, the US, Australia, Zimbabwe, Egypt (where he interviewed Anwar Sadat), Israel, Japan and Hong Kong. Among JY's awards are the Queen's Silver Jubilee Medal, the OBE, the Sony Award for Radio Programme of the Year in 1979 and Sony's Radio Personality of the Year in 1985. The JY Prog was voted Best Current Affairs Programme in the Daily Mail BBC National Radio Awards and in 1989 it was named Radio Programme of the Year by the Television and Radio Industries Club.

STEVE WRIGHT ▼

Steve Wright started out in radio on a pirate station, recording a show at home which was sent out to a ship to be broadcast. He then got a job as a news reporter at a commercial station in Reading, and worked at London talk station LBC before getting his own show in Reading. He joined Radio 1 in 1980 with a Saturday evening show. These days he is best known for the weird and wonderful Steve Wright in the Afternoon, transmitted on Radio 1 every weekday between 3 and 6pm. He has been Sony Radio Personality of the Year three times and is the current Variety Club Personality of the Year. An avid collector of miscellany, from old radios to hideous masks, Steve lives in Oxfordshire with his journalist wife and their young son Tommy.

JOHN PEEL ▲

John Peel started his incredible career as a DJ in America. He went to Texas after finishing his military service in 1962 and began working for WRR in Dallas. For the next three years he worked in different radio stations in America, among them KMEN outside Los Angeles. He joined Radio 1 when it started in 1967, quickly establishing himself with the late-night programme Top Gear. He currently presents two shows a week on Radio 1, and has a regular weekly programme for the BBC World Service. John has topped the Best DJ polls in the music press for the last ten years and was recently awarded an honorary degree by the University of East Anglia. He lives in Suffolk with his wife and four children, William Robert Anfield, Alexandra Mary Anfield, Thomas James Dalglish and Florence Victoria Shankly, all eccentrically named in honour of his great love, Liverpool FC.

◄ MANESSEH

DJs Nick Raphael, Bill Tuckey and Ed Maiden built their sound system as pupils of Westminster School. They quickly earned the respect of reggae enthusiasts, a rare achievement for white DJs. These days Nick and Bill alternate each Saturday night/Sunday morning to play the "graveyard shift" on Kiss FM and are renowned for their uncompromising selection of roots reggae. Nick is involved in reggae production, with his own studio and Riz label, and he also works as an artist under various aliases, most notably Sound Iritation. Bill is deputy editor and co-owner of Touch magazine.

CHRIS TARRANT ▲

After graduating from Birmingham University with an English degree Chris Tarrant became a teacher in a boys' school in London's East End. He then worked as a researcher and rose to become director of the Overseas Television Unit of the Central Office of Information. He joined ATV in 1972 and was appointed to present and produce the Saturday morning show Tiswas in 1974, which became a huge success. Since then he has produced and presented many shows for TV and radio, has written half a dozen best selling books, has a regular column in the Sunday Mirror and has received countless awards for his work. These include Radio Personality of the Year (TV and Radio Industries Club) in 1989 and Radio Personality of the Year (Sony Radio Awards) in 1990, Variety Club of Great Britain's Independent Radio Personality of the Year in 1991 and a silver medal at the Sony Radio Awards in 1992. The series Tarrant on TV and Tarrant's Ten Years on TV are scheduled for screening on LWT later in the year. Chris will also be with the Capital Radio Breakfast Show until mid 1993.

NORMAN JAY ↱

Norman Jay was one of the people responsible for the emergence of the mid-1980s rare groove scene. With his show on the then pirate station Kiss and the numerous house and warehouse parties he organised, a new trend was born. The rare groove sounds which Norman popularised influenced a generation of new DJs, artists and music lovers. Bands like the Brand

SIMON MAYO ▲

Simon Mayo started out in radio on a trainee scheme at BBC Radio Sussex. He then worked at Radio Nottingham before joining Radio 1 in 1986, with a Saturday evening show from 7.30 to 9.30. These days he is best known and loved for The Breakfast Show. Its True Confessions slot has become a national obsession, spawning two best-selling books. He was voted the Variety Club BBC Radio Personality of the Year for 1990 and Sony National DJ of the Year in 1991. His Pilgrimage To The Holy Land won the Best Programme Award at the International Radio Festival of New York in 1987. Simon is married with a two-year old son, Ben.

New Heavies and The Young Disciples are direct descendants of the scene Norman helped to create. Norman's Sunday afternoon show, The Musicquarium, combines classic Philly and other sounds from the 1970s and 1980s with his favourite new records.

SIR CLEMENT FREUD ▲

Sir Clement Freud started his working life as a cook at the Dorchester, and became in turn a soldier, night-club owner, journalist broadcaster, politician (Liberal MP 1973-1987) and author. He currently writes for the Times and is a hotel and restuarant consultant. He was Rector of Dundee University (1974-80) and Master of the Open University (1989). President of the Down Syndrome Association, he was knighted by the Queen in 1987. In his time, Sir Clement has been nominated Sports Writer of the Year (1964), has won the London to New York Air Race, and has been After Dinner Speaker of the Year (1974). He has held a licence as an amateur jockey. Sir Clement Freud is married with five children and lives in London, Suffolk and the Algarve.

RABBI LIONEL BLUE ▲

Lionel Blue was born and brought up in London's East End. He lectures on comparative religion at the Leo Baeck College, conducts Jewish-Christian retreats and is in

BARRY CRYER ▲

Barry Cryer was born and educated in Leeds. He attended Leeds University where he failed a degree in English, a failure which he attributes to the outbreak of war 16 years previously. He started work on "The Good Old Days", and was seen by a London agent who got him a job at the Windmill Theatre, where he appeared for seven months before leaving to appear in Expresso Bongo. He started writing revues, and wrote and appeared in night club shows for Danny la Rue. Barry joined the writing team on The Frost Report in the late 1960s and moved on to write and appear in The Frost Programme, Frost on Sunday, etc., until returning to the BBC to write The Two Ronnies. He has written for virtually every top comedian in the country, and for visiting celebrities, has been associated with winning bronze, silver and gold awards at Montreaux and has had a No. 1 record in Finland!

charge of the Ecclesiastical Court of the Reform Synagogue. He is vice-chairman of the Standing Conference on Jews, Christians and Moslems in Europe. His five-part television series, In search of Holy England, has been shown on Channel 4. He has written several books, often entitled by plays on words involving his name – Blue Heaven, Kitchen Blues, etc. His Pause for Thought and Thought for the Day spots on Radio 4 are always popular for his unique, quirky humour.

FREDDIE TRUEMAN ▼

Frederick Sewards Trueman was born in 1931 in Stainton, Yorkshire. He made his first class debut for the County at Cambridge University when he was 18, and was described in Wisden as a slow left-arm bowler – perhaps the biggest mistake that the cricketing bible has ever made! He was awarded his County Cap in 1951, and in the following year made his England debut in the series against India. In the third Test he totally demoralised the Indians by his sheer pace, taking 8 for 31, still a record in Tests between the two countries, and became the first bowler to take 300 wickets in 1964, when he took the wicket of Neil Harvey. Fred was the first to congratulate the unfortunate Harvey, and they have been great friends ever since. Other people have since passed Fred's record, but it is important to note that he took his 307 Test wickets in only 67 matches played over 13 years. He made 981 runs in Test matches, and held 64 catches. For Yorkshire, Fred took 1,745 wickets, and scored 6,852 runs. In all cricket his haul was 2,304 wickets, many more than any other fast bowler. His proudest moment was when he led Yorkshire to victory over the Australians in 1968, after which he retired. Always famous for his wit, Fred is an essential member of the Radio 3 commentary team, a newspaper columnist and a famous after dinner speaker.

◄ WILLIAM RUSHTON

William Rushton started his career as a political cartoonist but, in 1961, appeared in the play The Bed Sitting Room and received rave reviews. He was offered the chance of appearing in a new satirical programme, That Was The Week That Was, and has never looked back. Since the 1960s he has juggled his career as a cartoonist, writer and performer. His books Pigsticking – A Joy for Life and Superpig – A Gentleman's Guide to Everyday Survival were both best-sellers. He has written several novels and collections of drawings, and was a co-founder of Private Eye for which he is still a regular cartoonist. He reunited with David Frost in 1985 to co-present the International Ultra Quiz series, and has made numerous film and television appearances. His regular radio appearances include I'm Sorry I haven't a Clue and Trivia Test Match. He was nominated for the Observer Magazine's "Expert's Expert" as an after dinner speaker, and lists his recreations as "gaining weight, losing weight and parking".

DENIS NORDEN ►

Scriptwriter and broadcaster par excellence, Dennis Norden lists his recreations in Who's Who, a rival publication, as "reading and loitering" and his club as "Saturday Morning Odeon". Born in 1922, Dennis Norden's professional career is inseparable from that of his long-time collaborator Frank Muir, which started in 1947. For radio they wrote Take it From Here (1947-58) and Bedtime With Braden (1950-54), and for TV, And So To Bentley (1956), Whack-O! (1958-60), The Seven Faces of Jim (1961), and other series featuring Jimmy Edwards. They have collaborated on film scripts, TV commercials and revues. From 1960-64, they served as advisors and consultants to the BBC TV light entertainment department and, in 1961, jointly won the Screenwriters Guild Award for the Best Contribution to Light Entertainment. Since 1964 Dennis has been a solo writer for TV and films, presenting Looks Familiar and It'll Be Alright On The Night, and its various spin-offs, and scripting films including The Bliss of Mrs Blossom. He appears on the panel shows My Word and My Music, one of which seems to be on every time one turns on the radio. He has collaborated in many books and, in 1980, was voted Male TV Personality of the Year.

AFTER DINNER SPEAKERS

IVOR SPENCER ▸

Ivor Spencer has been life president of the Guild of Professional Toastmasters for 39 years. He is also the founder of the Guild. He has officiated at over 1,000 Royal events in the UK and overseas, the first toastmaster to have achieved this, and runs a school for professional toastmasters. He also runs a unique school for butler administrators/personal assistants in the UK and the USA. He created the Guild of Professional Toastmasters Best After-Dinner Speaker of the Year Award in 1966 and this most sought after accolade has been won by such speakers as

Sir Peter Ustinov, Baroness Thatcher and Bob Monkhouse. Ivor Spencer is the author of A Toastmaster's Story and Speeches and Toasts. He is listed in the Guiness Book of Records for having listened to over 40,000 speeches.

SIR PETER DE LA BILLIERE ▲

General Sir Peter de la Billière was born in 1934 and educated at Harrow School. He joined the KSLI in 1952 and was commissioned in the Durham Light Infantry, serving in Japan, Korea and, for two years, in the Suez Canal Zone and Jordan. In 1956 he joined the Special Air Service and fought the communist terrorists in Malaya. In 1959 he led a troop during the assault on Jebel Akdar, where he won his first Military Cross. From 1964 to 1966 General de la Billière commanded A 22 SAS Squadron on operations in Radfan and Borneo, gaining a Bar to his MC. He later returned to 22 SAS as Second-in-Command and, subsequently, as Commanding Officer. During the period 1969–74 he commanded operations in

Musandam and Dhofar, and was appointed a member of the Distinguished Service Order. In 1977 Sir Peter assumed command of the British Army training team in the Sudan. From 1979 to 1983 he commanded the SAS group that was in overall charge of the successful assault to release the hostages held in the Iranian Embassy in London. He was appointed CBE in 1983, and KCB in 1988. On October 6th, 1990, General de la Billière assumed command of the British Forces in the Middle East. After his return to the UK, after the Gulf War, he was appointed KBE, promoted to General and became special adviser to the Ministry of Defence on Middle Eastern matters. He retired from active service in June 1992 as the most highly decorated British serviceman.

JEFFREY ARCHER ▲

Jeffrey Archer was born in Somerset and educated at Wellington and Oxford, where he won an athletics Blue, and went on to represent Great Britain in 1966 at the 100 yards. After leaving Oxford he was elected as the youngest member of the GLC and, three years later, became the youngest member of Parliament. Resigning after five years, aged 34, he wrote his first novel Not a Penny More, Not a Penny Less – an instant best-seller – which has been followed by many other best-sellers. His play, Beyond Reasonable Doubt ran for 600 performances. He was deputy chairman of the Conservative Party 1985/86 and co-ordinated the Campaign for Kurdish Relief, raising £57 million for the Kurdish people. Jeffrey Archer was made a life peer in 1992, and lives with his wife and two sons at the Old Vicarage, Grantchester.

JOHN MORTIMER ▼

John Mortimer is a playwright, novelist and former practising barrister, who "took silk" in 1966. Born in 1923 and educated at Harrow, during WWII he worked with the Crown Film Unit. He has written novels, plays and television and film scripts ever since and it is seldom that some new offering from him is not before the public. Amongst his television work are six Rumpole series, for which he won the BAFTA Writer's Award in 1980, the autobiographical play A Voyage Round My Father and the highly acclaimed adaptation of Evelyn Waugh's Brideshead Revisited. His autobiography, Clinging to the Wreckage, won the York Post Book of the Year Award in 1982. Amongst his most recent novels, filmed for television, are Paradise Postponed, Titmuss Regained and A Summer's Lease. John Mortimer was appointed CBE in 1986.

SIR PETER USTINOV ▼

Born in 1921 in London, of Russian, French and Italian extraction, Peter Ustinov is probably the world's most versatile and talented contributor to the arts. As an actor, producer, director, novelist, playwright raconteur and ambassador-at-large for UNICEF,

to list but a few of his accomplishments, he has accumulated a considerable list of credits and awards, culminating in his knighthood in 1990. He has won two Oscars as Best Supporting Actor, three emmys for Best TV Performance, Grammy Awards for his recording of Peter and the Wolf, the New York Critics Award and Donaldson Award for Best Foreign Play for "The Love of four Colonels", the British Critics Award for "Romanoff and Juliet" and awards for the films Billy Budd and Hot Millions worldwide. To date Ustinov has written over 25 plays, ten books, nine movies scripts, and starred or been top-featured in over 34 films, and 25 plays, ten books, nine movie films, eight plays and ten operas. He has written and starred in his own radio shows, and appeared in top television shows all over the world. Multi-lingual, and functioning in so many capacities, he says "My card case is nearly as heavy as I am".

NED SHERRIN ▼

Ned Sherrin is a director, writer and presenter. He is best known on television for That Was The Week That Was and Song by Song. He produced The Virgin Soldiers, wrote, directed and appeared in Side by Side by Sondheim in the West End and on Broadway, and has also directed Mr and Mrs Nobody, Jeffrey Bernard in Unwell and Our Song. His most recent best-seller is Ned Sherrin's Theatrical Anecdotes. Ned presents Radio 4's award-winning Loose Ends. Renowned for his almost fearsome wit, it is unsurprising that he is the holder of the Benedictine Award for Best After Dinner Speaker.

LOOKALIKES

JOHN KERR ↑

Born in 1965, John Kerr has suffered for his art as the George Michael lookalike. He is one of the few who have actually had plastic surgery to improve their similarity to the original. It seems to have proved a worthwhile exercise, however, as George Michael has said on the radio that the likeness is "frightening", and John has performed at many top European and US venues and, he says, "fooled many people, famous and infamous".

ANDRE GROARKE ↑

Andre Groarke is 29 years old and Britain's Rambo lookalike, whose looks have led to foreign trips, TV commercials and success in numerous contests. Prizes in these have included a trip to New York, where he did not meet Sylvester Stallone. He is the assistant manager of a sports shop, and an active sportsman.

PATRICK JAMES ↑

Born in 1946, Patrick James is three years younger than John Major, the man to whom he bears such an uncanny resemblance. Patrick is the chairman of a recruitment company operating in London and the Home Counties, and has been appearing as a lookalike since John Major became Prime Minister. He has featured in advertising campaigns, TV shows and live shows, and made personal appearances throughout the UK and Europe.

ROD TAILBY ↓

Rod Tailby was born in Brazil in 1941, and educated at public school in England. After school, he returned to Brazil for a business administration course, and started acting and modelling there. He returned to England in 1964, and by 1967 was so well known as the man in the Hepworth's advertisement, that he was signing autographs wherever he went. Other modelling and film work followed, and his first Roger Moore lookalike job was a luggage ad on French TV in 1980, and worldwide commercials and personal appearances have followed, as well as films with Moore himself, one of which, Bullseye, caused Michael Caine to remark on TV: "Roger's double looks more like Roger Moore than Roger does!"

IAN ROSS ⬆

Ian Ross has been mistaken for Eddie Murphy so often that he has decided to make a career of it. He has developed his own stand-up comedy routine, which he is currently exercising on the London cabaret circuit.

ANTONY STOWELL ⬆

Twenty-four year old Antony Stowell is an actor and model, and the Tom Cruise lookalike. He started modelling in 1988, and has done TV commercials, photographic work, and personal appearances such as store openings. He has worked all over Europe, and toured with the cast of Home and Away. Antony is also a Sun newspaper "Page 7 Fella", and appears in the 1993 calendar.

MARTIN GOODYEAR ⬆

Martin Goodyear, 35, is a professional entertainer and Tom Jones lookalike. For as long as he can remember, people have told him how much he looks like Tom, and as he is a great fan, he has been more than happy to perform as Tom all over the country and abroad. Martin says that all the jobs he gets are different and great fun, and "as long as I can fit into my leather trousers, and keep my hair on, I'll carry on".

STEPHEN DREW ⬇

Stephen Drew is 28 years old. He runs a security business and is a body-building instructor and part-time model. Because of the numerous times that he has been mistaken for Patrick Swayze, he also practises as a Patrick Swayze kissogram.

⬅ PETER HUGO

Since 1981, the uncanny combination of his face, voice and mannerisms have resulted in Peter Hugo's full-time career being that of the International Impersonator to the Prince of Wales. During this time, he has appeared internationally on TV shows, made numerous personal appearances, featured in TV commercials abroad and made a multitude of after dinner speeches. Peter left school in 1966 and embarked on a career in marketing. In 1975 he drove from London to Nairobi and, upon his return, wrote and published his book Private Motor-Car Collections of Great Britain. He subsequently became self-employed selling classic cars which, together with food, remains his hobby. His ambition is to be The International Impersonator to King Charles III.

ADVENTURERS

CHRIS BONINGTON ▼

One of our most famous mountaineers Chris Bonington was born in London and went to University College, London and Sandhurst before joining the Tank Regiment from 1956 to 1961. His first mountaineering ascents were Annapurna II, Nuptse, Central Pillar of Freney, Mont Blanc, Central Tower of Pine, Brammah, Changabang, Mount Kongur, China, Shivling West and the first British ascents of the North Face of the Eiger and Mt Vinson in Antarctica. He has led or co-led many successful expeditions, including Annapurna South Face in 1970 and Everest in 1972 and 1975 (the south-west face) and reached the summit of Everest in 1985. He has been president of the British Mountaineering Council since 1988. His autobiography, Mountaineer, came out in 1989.
Photograph courtesy of BBC Photo Library

TOM SHEPPARD ▼

Tom Sheppard has, since 1960, accumulated over 65,000 miles of desert/overland experience, much of it off the beaten track, using his own sun compass and satellite navigation. Many of his expeditions have also, for logistical reasons, been solo, including two (in 1985 and 1991) by motorcycle. In 1975 he led the first ever west-east Sahara crossing for which he gained the Royal Geographical Society's Ness Award.
Photograph by Paul Harris courtesy Expedition Advisory Centre

ROBIN HANBURY-TENISON ▼

Explorer, writer and broadcaster Robin Hanbury-Tenison was brought up in Ireland and educated at Eton and Oxford. He came to prominence in the travel world when he achieved the first land crossing of South America at its widest point in 1958. During the 1960s he crossed the Sahara several times by camel in search of prehistoric paintings. His concern for Indian tribes led to him being one of the founding members of Survival International, of which he is now president. In 1971 he was invited by the Brazilian government to undertake a three-month expedition, and subsequently visited 33 tribes, publishing a report on their plight. He took part in the British Trans-Americas expedition in 1972, crossing the Darien Gap and writing a report on the impact of the road on the Cuna Indians. He led the RGS's Gunung Mulu (Sarawak) expedition 1977/78, a multi-disciplinary survey of a tropical forest ecosystem in a newly-created national park involving 115 scientists over 15 months. In the last few years he has ridden on horseback with his wife from Cornwall to Camargue, along the Great Wall of China, and South to North through New Zealand.
Photograph by Paul Harris courtesy Expedition Advisory Centre

SIR RANULPH FIENNES

Sir Ranulph Fiennes' departure from the Army in 1971 marked the beginning of a series of expeditions which were to earn him the Sultan of Oman's Bravery Medal in 1970, the RGS's Founder's medal, both the Livingstone Gold and Polar medals and the title of the World's Greatest Explorer in the Guinness Book of Records. His most famous expedition, the Transglobe (1979-82) described as "the world's last adventure" by the New York Times, is the first circumpolar journey round Earth. He is also the author of seven non-fiction books, including the best selling To the Ends of the Earth, has made several TV documentaries, is executive consultant to Occidental Oil International Inc and has been keynote speaker for over 400 professional and business groups.
Photograph by Paul Harris courtesy Expedition Advisory Centre

WILFRED THESIGER

Arabian explorer Wilfred Thesiger was born in Addis Ababa and educated at Eton and Oxford. He attended the Coronation of Hailie Selassie in 1930, and in 1933 returned to Ethiopia to hunt with the Danakil tribes, exploring the Sultanate of Aussa. In 1935 he joined the Sudan Political Service and while on leave travelled by camel across the Sahara to the Tibesti mountains. He was seconded to the Sudan Defence Force at the outbreak of WWII, and later served in Abyssinia, Syria and with the SAS in the Western Desert. From 1945 to 1950 he explored the Empty Quarter of southern Arabia and the borderlands of Oman with Bedu companions, which he described in The Marsh Arabs of Iraq. He first travelled in East Africa in 1961, and returned to live with tribal peoples there from 1968 onwards, occasionally returning to London. His travels elsewhere include the Zagros mountains of Iran, the Hindu Kush and Karakoram mountains, Pakistan, Afghanistan and Northern India.
Photograph by Paul Harris courtesy Expedition Advisory Centre

ADVENTURERS

ROBERT SWAN ▼

Robert Swan is the first person to have walked to the North and South Poles, surviving 56 days of tortuous travel, some of the worst ice conditions in years, appalling radio conditions, team illness, frostbite and fatigue. Robert first became interested in polar travel when he read about Scott's last journey into Antarctica as a student at Durham University. He spent the following decade raising funds and support for his own expedition: cycling from Cape Town to Cairo, cross-country skiing in Norway and joining a Royal Marine expedition on Mount Kenya in 1980. After his first journey to the South Pole he embarked on a worldwide lecture tour, published two books and produced an award-winning film of the expedition. Recognised internationally for his involvement with the Duke of Edinburgh's Award Scheme, he was also recently appointed the United Nations Environment Programme Goodwill Ambassador with special responsibility for youth activities.
Photographs: Icewalk Future Limited, Paul Harris courtesy Expedition Advisory Centre

WALLY HERBERT ▶

Arctic explorer Wally Herbert was brought up in South Africa and trained at the School of Military Survey. He spent two years in Egypt before joining the Falkland Islands Dependencies Survey in 1955 for two and a half years in Antarctica, travelling long distances by dog-sled. This was followed by expeditions to Lapland, Svalbard and Greenland. In 1960 he took part in the New Zealand Antarctic expedition which surveyed 26,000 square miles of Queen Maud Range, and commemorated the 50th anniversary of Amundsen's attainment of the Pole by following his return journey. He achieved the first surface crossing of the Arctic Ocean in 1968, a journey of 3,620 miles in 464 days, the longest sustained sledge journey in history. He has lived in the Arctic, with his wife and daughter, and filmed for long periods with the Inuit (Eskimos) and between 1978 and 1982 he made several attempts to navigate Greenland. He has written a number of books, including The Noose of Laurels (1989) on the Cook-Peary controversy.
Photograph by Paul Harris, courtesy Expedition Advisory Centre

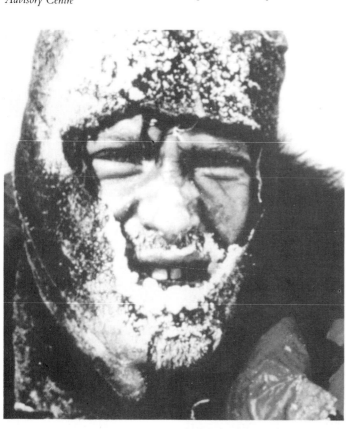

JOHN RIDGEWAY

The Trans-Atlantic oarsman and explorer John Ridgeway was educated at the Nautical College, Pangbourne, before joining the Merchant Navy. After National Service with the Royal Engineers he spent two years at Sandhurst and then received a commission in the Parachute Regiment. He served in Canada, Norway, Greece, the Arabian Gulf, Kenya and Malaysia. Among his feats as an oarsman and explorer are sailing the Atlantic single-handed to South America, leading an expedition that followed the River Amazon from source to sea and another which crossed the Chilean ice-cap.

TIMOTHY SEVERIN

The historian, traveller and writer Timothy Severin was educated at Tonbridge School and Keble College, Oxford, where he took a research degree in medieval Asian exploration. Since then he has recreated many voyages following the routes of early explorers and navigators, using ships and boats reconstructed to the original specifications, including those of St Brendan, the legendary Irish monk, Sinbad whose seven long voyages in an Arab dhow took him from Arabia to China, and the early Greek quests of Ulysses and Jason in a bronze age galleon. He holds the RGS Founders Medal and Livingstone Medal as well as the RSAA Sykes Medal.

ROGER PAYNE

Roger has climbed extensively throughout Britain and Europe and completed new routes and winter ascents in the Alps. He has also led and participated in trips to the Andes, Alaska, Tien Shan, the Himalayas and the Karakoram where he has climbed new routes and made first British ascents. In his most recent expeditions to some of the world's highest mountains in Pakistan, exploration has been combined with development work with the support of Eastern Electricity plc.

COLONEL JOHN BLASHFORD-SNELL

John Blashford-Snell, MBE, DSc(Hon), FRSGS, chairman of the Scientific Exploration Society and of the British Chapter of the Explorers Club, has been on over 60 expeditions. In recognition of his leadership of the Bue Nile, British Trans-America and Zaire River Expeditions, he received the Livingstone Medal and the Segrave Trophy. Since 1978, with the encouragement by the Prince of Wales, John and his colleagues have been organising mammoth expeditions to provide inspiring challenges for young people. The most famous of these are Operation Drake and Operation Raleigh, enterprises which, by 1992, had involved more than 7,000 young people from all over the world.
Photograph by Paul Harris courtesy Expedition Advisory Centre

CHARLES HARVEY ▲

Charles Harvey, a consultant astrologer since 1966 and President of the Astrological Association of Great Britain since 1973, uses astrology as a tool to assist individual growth, self-awareness and decision making. He also specialises in financial astrology and the astrology of world affairs. From 1977 to 1986, Charles was vice-president of the Faculty of Astrological Studies, for which he still teaches. He is co-director with Liz Greene of the Centre for Psychological Astrology. In 1980 he co-founded the Institute for the Study of Cycles in World Affairs, with Michael Baigent and Nick Campion. With these two authors he co-wrote Mundane Astrology and, with Mike Harding, Working with Astrology.

GEOFFREY CORNELIUS ▼

An early interest in occult philosophy and divination led Geoffrey Cornelius to investigate the I Ching and astrology. He pioneered the study of both in adult education in London. Geoffrey was President of the Astrological Lodge of London from 1980 to 1983, and edited its journal, Astrology. He co-founded the Company of Astrologers in 1983. His book, The Moment of Astrology, comes out later this year.

DEREK APPLEBY ▶

Consultant, author and lecturer, Derek Appleby has been in the field of serious astrology since the 1960s. He is one of a small group of British astrologers who, through their work with horary astrology, pioneered the introduction of traditional divinatory judgement techniques into modern European astrological practice. His contribution to the development of astrological knowledge is broad, encompasing innovative work on the effects of eclipses and national horoscopes. He is the author of Horary Astrology and co-author with Maurice McCann of Eclipses. Derek was also a founder member of the Company of Astrologers.

ROGER ELLIOTT ▲

Roger Elliott has covered the spectrum of astrology, from writing popular guides to computer-aided research. As well as having some 25,000 personal clients, he writes daily and weekly columns which are syndicated all over the world. He has written for TV Times, News of the World, Financial Times and Life magazine. Roger has appeared on TV and wrote and presented his 12-part video series Your Star Sign. He also runs a telephone astrology service in Europe, Australia and the USA (providing forecasts, tarot readings, biorhythms and answering questions) and Starlife, a worldwide computerised horoscope service. Among Roger's numerous books on astrology are Astrology for Everyone, Astrology and the Royal Family and How to Tell Your Own Fortune.

RUSSELL GRANT ▼

Russell Grant made TV history by becoming its first resident astrologer. Since the 1980s he has hardly been off the screen in series like A Question of Stars, The Zodiac Game and Star Choice. He has also written numerous astrology columns, now syndicated worldwide by 250 publications. In 1986 Russell launched his telephone horoscope service, the Russell Grant Zodiac Line, and joined TV-am as a regular presenter, looking at both the light and serious sides of astrology. He made successful TV debuts in the USA, Australia and New Zealand. Since then he has continued to write popular columns and best-selling books, provide telephone astrology services and still appears regularly on TV. Among recent projects is an Astro-tarot book, along with a tarot phone-in line. He is President Emeritus of the British Astrological Psychic Society, which he founded. Amazingly, every year Russell finds time for his other great love, appearing in pantomime.

DENNIS ELWELL ▼

In his 45 years as a research astrologer, Dennis Elwell has established an international reputation as a leading writer and lecturer. After working as a full-time newspaper journalist for most of that time, he set up an astrology-based, problem-solving consultancy. Aware of astrology's poor image, he wrote his first book, Cosmic Loom, to stimulate scientific and philosophical discussion of its fundamentals. The book's appearance in 1987 coincided with the wide publicity he received as a result of a feat of astrological foreknowledge. Three weeks before the Herald of Free Enterprise sank, he pleaded with the ship's owners, P & O, to avert the major disaster he foresaw. Sadly his warning was ignored.

NICHOLAS CAMPION ▼

Best known for his use of astrology in the analysis of history and for his record of accurate political forecasts, Nick Campion has been a professional for over 20 years. A graduate of Cambridge, he pursued post-graduate studies in politics and history at London University before becoming an astrological consultant and columnist, notably for the Daily Mail. His monthly columns also appear in New Woman and the American Harper's Bazaar and his work is syndicated worldwide. His books include The Practical Astrologer, a classic introduction to horoscope interpretation. Scheduled to appear in 1993 are two others – The Great Year: Astrology, History and Millenarianism in the Western Tradition, and Royal Astrology. President of the Astrological Lodge in London, he is in great demand as a lecturer, and among his engagements for 1993 is the World Astrology Congress in Lucerne.

ROBERT CURREY ▼

Educated at Eton and London's South Bank Polytechnic, Robert Currey was a commodity broker in the City from 1979 until 1981, when he founded Equinox. The first astrological company of its kind in Britain, it prepares astrological charts using text and computer software written by Robert, who has a Diploma of the Faculty of Astrological Studies. Equinox currently holds exclusive licences to market Astro Intelligence Psychological Analyses by Liz Greene and Astro Carto Graphy Maps and Reports by Jim Lewis. Operating from the Astrology Shop in Covent Garden and, with a branch in Sydney, Equinox currently has over 75,000 clients, including British and foreign royalty, national leaders, politicians and many celebrities in the media and the arts. Robert Currey and Equinox have been featured extensively on television, including Channel 4's series The New Age.

DAVE SMITH ▲

SPICE stands for Special Programme of Initiative, Challenge and Excitement and is an organisation founded by 38-year-old Dave Smith in 1980. Dave was a "beat bobby" for six years, but became increasingly disillusioned with the role of the modern policeman and went to live on a kibbutz, where he learned the value of living selflessly within a community. On his return to England, Dave became assistant director of Manchester YMCA, but again the limitations of a rigid system proved too frustrating and he set up as a freelance personal development tutor, building up an impressive list of corporate clients. He set up SPICE for ordinary people with a lot of energy, who wanted to do something extraordinary and most of his early members came from his corporate groups. Membership now numbers over 10,000 with ages ranging from 18 to 75, and several franchised companies. Activities – about 50 a month – range from bungee jumping to go-karting, abseiling to rambling. When Dave has a new idea, however "off the wall", he puts it in the pending file and, he says, it will always happen.

ROGER PEVERETT ▶

Roger Peverett spent seven years with Lunn Poly and 13 with Thomson Holidays before taking over as managing director of Blakes Cottage and Boating Holidays UK Ltd, on the retirement of David Court, in 1992. Blakes' reputation as the first name in boating has been well established since 1908 and their more recent success as market leader in the cottage holiday market has established them as a major force in British tourism, a position which Roger is set to consolidate.

STEPHEN REES-JONES ▼

Stephen Rees-Jones fell in love with Exmoor during his time as a cadet with the Somerset Police Force. On leaving the Force he became an adventure training instructor in North Wales, before moving to the Midlands, where he and his wife ran hotel boats on the inland waterways. The next move was to Gloucestershire, manufacturing patés for the catering trade. Following the death of his wife, Stephen and his two daughters moved to Somerset and he started his present business, Moorland Rover, specialising in taking small groups of people on tours to little-known and out-of-the-way places on Exmoor. The itinerary of Stephen's tours always includes the natural and social history of Exmoor, picnics, visits to country pubs and accommodation in farmhouses and small hotels. In 1993 he is adding a Glorious Gardens Tour, a Tarka Trail Tour and a special "safari" holiday, by Land Rover to his repertoire.

PETER COX ▼

His father being a lifelong employee of British Rail it was, perhaps, inevitable that Peter Cox should end up associated with leisure rail travel. From early days in Derbyshire, where rock climbing was his pasion, Peter has undertaken a number of sales and marketing assignments, but leisure has been his main area of expertise for much of the recent past, with several years spent working for the Rank Organisation in the 1980s. Currently, he is looking after the marketing of private rail charter for Flying Scotsman Services, organising trips on the most scenic railway lines in Britain, corporate hospitality and days at the races with personal Pullman carriages – by-gone luxury for today.

MARK DAVENPORT

Mark Davenport is the event co-ordinator for Catalyst Event Management, a team of competition designers who have bridged the gap between training, motivation and personal development. He joined the Kendal based company on an industrial placement scheme during his studies for a BA(Hons) degree in recreational management at Sheffield City Polytechnic. He took up his current position in 1990 and, with his design and practical skills, has been responsible for developing the visual presentation of equipment and paperwork within Catalyst. He has also built up a strong team of marshals to work on the company's events. Mark's appetite for life and meeting people is satisfied by working on Catalyst's more exotic events in the USA and France and his passion for paragliding, mountain biking and bridge jumping.

ROWLAND HARDWICK

English Country Cottages is a company which was set up to fill the increasing demand for up-market self-catering holidays. It began life in 1969 as Norfolk Country Cottages and adopted its present name in 1976. Country Cottages in Scotland and Welsh Country Cottages were incorporated during the 1980s and, in 1988, the company entered the European market. Rowland Hardwick joined ECC in 1980 as general manager, and was appointed managing director in 1983. He led the successful management buy-out in 1986, and is now group managing director. In 1988 English Country Cottages won the English Tourist Board's English Holiday and Travel Company of the Year Award.

JOHN RENNIE ▲

Born in Glasgow in 1929, John Rennie joined the Pullman Car Company as a kitchen boy at the age of 16. He worked on all the prestigious Pullman trains and, in 1947, his first Royal train, taking King George VI and his family to Portsmouth. Over the next 20 years John was a member of an elite corps of staff who worked Royal trains and VIP "specials". In 1970 he moved into management when he was appointed training officer for the train catering sector of British Rail. By 1979 he was responsible for train catering throughout the UK. John joined the Venice Simplon Orient-Express in 1983, as operations manager, having served on the British Rail committee responsible for liaising with them in the setting up of the company over the previous two years. He was promoted to general manager in 1986.

ROBIN LLYWELYN ▲

Robin Llywelyn has been managing director of Portmeirion Limited since 1983. He is the grandson of Sir Clough Williams-Ellis, the man whose vision and skill created the village on the Aber peninsula, starting in 1925, and finishing for his 90th birthday in 1973. Portmeirion enjoyed a celebrated clientele from its inception. George Bernard Shaw, H. G. Wells and Bertrand Russell were habitues, and Noel Coward wrote Blithe Spirit there. In the 1960s it became a cult amongst devotees of Patrick McGoohan's television series The Prisoner. Robin was born in 1958 and educated at the University College of Wales, where he gained a joint first in Welsh and English. In addition to his expertise as a hotelier, Robin won the Prose medal in the Royal National Eisteddfod in 1992.

DAVID LESSMAN ▲

A full-time licensed black cab driver since 1976, David Lessman won the title of London Taxi Driver of the Year (sponsored by S.P. Tyres Ltd) in 1989 and again in 1992, having narrowly missed carrying away the title in 1991. David has served for five years as Honorary Treasurer of the London Taxi Drivers' Fund for Underprivileged Children and, in 1990, as the London taxi trade's representative, he drove a black cab in a convoy of vehicles to Romania to ease the plight of young orphans. He was made a Freeman of the City of London

JIM BENSON ▶

To win the coveted title of JCB Driver of the Year, Nottinghamshire excavator operator Jim Benson had to do battle with 60 of Britain's top agricultural and construction drivers at the 1992 Royal Show in Warwickshire. In the preliminary rounds and the Grand Final the drivers were tested on three different JCB machines – a tractor, a backhoe and a telescopic handler – to even out any bias due to specialisation. In the Grand Final, Jim, who was a Driver of the Year finalist in 1989 and 1990, beat top agricultural driver Michael Bell to clinch the title and a holiday for two in Cyprus.

ANDREW HENDERSON PHILIP ◀

After military service in Cyprus and Hong Kong, Andrew Henderson Philip, BEM, started work with British Rail in 1961. His lifelong love of gardening served him well when he transferred to station duties after 19 years as a guard, for since 1981 he has won Scotrail's Best Kept Station Garden award every year, as well as many Best Kept Station awards, first at Markinch and for the past 11 years at Aberdour. The winner the previous year of British Rail's Best Small Station award, in 1990 Andrew took the Best Kept Station in Britain award, which was presented to him by Princess Anne. In 1991 he was honoured with the British Empire Medal for his work at the station and in the community of Aberdour.
Photograph by Bill Robertson

JOHN LOWE AND DAVID MARTIN ▶

John Lowe, who works at Leyton Garage for East London, a subsidiary of London Buses, was London Buses' Driver of the Year in 1992, while David Martin, based at London United's Fulwell Garage in West London, was the Midibus Driver of the Year. Sponsored by Optare, a major supplier of new vehicles to London Buses, and held in Battersea Park on 28 June, the contest to decide the winners of the awards involved practical manoeuvering exercises with a bus. These included pulling into bus stops between parked cars, avoiding overhead obstructions and making the best use of limited road space. Eighty-seven drivers from London Buses' subsidiaries qualified for the event by passing practical and written examinations. John and David both went on to compete in the National Bus Driver of the Year competition in September.

BRIAN EVANS ▼

Named the Automobile Association's Patrol of the Year in 1992, Brian Evans, from Aberystwyth, beat more than 3,000 road-side service patrols to clinch the award. Brian, who joined the AA in 1988, had to go through a gruelling series of tests, interviews and practical exercises to win the award. Along with the title, the AA's Director General, Simon Dyer, presented Brian with a brand new Land Rover Discovery. Bearing the Patrol of the Year logo, the vehicle will be used exclusively for attending the breakdowns of AA members in Wales.

COMMODORE CHRISTOPHER CRAIG

Commodore Christopher Craig, CB, DSC, first saw service in the Gulf, aboard HMS Ashanti, and then for several years flew helicopters and other aircraft, as well as teaching flying. After a period in the Ministry of Defence, he returned to sea and occupied a succession of important posts, including commanding HMS Alacrity. In this ship he saw action throughout the Falklands Campaign, winning the Distinguished Service Cross. In December 1990 Commodore Craig took command, as Senior Naval Officer Middle East, of all Royal Navy units afloat in the Gulf for Operation Granby – an appointment which lasted six months and included the Gulf War. For his part in the campaign he was made a Companion of the Military Division of the Most Honourable Order of the Bath.

SERGEANT LESLIE CARROLL ▼

Since he started parachuting in 1975, Sergeant Leslie Carroll has made 4,300 jumps. He holds 13 British national titles, the British paraski title and the British style and accuracy records. He has also been army champion 15 times (including an army record of five consecutive overall titles) Cyrus champion seven times and RAPA champion six times, as well as winning numerous competitions in Europe and representing Britian in six World Championships and two World Cup of Champions events.

Les joined the Artillery parachute team in the early 1980s, and is now a parachute instructor based in Wiltshire. He readily accepted this role and the task of forming the Army Classics team, as this allows him to pursue his personal interest and pass on his wealth of experience in the sport.

BRENDAN O'BRIEN ▼

A display flyer for nearly 20 years, Brendan O'Brien was with the Rothman's aerobic team and then the Marlboro team before starting the Fournier acrobatic duo – named after the long wingspan motor glider he flew. He introduced the truck-top landing display to Europe in 1987, participated in two paramilitary expeditions as a qualified military parachutist and flew research in personnel and equipment for the British Antarctic Survey. Brendan recently established 201 Fédération Aéronautique Internationale world speed records and appears in the Guinness Book of Records as the holder of more world records than any other flyer. He holds a commercial helicopter pilot's licence, and is also a balloonist and airshow commentator.

NIGEL LAMB ▲

A former Rhodesian Airforce pilot now living in Oxfordshire, Nigel Lamb flew in the Marlboro acrobatic team for eight years and is currently managing director of Aerobatic Displays Ltd. The company operates Team Toyota Aerobatics, with whose three-man display team he flies an Extra 300 monoplane as lead pilot. Nigel has been the British National Champion for eight successive years, and has represented Britain eight times in the European and World Championships. A silver medallist in the South African Masters, he was placed fourth in Switzerland's Breitling Masters.

CAPTAIN WILLIAM DENNIS (JOCK) LOWE ▲

After joining British Airways in 1970, Captain Jock Lowe transferred from VC10s to Concorde in 1976, becoming Concorde Division resource manager six years later. As general manager operations control, from 1986 he had total responsibility for day-to-day operation of BA's fleet, to which role was added that of operations co-ordinator Gatwick after the merger of BA and British Caledonian. Appointed chief pilot TriStar/Concorde/DC10 in 1990, the following year Captain Lowe, who lives in Oxfordshire, became director of Flight Crew.

THOMAS JUSTIN WILLS � arrow

Oxford-educated and now based in Timaru, New Zealand, where he is chairman of a company specialising in superfine merino wool, Thomas Justin Wills made his first solo glider flight in 1963. He holds numerous British gliding records, including the current distance record of 829km (York to Dijon). British champion in 1988 and 1992, and vice-champion in the 1989 World Gliding Championship. Thomas has also won major championships in Austria, France, Italy, Norway, Switzerland and the USA.

TREVOR JONES ▼

Trevor Jones, who in his six years in the Fleet Air Arm had flown Lynx and Sea King helicopters all over the world, became a hero overnight by saving the lives of Richard Branson and Per Linstrand when their trans-Atlantic hot-air balloon ditched in the sea. Tragedy struck Trevor when he broke his neck ski-ing in 1988, and he is now paralysed from the shoulders

down. But he has established his independence through the foundation of the Trevor Jones Trust, which has raised over £250,000 to buy specialist equipment for himself and others with similar injuries. In September 1992, in an amazing feat of bravery, he flew a Shadow Series C-D microlight aircraft, which can be controlled by hand, to publicise the Trust and raise funds.

DR DAVID BAREFORD ▲

A Birmingham-based specialist in haematology, the hot-air balloonist Dr David Bareford has competed in the British National Championship 13 times, coming first four times, second three times, third once, and always in the top ten. Selected ten times for the British team, he gained second and third place in the World Championship and a first, third and fourth in the European Championship. David has won the Great British Balloon Race four time and, in addition to holding six diplomas from the Fédération Aéronautique Internationale, was the British Balloon and Airship Club's Pilot of the Year in 1992.

SQUADRON LEADER ▼ LES GARSIDE-BEATTIE

Having worked in the RAF as a jet provost flying instructor, Squadron Leader Les Garside-Beattie flew Harriers for nine years. During this time he was promoted to Squadron Leader, awarded the Queen's Commendation for Valuable Service in the Air and was Harrier Display Pilot of the Year in 1988. Squadron Leader Garside-Beattie was Deputy Officer Commanding No. 1 (Fighter) Squadron before becoming the manager, in 1991, of the RAF aerobatic team, the Red Arrows. Based with the team at RAF Scampton, in Lincolnshire, he flies its tenth Hawk aircraft to each display and so is known as Red 10.

BRUCE GOLDSMITH ▲

A member of the British team since 1986, Bruce Goldsmith was world professional hang gliding champion (Super League) in 1990 and British champion in 1991 and 1992. More recently involved in paragliding, Bruce became the British distance record holder in 1991, setting a record of 129km that still stands. He is a director of Airwave Gliders, based in Newport, Isle of Wight, designing and testing paragliders, as well as representing Britain in this sport and hang gliding.

FLIGHT-LIEUTENANT DAVID JONES

Flight-Lieutenant David Jones won the Helicopter Club of Great Britain's National Helicopter Championship in 1992. The previous year he won the competition's slalom section, only to drop and shatter the trophy the very same day. So far he has managed to keep the 1992 trophy intact. David, who started flying in 1981, also flies Wessex and Puma aircraft and is based at RAF Shrewsbury, where he works in the Central Flying School, teaching helicopter flying instructors for the RAF, Army and Royal Navy.

RICHARD MEREDITH-HARDY

Having gained his licence to fly microlight aircraft three years earlier, Richard Meredith-Hardy won the British National Championship League (Open Class) in1987. The following year the Hertfordshire-based flyer became European Champion and carried off the British National Championship again. In 1990 he achieved a hat trick in the latter, as well as winning the World Championship (individual and team). The following year he set three Fédération Aéronautique Internationale world speed records and won the round-Britain Great Microlight Air Rally in 1991. Richard was elected secretary of the Association of Microlight Professionals in 1992.

RICHARD CARTER

In the mid-1980s Richard Carter took a course at Britain's first paragliding school and bought and repaired a damaged paraglider. He flew this for 18 months before buying a state-of-the-art machine with which he broke the British distance record and participated in several international competitions, his best result being a fourth placing. In 1991 Richard broke the distance record twice more, won the British Cross-Country League title for the second consecutive year and competed in the World Paragliding Championship. The following year he twice pushed the British record still higher, as well as winning the British Championship. Sponsored by Sky Systems of Brighton and the USA's Ultralight Products, Richard flies and competes all summer. During the winter he is employed by British Sugar plc.

277

DAVE BICKERS ▼

Dave Bickers was born in 1938 and has lived all his life at Coddenham in Suffolk. He left school when he was 16 years old to go into his father's garage and bus business. Always interested in two-wheeled sport, he started at the age of seven on the motorless variety. He rode his first motorcycle scramble in 1954. He went on to become European Champion in 1960 and 1961 and was British Champion nine times. In the mid-1970s he was asked to organise motorcycle stunts on the film Copter Kids, and this led to more work on films and to the formation of Bickers Action Enterprises, specialising in stunt engineering and other services to films, TV and commercial advertising. Dave has never officially retired from competition.

BARON STRATHCARRON OF BANCHOR ▶

Lord Strathcarron passed his driving test at the age of 16, in a 1934 Morgan three-wheeler, with the reverse gear blocked off, because it was illegal to go backwards before the age of 17. He has been a devotee of motorcycling all his life, and rides one on most days, particularly in London. For years, he and his wife took continental holidays towing a luggage trailer behind his BMW. Lord Strathcarron is the President of the Guild of Motoring Writers, and has written on motoring in The Field magazine for 38 years. He is the Chairman of the all-party Parliamentary Motorcycle Group, formed to protect motorcyclists against anti-motorcycling legislation.

PETER FISCHER ▶

Peter Fischer is an ex-fashion model, actor, interpreter and trained hotelier with a passion for British motorcycles. This passion took him from touring abroad to working as a despatcher in London for eight years on his Triumph Bonneville, during which time he learned to do all his own maintenance. The valuable engineering skills which he gained enabled him to start his own business restoring British motorcycles. The business also involves hiring out classic bikes, and co-ordinating and performing stunts, and acting as technical advisor and stylist, on film, television and video.

JIM DOWDALL ↑

Jim Dowdall bought his first motorcycle, a BSA C15, after precipitously leaving school at the age of 16. He took a succession of jobs, including working in a circus and as a film armourer before joining the Parachute Regiment in 1971. Invalided out with impacted vertebrae, he drove a mini-cab and did film extra work in order to acquire his Equity card and, in 1973, joined the stunt register and bought his first Harley Davidson, a 1942 ex-US Army bike which he still uses to visit WWII battlefields. His motorcycle collection now numbers 17 (nine Harleys), subsided by stunting on The Eagle has Landed and the Superman, Star Wars, Indiana Jones, Batman films and many TV series. Jim now specialises in car commercials and has completed over 100. His hobbies include falconry, shooting, military history and his amphibious Dukw.

RICHARD YOUNG ↑

Richard began biking 15 years ago. He learnt on a Yamaha. As soon as he passed his test he bought a secondhand Harley Davidson and over the years has owned ten of them. His current bike is an Ultra Classic Glide with stereo and CB. Richard loves going on long rides around Britain and France, but the highlight of his trips was to ride from the East Coast of America to Colorado and then to Milwaukee 1990, and would now like to take a different route from the west coast of American to the east coast. His profession is social and showbiz photography.
Photograph by Peter Rosenbaum

◄ CHAS GUY

Chas Guy has owned Vincent motorcycles for over 30 years and has ridden, rallied and raced all over the UK and the continent. He races a 1948 Vincent 1000cc HRD Twin, which he built and prepared himself, and competes in many classic and vintage events with, he says, pleasing results. Chas and his wife Ann became professionally involved with Vincent in 1980, when they acquired Conway Motors in Whitstable, one of the earliest Vincent dealers, appointed in 1936, and a company that still deals exclusively in Vincent HRD.
Photograph by Terry Howe

DAVID WILSON ▼

David Wilson, 40, has been riding motorcycles since 1966. A former RAF fighter pilot and aerobatic display pilot, he now flies Boeing 747 jumbo jets. David is a former British bobsleigh team driver and competed on the international circuit for several years. David sees a correlation between high performance motorcycling and flying a fighter – both are experiences which, he says, leave one with a satisfying fatigue which can clear the mind of everyday worries, and allow the internal batteries to recharge. He believes that motorcycling is one of the last legal "frontier spirit" pastimes available to everyone.

VINTAGE CARS

MARTIN STRETTON ▲

Martin Stretton left a career in insurance in 1988, to set up a flourishing business restoring and selling classic racing and sports cars. He first made his name racing vintage Frazer Nash cars, winning more than 80 trophies. He also won Britain's premier historic race at Silverstone in 1991 and 1992, driving a 1955 Grand Prix Connaught, and eight races in 1991/92 around Europe in a 1959 Formula 1 Cooper Climax. He races a wide selection of vintage and historic cars from various collections, and set the lap record at Cadwell Park in a 1932 Maserati.

ANTHONY MERRICK ▼

Tony Merrick was born in Leicestershire in 1939 and brought up in the family garage business. He became interested in older cars while studying engineering at Loughborough College. He started racing in 1960, in an MG and an ERA. In 1966 he set up a company restoring cars for the Donington Museum, and in 1969 joined Neil Corner, preparing his cars for historic events. In 1971 he reformed his own company in Berkshire, restoring historic racing cars of all types, and pre-war exotic road cars, with clients as far afield as Japan. He has raced historic grand prix cars for 30 years.

PETER HANNEN ▲

Peter Hannen left Eton and became a sugar trader in 1972, transferring to New York in 1976. He returned to London in 1986. Always a vintage car enthusiast, he started racing in his own Maserati 6CM in 1986. Successes include the 1987 Nurburgring and the 1990 Nuffield Trophy and he is the current Silverstone Club and GP circuit record holder. He was also the instigator of the "100 Mile Race" for front-engined GP cars pre-1959, which is held annually at five circuits around Europe.

BRUCE SPOLLON ▲

The son of an architect, Bruce Spollon qualified as an engineer in 1947, at Austin Motors, and started his own company, Merton Motors specialising in rebuilding and tuning pre-war sports cars. The obsession with these cars has remained. He was always interested in motor sports, and began competing in 1945 in trials, hill climbs and sprints. He is a regular competitor on all types of circuit, hill climb and trial events, driving an ERA, Bentley, Riley, Alfa Romeo or 30/98 Vauxhall.

DAN MARGULIES ▼

The Margulies family came from Bucharest to London in 1937, and Dan attended Highgate School and the College of Aeronautical Engineering, Chelsea. He started driving at the age of five, and by 15 owned and drove a 3 litre Bentley, and a 30/98 Vauxhall. His first competitions were in a Bugatti GP in 1946/47, and in the 1950s, his mechanic was Graham Hill. In long distance events his co-driver was David Piper. In 1957, after several accidents and a great deal of money spent on racing, Dan opened the doors of Dan Margulies (Vintage Cars) Ltd, specialising in the buying, selling and restoration of vintage and historic racing cars. The most important cars have passed through his hands. Between 1958-1981 Dan competed in over 50 international rallies. He is a member of the BRDC and the VSCC. A purist and great enthusiast, he still competes in his 1939 Maserati 4CL.
Photograph by Fred Scatley

TOM WHEATCROFT ▲

Frederick Bernard Wheatcroft, known to one and all as Tom, served with the 8th Army in the war, ending up in Germany where he met and married his wife. Leaving the Army, he returned to the plastering trade, and started his own business which mushroomed into the biggest private building company in Leicester. He bought his first vintage car, a 1929 SS Mercedes, in 1947. By 1957, he had the largest private collection of Mercedes Benz and changed direction, now owning the world's largest private collection of single seater grand prix cars. In 1970 he bought Donington Park, and restored it to its former glory, opened to the public in 1977, and is now rated as one of the best circuits in the country, especially by drivers. Now aged 70, Tom is still motor racing all over the world.

STANLEY MANN

Stanley Mann's enthusiasm for vintage cars, and particularly Bentleys, was nurtured as a child and, in 1966, he gave up his career as a fashion pl.otographer to turn his hobby into his business. For the past eight years he has run the most successful vintage Bentley dealership in the world, from his working showroom in Radlett. Among his recent racing achievements, in the past three years, he has taken various British records in vintage Bentleys with speeds of up to 136mph, including the British Class B 1,000 mile record, in a team headed by HRH Prince Michael of Kent.

LORD MONTAGU OF ▼ BEAULIEU

The son of a leading motoring pioneer, Lord Montagu inherited the Beaulieu Manor Estate in 1951, and decided to open the Palace House to the public. Beginning with a few vintage cars, he founded the Montagu Motor Museum in memory of his father and, in 1972, it became the National Motor Museum, which is administered by a charitable trust. The museum, Palace House and Abbey ruins attract over 500,000 per annum. In 1974 the museum won the Museum of the Year Award. From 1973 to 1978 Lord Montagu was founder president of the Historic Houses Association, and from 1982 to 1984, he was president of the Museums Association. From 1983 to 1992 Lord Montagu was the first chairman of English Heritage. He is president of the Southern Tourist Board, the Tourism Society, the Federation of British Vehicle Clubs, and of the Historic Commercial Vehicle Society. The positions he holds in the various fields of sailing, wine and conservation are myriad. He is the author of many books on motoring, and an active member of the House of Lords.

SIR JOHN VENABLES- ▼ LLEWELYN, Bart

Sir John is very much associated with the Marque Bugatti, is a member of the Main Council and Chairman of the Bugatti Affairs Committee, and an official of the Bugatti Owners Club. A successful racer for many years, Sir John's most notable triumphs have been with a Type 51 Bugatti, in which he has won the Williams Trophy for several years at Cadwell Park. He also won the famous 1984 Bugatti Race at Monaco. Apart from the Type 51, Sir John also competes in a Type 35 Bugatti, and has been a front runner for years in his 2 litre ERA.

HARRY DODSON ▲

Harry Dodson was head gardener at Chilton Hall in Hungerford for more than 40 years. It would be no exaggeration to say that he is one of the few surviving links with the golden age of the Victorian kitchen garden. He is the nephew of the head gardener to the Earl of Selbourne and two other uncles of his were also head gardeners. Harry is like a walking encyclopaedia of their now forgotten skills and he played a major part in the recent restoration of the garden at Chilton Hall, documented for the BBC TV series The Victorian Kitchen Garden. He has spent more than 50 years as a gardener on private estates and, although retired, he is still associated with the garden at Chilton. Harry has been awarded the Royal Horticultural Society's Gold Medal of Honour.
Photograph by BBC Photo Library

ALAN AND ADRIAN BLOOM ▼

Nurseryman and steam engine enthusiast Alan Bloom was born in 1906 in the Ouse Valley. He started working at the Wisbech nursery in 1921, establishing a wholesale business with his father in 1926. In 1939 they were growing nearly 2,000 varieties of alpines and perennials. He bought Bressingham Hall in Norfolk in 1946, which is now the UK's largest grower of perennials. Alan and his sons Adrian and Robert have introduced more than 70 new species to cultivation and raised and named some 170 new cultivars. He and Adrian have been awarded the Victoria Medal of Honour. Although retired he is life president of the Hardy Plant Society. Alan has written for the gardening press and published two novels.
Photograph by Ed Barber courtesy of Harper Collins Publishers

◄ ALAN TITCHMARSH

Alan Titchmarsh is well-known for his many appearances on TV as a gardening expert. His broadcasting career began on Radio 4's Down to Earth and he can be heard on Radio 2's Arts Programme and A House in a Garden. He first appeared on TV on BBC Breakfast Time and since then has presented Open Air, Daytime Live and Pebble Mill as well as the BBC's annual Chelsea Flower Show programme. He was seen most recently in his enjoyable series Titchmarsh's Travels. Alan taught at the Royal Botanic Gardens in Kew, where he was trained, before becoming a horticultural journalist. An author and correspondent for the Daily Mail, he was named Gardening Writer of the Year in 1980 and 1983 and was awarded the Royal Horticultural Society's Gold Medal in 1985.

SIR GEOFFREY JELLICOE ▲

Sir Geoffrey Jellicoe was a founder member of the Landscape Institute and its president between 1939 and 1949. Sir Geoffrey has designed gardens at the Royal Lodge, Windsor, Chequers and at the Royal Horticultural Society's central area in Wisley. He was formerly senior partner of Jellicoe and Coleridge Architects. The first president of the International Federation of Landscape Architects in 1948, he was a member of the Royal Fine Arts Commission between 1954 and 1968, and a Trustee of the Tate Gallery between 1966 and 1973. A prolific author on the subject of landscape architecture, he was awarded the CBE in 1961 and knighted in 1979.
Photograph by the Landscape Institute

ARTHUR HELLYER ▼

A noted gardening correspondent, Arthur Hellyer is a practical gardener first and writer second. He left Dulwich College in 1916, grew tomatoes in Guernsey, worked as a farm labourer in Jersey, and as a salesman for market gardeners Isaac House and Sons. He decided to become a horticultural journalist in the mid-1920s. He became assistant editor of Amateur Gardener in 1930. In the same year he revised Sanders' Encyclopaedia of Gardening and wrote The Amateur Gardening Pocket Guide, which is still in print today. Editor of Amateur Gardener since 1946, he retired from the magazine in 1966. He was awarded the MBE in 1976.
Photograph by Alan Titchmarsh by courtesy of Dr Brent Elliot

ROBERT J. CORBIN ▲

Robert Corbin was the horticultural manager of the Greater London Council's housing department for more than 30 years. On his retirement in 1980, he was managing more than 350 staff, administering an annual budget of nearly £3 million and was responsible for the outstanding appearance of many of London's open spaces. He founded the Institute of Groundsmanship, is a member of the International Federation of Parks and Recreational Administration, committee chairman of the Royal Gardeners' Orphan Fund and a council member of the Gardeners' Royal Benevolent Fund.
Photograph by Anita Corbin

GRAHAM STUART THOMAS ▲

Graham Stuart Thomas has been the Gardens Consultant of the National Trust since 1974. He is the vice-president of the Garden History Society, vice-patron of the Royal National Rose Society and honorary president of the Historic Roses Group. He has written many books and, as an artist, his work has been collected in The Complete Paintings and Drawings of Graham Stuart Thomas, published in 1987. He has been awarded the Royal Horticultural Society's Veitch Memorial Medal, the Victoria Medal of Honour and the Natural Rose Society's Dean Hole Medal. He was awarded the OBE in 1975.
Photograph by Country Life

ROY LANCASTER ▼

Roy Lancaster, youngest winner of the Royal Horticultural Society's prestigious Victoria Medal, lived and studied in East Asia for several years and is an authority on much of the region's plant life. A renowned plant collector, fascinated by the astonishing diversity of flora in China and Nepal, he has chronicled his great curiosity in two books: Travels in China and Plant Hunting in Nepal. Co-author of several other books,

NEIL HEWERTSON ▼

Garden designer Neil Hewertson was born in Lancashire in 1960. Educated at Yarm Grammar School he graduated from Liverpool University with a degree in botany in 1981. Neil soon joined Drummonds of Codland, Hampshire, working on the rediscovery and renovation of their Capability Brown park. He moved to the Cotswolds in 1985, where he designed and built an extraordinary garden at Stowell Park for Lady Vestay. This well-documented commission led, in 1988, to the formation of Neil Hewertson Garden Design. The company specialises in designing and building gardens for "houses of character". Since 1988 Neil Hewertson has had more than 20 private commissions, from

including Mediterranean Plants and Gardens, he writes for the gardening press and contributes to Country Life. He appears regularly on TV, notably on the BBC's Gardener's World and Channel 4's The Gardening Club. Roy was the curator of the Hillier Arburetum, especially well-known for its trees and shrubs. On the death of Sir Harold Hillier and while Roy was still curator, the Hillier Arburetum became a public garden.
Photograph by The Landscape Institute

Devon to the Scottish Highlands. He has worked for clients including Sir Phillip Payne Gallway at Boxford in Oxfordshire and the Harts at Hambledon Hall. With each new commission testing his understanding of scale and his knowledge of plants, he is perhaps the UK's foremost garden designer. Neil, who is a member of the Institute of Horticulture, lives on the Stowell Park estate.
Photograph by the Royal Horticultural Society

CHRISTOPHER DAY ▲

Christopher Day qualified as a vet at Cambridge in 1972 and soon joined his parents' pratice in Oxfordshire. Here, with an interest in homoeopathy dating back to when he was 13, he used homeoepathy increasingly and by 1982 rarely needed to adminster drugs. In 1987 Christopher became a member of the Faculty of Homoeopathy, starting courses for vets. He became Veterinary Dean and then a Fellow, for services to homoeopathy. From 1980 he studied acupuncture, which is now a major part of his practice, along with herbalism and other alternative techniques. Christopher was the first President of the International Association of Veterinary Homoeopathy and is Secretary to the British Association of Homoeopathic Veterinary Surgeons. A leading expert on veterinary homoeopathy, he lectures throughout the world and has written four books on alternative medicine.
Photograph by Tim Bryce

GARY CLAYTON JONES ▼

After qualifying at the Royal Veterinary College in 1965, David (Gary) Clayton Jones taught surgery there until 1990, eventually becoming senior lecturer. In 1986 he was made the first director of the Queen Mother Hospital for Animals. The recipient, among other honours, of the British Small Animal Veterinary Association's Simon Award in 1976 and the Royal College of Veterinary Surgeons' Francis Hogg Award in 1979, Gary is also the holder of diplomas in veterinary radiology and small-animal orthopaedics. He became a partner in Ogle, Clark and Partners in 1991, based in Tenterden, Kent, and began a referral surgical practice. Gary has lectured internationally, published over 60 papers and appeared on television and radio.

PETER KERTESZ ▼

A dental surgeon, who trained at London's Kings College Hospital and qualified in 1969, Peter Kertesz runs a private practice in the West End. Having first become involved in the dental treatment of animals in 1977, he is now the world's foremost expert in the field, and is a consultant to some 16 zoos and wildlife establishments in Britain and abroad. An Honorary Research Fellow of the Zoological Society of London, Peter wrote the definitive work on his subject, *A Colour Atlas of Veterinary Dentistry and Oral Surgery*.

DAVID McCARTNEY ▲

Having qualified in Edinburgh in 1946, Ulsterman David McCartney returned to Belfast in 1949 to run an established practice with Eric Bryson for ten years. During this time David had developed a special interest in orthopaedics and physiotherapy, and now began to concentrate on cryosurgery and ophthalmology. He went on to acquire another long-established Belfast practice. David started using homoeopathy in 1980 and from 1987 studied at the Faculty of Homoeopathy and, in 1984, gained the Certificate in Veterinary Ophthalmology. Recently semi-retired from Belfast's Cedar Grove Veterinary Clinic, David is currently developing an alternative veterinary medicine clinic, while the practice is being carried on by his daughter Pat Hart and Gordon McKnight.

KEITH BUTT ▼

With a practice near Kensington Gardens, Keith Butt has treated the pampered pets of central London since 1963, having qualified at Cambridge two years earlier. Ably supported by an assistant vet, three nurses, two receptionists and Serena, who lives and works with him, organising the practice, Keith has a referral surgical facilitiy in Putney and links with the busy Elizabeth Street Emergency Clinic. He has himself kept a wide variety of dogs, cats and monkeys, Burmese cats being particular favourites.

PETER NEVILLE ▼

Currently Visiting Animal Behaviour Therapist at Bristol University's Veterinary School, Peter Neville has referred and treated pet behavioural problems for over eight years and is the Honorary Secretary of the Association of Pet Behaviour Counsellors, which he co-founded. In addition to producing many specialist papers on pet and feral cat behaviour, Peter writes for leading pet magazines, and has published four internationally successful books, the latest of which is *Pet Sex – the Facts of Life for the Family Dog, Cat and Rabbit . . .*, and has lectured in four continents on pet behaviour therapy. He is also a frequent broadcaster on radio and television. Peter is a partner with his wife, the veterinary journalist Claire Bessant, in the Bessant Neville Partnership, a small, UK-based international company specialising in public relations and editorial services in the pet services market.

◄ ROGER MUGFORD

Roger Mugford's Chertsey-based Animal Behaviour Centre is the leading institution of its kind for the treatment and study of behavioural problems in animals. Trained as a psychologist, Roger sees such difficulties as most often due to a mismanagement of attachment and love by the pet's owner. His use of the latest scientific techniques for behaviour modification is described in *Dr Mugford's Casebook*, published in 1991, while his more recent *Never Say No* focuses on behavioural problems in dogs. Roger is a frequent guest speaker and broadcaster on animal care and behaviour, and an opponent of wild animals' treatment in zoos and other forms of commercial exploitation. He holds a part-time lectureship at the Royal Veterinary College and is a consultant to many of the world's humane societies and animal charities.

JERRY DAVIES ▼

Awarded a mark of distinction in Veterinary Surgery on graduating from the Royal Veterinary College in 1974, Jerry Davies went on to gain his PhD in 1983 and two years later a Diploma in Veterinary Radiology. Formerly senior lecturer in veterinary surgery at the Royal Veterinary College, Jerry is a Royal College of Veterinary Surgeons Specialist in Veterinary Radiology and Small Animal Surgery and Clinical Director of Ridgway Referrals in Bedfordshire, possibly Britain's first private referral clinic.

JOHN FISHER ▲

Surrey-based John Fisher is a canine behaviour counsellor and the current chairman of the Association of Pet Behaviour Counsellors. The APBC, whose members work strictly on veterinary referral, has over 40 clinics in Britain and Ireland and combines expertise in veterinary medicine, clinical psychology, biology, zoology, ethology and animal training. John, who has had over 20 years' experience of working professionally with dogs, is the author and tutor of a correspondence course on canine behaviour. He has written two books on the psychology and behaviour of dogs and another, recently published, which challenges the established theories of dog training.

PETER BEDFORD ▲

A graduate of the Royal Veterinary College, Dr Peter Bedford is currently its GDBA Professor of Canine Medicine and Surgery. He gained a PhD in aetiology, pathology and the treatment of canine glaucoma, and his teaching and referral work focuses on ophthalmology in all species and conditions of the head and neck in small animals. Past President of the British Small Animal Veterinary Association and the European Society of Veterinary Ophthalmologists, Peter is the current President of the World Small Animal Veterinary Association.

MIKE REYNOLDS

Mike Reynold's career has taken some remarkable turns since he left Sandhurst to serve with the Royal Artillery for five years. For 15 years he worked in advertising, rising to creative director for a major international agency. Mike was the man who brought us the "Milky Bar Kid", but there is no suggestion that it was an act of atonement which led him, in 1970, to move to Cornwall and open a bird garden. "Bird Paradise" opened its gates in 1971 and has since changed its name to "Paradise Park". It is a breeding and conservation centre for birds, and one of Cornwall's four top tourist attractions. In 1989 Mike established a charity, "The World Parrot Trust", funding parrot conservation projects worldwide.
Photograph by Andrew Besley

KEN JONES

Ken Jones started his working life as a miner, and he says that there have often been times in his subsequent career as a "Seal Doctor", when mining has seemed a comfortable alternative. In the 30 years since they rescued Cindy, their first seal, Ken and his wife, Mary, rescued hundreds of seals, and set up the Cornish Seal Sanctuary, in Gweek, Cornwall, where Ken is the curator.

BILL JORDAN

In 1984 Bill Jordan founded Care For The Wild, a charity registered with the aim of tackling the problems of suffering and exploitation of wildlife caused by man. In 1991 Care Of The Wild offices were opened in the USA and Denmark. Born in 1924, William Johnston Jordan attended Edinburgh University (BSc), the Royal Veterinary College (MRCVS) and Liverpool University (MVSc). In the 1950s, while in private practice, he became very concerned about the negative attitude towards wildlife. He became a founder member of the British Veterinary Zoological Society, and made a study of the many substandard zoos that existed at that time in England and, with Stefan Ormrod, wrote "The Last Great Wild Beast Show", highlighting their plight, and initiating the process which finally resulted in the Zoo Act. "Care of the Wild" was formed by Bill as a result of his being appointed chairman of the National Society Against Cruel Sports – a post which he accepted on condition that he could form a society to help all wildlife.

KEITH SANDERS

Keith Sanders, now 48, has variously been a newspaper man, car salesman, transport manager, mobile crane driver, smallholder and photo-journalist. He now has the Northcote Heavy Horse Centre in Lincolnshire on the family smallholding, where he has representative horses from all of the British breeds, as well as rare breed farm animals – endangered rather than exotic. The Centre is open from March to September.

BOBBY DALZIEL

Bobby Dalziel was born in 1955, and is a shepherd on an 850 Ewe (200 ewe lamb) farm in Selkirk. He started competing in sheepdog trials in 1975, and in 1979 entered the Scottish National for the first time, and won the Scottish Shepherds' title with a dog called Joe. He went on to win the International Shepherds Title in 1985 with a bitch, Nell. He ran Whisp, his present dog, in 1989 when he won the Scottish Shepherds title and the Supreme Championship, a feat which he repeated in 1992, adding to it the International Shepherds' title.

CHRISTOPHER MARLER

Christopher Marler has been breeding wild and domestic animals for more than 40 years. With pedigree cattle, his successes have included eight Royal champions and four Royal Highland champions, all with his homebred Belted Galloway cattle. He established his Flamingo Gardens and Zoological Park in 1960, and has achieved international recognition with rare bird breeding. In 1977 he won the Outstanding Swan Breeding Award for being the first person to breed all four varieties of Arctic Swan in captivity. His UK first breedings include Painted Storks, Black Spurwinged Geese, Whistling Swans and American Bald Eagles. The Park now maintains a collection of 150 bird species, and 1992 successes included two Bald Eagle chicks and six Flamingo chicks.

GRAHAM DANGERFIELD

On leaving school in Oxford, Graham Dangerfield immediately went to Tanganyika, joining Jonathon Kingdon on a series of safaris. He then joined ATV for eight years, presenting animal shows mainly for children, before returning to Tanzania to spend two years as a warden at Serengeti National Park. In 1965 he wrote The Unintended Zoo and, in 1981, co-wrote Tarkina The Otter and Rajah of Bong and Other Owls. Graham founded The Graham Dangerfield Wildlife Trust in 1989, which deals with several hundred orphaned and injured animals a year, and set up the Wildlife Breeding Centre in 1968, in which he has bred large numbers of endangered species of wild cat, and now breeds Golden Eagle and White-Bellied Sea Eagle – the world's first. Graham has worked on the soundtracks of numerous films and documentaries, and currently films in Cornwall and longs for Africa.

Photograph by Maria Zegallo-Tufnell

GERALD DURRELL

Gerald Durrell was born in India in 1925, and educated on the Continent by private tutors, with a special emphasis on natural history. In 1945 he joined Whipsnade Park, London, as a student keeper. In 1946 he inherited £3,000 and embarked on his career leading collecting expeditions to remote parts of the world. He acquired specimens for the major zoological gardens of Europe and America, and contributed 22 new species to the collection of the Zoological Society of London. In 1959 he created his own Zoological Park in Jersey, and in 1963 he founded the Jersey Wildlife Preservation Trust, with a view to the captive breeding of endangered species. There are facilities for research, and for the training of students, of whom 274 from 64 countries had received training by 1989. A prolific and best-selling author, probably Gerald Durrell's best known title is "My Family and Other Animals" (1956). He was appointed OBE in 1983.

FARMING

ROBERT SUTTON

Born, as he says, with "silver cutlery protruding from every orifice" Robert Sutton inherited a third of his father's 1,000 acre farm when he was 16 years old. The farm grew until it could be divided equally and still leave him 1,250 acres. Robert learned serious lessons in business by dabbling unsuccessfully in spec building and free range eggs. The principal lesson was to concentrate on the core business. His land in Nottinghamshire is too heavy to grow anything below ground and he is, he says, too lazy for livestock, so the main crops have been wheat, rape and oats. Robert's on-going business philosophy is that cost cutting is most effectively achieved by substituting management for expenditure. He is a non-executive director of Sentry Farming Ltd, chairs two discussion groups and is an occasional farming journalist.

PETER MORRISH

A career land agent in a previous incarnation, Peter Morrish started farming in 1955, at Horsmonden, near Tonbridge in Kent. When he took over, the acreage of hops on Castlemaine Farm had been whittled down from 65 to 14, largely because of hop verticillium wilt. By meticulous hygiene he now grows 35 acres of mixed varieties of hops, most of which can no longer be grown elsewhere in the Weald of Kent. In 1986, following the abolition by Brussels of the Hop Marketing Board, Peter set up a new marketing group, Wealden Hops Ltd, which was shortly followed by the creation of three more groups, and is now the second biggest marketing company in the country and attracting members all the time.

JOE HENSON

Joe Henson gained an MRAC and worked as a farm manager before taking on the tenancy of a 1,000 acre farm in the Cotswolds. His interest in rare breeds led to his being invited to join a working party, set up by the London Zoo Society and the RASE, to look into ways of preserving the nation's rare breeds. This working party became the first council of the Rare Breeds Survival Trust of which Joe was the founder chairman and is still a vice-president. In 1971 Joe opened the first collection of rare breeds to the public on part of his farm, which he called the Cotswold Farm Park and which now welcomes over 100,000 visitors every summer. His work for the BBC as a presenter of countryside programmes has done much to publicise the importance of the work for rare breeds survival in Britain and worldwide.
Photograph by the Cheltenham Newspaper Co Ltd

MICHAEL MORTIMER ↑

After leaving Nottingham University with an agricultural degree, Michael Mortimer joined a feed compounder, E. Billington & Son, as a nutritionist. He worked there for ten years, finally emerging as managing director of one of their feed mills. In 1987, with a partner, he formed Balanced Feeds. The company uses waste materials from the human food industry – biscuits, breakfast cereal and sweets – combined with conventional animal feed ingredients to provide a balanced ration for cattle and sheep. Within four years the business was turning over £5 million, at which point Michael's co-director decided to retire and Michael and his wife Catherine, bought out his share. The mill is situated at Chelford in Cheshire and the Mortimers live nearby in Macclesfield.

JOHN WARNE ↑

John Warne has been farming 150 acres of mixed livestock farm in the heart of Cornwall for over 40 years and has always been involved with breeding, showing and judging pedigree cattle. Having had considerable success with South Devon cattle, he is now involved with rare and minority breeds and is currently chairman of the Longhorn Society. Amongst the other breeds he keeps are the Beef Shorthorn and Leicester Longwool and Norfolk Horn sheep as well as commercial livestock. His showing successes include breed championships at the Royal and Smithfield Shows, Interbreed Championships at the Devon County and Royal Cornwall Shows and the Rare Breed Show and Sale at Stoneleigh. John has been a judge on four occasions for different breeds at the Royal Show. His main objective in breeding pedigree livestock is to improve the commercial potential whilst retaining the true breed character.

PETER ROBERTS ➤

Peter Roberts once found himself in charge of 600 mules, the animals that Orde Wingate had used in Burma, transporting them from Burma to Greece. Years later he would contrast the care which these animals received from the Royal Army Veterinary Corps with the indifference with which they were treated by dealers around the world. He learned the scientific side of farming at Harper Adams Agricultural College and the practical side as a cowman and farm manager, before farming on his own account, with his wife Anna, for eight years in Hampshire. They became so disillusioned with the lifelong treatment of farm livestock and the spread of chemical dependent crops that they started Compassion in World Farming, a campaigning trust, and the Athene Trust, an educational charity, the joint aims being to improve the lot of the animal as food. They became vegetarian and then moved out of farming altogether. Peter reasoned that machines could

convert prime quality crops into "meat" for human consumption more efficiently than animals and set up a company which launched the first soya based convenience foods, Protoveg and Sosmix, on to the British market. He anticipates that soya bean technology will one day be applied to the field bean, pea and white lupin, establishing a new market for British grown crops.

FARMING

MALCOLM READ

Malcolm Read has lived all his life on the South Wiltshire farm previously occupied by his father and grandfather. From the chalk downland ridge which forms the southern boundary, he remembers his grandfather pointing out Southampton Water and the Isle of Wight. As a young man he worked hard for 20 years tending a large flock of sheep on these downs, which are now designated a Site of Special Scientific Interest, and now he enjoys nothing more than to spend time there with his own grandchildren, among the bee orchids and picnic thistles. As a District and Parish Councillor he has fought for many years to protect the countryside around Salisbury. Malcolm Read loathes "agribusiness" – large farming companies – and slick land agents who extract too much rent from tenant farmers. He likes traditional landowners. His great passion is for the novels and poems of Thomas Hardy and the music of Edward Elgar because, he says, they evoke the true spirit of the English countryside and culture.

COLIN EVANS

Colin Evans farms 166 acres in the Brecon Beacons National Park. He took over the farm in 1989, at the age of 20, following the untimely death of his father. The land lies between 700 and 900 feet above sea level and is severely disadvantaged in the less favoured areas. In addition to his 430 breeding ewes, Colin has 40 trekking ponies on the farm, adding to the tourist facility which includes bed and breakfast accommodation and a caravan site. He has recently constructed an outdoor riding arena for tuition. Colin is a top class rugby player and has represented Wales in the tetrathalon.

DAVID HORMANN

David Hormann has worked at Fan Farm in Llandovery, Dyfed, initially with his father, Fritz, since leaving school in 1977. His father is now retired and David manages the farm with Sarah, his wife. Major investment in buildings and pollution control, together with genetic improvement in livestock, were rewarded when David won the British Grassland Society UK Silage competition and the Farmers' Weekly Beef Farmer Award for 1992. The farm is run in harmony with the countryside and this, together with David's willingness to host farm walks and give talks to students and other interested groups, helps promote the British farmer in a positive way. This was recognised in 1992, when David was awarded the title of Farmers' Weekly Farmer of the Year.

STEPHEN CARR

Stephen Carr runs his 1,000 acre cereal, beef and sheep farm in Polegate, East Sussex, with two very basic management criteria: minimum effort and maximum profit. He has been farming since 1979. In 1988 a friend suggested to him that he should enter a writing competition and now he is a regular contributor to Farmers' Weekly and Crops magazines and he broadcasts frequently on Radio 4's farming programmes.
Photograph by Raymond Austin

EDDIE NICHOLSON ▼

When Eddie Nicholson was four years old his farmworker father moved the family to a council-owned smallholding of 50 acres, near Middlesborough. By the time Eddie left school the family had moved up the farming ladder to a 120 acre tenancy on a small estate near Whitby. Eddie worked at home for two years while taking a day release course locally. In 1980, when he was 18 years old, Eddie took a one-year National Certificate of Agriculture course and, the following year, went to agricultural college and completed a dairy herd management course. In 1986 he took on the tenancy of a 330 acre farm and, over the last six years, has concentrated on increasing the dairy cow numbers from 85 to the present 232 and buying milk quota, enabling him to sell over 1.4 million litres of milk per year. The herd is now pedigree Fresian Holsteins and all replacements are bred on the farm. Eddie, and his wife Carol, also run a small flock of 75 sheep, enabling them to rear 120 fat lambs a year.

◄ JOHN BERRY

Having been interested in wildlife and landscape since the early 1970s, John Berry has devoted a great deal of time and effort to conservation on the farm which he runs with his wife, Rosemary, and which is rented from the Duchy of Cornwall. Initially, two small lakes and a number of ponds were created in an unspectacular wet area, the banks planted with native hardwoods and the lakes stocked with trout and carp for fishing. The conservation area now covers 12 acres and a total of 22,000 trees have been planted since 1979. John has allowed the hedges to get taller and thicker, some left to grow for ten years, before cutting and laying. He leaves hardwood in the hedges and new hedges have been planted. John has received numerous awards for conservation, including the Country Life Silver Lapwing Award and the Royal Association of British Dairy Farmers Landscape Conservation Award. At Billingsmoor Farm, John and Rosemary Berry introduce school children, students and adult groups to successful modern farming combined with conservation.
Photograph by Tiverton Gazette

SIR ALAN COOK ↑

Born in 1922 Alan Hugh Cook is the Master of Selwyn College, Cambridge. He graduated from Corpus Christi in 1943 and worked on radar development at the Admiralty Signal Establishment. He continued research into geophysics at Cambridge (PhD 1950, ScD 1967) and at the National Physical Laboratory from 1952-69 (as superintendent of the Division of Quantum Metrology 1966-69). He was the first Professor of Geophysics at Edinburgh University 1969-72 and Jacksonian Professor of Natural Philosophy at the University of Cambridge 1972-90. Sir Alan was a Fellow of King's College, Cambridge, from 1972 before becoming Master of Selwyn College in 1983. He was Visiting Fellow to the Joint Institute for Laboratory Astrophysics at Boulder, Colorado, 1965-66 and Visiting Professor to the University of California 1981-82. He is a former member of the Natural Environment Research Council and of the Science and Engineering Research Council, where he was Chairman of the Astronomy and Space Board. Sir Alan is the author of about 180 articles in various journals and seven books on astronomy, the latest of which – Gravitational Experiments in the Laboratory – is published in 1993.

SIR BERNARD LOVELL ▼

Sir Bernard Lovell's appointment as Director of Jodrell Bank Experimental Station (now Nuffield Radio Astronomy Laboratories) in 1951 coincided with the start of the "TV age", so he was the first astronomer to become a household name (and face) to a whole generation. He remained Director until 1981. He is Emeritus Professor of Radio Astronomy at the University of Manchester. In a distinguished career, Sir Bernard has received the Guggenheim International Astronautics Award (1961), the Churchill Gold Medal (1964) and the Gold Medal of the Royal Astronomical Society (1981) among many others. He was knighted in 1961. His many books include The Origins and International Economics of Space Exploration (1973) and Emerging Cosmology (1981). His autobiography, Astronomer by Chance, was published in 1990. He is a keen musician and was President of the Guild of Church Musicians from 1976-89.

PATRICK MOORE ▼

Dr Patrick Caldwell-Moore was born in outer London in 1923, but has lived almost all his life in Sussex. Due to ill health, he was educated privately at home. At the start of the war he joined Bomber Command and flew as a navigator. After the war he set up an observatory at home, and has concentrated ever since on observations of the Moon and the planets. Patrick Moore's lunar charts have been used by lunar astronauts from the USA and the USSR. From 1964 to 1968 he was Director of the Armargh Planetarium and from 1982 to 1984 was President of the British Astronomical Association. A prolific author, Patrick Moore has presented BBC Television's monthly progamme The Sky at Night since 1957. He was awarded the OBE in 1967 and the CBE in 1988. His hobbies include cricket and music – his enthusiastic xylophone playing has featured in many TV programmes.

SIR FRED HOYLE ▼

Yorkshireman Sir Fred Hoyle intended to study chemistry after winning a place at Emmanuel College, Cambridge, when he was 18 years old. Instead, he switched to mathematics and came top of the whole university in his final examinations. During WWII he helped to develop radar for the Navy. His post-war achievements include helping to develop the Steady-State Theory of the Expanding Universe (with Hermann Bondi and Thomas Gold) and working on the formation of heavy elements in stars (which gained worldwide fame as the B^2FH paper of 1957). He went on to become a Senior Professor at Cambridge, a Fellow of the Royal Society and a foreign member of the US Academy of Sciences. He is also well-known as an author, having produced numerous science fiction novels including The Black Cloud, A for Andromeda (which became a celebrated TV serial), Rockets in Ursa Major (which became a play) and various children's stories. His collaborator on many of these is his son Geoffrey.

DR PAUL MURDIN ▲

After studying for a PhD in astronomy at the University of Rochester, New York, Croydon-born Dr Paul Murdin joined the Royal Greenwich Observatory in 1971 and co-discovered the first identified "black hole" in the star Cygnus X-1. He was on the scientific staff of the Anglo-Australian Telescope in New South Wales in 1974-78 and worked on supernovae. Back in the UK in 1979, he was chosen as the first head of Britain's observatory (which he set up) on La Palma in the Canary Islands. He was awarded an OBE in 1988 and appointed Acting Director of the Royal Observatory in Edinburgh in 1991. He is married with three grown-up children.

SIR FRANCIS GRAHAM-SMITH ▼

Astronomer Royal from 1982-90 and currently Secretary of the Royal Society, Sir Francis Graham-Smith is one of the most distinguished men in his field. He was Director of the Royal Greenwich Observatory from 1976-81 and Professor of Radioastronomy and Director of Nuffield Radio Astronomy Laboratories at Jodrell Bank from 1981-88. His books include Pulsars (with Sir Bernard Lovell) and Pathways to the Universe. He was awarded the Royal Medal of the Royal Society in 1987 and the Glazebrook Medal of the Physical Society in 1991. He is married with four children and nine grandchildren and lives in Macclesfield, Cheshire.

ARCHIE ROY ▲

Archie Roy joined the Department of Astronomy at Glasgow University, where he was Professor of Astronomy for many years. He is now Honorary Senior Research Fellow in the Department of Physics and Astronomy. He is also a Fellow of the Royal Astronomical Society, the Royal Society of Edinburgh and the British Interplanetary Society, as well as being the current President of the Society for Psychical Research. He conducts research in astrodynamics and astro-archaeology and has published numerous books.

SIR HERMANN BONDI ▼

Vienna-born Sir Hermann Bondi was Secretary of the Royal Astronomical Society from 1956-64 and Director General of the European Space Research Organisation from 1967-71. He is Emeritus Professor of Mathematics at King's College, University of London. His scientific research has been mainly in gravitation, astrophysics and cosmology. He is President of the British Humanist Association, Chairman of the International Federation of Institutes for Advanced Study and Chairman of the Advisory Council of the Royal Naval Engineering College. In 1988 he was awarded the Gold Medal of the Institute of Mathematics and its Applications. He is a Fellow of Churchill College, Cambridge.

LAWYERS

Unusually Vanni Treeves is a solicitor *and* an industrialist. Born in 1940 and a graduate of Oxford University, he took a Master of Law degree at the University of Illinois as Fullbright Scholar. Qualifying in 1965 he joined Macfarlanes' Corporate Department and was seconded to White and Case in New York for a year. He has been senior partner at Macfarlanes since 1987. As chairman of BBA Group and McKechnie, and director of Oceonics, he is exceptionally qualified to specialise in Business Law. A Trustee of the Getty Charitable Trust, his corporate clients include the Dun and Bradstreet Corporation, Saatchi and Saatchi and the Royal Academy. He is the Treasurer of the London Federation of Boys' Clubs and works for many other charities. Vanni Treeves, married with two sons and a daughter, includes "eating too much and walking off the effects of doing so" among his many recreations.

PETER CARTER-RUCK ▲

A libel lawyer with a high media profile, Peter Carter-Ruck is one of the legal profession's most revered figures. Admitted as a solicitor in 1937, he spent much of the war in the Royal Artillery. He joined Oswald Hickson Collier in 1945, leaving in 1981 to form Peter Carter-Ruck and Partners. The practice has represented Randolph Churchill, Robert Maxwell and many other well-known clients. A former president of the City of Westminster Law Society, Peter Carter-Ruck is Solicitor to the Supreme Court. A member of the Livery of the City of London Solicitor's Company, the Council of Justice and the British Section of the International Commission of Jurists, he was a specialist member of the Council of the Law Society. His book, Libel and Slander, now in its fourth edition, is one of the standard texts on the subject. A passionate yachtsman, he was Commodore of the Ocean Cruising Club, and enjoys the unusual distinction of being one of the few yachtsmen to have sailed to Iceland.

◀ RODGER PANNONE

Through Pannone Napier, Rodger Pannone has acted in most of the major disaster cases of recent years: Thalidomide, Opren, King's Cross, Piper Alpha, Lockerbie, Zeebrugge and many others. His practice often represents public figures, including John Stalker and Ernest Saunders. He has recently been instructed to defend Asil Nadir, and has acted for multi-nationals and trade unions on product liability and labour law issues. Together with other professionals, Rodger Pannone has formed an economic interest group to examine how lawyers can practise most effectively in the single European market. Vice-president and president elect of the Council of the Law Society, he is a former chairman of the Council's Contentious Business and Law and Procedures Committees. A past member of the Supreme Court Rule Committee, he was the solicitor member of the Lord Chancellor's Advisory Committee and a Governor of the College of Law. He is married.

ANTHONY SCRIVENER ▼

Anthony Scrivener, QC, called to the Bar in 1958, lectured in Ghana for several years before he began to practise in 1961. He has acted for striking miners and for Westminster Council against the GLC. His Common Law practice has dealt with a wide variety of Civil and Commercial and Public Law work, including appeals in the West Indies and Hong Kong. He has made more than 40 appearances for the prosecution in the House of Lords. A veteran of numerous fraud and corruption trials, appearing in more than 40 murder trials, Anthony Scrivener became a Queen's Counsel in 1974. He has represented the Governments of Jamaica and Trinidad, as well as Winston Silcott, Gerry Conlon of the "Guildford Four", the plaintiffs in the first civil murder case and the defendant in the first civil rape case. Born in 1935 and a graduate of University College, London, he is a Bencher of Lincoln's Inn and was made chairman of the Bar in 1991.

ANTHONY SALZ ▼

Anthony Salz is a solicitor at Freshfields, where he leads the Corporate Finance Group. He read law at Exeter University after teaching for nine months in Devon. Articled with Kenneth Brown Baker Baker, he was admitted as a solicitor in 1974 and joined Freshfields in 1975, working on the solvency problems of Burmah Oil and several banks. He moved to New York for a year in 1977, working for the Wall Street firm of Davis Polk and Wardell as a corporate lawyer, dealing with equity, debt financing and acquisitions. A Freshfields partner since 1980, and head of the Corporate Finance Group since 1990, his work has focused increasingly on corporate finance, particularly the mergers of SmithKline with Beecham, BSB with Sky and Reed with Elsevier, as well as British Petroleum's 1987 rights issue. Married with a son and two daughters, he was born in Devon in 1950.

CLIVE THORNE ▼

A Cooper's Law Studentship graduate of Trinity College, Cambridge, Clive Thorne was born in 1952. Articled in 1975, he qualified as a solicitor in 1977 and has practised law as a solicitor and barrister in Hong Kong and Australia. He is currently head of the Intellectual Property Litigation Group at Denton Hall Burgin and Warrens. An authority on intellectual property and copyright, author of Intellectual Property – the New Law (A Guide to the Copyright and Patents Act 1988), contributor to The Sony Guide to Home Taping, his articles on intellectual property law and litigation have appeared in the European Intellectual Property Review and other professional journals. Clive is a member of the International Bar Association, the United States Trade Mark Association, the Computer Law Group and is a former member of the Anti-Counterfeiting Group Law Reform Committee. A member of the United Oxford and Cambridge Club, he plays the flute and enjoys music, especially opera.

JOHN ROWSON ▶

Master of the City of London Solicitors' Company and President of the City of London Law Society, John Rowson is senior partner at Herbert Smith Solicitors. Married with two sons and a daughter, he was born in 1930. Educated at the College of Law, he was admitted as a solicitor in 1959. A partner at Herbert Smith since 1960, he was elected senior partner in 1988. A specialist in Company, Commercial and Tax Law, he has also been responsible for the practice's management, particularly its partnership, constitutional, financial and taxation affairs. For four years he was Chair of the City of London Solicitors' Company, which is the Local Law Society for the City of London and a City Livery Company. He has also been Chair of the Society's Taxation Committee and served on the Law Society's Standing Committee on Taxation. A recently elected Fellow of the Royal Society of Arts, he enjoys music and is a member of the Athenaeum and the Royal Thames Yacht Club.

SIMON OLSWANG

Established in 1981, Simon Olswang and Company is one of the UK's leading media and entertainment law practices. The company, co-founded with Mark Deveraux, represents corporate clients involved in film, TV, video and multi-media transactions worldwide. Simon Olswang's specialist practices extend to Corporate Finance, Litigation, Property and Taxation Law. A star performer in The Legal 500 – The Client's Guide to UK Law Firms, he is an innovative manager and believes in involving the company's partners and lawyers in the long-term development of the business. Something of a professional maverick, he practises in Great Cumberland Place, arguing that commercial law is not a City of London monopoly.

JOHN GRIEVES

John Grieves has been Freshfields' senior partner since 1990. Educated at King's School, Worcester, he is a graduate of Oxford University. In 1979 he was a postgraduate student at the Harvard Business School, where he took the Advanced Management Program Course. He was articled with Pinsent and Company in Birmingham and joined the Freshfields practice in 1963, becoming a partner a year later. He worked as managing partner of the Company department for a short time before succeeding as managing partner, which he remained for six years. Before being elected senior partner, he was head of Freshfields' Corporate Finance Group. Born in 1935, John Grieves is married and has a son and a daughter. He enjoys the arts, especially music. He was appointed to the Board of British Invisibles in 1992.

MICHAEL FLINT

A former vice-president of Paramount Pictures, Michael Flint specialises in film, television and related entertainment law issues, and is an authority on telecommunications law. He has written many articles, is the author of A User's Guide to Copyright and co-author of Intellectual Property: the New Law and Television by Satellite – Legal Aspects. A former chairman of the Intellectual Property and Entertainment Committee of the International Bar Association, he was a Founder Council Member of the Common Law Institute of Intellectual Property. A partner of Denton Hall Burgin and Warrens since 1960, he is now chairman. Michael Flint has also acted as a consultant on audio-visual matters to the European Commission. He was the first chief executive of Capital Radio and formed the Association of Independent Radio Contractors. He is a Fellow of the Society of Antiquaries and the vice-president of the British Archaeological Association. He is married with three children.

DOUG McAVOY

Doug McAvoy started his teaching career at secondary schools in Newcastle in the early 1960s. He taught PE, maths and science. Prior to taking up his appointment as deputy general secretary of the NUT he lectured in maths at Newcastle College of Art and Technology. He was a member of the NUT Executive from 1970 to 1974 and served on the Membership and Public Relations Committee, and as chairman of the Finance and General Purposes Committee. He was appointed deputy general secretary of the NUT in 1974, with special responsibility for developing the Union's conditions of service and health and safety policies. From 1984 he was responsible for all negotiations with the local authorities and government. He led the teachers' side in the campaign and negotiations which produced the 1987 agreement, which was set aside by the Secretary of State. In 1989 he was elected to the post of General Secretary, becoming the first elected General Secretary in the 120-year history of the NUT.

PROFESSOR STEWART ROSS SUTHERLAND

The present vice-chancellor of the University of London and HM Chief Inspector for Schools in England, Professor Stewart Ross Sutherland is currently titular professor of history and philosophy of religion at King's College London. He holds honorary degrees from the College of Wooster, Ohio (Hon LHD), the Commonwealth University of Virginia (Hon LHD), the University of Aberdeen (Hon LLD) and the National University of Ireland (Hon LLD). He is an honorary Fellow at Corpus Christi, Cambridge, and at University College, Bangor, a Fellow of the Royal Society of Arts, a Liveryman of the Goldsmith's Company and a Fellow of the British Academy. He has chaired the British Academy Postgraduate Studentships Committee in 1987, the Ethiopian Gemini Trust in 1987, Council Royal Institute of Philosophy (1988) and the London Conference on Overseas Students (1989). He is

Universities Council, the British Council Committee for International Cooperation in Higher Education, the Hong Kong Council for Academic Accreditation, and the North West Thames Health Authority. He has written several books on theology and numerous articles in books and journals. He is also president of the Society for the Study of Theology.

PROFESSOR BRIAN COX

Brian Cox became famous (or infamous) in 1969 when he published the Black Papers on education, an attack on the permissive methods of teaching fashionable at the time. He tells the full story of the debate in his autobiography The Great Betrayal (1992). He entered the limelight again in 1989 when he chaired the National Curriculum English Working Group. This proved very popular with teachers, but was attacked by the right wing of the Conservative Party. Brian has published two books of poetry, Every Common Sight and Two-Headed Monster, and has been an

editor of the literary journal The Critical Quarterly for over 30 years. He is currently John Edward Taylor Professor of English Literature at the University of Manchester.

PROFESOR E C WRAGG ▼

After graduating from Durham University with a First in German and a First Class Diploma in Education, Professor Wragg taught at Queen Elizabeth Grammar School, Wakefield and Wyggeston Boys' School, Leicester, before taking a lectureship at Exeter University and becoming, when appointed to Nottingham University at the age of 34, the youngest professor of Education in the country. He gained his MEd at Leicester University, his PhD at Exeter University and an honorary doctorate at the Open University. He is the author of over 20 books, several hundred articles and has a regular column in the Times Educational Supplement. He has acted as specialist adviser to a parliamentary select committee, to the Council of Europe, and been president of the British Educational Research Association, chaired the Educational Broadcasting Council for the UK, and been a member of several national committees, including the Speaker's Commission on Citizenship. In 1991 he was awarded the prestigious Jerwood award.

CHRIS WOODHEAD ▼

Chris Woodhead was educated at Wallington County Grammar School and Bristol University. He subsequently spent seven years teaching English in secondary schools before taking up a lecturing post at Oxford University. In 1982 he began working for LEA, serving as chief adviser in Shropshire, and deputy education officer in Devon and then Cornwall, before coming to the National Curriculum Council (NCC) as deputy chief executive in 1990. From August 1991 he served as acting chief executive before being appointed chief executive in October 1991. His directorships include the City Technology Colleges Trust, the Elmhirst Trust and the NCC Enterprises Ltd. He is a Fellow of the Royal Society of Arts and a member of the Royal Overseas League. He has written numerous books and articles on a range of educational issues and in December 1991 was invited by the Secretary of State, along with Robin Alexander and Jim Rose, to make recommendations about curriculum practice in primary schools.

PAUL CORDY ▲

Paul Cordy, who lives in Barry in Wales, where he was born, believes that his job as a bank official helped him to win the UK Monopoly Championship in 1991, which was played with real money in the Bank of England. His success came shortly after he scooped the Welsh National Championship at his first attempt. Victory eluded Paul, however, in the 1992 World Championship in Berlin.

JOHN ARMSTRONG ▼

It was at Cambridge, where he gained a first-class honours degree in mathematics, that John Armstrong became an enthusiastic bridge player. Four years later, in 1977, began the partnership with Graham Kirby which continues to this day. John and Graham have represented Britain in four World Bridge Championships, taking second place in the 1987 Bermuda Bowl, and in five European Championships, culminating in victory for Britain in 1991. They have also won 23 Camrose matches for England – a record for a partnerships – and four Gold Cups.

DEREK OLDBURY ▲

Widely acknowledged as Britain's draughts ambassador, Derek Oldbury scored his first victory in the Scottish Open in 1950, which he followed by taking three English titles, in 1953, 1955 and 1957. In 1955 he became the first, and so far the only, holder of the British Match Championship, and won World titles at the three opening conventions: 1974 (11-man ballot), 1976 (Go-as-you-please) and 1991 (3-move). Disabled from birth, wheelchair-bound Derek, who lives in Devon, has flown the Atlantic 30 times to compete in matches and top-class tournaments in the USA. The author of The Complete Encyclopedia of Draughts, he edits the games magazine Alpha-Beta.

TONY SOWTER ▲

Tony Sowter combinés his career as a consequential loss consultant with numerous positions in the bridge world. He is managing director of Probray Press, the publishers of International Popular Bridge, which he edits. From 1969 to 1971 he won the Sunday Telegraph Salver for the most masterpoints in England. He has represented England and Great Britain, most notably as European Open Teams Champions in 1991.

ANDREW ROBSON ▲

Andrew Robson, who won the World Junior Team Championship in 1989 and the European Team Champion's title in 1992, teaches bridge at all levels from beginner to international standard. A psychology graduate and trained secondary school maths teacher, he has written several books on bridge as well as contributing regularly to specialist magazines. He also actively promotes bridge to younger players, and is a member of the game's National Youth Committee. London-based Andrew and his partner Anthony Forrester, considered one of the strongest pairs in the world, have won many tournaments, including in 1991 the Slater Bank and The Sunday Times Tournaments.

RICK JANOWSKI ▼

Rick Janowski, 1992 British Open Champion and widely regarded as one of backgammon's leading theoreticians, first played when he was 17. But it was not until he was repeatedly beaten by a black box that he really decided to perfect his game, eventually thrashing his computerised adversary. Between 1986 and 1990 Rick, who was born in England of Polish parents, put backgammon on a back burner to pursue his professional training as a bridge design engineer. In 1990 he attended his first BIBA tournament, since when he has built up a reputation as one of the country's leading players, competing in BIBA tournaments in Britain as well as in competitions all over Europe.

DARREN RAY ▲

Darren Ray was born in Handcross, West Sussex, the home of the longest-playing marbles team, the Handcross Rebels, who have competed in the past 40 British Championships and have won the title three times. His father, Barry, is their captain and has taken the singles title four times. He also trained Hereford and Worcester's Hoarwithy Forty-niners, with whom Darren has played since 1984. Darren won the British singles championship in 1991 and 1992 and, in 1991, gave exhibition matches at a marbles exhibition in San Francisco.

ANTHONY FORRESTER ▲

European bridge champion of 1992 Anthony Forrester is a full-time player, lecturer and writer on the subject, and has appeared on several television series and programmes. Based in Suffolk, he writes regularly for bridge magazines, contributes to newspapers including The Daily Telegraph and The Guardian. Anthony, a mathematics graduate, member of the Chartered Institute of Public Finance and Accountancy and a Justice of the Peace, was the World Vice-Champion in 1987, and the winner of The Sunday Times Tournament in 1991.

ALAN HIRON ▼

Original a pure mathematician, Alan Hiron lectured before switching to computers in 1959. He later became a full-time journalist, writing about, teaching and playing contract bridge. Headmaster of the London School of Bridge from 1962 to 1991, he represented England and Britain several times, and was non-playing captain of British teams in 1968, 1969 and 1974. His bridge wins include all the major British events and the World Senior Pairs Championship in 1990. The editor of Bridge Magazine from 1985 to 1990 and bridge editor of the Independent and the Independent on Sunday since their inception, Alan has written several books on bridge and other subjects, such as Winning at Kensington. With his wife Maureen (pictured below with him), he has written, among other titles, Beginning Bridge, An Easy Guide to Bridge and several books on the quiz game Trivia.

GEOFF MYERS ▲

Currently computer-rated the world's top tiddlywinks player, Geoff Myers leapt to prominence in the 1987 National Singles, qualifying for the final after playing for less than a year. He represented Cambridge University, where he gained a first-class honours degree in economics, as well as Oxford, where he went on to take his master's degree before joining the Office of Fair Trading. Geoff, who lives in London and is the Chairman of the English Tiddlywinks Association, won the National Singles title in 1991 and 1992. With Andy Purvis, he is also the current holder of the National Pairs title, which the duo have taken for an unprecedented three years in succession (1990-92), and of the World Pairs title. In 1992 Geoff beat the reigning world champion, American Larry Kahn, in the contest for the title of World Singles Champion.

DR YEHUDI GORDON ⬆

Yehudi Gordon graduated in Johannesburg and was later awarded the Royal College of Obstetricians' Blair Bell research fellowship in London. His biochemical research into the well-being of the baby led to the development of a number of biochemical tests for wellbeing during pregnancy. A founder member of the Active Birth Unit Yehudi is a pioneer in the field of natural active birth in the UK. He has created a unique antenatal programme which includes yoga for preparation for birth and for recovery in the post-natal period, baby massage and swimming as well as a weekly discussions group attended by yoga teachers, midwives, obstetricians, parents and new babies.

MATTHEW MANNING

Probably the most extensively tested healer in the world Matthew Manning has successfully demonstrated his ability to influence cancer cells, enzymes and mould samples under laboratory conditions. He has lectured worldwide, made numerous TV appearances and has the rare distinction of being invited to address the Royal Society of Medicine in 1985. His first book, The Link, published in 1974, sold over a million copies and was translated into 16 languages. It was followed by In The Minds of Millions (1977) and The Strangers (1978). Matthew Manning's Guide to Self-Healing came out in 1989 and is now in its sixth edition.

CLIFFORD ANDREWS ⬇

Clifford has been studying, practising and teaching shiatsu for more than ten years. He served a full-time apprenticeship with Pauline Sasaki in 1986 and became the first non-American graduate of her teaching programme. Since then he has worked at developing the syllabus at the Shiatsu College in London, and has also established a shiatsu practice in Norwich, which has grown to include three full-time practitioners. During this time he has acquired a growing international reputation which has brought him invitations to teach in the US and all over Europe. He is a member of the Shiatsu Society's Assessment Panel.

WALTER CARRINGTON ⬆

Walter Carrington met F M Alexander, the originator of the technique that bears his name, in 1935 and worked with him from 1936 to 1939. He served as a pilot in the RAF from 1941 to 1946 – during which time he was shot down and taken prisoner in Hungary. He resumed his work with Alexander in 1946 as an assistant teacher, subsequently with special responsibility for the Teachers' Training Course. After Alexander's death in 1955 he worked with other assistants until the incorporation of the Constructive Teaching Centre in 1960 when, together with his wife, Dilys, also an Alexander teacher he continued the Teachers' Training Course and the private practice with which they are still involved today.

DAVID REPARD

Chairman of the Confederation of Healing Organisations David Repard discovered (with alarm) his own healing ability when he read an article on the subject and promptly cured his daughter of a back injury. The success of the CHO has been such that both the General Medical Council and the government have recently adjusted their policy to incorporate healing on the NHS. Prior to setting up the Confederation David worked for Kodak, responsible for administration and training and served in the Royal Navy for some 30 years.

IAN McDERMOTT ▼

An expert in neuro-linguistic programming Ian McDermott has a background in business, higher and further education, counselling and psycotherapy. He has been invited to set up a major senior management training programme for Gallaher; to show how NLP could improve communication and save lives in disasters and emergencies by the UN Disaster Relief Co-ordinator and the Institute of Civil Defence; to train executives at Saatchi and Saatchi; run a one-month NLP programme for doctors in Italy; and train counselling trainers and supervisors in the use of NLP. He is director of ITS and a certified trainer with the Society of Neuro-Linguistic Programming.

PATRICK HOLFORD ▼

Patrick Holford started his academic career in the field of psychology. While completing his bachelor's degree in Experimental Psychology at the University of York he researched the role of nutrition in mental illness. Since then he has carried out research into mental health, pre-menstrual syndrome, athletic performance, weight control, hair mineral analysis and the importance of trace elements such as zinc. In 1984 he founded the Institute for Optimum Nutrition, a charitable and independent trust for the furtherance of education and research in nutrition where he now teaches and practices.

HOWARD KENT ▲

Howard Kent started his career in journalism, editing local newspapers. He joined News Chronicle in 1955 and became chief picture editor. He then became involved in films (working on Lawrence Of Arabia), stage and TV, before running Intimate Theatre, Palmers Green as a West End tryout theatre. He became interested in yoga when he became a member of the Indian Freedom Campaign National Executive. He produced the TV series Yoga For Health in 1969 and started the organisation which became a charity Yoga For Health Foundation in 1976. The Foundation now operates in many parts of the world. He founded a centre for yoga at Ickwell Bury, Bedfordshire, in 1978. Kent is the author of four books on yoga (a fifth is due to appear in 1993) and one on the filming of Lawrence Of Arabia.

◄ TONY PINKUS

Tony Pinkus graduated from the London School of Pharmacy in 1980. He spent four years in pharmacy before joining Ainsworths Homoeopathic Pharmacy. He became managing director of Ainsworths in 1989, acquiring three Royal Warrants. He is involved with counselling, prescribing and manufacturing homoeopathic remedies, teaching pharmacists, doctors, vets, dentists and the public about homoeopathy. He is a member of the Council and Executive of the Homoeopathic Trust and is a member of the committee of International Homoeopathic Pharmacists.

PARANORMAL

BOB RICKARD AND ▼ PAUL SIEVEKING

The editors of Fortean Times, Bob Rickard, 48, and Paul Sieveking, 43, were both influenced in some way by life in the East. Bob was brought up in the Far East, and learned from a Dyak magician and reformed headhunter about the frontiers of the known and unknown. He discovered the writings of Charles Fort in the early 1960s, and set up the newsletter which was to become Fortean Times in 1973. Paul joined him at FT, after spending a year in India in 1978, and together they continued the work of Fort, collecting data embarrassing to orthodoxy and unusally swept under the scientific carpet. Circulation of the FT was predominantly by postal subscription until 1990, when a deal with John Brown Publishing Ltd made the magazine available through the news trade. Their ambition is to make Fortean Times a truly international journal of reliable news and investigation into the whole spectrum of weird phenomena, and to do so with humour, sensitivity and intelligence.

PAUL DEVEREUX ▲

Born in 1945, of Anglo-Irish descent, Paul Devereux left a teaching career in 1986 for full-time geomancy/Earth mysteries research and freelance lecturing and writing. The author of several books on the subject, he has edited The Ley Hunter journal since 1976. It is a specialist publication dealing with the multi-disciplinary area known as Earth Mysteries. This area involves wide-ranging investigation into the nature of ancient sites and landscapes. He has organised and hosted 14 annual conferences, which have attracted leading academic and mainstream speakers as well as new age workers of merit. Paul is also a painter and photographer of note, using ancient sites and their groundplan geometry as a source of inspiration. He is the founder/director of The Dragon Project Trust, studying the various cliams and ideas of unusual energies at prehistoric sites, which he started in 1977. A current Anglo-American Dragon project is the study of dream consciousness at sites selected for unusual geophysical properties in Cornwall. Paul is also a director of Environic Foundation International, based in Indiana, USA.
Photograph by Ashley Peters

HILARY EVANS ▲

Born in 1929 and educated at Cambridge and Birmingham universities, Hilary Evans' interest in anomaly research began during his student years and he has been actively involved since the late 1960s. His special area of interest is UFOs and alleged encounters with other worldly beings, although he considers himself rather sceptical. He does, however, believe that many claims of the paranormal are based on fact and that scientific anomaly research can dramatically extend our knowledge of ourselves and our universe. Amongst Hilary's many books on the subject are: UFOs – The Greatest Mystery (1979); The Evidence for UFOs (1983); Visions, Apparitions, Alien Visitors (1984) and Frontiers of Reality (1989).

ANDREW COLLINS

Thirty-four year old Andrew Collins became a journalist on the magazine Strange Phenomena in 1979. He teamed up with fellow writer and parapsychologist, Graham Phillips, and together they uncovered a green, talismanic jewel, known as Meonia, and a sword bearing a monogram designed by Mary Queen of Scots. The events leading to the discovery of these artefacts are chronicled in Andrew's 1991 Book of the Seventh Sword. Andrew coined the term psychic questing to describe this unique method for unearthing hidden artefacts and solving historical enigmas using information gained through psychic processes. Andrew is a full-time author and publisher of his own books. In 1989 he published The Black Alchemist, which became a cult hit selling 15,000 copies in hardback.

PROFESSOR ARTHUR ▼ ELLISON

Professor Ellison has spent most of his working life concerned with the research and design of electrical machines, in small and large industry. He was head of the Department of Electrical and Electronic Engineering at City University and was a member of the Institution of Electrical Engineers for three years. In parallel with this, he has been a researcher into aspects of the paranormal and is a long-term member of the Society for Psychical Research, where he was chairman for two three-year terms, and of the Parapsychological Association. Professor Ellison is the author of some 100 papers and articles on engineering and psychical research and of several books, including The Reality of the Paranormal (Harrup 1988). Now aged 73, Professor Ellison is still active as a consultant engineer, lecturer and author.

MAURICE GROSSE ▶

Maurice Grosse has made a scientific study of paranormal activity for over 50 years. Following the accidental death of his daughter, Janet, in 1976, which led to a number of inexplicable phenomena, he joined the Society for Psychical Research. He was chief investigator in the Enfield Poltergeist Case, which is recognised as the most thorough investigation into poltergeist activity this century. He is a member of the Royal Institution; the Institute of Patentees and Inventors; chairman of the Spontaneous Phenomena Group of the SPR and a fellow of the College for Psychic Studies. Born in 1919 of a Romanian father and a Lithuanian mother, Maurice Gross is one of the world's leading authorities on poltergeist activity.

BRIAN INGLIS ▼

Best known as a television presenter and journalist, Brian Inglis was born in 1916, and educated at Shrewsbury and Magdalen College, Oxford. After distinguished wartime service in the RAF, he took his PhD at Trinity College, Dublin, and worked as a lecturer for some years before returning to journalism, becoming editor of the Spectator in 1962. He has a long held interest in the paranormal and has been a trustee of the Koestler Foundation since 1983. A prolific author, his published works on the paranormal are: Natural and Supernatural: a History of the Paranormal from 1914 to 1939 (1984); The Hidden Power (1986); The Unknown Guest: the Mystery of Intuition (1987); Trance: a Natural History of Altered States of Mind (1989); The Power of Dreams (1987) and Coincidence: a Matter of Chance – or Synchronicity? (1990).

PALMISTS/GRAPHOLOGISTS/MEDIUMS

GORDON HIGGINSON

A child medium who was demonstrating his gifts at the age of 12, Gordon Higginson continued his work while serving in the forces. Now, at the age of 73, he is president of the Spiritualist National Union and has filled the Royal Albert Hall to capacity five times. He is also principal of the Arthur Findlay College, to which people from all over the world come to see demonstrations and learn from "the ambassador of the Spirit World". He is single and lives in Stoke-on-Trent.

JOHN CHRISTOPHER TRAVERS

John Christopher Travers has been a noted clairvoyant for more than 20 years. Starting out as a healer, he was resident psychic consultant at Zodiac, the astrological emporium in London, from 1974-80. He has appeared at the Festival of Mind, Body and Spirit in London and New York and at psychic fairs all over the UK. He lives in Hove, Sussex, and runs a successful Tarot consultancy, Oracles, which was a feature of Brighton life in the 1980s. He has been a regular writer on the Tarot for Prediction magazine for the last ten years. For his consultations he uses Tarot cards, crystal ball, palmistry and clairvoyance.

ROBIN STEVENS

A retired health service administrator, Robin Stevens is president of the International Spiritualist Federation and has been a practising medium for 35 years. He is president of the West London District Council of the Spiritualists' National Union and a regular contributor to Psychic News. He has demonstrated his skills as a medium in most European countries and the USA and is a leading authority on the aura and aura reading. Robin first gained prominence in the 1970s as the youngest medium invited to demonstrate at London's Royal Albert Hall in front of 6,000-plus people. He is a director of Psychic Press Ltd and a trustee of the Spiritual Truth Foundation. He lives in Ruislip, Middlesex, and is unmarried.

GLYN EDWARDS

Born a Catholic in Liverpool in 1949, Glyn Edwards' earliest ambition was to be a priest but he realises now that this desire was part of "the growing awareness towards spiritual things". He says he has experienced psychic happenings all his life but did not understand their significance until he had a private sitting with a medium when he was 19 years old. Soon he was travelling around the country demonstrating his abilities and this led to an association with the Arthur Findlay College where he has been a tutor for the past 17 years. Glyn has worked in the USA, Switzerland, Germany, Denmark, Australia and India. He is a local education officer of the Spiritualist National Union and runs his own psychic centre in Southport. He sees his main role in life as educating people to understand that they do not die – and what that implies.

PETER MARSHALL ▼

Peter Marshall started out as a graphic designer in the film industry before WWII, but gave it up after meeting a German psychologist who analysed his handwriting. His new obsession became his career and he has taught it ever since, performing analyses for numerous companies and authorities. He recalls a case in the 1970s when a newspaper asked him to analyse the handwriting of a Russian spy. He concluded that the man was well educated and had a razor-sharp mind – perfect spy material! Now aged 81, Peter can look back on a long career in which he has dealt with all aspects of personality assessment and character diagnosis. He is married and lives in Pulborough, Sussex.

STEPHEN O'BRIEN ▼

Still in his 30s, Stephen O'Brien has been described as the logical heir to the crown of the legendary Doris Stokes. He claims to have been a naturally psychic child, born "to a poor Welsh family during a thunderstorm". A quiet man who lives a reclusive life in a remote part of Wales, he nevertheless fills some of the country's leading theatres as he demonstrates his gifts to an ever-larger following. He is the author of three best-selling autobiographical books – Visions of Another World, Voices from Heaven and In Touch with Eternity – and has appeared on the major TV chat shows. He claims to have reunited more than 35,000 people "in the Beyond" with their families, encountering the occasional celebrity along the way – Marlene Dietrich, Marilyn Monroe and Judy Garland to name but three.

IVAN STAFFORD ▲

In the past few years numerologist Ivan Stafford says he has forecast a number of notable events – the 1987 stock-market crisis, the Gulf War, the break-up of the Soviet Union and the collapse of the housing market. He has studied numerology for almost 20 years and has demonstrated his abilities on many radio shows in the UK and Eire. Among the publications for which he has written are the Daily Star, Daily Mirror, Woman, Chat and Radio Times.

MALCOLM ESDALE ▼ WRIGHT

Psychic and palmist Malcolm Esdale Wright is a consultant member of the British Astrological-Psychic Society and co-author of two books, The Living Hand and Living Palmistry. He has been a reader at Mind, Body and Spirit festivals in Britain and the USA for many years and functions as a researcher on health problems. A much travelled lecturer, he has conducted workshops on palmistry and allied subjects.

◄ BARRY BRANSTON

Barry Branston has been involved in handwriting analysis since 1969. He is a founder member of the Graphology Society in London and is the author of Graphology Explained. Barry, who is a consultant to recruitment agencies, also claims to be able to spot any forgery and has helped to identify blackmailers and graffiti vandals.
Photograph by Graham Morton

NATURAL PHILOSOPHERS/SCIENTISTS

BRIAN GOODWIN ▼

Canadian-born Professor Brian Goodwin won a Rhodes Scholarship to Oxford where he read Mathematics. From 1960 he worked towards a PhD on the dynamics of embryonic development and his thesis was developed into a book, Temporal Organisation in Cells, published in 1963. After research fellowships in Canada, he returned to the UK to take up a lectureship at Edinburgh University (1964-65) and then a Readership in Development Biology at Sussex University where he remained until 1983. He was then appointed to Chair of Biology at the Open University. His research interests cover development and evolution, understanding how biological form is generated and making biology more of an exact science. He is married with four children and lives in Buckinghamshire.

JOHN BARROW ▲

John Barrow has been Professor of Astronomy at Sussex University since 1989. A First Class Honours graduate in Mathematics at Durham University, he began research at Oxford, completing his doctorate in 1977. A research fellowship took him to the University of California and he joined the Astronomy Centre at Sussex University on his return. His primary research interest is in cosmology and ranges from the study of elementary particle interactions in the early stages of the Big Bang to observational studies of galaxy clustering. He has published more than 150 papers on cosmology and astrophysics. In 1989 he was awarded the Samuel Locker Prize for his contributions to astronomy. He has written a series of books which include The World Within the World and The Left Hand of Creation. He has delivered the Centenary Gifford Lectures at Glasgow University and the Collingwood Lecture at Durham. In 1992-93 he will be a Leverhulme research fellow of the Royal Society. He is married with three children and lives in Brighton.

COLIN BLAKEMORE ▲

Born in Stratford-upon-Avon in 1944, Colin Blakemore studied medicine at Cambridge and completed his PhD at the University of California. He taught at Cambridge for 11 years before taking up the Chair of Physiology. He is also Director for the McDonnell-Pew Centre for Cognitive Neuroscience in Oxford and vice-president of the British Association for the Advancement of Science. His research has been in the many aspects of vision and he is known for his work on the influence of visual experience on the brain after birth and on the causes of common forms of childhood blindness. He has been awarded the Robert Bing Prize from the Swiss Academy of Medical Sciences, the John P McGovern Science and Society Medal and the French Académie Nationale de Médecine's Prix Netter. In 1989 he won the Michael Faraday Award for furtherance of the public understanding of science. He is a Fellow of the Royal Society and author of books including Mechanics of the Mind and the Mind Machine.

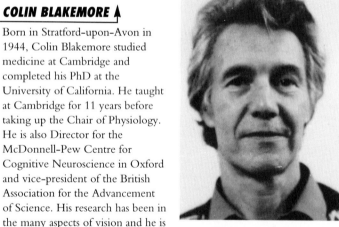

◄ RUPERT SHELDRAKE

Biochemist and teacher Rupert Sheldrake is a Fellow of Clare College, Cambridge, and past principal plant physiologist at the International Crops Research Institute for the Semi-Arid Tropics in India. He is the author of A New Science of Life, The Presence of the Past and The Rebirth of Nature. He has long argued that mankind should "re-establish our relationship with the planet as a sacred relationship. In this way we may be able to continue to be here". he is a regular contributor to publications in his field.

PAUL DAVIES ►

London-born Paul Davies is Professor of Mathematical Physics at the University of Adelaide. He held appointments at Cambridge and London and was Professor of Theoretical Physics at the University of Newcastle-upon-Tyne prior to emigrating in 1990. He has published around 100 research papers on cosmology, gravitation and quantum field theory, with special emphasis on black holes and the origin of the universe. He is the author of 20 books including God and the New Physics, The Cosmic Blueprint and The Mind of God. His books explain advanced scientific concepts in simple terms and explore the philosophical consequences of new research. Professor Davies is married with four children.

MICHAEL ROWAN- ▼ ROBINSON

Edingburgh-born Professor Michael Rowan-Robinson works mainly on cosmology and infra-red astronomy at the School of Mathematics and Sciences at the University of London. He was a member of the science team for the Infra-red Astronomical Satellite from 1976-84 and since then he has led the ground-based follow-up

DR PERCY SEYMOUR ▼

Dr Seymour studied at Manchester University, specialising in physics and astro-physics. He pioneered the use of mathematical techniques to investigate the magnetic field of the Milky Way. After a few years as a teacher, he became senior planetarium lecturer at the Old Royal Observatory, Greenwich. He is currently principal lectuer in astronomy at Plymouth University. His recent work is formulating scientific theories to explain aspects of the paranormal and astrology. His books include Adventures with Astronomy and Astrology: The Evidence of Science.

THOMAS GOLD ▲

Although he was briefly chief assistant to the Astronomer Royal, Professor Thomas Gold has spent most of his career in the USA. He was Professor of Astronomy at Harvard, then moved to Cornell University to found its Centre for Radiophysics and Space Research and to be chairman of the Astronomy Department. He was responsible for the construction of the Arecibo Radio Observatory in Puerto Rico. Born in Vienna in 1920, he studied Mechanical Science at Cambridge and worked on radar research during WWII. He later did research into the mechanism of the inner ear. In 1948 he was co-author of the Steady-State Theory of the Expanding Universe. Professor Gold was elected to the Royal Society Fellowship in 1964 and to the US National Academy of Sciences in 1968. He received the gold medal of the Royal Astronomical Society in 1985 and was appointed Honorary Fellow of Trinity College, Cambridge, in 1986. Now retired from Cornell, he is married with four daughters and lives in Ithaca, New York.
Photograph by Charles Harrington

of the IRAS survey using telescopes in La Palma, Hawaii, Australia and New Mexico. He is the author of Universe, Cosmic Landscape and Fire and Ice: The Nuclear Winter. He is a regular broadcaster and was vice-chair of Scientists Against Nuclear Arms from 1987-92. Married with three children, he lives in Muswell Hill, London.

JONATHAN ROSS ↟

Jonathan Ross's East End accent was just right for the second half of the 1980s, when working-class voices and street cred became all but compulsory. The loose format and informal atmosphere of Channel 4's The Last Resort brought him instant success, with personalities such as Jerry Hall, Steve Martin, Paul McCartney and Sean Connery among his guests in a four-season run. He went on to exploit his interest in obscure American film directors with The Incredibly Strange Film Show and its sequel, Son of the Incredibly Strange Film Show. Another success was One Hour With Jonathan Ross and he soon found himself invited to take over the Wogan hot seat when its eponymous star took a break. The familiar host of industry awards ceremonies, Jonathan, now aged 32, is rarely inactive. Recent projects include four documentaries on international film-makers, a documentary on the Elvis Presley phenomenon and an exclusive interview with Madonna. His fascination with the USA continued in his Channel 4 series Americana and he has hosted a live comedy series, Saturday Zoo. He is married to journalist Jane Goldman and they have a young daughter. *Photograph by Brian Aris*

PAUL DANIELS ↟

No-one has done more than Paul Daniels to popularise magic on British television. One of the most accomplished practitioners he performs with a natural wit that sets him apart from the traditional over-dramatic performers. Born in South Bank, Cleveland, where his parents managed the local Hippodrome theatre, Paul became fascinated by magic tricks at the age of 11. After leaving school he worked in local government but devoted his spare time to developing his technique. He turned professional after being offered a summer season in Newquay. Paul made his TV debut on Opportunity Knocks. More TV work followed and his catchphrase – "You'll like it . . . not a lot . . ." – really caught on with the viewers. His magic shows for the BBC became ratings-toppers throughout the 1980s and an Easter special won the coveted Golden Rose of Montreux in 1985.

DES O'CONNOR ↡

From Butlin's redcoat to international entertainer is quite a leap but Des O'Connor made it, mainly by being a perfect judge of what middle-of-the-road audiences want. His early successes in the 1960s included compering touring pop packages (including Buddy Holly's only visit to the UK) and TV's popular Sunday Night at the London Palladium, but the real breakthrough came in 1977 when he landed his own chat-and-variety show on BBC 2. His easy-going style with guests was an instant hit and he later took this format to Thames TV, in order to reach a bigger audience. Des O'Connor Tonight is now a mainstay of the ITV network. Des also landed the job of compering Take Your Pick, a revamped version of one of the early TV quiz-show successes, and the continuing popularity of both shows brought him the Presenter of the Year title in the 1992 British Comedy Awards, by no means his

first such accolade. One of the few British TV performers known to American audiences, he was honoured to be invited to appear in an all-star gala at the MGM Hotel in Las Vegas.

JIMMY GREAVES ▼

To most followers of the game, the opinions of a soccer "pundit" are worth hearing only if he has played with some degree of success himself. When he is one of the legendary figures of football, every word becomes gospel. Born in East Ham, London, Jimmy made his Football League debut for Chelsea in 1957, later playing for Tottenham Hotspur, AC Milan and West Ham. One of the most prolific goalscorers of his generation, he found the net 491 times in competitive games. Personal problems, including a much-publicised battle with alcohol, saw him drift into non-league football but his comeback via newspaper columns and TV appearances has been a revelation. By the mid-1980s he was one of the most familiar faces on the small screen. A good rapport with Ian St John in On The Ball led to the pair getting their own lunchtime Saturday slot.

◀ PHILLIP SCHOFIELD

No children's TV personality has had quite such a spectacular rise as Phillip Schofield. After leaving school he bombarded the BBC with letters asking them to take him on and, in 1979, he was offered a job as a radio outside-broadcasts booking clerk. When his family emigrated to New Zealand, he broke into TV there, presenting pop shows. Within four years he was back in Britain fronting Children's BBC. The sheer volume of fan mail persuaded the BBC that they were on to a winner with the clean-cut Schofield and he was "promoted" to Going Live! His other shows have included Take Two, The Movie Game, Schofield's Europe and Television's Greatest Hits. He has won the BBC/SOS Top Man on TV award three times and various TV Times awards since 1988. When pop idol Jason Donovan left the hit show Joseph And The Amazing Technicolour Dreamcoat at the London Palladium, Phillip was offered the leading role, although he had no track record as an actor or singer. The result, however, has been yet another remarkable success story.

IAN ST JOHN ▼

One of the legendary names of Liverpool FC in the 1960s, Ian St John has continued to have a high profile in the soccer world. In a made-in-heaven partnership with Jimmy Greaves he co-hosted the series Saint and Greavsie, which proved to be essential viewing for enthusiasts until last year's financial wranglings saw ITV lose its hold on Football League matches. Ian can still be seen on big-match occasions. Born in Motherwell, he signed for his home-town team in 1956. The move to Liverpool came five years later and he was a member of the Championship teams of 1964 and 1966.

MICHAEL PARKINSON ▲

In the 1970s Michael Parkinson set the standard by which TV chat shows have been judged ever since, attracting the biggest names to his late-night BBC slot. The turning point in his career was his involvement in the embryo TV-am and the failure of the so-called Gang of Five (Parkinson, Anna Ford, Angela Rippon, David Frost and Robert Kee) to live up to their hype. Since then, Michael has adapted his skills to radio, commanding a decent audience for his morning show on London's LBC. Born in Cudworth, Yorkshire, in 1935, he was educated at Barnsley Grammar School and broke into journalism via local newspapers. He joined what was then the Manchester Guardian, then moved to the Daily Express in London. His early experience in TV reporting was with Granada and he was later a presenter of their pioneering Cinema programme. He wrote a lively sports column in the Sunday Times and this material later surfaced in several books. More recently he has written for the Daily Telegraph. Other published work includes a biography of his friend George Best and a children's story, The Woofits. In 1979 he co-founded Pavilion Books (with Tim Rice and Colin Webb). Michael is married to Mary, a successful broadcaster in her own right, and they live in Bray, Berkshire. They have three sons.

PROPERTY

STUART LIPTON ▼

Born in 1942 Stuart Lipton has been responsible for many of the major developments which have taken place in and around London in the last 15 years. As joint chief executive of the Greycoat Group between 1976 and 1983, he was responsible for the redevelopment of Victoria Station and several other central London building works, including 250 Euston Road, a 300,000 square feet mixed office and residential development. Since 1983 Stuart has been chief executive of Stanhope Properties plc and the scale of the developments has increased considerably, notably: Stockley

Park, a 400 acre site near Heathrow Airport, formerly a rubbish tip and now redeveloped into 125 acres of business park and a 275 acre golf course; Broadgate, a 14 phase five million square feet City of London development and a 125 acre mixed use project at Kings Cross. Stuart Lipton holds several prestigious positions associated both with property and the arts: he is a Trustee of the Whitechapel Art Gallery; a Trustee of the Architecture Foundation; a member of the governing body of Imperial College; a member of the National Theatre board and a commissioner of the Royal Fine Art Commission, amongst very many others.
Photograph by Sidney Harris

KIT MARTIN

Kit Martin was born in 1947, the son of two distinguished architects and grandson of another. Educated at Eton and Cambridge, he received his Architectural Diploma in 1972 and his MA in 1973. He formed the architectural practice Martin & Weighton in 1969 and was involved until 1976 in numerous projects to restore and save historic buildings in the UK, France and Italy. From 1974, as chairman of Lucca Wines Ltd, he has initiated and organised the rescue, restoration and conversion of a number of listed buildings of outstanding architectural and historic interest, including: Dingley Hall, Northants (1976-79); The Hazells, Bedfordshire (1981-83); Gunton Park, Norfolk (1980-84); Cullen House, Banffshire (1982-85); Tyninghame House, East Lothian (1988-92) and Burley, Rutland (1992-). Kit has won a number of local, national and European awards.

312

JOHN RITBLAT ▼

As well as his positions as chairman of The British Land Company plc and founder and senior partner of Conrad Ritblat & Company, consultant surveyors and valuers, John Ritblat's career has consisted of chairmanships of a variety of banking, financial, industrial and retail companies, including W. Crowther & Sons plc and Dorothy Perkins plc. He founded Conrad Ritblat in 1959 and has been chairman and managing director of British Land since 1971. British Land was sponsor of the notable Wright of Derby Exhibition at the Tate Gallery in 1990.

ANDREW LANGTON ▲

Born in Norfolk in 1943, Andrew Langton spent two years in the Middle East after leaving school. He started his working life in the UK as a stockbroker before going into property with Harrods Auction Office. He created Aylesford & Co, the estate agents, surveyors and valuers in Chelsea in 1963 and, over the next five years, acquired Frank Bateman & Co of Wimbledon and Putney and John Hollingsworth & Co of Fulham. In 1970 Andrew opened an Aylesford office in Marbella and now has an associate office in Hong Kong. Andrew Langton lives in London with his wife Carole and their three children.

ERNEST HALL

Composer, pianist, philanthropist, textile manufacturer, property developer and patron of the arts, Ernest Hall was born in 1930. He was educated at the Royal Manchester College of Music, where he was awarded the Royal Patron's Fund Prize for composition. He has continued his career as a pianist and composer, but has also diversified. In 1983 he took over Dean Clough, the derelict site of Crossley Carpets in Halifax, comprising 16 major buildings and over a million square feet. In less than a decade Dean Clough had become home not only to 200 companies and 3,000 workers but also to two major art galleries, two theatre companies and more than 20 artists in residence with a permanent art collection of over 600 works. Ernest Hall is a member of the Arts Council of Great Britain and chairman of Yorkshire and Humberside Arts. He has an honorary doctorate in Law from the University of York, and in 1986 was awarded an OBE.

ANDREW WADSWORTH ▲

In 1979, at the age of 22, Andrew Wadsworth bought New Concordia Wharf, which was to be the first major Victorian riverside warehouse conversion in Docklands and the only building in the UK ever to win three major conservation awards. Working from his unique office on board an Edwardian customs pontoon by Tower Bridge, his other innovative projects have included China Wharf, Little London and Jubilee Yard. Andrew's other activities include Jacob Street Studios Ltd, the major London film studio, the Waterhouse Group plc and a directorship of The urban Village Company, set up at the request of the Prince of Wales. Andrew organised the first Docklands Ball and The Globe Royal Gala, raising over £200,000 for local charities. Brought up in Cheshire, the son of a psychiatrist father and a psychoanalyst mother, Andrew is a non-drinking, non-smoking vegetarian. He lives in London with his wife, painter Julie Balmforth, and their three young children.

JOHN MAJOR ▼

Grammar school educated John Major cut his political teeth in Lambeth and Brixton – hardly the Conservative heartlands. He was elected a councillor of the London Borough of Lambeth in 1968 and served on the Housing and Finance Committees. In 1969 he became Chairman of the Accounts and the Housing Committees, presiding over the establishment of a pioneer Housing Advice Centre. He had been successively treasurer, vice-chairman, political officer and chairman of the Brixton Young Conservatives between 1960, when he was 17 years old, and 1964, and, in 1965, founded the Lambeth Borough Young Conservatives and was their first chairman. He was chairman of the Brixton Conservative Association from 1970 until its dissolution, following the report of the Boundary Commission in 1971. He was a senior executive in a large British overseas bank and is an Associate of the Institute of Bankers. Having contested St Pancras North in the two elections of 1974, John Major was adopted as candidate for Huntingdon in 1976 and elected to Parliament as MP for Huntingdon in 1979. In March 1981 he was elected PPS to the Ministers of State at the Home Office. In 1983 he was appointed an assistant Government Chief Whip and, in 1984, was made Lord Commissioner to the Treasury. He became Parliamentary Under-Secretary of State, Department of Health and Social Secuirty in 1986. His meteoric rise after the 1987 General Election took him from Chief Secretary to the Treasury to Foreign Secretary in July 1989, Chancellor of the Exchequer in October 1989 and Prime Minister in November 1990. He led the Party to victory in the 1992 General Election.

PADDY ASHDOWN ▲

Born in India in 1941, Paddy Ashdown came to the UK in 1946, was brought up in Northern Ireland and educated at Bedford School. He served as a Royal Marine officer between 1959 and 1972 and saw active service as a commando in Borneo and the Persian Gulf. He commanded a Special Boat Section in the Far East. He undertook a full-time course in Chinese and, in 1970, became the youngest Royal Marine officer since the war to command a Commando company. In 1972 he left the Royal Marines and joined the Foreign Office, where he worked for the British Mission to the United Nations in Geneva until 1976. After spells in local industry, local government and a taste of unemployment, he was elected Liberal MP for Yeovil, in 1983, at the second attempt. He was elected leader of the Liberal Democrats in 1988 and a Privy Councillor in 1989.

NORMAN LAMONT ▲

Educated at Fitzwilliam House, Cambridge, Norman Lamont, 50, was president of the Union in 1964 and toured the United States with the Union debating team in 1965-66. He was a research assistant to Duncan Sandys at this time and joined the Conservative Research Department in 1966. He worked for N M Rothschild & Sons Ltd until his election as MP for Kingston-upon-Thames in 1972. He was chairman of the Bow Group in 1972. He was appointed Parliamentary Under-Secretary of State at the Department of Energy in 1979; Minister of State at the Department of Industry in 1981; Minister of State for Defence Procurement at the Ministry of Defence in 1985 and Financial Secretary to the Treasury in 1986. A Privy Councillor, Norman Lamont was appointed Chancellor of the Exchequer on November 28th, 1990.

MICHAEL HESELTINE ▼

Michael Heseltine was born in 1933 and read Politics, Philosophy and Economics at Oxford University, where he was president of the Union in 1954. In 1959 he did his National Service and was commissioned into the Welsh Guards. Before joining the government, Michael Heseltine was chairman of the Haymarket Publishing Group. Having fought Gower in 1959 and Coventry North in 1964, in 1966 he was elected as Conservative MP for Tavistock. He has represented Henley since 1974. He was appointed Parliamentary Under-Secretary of State at the Department of the Environment in 1970 and Minister for Aerospace in 1972. In Opposition in the 1970s, he held the brief for Industry and then the Environment. From 1979 until 1983 he was Secretary of State for the Environment. He held the post of Secretary of State at the Ministry of Defence from 1983 until his celebrated resignation in 1986. From 1990 to 1992, under John Major, he was Secretary of State at the Department of the Environment and, since the 1992 election, has been President of the Board of Trade and Secretary of State for Trade and Industry. He is a Privy Councillor.

◄ CHARLES KENNEDY

Born in Fort William in 1959, Charles Kennedy was educated at Glasgow University, where he was president of the Union and winner of the Observer Mace for debating. He won a Fullbright Scholarship to Bloomington University, Indiana, where he taught British politics and speech communication. He was selected as SDP candidate for Ross, Cromarty and Skye while still in Indiana and, in 1983, at the age of 23, became the youngest member of the House of Commons. He proposed the successful motion at the 1987 SDP conference which led to the Party's merger with the Liberal Party and, in July 1990, won the first of his two year terms as President of the Liberal Democrats. He has held most of his party's front bench posts and is currently Liberal Democrat spokesman on Europe.

ROBIN COOK ▼

Born in 1946, Robin Cook attended Edinburgh University, where he gained an MA (Hons) in English Literature. He joined the Labour Party in 1965 and was an Edinburgh Town Councillor from 1971 to 1974, where he chaired the Housing Committee. He chaired the Housing Sub-Committee of the Scottish Labour Group from 1974 until 1980. He entered Parliament as MP for Edinburgh Central in 1974 and became MP for Livingston in 1983. He has been Opposition front bench spokesperson on: Treasury affairs (1980-83); European and Community affairs (1983-84); the City (1986-87); Health and Social Security (1987-89) and Health (1989-92). Since the 1992 General Election, Robin Cook has been Opposition front bench spokesperson for Trade and Industry.

JOHN SMITH ▲

John Smith, QC, has been MP for Monklands East since 1983. He was born in 1938 and educated at the University of Glasgow, where he gained an MA (Hons) in History and an LLB. He joined the Labour Party in 1955. Admitted to the Faculty of Advocates in 1967, he entered Parliament as MP for North Lanarkshire in 1970. He was Under Secretary for the Department of Energy from 1974 to 1975, Minister of State for the Department of Energy from 1975 to 1976, Minister of State, Privy Council Office, with special responsibility for devolution from 1976 to 1978 and Secretary of State for Trade from 1978 until the 1979 General Election. In Opposition, he has been spokesperson on Trade (1979-82); Energy (1982-83); Employment (1983-84) and Trade and Industry (1984-87). He was Shadow Chancellor of the Exchequer until the 1992 General Election, after which he succeeded to the Leadership of Her Majesty's Loyal Opposition. He is a member of, and sponsored by, the GMB. He became a Privy Councillor in 1978.

DOUGLAS HURD ▼

Born in 1930, Douglas Hurd took a first class honours degree in history at Trinity College, Cambridge. He was chairman of the Cambridge University Conservative Association in1951 and president of the Union in 1952. He passed top of his year into the Diplomatic Service for that year and remained in the service until 1966. After a period in the Conservative Research Department, he was appointed head of Edward Heath's private office in 1968. He became the Prime Minister's private secretary after the general election victory for the Conservative Party in 1970 and remained in that post until his election as MP for Mid-Oxfordshire in 1974. He was appointed CBE in the same year. He contested the new seat of Witney following the redistribution in 1983. In 1976 he was appointed Opposition front bench spokesman on Europe. Following the General Election of 1979, Douglas Hurd was appointed Minister of State at the Foreign and Commonwealth Office. He was made a Privy Councillor in 1982 and, in 1983, was appointed Minister of State at the Home Office, with particular responsibility for police and broadcasting. He was appointed Secretary of State for Northern Ireland in 1984, Home Secretary in 1985 and Foreign Secretary in 1989.

DAVID BLUNKETT ▲

Opposition front bench spokesperson on Health, David Blunkett has been MP for Sheffield Brightside since 1987. He was born in 1947 in Sheffield and gained a degree in Political Theory and Institutions at Sheffield University. He joined the Labour Party in 1963, at the age of 26, was a Sheffield City Councillor from 1970 until 1988 and Leader of the Council from 1980 until 1987. He was a South Yorkshire Metropolitan County Councillor from 1973 until 1977. He has been a member of the Labour Party National Executive Committee since 1983 and is a member of, and sponsored by, NUPE. Until the 1992 General Election, David Blunkett had been Opposition front bench spokesperson on Local Government since 1988.

GORDON BROWN ▶

MP for Dunfirmline East since 1983, Gordon Brown has been Shadow Chancellor of the Exchequer since the 1992 General Election. Born in 1951 he was educated at Edinburgh University, where he gained an MA and a PhD. He joined the Labour Party in 1970 and was a member of the Scottish Executive Committee from 1977 until 1984. He contested Edinburgh South for Labour in 1979. He was chair of the Scottish Labour Party from 1983 to 1984 and Shadow Chief Secretary to the Treasury from 1987 to 1989, before becoming Shadow Secretary of State for Trade and Industry, the post he held until the last election. Gordon Brown is a member of, and sponsored by, the TGWU. He is the author of Maxton and Where There is Greed and co-author, with Robin Cook, of The Real Divide.

TIM SILVERTHORNE

In 1963, at the age of 16, Tim Silverthorne joined the family fish business in Worthing. He left for a brief spell as management trainee at the Ford Motor Company, but rejoined on his uncle's retirement and has been involved with all aspects of fishing industry ever since. For the past two years, he has been president of the National Federation of Fishmongers and he serves on various committees of the Sea fish Industry Authority and on the Independent Food Retailers Federation. He is, he says, a dedicated shopkeeper.

STEVE HATT

Born in 1952, Steve Hatt is the fourth generation running Steve Hatt Fishmongers, in Islington. His father, also Steve Hatt, still takes an active interest in the business, which was started by his father-in-aw. Steve junior has grown up with fish and provides the same excellent service as his predecessors, with smoking of fish still taking place on site and absolute integrity exercised when it comes to freshness. He is delighted to have the advantage over his forebears of modern communications, essential for ensuring supply with an ever-decreasing quantity of prime quality fish.

GEORGE BENNELL

George Bennell's love affair with France began in 1975, when he was seven years old and his family moved to Paris. He was educated in England, but returned to Paris to study as a chef. Returning to England again, he worked under Phillip Britten at the Capital Hotel. While on a visit to Provence in 1990, he was struck by the richness of the olive harvest and determined that tinned olives in England should become a thing of the past. Within months, the Fresh Olive Company of Provence was born and soon many of London's top restaurants would take nothing but George's olives and olive oil, while delicatessens all over the country clamoured for them.

MICHAEL HORRELL ⬆

Michael Horrell, 57, received an agricultural education at Cambridge and Reading universities and then flew jets in the RAF, before joining the family farm in Cornwall in the early 1960s. By the early 1980s, the farm had 500 head of milking cows. After an overseas tour as a Nuffield farming scholar, Michael and his wife, Margaret, went into the production of nettle-coated Cornish Yarg and its sister cheeses. They are amongst the leaders of the new breed of farmhouse cheese producers and frequently visited by those who wish to see the cheese in production. Outside the farm, Michael has become a director of food and agricultural co-operatives and frequently involved in speaking engagements, both live and through the media.

JOHN SULLIVAN

Vin Sullivan Foods Ltd was started by John's father in 1960. Vin Sullivan died in 1964, when John was 18 years old, and he and his mother had to take over what was then, predominantly, the fish business. Thrown in at the deepest end, John learned the business and gradually expanded it by dealing increasingly with trade customers and diversifying into exotic fruits and vegetables, game, poultry and delicatessen fare. The firm now employs nearly 60 staff at its catering depots at Abergavenny and Exeter and has a range of over 4,500 food lines, supplying top class hotels and restaurants as far afield as Scotland and East Anglia. The shop in Abergavenny is still the centre of the company and carries some 70 different species of fish and shellfish and specialities from truffles to tuna and mallard to mullet.

COLIN BOSWELL

Colin Boswell joined his father on the farm at Newchurch, on the Isle of Wight, in 1976, when he was 24 years old, after a few years in market research and advertising. Martin, Colin's father, had pioneered the growing of sweetcorn since the early 1960s and they searched for a compatible crop to grow alongside it, experimenting with garlic. They found that garlic grew very well on the island and Colin now offers garlic and sweetcorn 12 months of the year. He is the main supplier of his two crops to Tesco, Sainsbury, Marks and Spencer and Safeway and the major UK supplier of fresh peeled and pureed garlic to food manufacturers throughout the country. The latest innvoations are oak-smoked garlic and Mr Boswell's Oak-Smoked Garlic Butter. Every year, Colin celebrates the garlic harvest with the Garlic Festival, which attracted 30,000 people in 1992.

ARTHUR CUNYNGHAME

Managing director of Paxton and Whitfield Ltd, cheesemongers since 1797, Arthur Cunynghame was born in 1951. In 1969, with his brother, he started City Vintagers, the wine merchants. By the time they sold the company to Trusthouse Forte, in 1985, the turnover had risen from £150,000 to £15 million per annum. He acquired Langmans, a business specialising in British farmhouse cheese, in 1988, and opened three shops in Stratford-on-Avon, Solihull and Bath, building a reputation and generating excellent business. He acquired Paxton and Whitfield, in Jermyn Street, London, in 1992.

ALAN PORTER ↑

Alan Porter's first venture into catering involved cooking for a grouse shoot on the Yorkshire Moors, which provided a lot of fun but no money. He opened his first business in 1972, at 22, the Real Food Shop in Knaresborough. Between 1974 and 1980, he opened various real food shops in Yorkshire; he developed a passion for traditional quality food, and started exporting British cheese to France. He opened as a wholesale supplier in 1984, sending goods all over the UK. He currently has four thriving businesses: The Original Porter Provisions Company; The Porter Chocolate Company – manufacturing, sourcing, importing, marketing and developing the finest products for the patissier, chocolatier and confectioner; The Chocolate Society – improving people's awareness of quality chocolate and Bankside Imports Ltd – with Justin de Blanc – developing the sale of traditional quality food products on behalf of selected manufacturers.

TONY CHECKETTS

Tony Checketts joined the butchery business started by his grandfather in 1902, in 1964 at the age of 16. He set about learning every aspect of the business and became a director in 1972 and managing director in 1985. The business is based on providing the finest quality meat and meat products, which involves selecting the livestock and slaughtering it in their own abattoir, thereby ensuring hygiene, handling and maturation. In 1987, the company was admitted to the "Q" Guild of butchers, a body dedicated to an exceptionally high standard of butchery.

NIGEL JERREY ↑

Born in Suffolk in 1948, Nigel Jerrey has lived in the county all his life. He worked as an office clerk in a fruit and vegetable wholesalers on leaving school at 16 and, 12 years later, joined his father in the family business, Emmett's Stores. He learned the business of pickling and smoking hams from his father and took over the business in 1981. He has expanded the business by introducing two further hams, a cider pickled and a mild cured, both oak-smoked like the original Suffolk sweet pickle. The company has carried a Royal Warrant, since 1970, for supplying sweet pickled hams to HM Queen Elizabeth the Queen Mother. Nigel has introduced a postal service for all his home smoked and cured produce, which was given a boost by his 1990 appearance on Delia Smith's Christmas programme on BBC TV.

HAMISH ROBERTSON

Struan Apiaries, started 15 years ago by Hamish Robertson, has evolved from a hobby into a thriving business. Hamish, with his wife Joan and his two sons, now collects between 10 and 30 tons of honey each year from hundreds of hives distributed throughout the Highlands of Scotland. The bees forage on a wide range of flowers and blossoms, notably heather, offering the consumer an unrivalled selection. Hamish supplies attractively packaged honey, honey flavoured with malt whisky and marmalade with honey to exclusive shops and hotels worldwide. He has won a gold award for packaging design and the Small Business section of the Scottish Marketing Awards competition.

RICHARD WOODALL ↓

Richard Woodall is the senior partner and representative of the seventh generation of the firm of Cumbrian butchers which bears his name. Royal Warrant holders as suppliers of traditional Cumberland sausages to HM The Queen, the firm also specialises in traditional dry-curing of Cumberland hams and bacons. A particular speciality is the Cumbria Air Dried Ham, which is matured for 12 months after curing and, served with melon or avocado, is similar in taste and texture to Italian Parma Ham.

FOODBILL O'HAGAN ▼

When Bill O'Hagan first came to England from South Africa, as a journalist, 22 years ago, he was appalled by the standard of the British sausage. At the age of 11, he had learned the sausage-making art at a local Yorkshire butchers in South Africa and set up a make-room in a shed in his English garden. His Fleet Street friends were fascinated by his hobby and soon it took over as his profession, although he still finds time to work one day a week for The Sunday Telegraph. In 1988, he opened the first, specialist sausage shop in Britain, in Greenwich. Bill is a purist and will allow no artificial additives or preservatives – not even artifical parsley in the shop window to enhance the multi-coloured display of his 34 sausage varieties. He has a library of over 2,000 sausage recipes and enjoys experimenting with new sausages, often sent in by sausage fans around the world. His ambition is to set up a working Museum of Sausage Making, exhibiting all he antique equipment he has picked up over the years.

MAYNARD DAVIES ▲

Master curer Maynard Davies was born in 1934 and served an eight year apprenticeship to a curing firm before becoming a manufacturing butcher and setting up on his own. He travelled extensively in Europe and North America, working and observing cultural practices, before farming and curing for 14 years in Derbyshire. Maynard's Farm Bacon, the product of forty years experience, is now situated in Weston-under-Redcastle, in Shropshire.

LORD JOHN MANNERS ▼

Educated at Eton and Oxford, Lord John Manners served five years in the army during the last war. In 1946, he started the Haddon Concrete Company, making lightweight blocks. In 1947, he launched the Belvoir Grass Drying Company, making dried grass cubes. Ten years later he could be found producing Beltsville white turkeys at Belvoir Farms and doing general farming. Many years later, in 1982, as a diversification from arable farming, Lord John started the Belvoir Fruit Farms, a pick-your-own and general soft fruit enterprise selling to multiple stores and other shops. In 1984, he started to produce elderflower cordial and, since then, has added raspberry, strawberry, blackcurrant, lemon, bitter lemon, passion fruit and ginger cordials. They are the only pure fruit cordials in the country and each bottle contains 2lb of fresh fruit.

CHRIS REES

Born in 1958, Chris Rees left school at 16 to join the Welsh produce merchant business, which his parents had started in 1962. The family had been involved in bacon and ham curing for many years and had developed a speciality, the Carmarthen Ham. In 1989, the business was split, locationally, between Chris and his brother, with Chris in Carmarthen and Pembroke Dock. Since then, he has diversified to include home-brew supplies and an off-license, specialising in Welsh produce. He is currently involved in a total refit of his Carmarthen shop.

These nominations courtesy of Henrietta Green. 'The Food Lovers Guide To Britain' published Autumn 1993 by BBC Publications.

RICHARD GUY

Managing director and co-founder of the Real Meat Company Ltd, Richard Guy was born in 1954. After leaving school, he abandoned his medical studies after one year and read Chemistry at Manchester University, where he gained a BSc in 1876. He bought, reared and consumed his first pig, Boarman, in 1976 and took the tenancy of a farm in Wiltshire three years later. He met his wife, Gilly, a grain commodity trader who also kept pigs in 1984. In 1985 they were married and Gilly moved her pigs to Richard's farm – and the Real Meat Company was born.
Photograph by David Wiltshire

PAUL KELLY ▼

Thirty year old Paul Kelly runs Derek Kelly Turkeys, the company started by his father in Essex. He is dedicated to the breeding and production of high quality strains of turkey, with concern for flavour and texture paramount and economics a secondary consideration. In the early 1980s, the company added to its white turkey flock by buying up the small flocks of bronze and black feathered birds which were still available, refining them and expanding their numbers. Kelly's turkey feed contains no growth promoters, hormones or animal protein and welfare of the animals has always been important to their farming. Although more expensive to produce, all Paul's customers think his product is worth a little extra.

WILLIAM BUCHANAN ▼

With his younger brother, Geoffrey, 24 year old William Buchanan runs Green Label Poultry at Woodbridge in Suffolk, producing some 7,000 ducks a week for the table. With a family tradition in the poultry business, William studied agriculture at Reading University and decided to go into the duck business because the market was easier to control than that of the chicken. They principally produce the Gressingham Duck, a large, gamey bird developed by Peter Dodd, and, amongst their direct restaurant customers, number Le Gavroche, Kensington Place and Leith's. Their turnover is now around £1 million per annum.

ROBERT SPINK ▲

Born and educated in Arbroath, Robert Spink joined the family fish business when he left school, working in every capacity from fish filleter to long distance lorry driver. He was called up for national service in 1958 and served with RAF Signals Intelligence in the Far East. He returned to the business and became a partner in 1965, when he was 26 years old. He assumed control of the company when his father retired in the early 1970s. In 1989, when the limited company was formed, Robert became managing director of R R Spink & Sons Ltd. His son Iain, the transport and stock control director, is the representative of the fifth generation of the family to be in the business. A keen fisherman, Robert is chairman of the Arbroath Fish Processors Association and a founder director of the Federation of Scottish Fish Merchants Assocations.

MARK JONES ⬆

The firm of Wm Jones & Sons was
established in 1874 as a market stall,
and moved to its present premises
in Newtown, Powys, in the 1950s.
Mark Jones, 35, runs the business
with his mother. He sells local
lamb, beef and pork, all sufficiently
matured and a large selection of
lamb and cooked meat products.
The sausage counter boasts
15 varieties and Mark produces six
types of burger, including lamb and
garlic burgers, with either mint or
rosemary. Salt beef, baked cider
ham and honey roast ham are also
all prepared on the premises, as are
Mrs Jones's famous home-made
lamb pasties.

DAVID LOUDEN ⬆

Graduating MA from St Andrew's
University, David Louden worked
in the Royal Bank of Scotland and
the First National Bank of
Chicago, retiring as a vice-
president in 1987. He bought
Smoked Salmon of Perth from its
founder, Major Jamie O'Connor,
in 1988, and renamed it Dunkeld
Smoked Salmon. The company
specialises in smoking anglers own
salmon and selling other wild fish.

PRINCE OF WALES ▲

Prince Charles, heir to the throne, experienced a year he would never forget in 1992. His separation from the Princess of Wales, long speculated on by the press, was finally announced and allegations of an intimate phone call to Camilla Parker-Bowles only served to compound the scandal. Born at Buckingham Palace on 14 November 1948, he was made Prince of Wales ten years later.

◄ PRINCE MICHAEL OF KENT

Born in Buckinghamshire on 4 July 1942, Prince Michael of Kent trained for the army at Sandhurst and, after six years' service, joined the Ministry of Defence later working in the Defence Intelligence Service. In 1978 he relinquished his right of accession to the throne when he married Baroness Marie-Christine von Reibnitz, a Roman Catholic.

DUKE OF YORK ▲

The announcement of the Duke and Duchess of York's separation, preceding that of his brother's from the Princess of Wales, came as a surprise to most Royalists in 1992, six years after their wedding at Westminster Abbey. Born at Buckingham Palace on 19 February 1960, Prince Andrew attended Gordonstoun – like his father and elder brother – then joined the Navy and was a helicopter pilot on HMS Invincible off the Falklands during the war against Argentina.

PRINCE EDWARD ▼

Born on 10 March 1964, the Queen's youngest son, Prince Edward, was educated at Gordonstoun and Jesus College, Cambridge, became a house tutor and junior master at Wanganui Collegiate School, in New Zealand, and served in the Royal Marines, before opting for a theatrical career. He joined Andrew Lloyd Webber's Really Useful Group, working on Starlight Express, and subsequently helped to set up a new production company.

COMMANDER TIM LAURENCE ▲

The Princess Royal's marriage to Commander Tim Laurence, on 12 December 1992, was one cause of rejoicing for the Royal Family in a year of much domestic unhappiness. The officer, a former equerry to the Queen, had joined the Ministry of Defence's planning department in March 1992, after commanding the frigate Boxer.

DUKE OF EDINBURGH ▶

Son of Prince Andrew of Greece and Princess Alice of Battenberg, born in Corfu on 10 June 1921, Prince Philip was nephew of Lord Mountbatten and moved with his family to Paris when he was just three months old. He was subsequently educated in Britain and Germany, and served in the Royal Navy. On 20 November 1947, he married Princess Elizabeth, the future Queen, adopted the surname Mountbatten and was made Duke of Edinburgh.

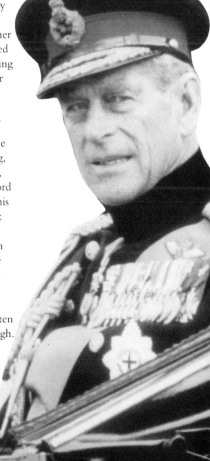

MICHAEL PALIN ▲

Since his Monty Pyton TV and film days, Michael Palin, born in Sheffield on 5 May 1943, has found all-round success as a comedy actor and writer, as well as a presenter of the BBC series Around the World In 80 Days and Pole To Pole, with best-selling books to accompany both. His films include The Missionary, A Private Function and A Fish Called Wanda, but he also made a huge impression as teacher Jim Nelson in Alan Bleasdale's disturbing TV series GBH.

CLIVE ANDERSON ▼

The genial host of the radio show Whose Line Is It Anyway?, barrister Clive Anderson, born in Stanmore, Middlesex, in 1953, was an instant hit when the programme transferred to television and has become Channel four's chat-show king, with Clive Anderson Talks Back, as well as hosting Notes and Queries With Clive Anderson, on BBC 2. He is married to a doctor, Jane, and has two daughters.

ROY CASTLE ▲

Beating lung cancer and growing his hair back was Record Breakers presenter Roy Castle's greatest feat. The Yorkshireman, born on 31 August 1932, stooged for Jimmy James and Jimmy Clitheroe, before making his name in the 1958 Royal Variety Performance and in singer Dickie Valentine's TV show. As well as his own television programmes, he has appeared in films such as Dr Who and the Daleks and Carry On Up the Khyber.

◄ GEORGE COLE

A discovery of Alastair Sim at the age of 15, George Cole, born in London on 22 April 1925, became an overnight star as the cockney evacuee in the play and subsequent film Cottage To Let, then appeared in the St Trinian's screen comedies. Fame came second time round when he landed the role of Arthur Daley in the hit TV series Minder. He was awarded the OBE in 1992.

LENNY HENRY ▲

Getting his break as a winner on the TV talent show New Faces at the age of 16, Lenny Henry, born in Dudley on 29 August 1958, went on to become a regular in the chaotic children's programme Tiswas, the rather more adult OTT and the alternative Three of a Kind, before starring in his own small-screen programmes and films such as True Identity. Married to actress-comedienne Dawn French, he has also appeared in Oxford – a Comic Strip Presents . . . Channel Four film – and was the subject of The South Bank Show.

DAVID JASON ▲

Taking over Ronnie Barker's mantle as Britain's top situation-comedy actor, David Jason, born David White in London on 2 February 1940, followed his role as Del Trotter in the long-running Only Fools and Horses with that of Pop Larkin in The Darling Buds of May. He also featured as Granville, alongside Barker, in the comedy series Open All Hours. Showing his versatility, he played straight roles as Skullion in Porterhouse Blue and Det Insp Jack Frost in A Touch of Frost.

◄ PETER COOK

His performances in the Oxbridge revue Beyond the Fringe led Peter Cook, born in Torquay on 17 November 1937, to open his own Establishment club, become a founder-director of the satirical magazine Private Eye and team up with Dudley Moore on TV in Not Only. . . But Also. Less prominent now, he popped up in the film Whoops Apocalypse and, in 1992, the ITV series Gone To Seed.

JOHN CLEESE ▼

As the man at the Ministry of Silly Walks, John Cleese, born John Cheese in Weston-super-Mare on 27 October 1939, was one of the Monty Python team's most inventive members. He went on to create the legendary Basil Fawlty in Fawlty Towers and star in films such as Clockwise and A Fish Called Wanda, but his appearences became less frequent after developing an interest in psychology, writing a best-selling book, Families and How To Survive Them, with his psychotherapist, Robin Skynner.

KENNETH BRANAGH

The bright young man of the British cinema, actor-director Kenneth Branagh, born in Belfast on 10 December 1960, formed his own Renaissance Theatre Company after disenchantment at working with the RSC. He has starred on TV as Billy Liar and in Fortunes of War. However, he made his name in films after his lead role in A Month In the Country and is married to his frequent co-star Emma Thompson, seen with him in a TV version of Look Back in Anger and his acclaimed three-hour film epic Henry V, which he also directed. He followed it by acting in and directing the Hollywood film Dead Again.

DANIEL DAY-LEWIS

Grandson of film-maker Sir Micheal Balcon and son of former Poet Laureate Cecil Day-Lewis and actress Jill Balcon, Daniel Day-Lewis, born in London in 1957, first made an impression in the stage play Another Country. He appeared in the film Gandhi but really made his mark on screen in My Beautiful Laundrette and A Room With a View. Since then, his films have included The Unbearable Lightness of Being – a a Czech neurosurgeon – and My Left Foot, with his role as cripple Christy Brown winning him a Best Actor Oscar.

MICHAEL CAINE

Most famous on screen for being plain old Michael Caine, the star was actually born Maurice Micklewhite in Bermondsey, South London, on 14 March 1933. He followed Sixties and Seventies films such as Alfie, The Italian Job, The Eagle Has Landed and A Bridge Too Far with more interesting roles in Educating Rita, Mona Lisa and Hannah and her Sisters, which won him an Oscar as Best Supporting Actor. His occasional forays into TV have included Jack the Ripper and Jekyll and Hyde. He and wife Shakira have a daughter, Natasha, and he has another daughter , Dominique by his first wife, actress Patricia Haines, from whom he was divorced. He was made a CBE in 1992.

TOM CONTI

Switching from ideas of becoming a classical pianist, Tom Conti, born in Paisley on 22 November 1941, found fame on TV in The Glittering Prizes and The Norman Conquests, before starring in films such as Reuben, Reuben (winning him an Oscar nomination) and Shirley Valentine.

SEAN CONNERY ⬆

Most famous as the first screen
James Bond, Sean Connery, born
in Edinburgh on 25 August 1930,
worked as a lifeguard and a model
before getting a role in the chorus
of the London production of South
Pacific. He starred in the first Bond
film, Dr No, in 1962, and followed
it with another six. He later won
an Oscar as Best Supporting Actor
for The Untouchables. Twice
married, his son Jason has followed
him into acting.

PETER O'TOOLE ▶

Labelled as one of Britain's 'hell-
raising' group of actors, Peter
O'Toole, born in Ireland on
2 August 1932, enjoyed his greatest
screen successes in the Sixties. He
has been nominated for seven
Oscars, for his performances in
films such as Lawrence of Arabia,
The Lion In Winter and Goodbye
Mr Chips, but has never won one.
More recent parts include that of
the English tutor in The Last
Emperor, winner of nine Oscars,
and the title role in the TV movie
The Pied Piper. He is divorced
from actress Siân Phillips.

◀ ROBERT LINDSAY

Since his TV comedy days as teddy
boy Jakey Smith in Get Some In
and Tooting revolutionary Wolfie
in Citzen Smith, Robert Lindsay,
born in Ilkeston, Derbyshire, on
13 December 1949, has become a
leading light on the stage, wowing
Broadway in Me and My Girl and
taking the title role in Cyrano de
Bergerac, as well as playing the
sinister Michael Murray in Alan
Bleasdale's G.B.H. on TV.
Divorced from actress Cheryl Hall,
he has a daughter, Sydney, from his
long-term relationship with actress
Diana Weston.

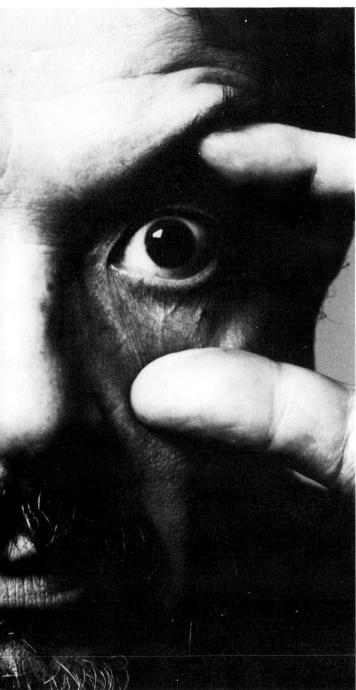

SIR DAVID FROST ▲

TV presenter and media entrepreneur David Frost, born in Tenterden, Kent, on 7 April 1939, was an overnight success as host of the 1960s satirical series That Was the Week That Was. He quickly became one of TV's top interviewers, taking on such heavyweights as Harold Wilson and Richard Nixon. He was awarded the OBE in 1970 and knighted in the 1993 New Year's Honours List. Divorced from actress Lynne Frederick, he subsequently wed Lady Carina Fitzalan, daughter of the Duke of Norfolk.

DAVID BAILEY ▲

After making his name as a fashion photographer, David Bailey, born on 2 January 1938, made television documentaries on Beaton, Warhol and Visconti, and has directed TV commercials since 1966. In recent years these have won him many awards, including an Emmy in America. Divorced three times, his second and third wives were actress Catherine Deneuve and model Marie Helvin.

NIGEL KENNEDY ▶

With a repertoire from classical to pop, Nigel Kennedy, born 28 December 1956, announced in 1992 that he was leaving the classic concert stage to concentrate on pop music, bowing out with a performance of Beethoven at the Festival Hall, London. He also abandoned the spiky-haired punk look. His recording of Vivaldi's The Four Seasons accounts for half of the two million-plus albums he has sold in less than ten years. He lives in Malvern, Worcestershire.

SIR PETER HALL ⬆

As a founder director of the Royal Shakespeare Company and first director of the National Theatre, Sir Peter Hall, born in Bury St Edmunds on 22 November 1930, succeeded in bringing contemporary plays to the London stage, as well as the classics. He has also directed such films as The Homecoming and Covent Garden operas, and was presenter of the 1970s TV arts series Aquarius. He was made a CBE in 1963 and knighted in 1977.

DAVID MELLOR ⬆

An affair with Spanish actress, Antonia de Sancha, did nothing to harm the wider opportunities for a media career for former Heritage Secretary David Mellor, born 12 March 1949. He survived the storm to stay with wife Judith and has since had regular guest spots on TV and radio shows. Called to the Bar in 1972, he became a QC 15 years later and has been Conservative MP for Putney since 1979. He resigned as Heritage Secretary in 1992, after revelations about his affair.

ANDREW MORTON ⬆

The man who made 1992 a year to remember for Royal followers, Andrew Morton – a University of Sussex graduate and former Royal reporter on the Daily Star – was the author of Diana: Her True Story, which claimed to reveal the innermost thoughts of the Princess of Wales on her marriage and was backed up with authoritative sources. It was followed by a paperback that included more revelations and, ultimately, by an official announcement of the Royal couple's separation. A TV drama was also made of the best-seller, which by the end of 1992 had sold more than two million copies.

STEPHEN FRY ⬆

A member of the Cambridge Footlights revue and a former contestant on TV's University Challenge, Stephen Fry, born in Hampstead, London, on 24 August 1957, teamed up with Hugh Laurie for two television series, A Bit of Fry and Laurie and Jeeves and Wooster. He also starred in This Is David Lander and appeared in the films A Handful of Dust and A Fish Called Wanda, as well as rewriting the script for the hit 1980s musical Me and My girl.

⬅ MARCO PIERRE WHITE

Marco Pierre White arrived at le Gavroche at the age of 19, with £5 in his pocket and a determination to achieve. Six years later, he opened Harvey's and, in 1990, became the youngest chef ever to win two Michelin stars. His objection to the media has been much in evidence in 1992.

SIR DAVID ENGLISH ▲

Architect of the modern-day Daily
Mail, Sir David English, born on
26 May 1931, was the editor who
groomed the paper into a successful
middle-market tabloid following its
transition from a broadsheet. In
1992, after 21 years as editor, he
became chairman of Associated
Newspapers, which owns the Mail,
as well as his existing post as the
group's editor-in-chief. He was
previously editor of the now
defunct Daily Sketch.

ROBERT SANGSTER ▶

Racing tycoon Robert Sangster
was born in Cheshire in 1936, only
child of Vernon Sangster, who
founded Vernons Pools. He
worked for the family business
until, at the age of 39, he started
breeding horses, building it up to
an 800 thoroughbred enterprise.
He became Britain's leading
racehorse owner, with two Derby
winners and three Arc de
Triomphe victories.

SIR SIMON HORNBY ⬆

Chairman of the W H Smith Group, Sir Simon Hornby, born on 29 December 1934, was educated at Eton and Oxford, and served in the Grenadier Guards. He joined W H Smith & Son, where his father was once deputy chairman, as a graduate trainee in 1958, later becoming a director and, in 1982, chairman. Under his control the group has bought the Our Price record chain and a controlling interest in Waterstone's, as well as moving into European TV production.

LORD KING ⬆

After becoming chairman of British Airways in 1981, Lord King of Wartnaby transformed it from being a loss-making nationalised business into the world's most profitable airline. Born John King, he started his career in small-scale engineering, worked as a car salesman, then bought Pollard Bearings, which he turned into that industry's third largest British company. He ran Babcock and Wilcox and Dennis Brothers, and was knighted in 1979, before Prime Minister Margaret Thatcher chose him to take over at British Airways.

LORD WHITE ➤

As business partner to Lord Hanson, Lord White of Hull helped to turn the Hanson empire into an £11 billion conglomerate and became its boss in America in 1973. Born in Hedon, near Hull, on 11 May 1923, Gordon White started a publishing business, then teamed up with James Hanson to found the greetings card firm Hanson White, before making the Hanson industrial concern a huge commercial success. He is also on the board of British Airways.

LORD OWEN ▼

Following membership of two political parties, leaving Labour and finding himself the only surviving member of the SDP, which he had founded in 1981, David Owen, born in Plymouth on 2 July 1938, was elevated to the House of Lords and became European Community peace negotiator in the former states of Yugoslavia. A former doctor, he is used to healing wounds. He was successively health minister and foreign secretary in the 1974-79 Labour government and is married to literary agent Deborah.

JACKIE MANN ▲

Frail and unsteady, Jackie Mann was one of the last bunch of Western hostages to be released from Beirut. The former Battle of Britain Spitfire pilot married wife, Sunnie, in 1943 and subsequently moved to Beirut, where he flew jets for Middle East Airlines. On 12 May 1989 he was kidnapped on his daily trip to the bank and was not released until 24 September 1991, after an 865-day ordeal. He was made a CBE in 1992, the year that also saw the death of his wife Sunnie (Dilys) from lung cancer.

CHRIS PATTEN ▼

After losing his seat at the 1992 General Election, former Conservative Party chairman Chris Patten, born in Ealing, West London, on 12 May 1944, was rewarded with the post of Britain's last ambassador to Hong Kong, before China takes over the territory in 1997. He graduated in history from Balliol College, Oxford, and worked in the Cabinet Office and Home Office before being elected Conservative MP for Bath in 1979, when the Tories returned to power after five years of Labour rule. He rose from being a parliamentary private secretary to become Environment Secretary in 1989 and Conservative Party Chairman and Chancellor of the duchy of Lancaster in 1990, masterminding the Tories' General Election win two years later. He and his wife, Mary, have three daughters.

JOHN McCARTHY ▲

Television journalist John McCarthy was the smiling, young face among the Western hostages held in Beirut. As acting bureau chief for the agency Worldwide Television News, he was captured on 17 April 1986 while trying to get out of the city, two days after the American bombing of Lebanon. He spent 1,943 days in captivity and was finally set free in August 1991, resuming his relationship with fellow-journalist Jill Morrell, who had campaigned relentlessly for his release. He was made a CBE in the 1992 New Year's Honours List.

TERRY WAITE ▲

The Archbishop of Canterbury's envoy, Terry Waite, borne on 31 May 1939, went to Beirut to seek the return of Western hostages but ended up as one of their number. He was captured on 20 January 1987 on a mission to meet a hostage-taking group and was not released until 18 November 1991, after 1,763 days in captivity. He had been adviser to the Archbishop of Canterbury on Anglican Communion Affairs since 1980, following posts as adviser to the Archbishop of Uganda and co-ordinator of the Southern Sudan Relief Project, as well as work as an international consultant with the Roman Catholic Church. Made a CBE in 1992, he and wife, Frances, have three daughters and a son.

JOHN BIRT ▲

Director-General of the BBC since the beginning of 1993, John Birt, born in Liverpool on 10 December 1944, decided the Corporation was in need of a clean sweep. A former editor of World In Action, he joined the BBC in 1987 as Michael Checkland's deputy, after five years as director of programmes at LWT, where he had previously been responsible for the launch of Weekend World. One of his first acts at the BBC was to combine news and current affairs into a single division.

STEPHEN HAWKING ▲

When Britain's best-known scientist, Professor Stephen Hawking, wrote his book A Brief History of Time – contending that time does not exist – it became an all-time best-seller after its publication in 1988. Lucasian Professor of Mathematics at Cambridge University, born in 1942, he has suffered motor neurone disease since his early 20s and was told he would not live beyond the age of 30. Twenty-one years later, he is still alive and lecturing with the aid of a voice synthesiser, which he also used during a guest appearance on the radio show Desert Islands Discs in 1992.

MICHAEL GRADE ➤

Son of the late, great agent Leslie Grade and nephew of TV mogul Lord Grade, Michael Grade, born in London on 8 March 1943, started his career as a newspaper journalist and was a sports journalist on the Daily Mirror, before becoming an agent with the Grade Organisation. In 1973 he moved into television with LWT, where he was deputy controller, then director of programmes. After gaining experience in Hollywood with his father's companies, Embassy Television and The Grade Company, he joined the BBC in 1983 as controller of BBC 1, then director of programmes, gaining a reputation as a scheduling whiz-kid. He became Channel 4's chief executive in 1987.

NIGEL THOMSON

Fearless news cameraman Nigel Thomson was awarded an OBE in the 1993 New Year's Honours List, following a year when he was twice wounded while covering the civil war in the former states of Yugoslavia. In 1992 he also received the Royal Television Society's Cameraman of the Year award, for the second time. Previously a sound recordist, he is married to ITN colleague Carol Barnes, with whom he has a son, James, and step-daughter, Clare, and the family live in Brighton.

MICHAEL GREEN

Chairman of Carlton Television, which ousted Thames from its London ITV franchise at the beginning of 1993, Michael Green, born in London on 2 December 1947, was a business tycoon at the age of 20, when he bought a loss-making printing company, sold its headquarters at a profit, bought new equipment, increased the staff and renamed it Tangent Industries. He expanded into photography and video and set up Carlton Communications, which in 1988 bought Technicolor. Married twice, he has two daughters.

MICHAEL NICHOLSON

Three times Television Journalist of the Year, Michael Nicholson, born in Romford, Essex, on 9 January 1937, has covered more wars than any other correspondent. From Vietnam to Biafra, Cambodia, the Middle East, the Falklands and the Gulf, he has brought news from the front-line to ITN viewers since the mid-1960s. Winner of the coveted BAFTA Richard Dimbleby Award in 1982, he was also awarded the OBE in 1991.

MARCUS PLANTIN

ITV's first network director, Marcus Plantin is one of the most powerful people in television. He came to the job in 1992, with the creation of a new central commissioning unit for ITV programmes, after seven years at LWT, first as head of light entertainment, then as director of programmes. He started his career working behind the scenes in the theatre, before joining the BBC as a floor manager and rising to become a light entertainment producer and director.

PAUL CONDON ▾

On January 31st, 1993, at the age of 45, Paul Condon was appointed Commissioner of Police for the Metropolis. He joined the Metropolitan Police in 1967 and between 1972 and 1975 was a Bramshill Scholar at St Peter's College, Oxford, where he gained a BA and an MA in jurisprudence. From 1978 to 1981, Mr Condon served with the Community Relations Department of New Scotland Yard. Following a series of promotions, he left the Metropolitan Police in 1984 to join Kent Constabulary as Assistant Chief Constable, as which he formulated the plans for the policing of the Channel Tunnel and was Head of Operations when the Fixed Link Treaty was signed. He returned to London in 1987 as Assistant Deputy Commissioner and then Deputy Commissioner before becoming Chief Constable of Kent in 1989.

IAN BOTHAM ▴

In a controversial cricketing career that has frequently seen him at odds with officialdom, Ian Botham, born in Heswall, Cheshire, on 24 November 1955, was acknowledged as England's leading all-round cricketer. In Test matches he achieved a then record 1,000 runs and 100 wickets in 21 matches. He has also captained England, played in county matches for Somerset and Durham, and was awarded the OBE in 1992.

SIR MARTIN JACOMB ▾

Knighted for services to the City of London in 1985, Sir Martin Jacomb is chairman of The British Council and of Postel Investment Management Ltd. He was born in 1929 and educated at Eton and Worcester College, Oxford and was called to the Bar in 1955, after completing his military service. He practised as a barrister until 1968, when he joined Kleinwort Benson, becoming vice-chairman in 1976, a post he held until 1985, when he left to become deputy chairman of Barclays Bank. He assumed the chairmanship of Barclays de Zoete Wedd Ltd at its inception in June 1986 until retiring from the position in 1991. He remains a deputy chairman of Barclays Bank plc. Sir Martin is deputy chairman of the Commercial Union plc, a director of the Bank of England, The Daily Telegraph plc, Marks and Spencer plc and the RTZ Corporation plc. He is a member of the finance committee of the Oxford University Press and a trustee of the National Heritage Memorial Fund. Sir Martin was made an Honorary Bencher of the Middle Temple in 1987.

LORD SIEFF OF BRIMPTON

Lord Sieff retired from the board of Marks and Spencer plc in 1985, when he was appointed honorary president. His term as chairman, from 1972, was marked by extensive merchandising development and the company's expansion overseas. One of his great contributions was to strengthen the company's policy of good human relations with staff, suppliers and the community. Marcus Sieff joined Marks and Spencer in 1935, after leaving Cambridge. During WWII, he served with the Royal Artillery, rising to the rank of Colonel and receiving the OBE in ·1944. He was created a knight bachelor in 1971 and a life peer in 1980. Lord Sieff has been associated for over 50 years with the development of first Palestine and then Israel and is the Chancellor of the Weizmann Institute of Science in Israel. Among his many awards and distinctions, Lord Sieff received the first Management Centre Europe Award for "an outstanding contribution to the social responsibility of business in Europe" in 1974; Hambros' Businessman of the Year Award in 1976; the International Retailer of the Year Award, presented by the National Retail Merchants Association of the USA in 1982 and the British Institute of Management's 1983 Gold Medal. He is an Honorary Master of the Bench of the Inner Temple, an Honorary Fellow of Corpus Christi College, Cambridge, Manchester Polytechnic and the Royal College of Surgeons and holds many honorary degrees.

FRANK BRUNO

After starting his boxing career with Wandsworth Boys' Club and subsequently joining Sir Philip Game's Amateur Boxing Club, Frank Bruno, 31, turned professional in 1982 and became the European heavyweight professional in 1982 and became the European heavyweight champion three years later. He has lost only a handful of fights and, by the end of 1992, had twice unsuccessfully challenged for the world heavyweight title. Branching out into acting, he appeared in the pantomime Robin Hood with Little and Large. He was made an MBE in 1990 and is married with two daughters.

DAVID BRYANT

The familiar, pipe smoking figure of David Bryant has become the image of bowling around the world. With calm, unflappable good humour, he remains one of Britain's great sporting ambassadors. In the sport which he has done so much to popularise, he has won three World Singles Championships, three World Indoor Singles Championships and, in 1993, reached the finals of the World Indoor Doubles Championships, a title which he has won five times since its inception in 1986. Added to these, David Bryant, now aged 61, has won numerous Masters and National titles. A former schoolmaster, David has published four books on bowls and spends his leisure hours gardening and angling.

NOMINATION FORM

I would like to nominate the following person for inclusion in the Best of British Guides 1994.

Name _____

Address _____

_____ Postcode _____

Tel No. (Home) _____ Tel No. (Work) _____

Occupation _____

Category of Nomination

Reason for Nomination

Proposer's Name _____

Address _____

_____ Postcode _____

Tel No. (Home) _____ Tel No. (Work) _____

Occupation _____

Signature _____

INDEX